REVELATION UNLOCKED

KEYS TO UNDERSTANDING END-TIME EVENTS

BOB KOLLIN

21ST CENTURY
PRESS

REVELATION UNLOCKED

Published by 21st Century Press
Springfield, Missouri U.S.A.
Printed in U.S.A.

21st Century Press is an evangelical Christian publisher dedicated to serving the local church with purpose books. We believe God's vision for 21st Century Press is to provide church leaders with biblical, user-friendly materials that will help them evangelize, disciple and minister to children, youth and families.

It is our prayer that this book will help you discover biblical truth for your own life and help you meet the needs of others. May God richly bless you.

21st Century Press
2131 W. Republic Rd.
PMB 41
Springfield, MO 65807
800-658-0284

ISBN: 0-9728899-1-4

Cover: Lee Fredrickson
Book Design: Terry White
Visit our web-site at: 21stcenturypress.com and 21stcenturybooks.com
For great children's books visit: sonshipbooks.com

21ST CENTURY PRESS

3308 S. Meadowlark Ave.
Springfield, MO 65807
lee@21stcenturypress.com

DEDICATION

This book is dedicated to my wife, Stephanie and my mother, June for their ever continuing support and love. Thank you for your faithfulness and steadfastness in the Lord.

Revelation 21:5-6 – *"Then He who sat on the throne...said to me, Write, for these words are true and faithful...It is done!..."*

ACKNOWLEDGEMENT

My appreciation to these special friends, Fran Richardson Cary, Jorge Valladares, Diane Richard, Brad Hammack, Julie Olsen, and Lany Setiawan, for their commitment to the Word of God and encouragement to me on this project.

Revelation 22:14 – *"Blessed are those who do His commandments, that they may have right to the tree of life, and may enter through the gates into the city."*

A special thanks to Lee Fredrickson and James Combs who were used by God as vessels of honor to open the door so this book could come to fruition.

Revelation 3: 8 – *"...See, I have set before you and open door, and no one can shut it..."*

TABLE OF CONTENTS

Foreword

Considering the Key Rings...9

Introduction

The Finalization of God's Redemptive Plan for Man.............12

Overview

God's Prophetic Time Chart 18

PART ONE
A VERSE-BY-VERSE GUIDE TO
THE BOOK OF REVELATION

Chapter 1 - The Alpha and Omega 39

Chapter 2 - Messages to the Church 47

Chapter 3 - Hear What the Spirit Says 59

Chapter 4 - The Church in Heaven 69

Chapter 5 - The Seven Sealed Scroll 77

Chapter 6 - The Seals Opened 83

Chapter 7 - Evangelism in the Tribulation 93

Chapter 8 - The Trumpets Sound 101

Chapter 9 - Demonic Activity 107

Chapter 10 - The Little Book............................. 115

Chapter 11 - The Two Witnesses 119

Chapter 12 - Five Personalities 129

Chapter 13 - The Two Beasts............................. 137

Chapter 14 - Angelic Activity............................ 145

Chapter 15 - Heavenly Activity 153

Chapter 16 - The Last Plagues............................ 157

Chapter 17 - The Harlot Religion 165

Chapter 18 - Destruction of Babylon 173

Chapter 19 - Armageddon 181

Chapter 20 - The Millennium and Final Judgment 189

Chapter 21 - The New Jerusalem 197

Chapter 22 - Behold, I Come Quickly. 205

PART TWO
PROPHETIC KEYS

1.   Millennial Viewpoints 213

2.   Letters to the Churches 217

     Comparative Overview of
     Churches of Revelation 2-3 (Chart) 219

3.   Setting the Stage 220

4.   Rapture 233

     Comparison of the Rapture and
     the Second Coming (Chart) 244

5.   United States in Prophecy 245

6.   The Antichrist 247

7.   Tribulation Period 254

     Events and Conditions on Earth
     During the Tribulation Period 256

     Tribulation Judgments (Chart) 263-264

     Timeline Overview (Chart) 265-267

8.   Groups of Believers 268

9.   Three Major Military Campaigns 272

10. Daniel Military Campaign 275

11. Magog Military Campaign 281

12. End-time Alignment of Nations .285

13. Day of the Lord 293

14. 200 Million Horsemen Army of Revelation 9:16 304

15. Male Child 306

16. Beasts – Seven Heads and Ten Horns 309

17. Religious and Literal Babylon 311

18. Conditions on Earth at Armageddon 314

19. Armageddon 317

      Event Chronology at Armageddon (Chart) 321

20. Marriage Supper of the Lamb .322

21. Millennium 325

22. Renovation of Heaven and Earth 333

23. Postmillennial Earth or Eternity Future 336

24. Natural and Supernatural Disturbances 339

      Persecutions, Judgments, and Signs
      in Revelation 4-22 (Chart) .342-343

25. Nether World Regions and Eternal Hell
      (with Chart) 344

26. Book of Matthew

      Matthew 24-25 346

27. Book of Daniel

      Daniel Overview (Chart) 357

      Daniel 2: 28-45 357

      Daniel 7 361

      Daniel 8 368

      Daniel 9:24-27 – Prophecy of the
      Seventy Weeks of Years 373

      Selected Verses from Daniel 10 380

Selected Verses from Daniel 11 381

Daniel 12 386

Comparison of Kingdoms and Beasts in
Revelation and Daniel (Chart) .391

28. Book of Ezekiel

Ezekiel 38-39 (with Chart) 392

Glossary 405

Author's Salvation Statement 413

References and Additional Study Materials 415

Subject Index 418

 FOREWORD

CONSIDERING THE KEY RINGS

The Revelation of Jesus Christ is the Holy Spirit inspired concluding book of the Word of God, penned by the exiled Apostle and Prophet John and sent forth initially to the churches where he had ministered.

It was and is, of course, an *apocalypse*, the unveiling and revealing of the person of Christ Himself and of the unfolding panorama of events, which will climax the history of the world in the end times.

In this volume, you will enter the portals of infallible truth, as researcher and scholar Bob Kollin unlocks the profound mysteries of Revelation for both teachers and laypeople, that all may understand.

The Apocalypse contains 913 distinct words, or excluding the names of persons and places, 871. Of these 871 Greek words, 108 are not used elsewhere in the New Testament.

While there are no specifically cited references to the Old Testament in the Apocalypse, some Greek scholars have noted that as many as 278 verses out of 404 contain allusions from 27 out of 39 Old Testament books. An allusion is a reference to something without indicating its source. It may be a near quotation, an apparent paraphrase, or the mention of an OT person, place or event with new insights. It is easily recognizable in Greek (the Septuagint or LXX translation of the Hebrew originals), but is noticeable in English versions and other languages.

It is most amazing that interwoven into this logical narrative are these ancient expressions, fitly framed into the whole pattern smoothly, appropriately, becoming an integral part of the whole. Surely, it would take more than human genius and even an ency-clopedic grasp mentally of the Old Testament to produce this mas-terpiece. It must be, it is divinely inspired by the Holy Spirit.

Imagery From Life Key

This is a book of vivid imagery from real life, drawing from virtual-ly all categories of nature and life.

The animal kingdom is used: horses white, red, black, pale; the lamb and the calf, the lion, leopard, the bear, the locust, the scorpi-on and the frog, the eagle, the vulture, the birds of the air and fish-es of the sea.

The vegetable kingdom is presented with its trees, herbs, and grass.

The mineral kingdom with gold and many precious stones both from Earth and the sea (pearls), which will have a grander counterpart in the Celestial realms. The sea is seen under judgment, a sea of glass is beheld in heaven, and a river flows from the throne of God.

The sky yields its stars, now shining in the firmament, now falling to earth, now forming a cluster in the right hand of Jesus, (whose face shines as the sun), now forming a crown on the head of the Woman (Israel). Across the heavens there sweeps from time to time a storm of thunder, lightning and hail, followed by an earth-quake.

The human realm supplies an abundance of imagery. We see the mother and the child, the harlot and her lovers, the bride arrayed for her husband.

Crowned heads wear the *stephanos* or the diadem; warriors carry the sword; the shepherd appears with his iron-tipped staff, the reaper with his sickle, the herald with his trumpet, the builder with his meas-uring rod, the musician with his flute and harp, the reveler with a golden cup, the king with his scroll, written within and on the back-side and sealed until the time to open. Figures move across the stage attired in the long belted robe of kingly or priestly dignity, or in shining white garments; two are dressed in sackcloth; one wears purple and scarlet and is decked with gold and precious stones and pearls.

Imagery from the Old Testament Key

A large proportion of this imagery is drawn from the Old Testament. Places, persons and objects, which occur in historical books, now reappear in Revelation as with additional significance for end times. Familiar place names meet us here and there-Euphrates, Egypt, Sodom, the Hill and Valleys of Megiddo, Babylon, Jerusalem. The seven-branched candlestick of the Tabernacle suggests the golden heavenly Menorah (and the sevenfold ministry of the Holy Spirit upon Christ *Isaiah 11:1, 2*), the seven churches of Asia. Balaam finds his analogue in the Nicolaitans, and in Jezebel the Thyatirian prophetess. The world and Israel are confronted by a new Babylon and the Bride of Christ lives in the New Jerusalem. The 24 elders answer to the 24 courses of priests that served in the Tabernacle and Temple. The two witnesses exercise powers like Elijah and Moses.

In other instances, the Revelation echoes the Old Testament, yet adds new truth in such expressions as the Tree of Life, the Book of Life, the Water of Life, or the prophetic fulfillments of Old Testament types of the Lord such as the Lamb and the Lion of the Tribe of Judah, and the Root of David.

Symbolism, Realities and Prophecies Key

The use of symbols does not deny, but rather reinforces the fact of realities. In some cases, the writer interprets the symbol (1:20; 4:5; 5:6; 12:9; etc.). In others, the symbolical meaning and application is only half-veiled (4:2). In all of these, both the symbol or type and the reality can be compared. If the language is plain and appears to be a prediction of cataclysmic or future historical events, remember to interpret literally.

It is the nature of apocalyptic literature to involve some measure of obscurity. This leads to the exercise of judgment, logical research and examination, with the spirit's guidance.

Numbers in the Apocalypse Key

It appears that numbers, so frequently occurring, carry a certain message.

The following numbers are found in the book: 2; 3; 3 1/2; 4; 5; 6; 7; 10; 12; 24; 43; 144; 666; 1000; 1260; 1600; 7000; 12,000; 144,000; 100,000,000; 200,000,000. The predominant number is *seven*, which occurs 54 times. We find 7 candlesticks (lampstands), 7 stars, 7 angels, 7 Spirits of God, 7 seals, 7 eyes and 7 horns (the Lamb), 7 trumpet blasts, 7 last plagues, 7 heads, 7 diadems, 7 bowls, 7 mountains or 7 kings. As you read the book, underline every use of the word *seven*.

Ten is another favorite number. We find 10 days, 10 horns, 10 kings, *Four* is significant: 4 beasts (zoa), 4 angels, the foursquare city, 4 corners of the earth, *Three* is less prominent: 3 woes, 3 parts, 3 gates on each wall of the New Jerusalem.

Theological Ideas Key

In Revelation, we discover the last revealed truths in the Bible of a doctrinal, theological nature. We learn much of Theology itself, about who God is and what He does; we learn more of Christology, the study of the person and work of Christ; we learn aspects of Pneumatology, the study of the Holy Spirit; we learn much of angels or Angelology, of Satanology, and of Demonology.

Of course, we read the final word about *Eschatology*, the study of last things.

These are but a few of the fascinating facts, figures, and symbols and realities you are going to explore as you learn to use the KEYS TO UNDERSTANDING THE END TIMES, so lucidly presented in this volume.

—Jim Combs, DMIN, LITTD
Provost of *Louisiana Baptist University and Theological Seminary*
Executive Director of the *Center for Advanced Prophetics*, Shreveport

Some material for this foreword has relied on the writings of H.B. Swete.

INTRODUCTION

THE FINALIZATION OF GOD'S REDEMPTIVE PLAN FOR MAN

Bible prophecy, as revealed in the Book of Revelation, Book of Daniel, Matthew 24, Ezekiel 38-39, and other key passages in the Word of God, describes end-time events in God's redemptive plan for man. Since these events will occur in the future, the precise manner and time of their occurrence cannot be exactly known. Scholars have made their best attempts at interpreting the scriptures, but in many cases, outstanding prophecy experts differ on the application of scripture, or more specifically, on the timing of a particular event. An approach that will minimize confusion is to first look at the events that are considered "fact" and generally agreed upon by prophecy scholars who adopt the Futuristic school of interpretation with a Premillennial, pre-Tribulation viewpoint, which is the position espoused in this book. For example, those holding this viewpoint would acknowledge the following events as fact:

- Revelation 1:19 represents a general outline to the Book of Revelation.
- The Rapture of the Church will occur before the Tribulation begins.
- The Rapture is imminent, i.e., that no prophecies need to be fulfilled before the Rapture can occur.
- The Rapture will be the last event of the Church Age.
- The Tribulation will last for seven years following the Rapture.

- Three sets of seven judgments will occur in consecutive order during the Tribulation.
- The Antichrist will appear on the scene of history and broker a seven year covenant with Israel.
- The Antichrist will break the seven year covenant after three and one half years.
- The Antichrist will enter the temple and proclaim himself to be God.
- God will send two witnesses or prophets that will minister during part of the Tribulation.
- The Second Coming of Christ will occur at the end of the Tribulation.
- Christ will defeat the armies of the Antichrist at the battle of Armageddon.
- A remnant of Israel will be saved at the end of the Tribulation, completing the spiritual family of God.
- Satan will be bound in the abyss for 1000 years.
- Christ will literally rule on earth for a 1000-year period called the Millennium.
- Satan will be released from the abyss for a short time after the end of the Millennium.

Generally, no two prophecy experts agree on every point. Prophecy is history in advance, and many events cannot be considered absolute fact, because not enough information is provided to lead all experts to the same conclusion. Therefore, these passages must be interpreted. When the facts are not absolutely clear from the Biblical text, the next step is to form assumptions and make speculations, which is how the variance in interpretation occurs. For example, less consensus will be found on the following events:

- Will Old Testament saints participate in the Rapture?
- Who are the elders in heaven?
- Are the 144,000 Jews evangelists?
- Who is the beast in the abyss?

- Who are the two witnesses?
- Who is the woman?
- Who is the male child?
- Is Satan cast out of the second or third heaven?
- What country or region will the Antichrist come from?
- Will the Antichrist have a fatal wound that is healed?
- Will the Antichrist be resurrected?
- What is the mark of the Beast?
- What do the seven heads on the Beast represent?
- Is Mt. Zion of Revelation 14 in heaven or on earth?
- When will the day of the Lord begin and end?
- When does the battle in Ezekiel 38-39 occur?
- What nations are engaged in the Ezekiel 38-39 conflict?
- When will the battle between the Antichrist and the King of the North and the King of the South occur?
- Will the city of Babylon be rebuilt?
- Who will enter the Millennium?
- Will the earth be completely destroyed by fire?

The following examination of the Book of Revelation and supporting prophetic scriptures and topics will address these and other controversial questions in a logical and rational manner that hopefully can be easily understood by the lay reader. Debate and controversy over application and interpretation of Greek words have been purposely avoided, being left to the Greek scholars.

As noted, this analysis follows the Futuristic, Premillennial school of interpretation, which espouses that most events of Revelation will occur in the future and have yet to occur, and that the Tribulation Period (a.k.a "Tribulation") or seventieth week of Daniel precedes the Millennium. Additionally, the Rapture position expounded in this book is pre-Tribulation, that is, the Rapture of the Church will occur before Daniel's seventieth week begins. The interpretative method used will apply scripture literally wherever possible and let the Word prove itself. The same meaning of words should be applied to prophecy as to other passages of scripture. Literal meanings are not to be spiritualized; i.e., an earthquake is an earthquake, not the breaking up of society, and hidden meanings of scripture are not sought out, such as finding the United States in the word "Jerusalem." The judgments in Revelation are viewed as a succession of consecutive, not concurrent events taken in the order God gave them.

As previously stated, scholars differ in their interpretation of various passages of scripture. God's prophetic Word is an account of history recorded in advance, but many events are not totally described, especially in regard to their occurrence on the prophetic timeline, location, historical versus future application, symbolic representation, etc. Although scholars strive for prophetic accuracy, there will be surprises as history unfolds. No one has all the answers. Even the best prophetic teachers do not have the full revelation and will probably be shocked as events occur. As time progresses and the study of prophecy expands among believers, the body of Christ collectively will possess a more complete revelation of the future. Since God is logical and orderly, this same method or approach has been adopted for this text when examining prophetic scriptures and events, as well as interpretations by leading prophecy scholars. This book is designed to be a companion study-aid to assist students in formulating their own conclusions about current prophetic thinking and interpretative positions. The hope is that this book will provide the lay reader with an overall understanding of end-time events in an easy to follow format, while identifying areas where scholars have differing opinions. Several positions provided in this writing will differ from those adopted by recognized prophecy teachers, but the purpose is not to be dogmatic on interpretation of prophetic events or positions, but to provide options and to challenge readers to think about prophecy and continue their search of the prophetic scriptures, because greater revelation is available to the diligent student.

BACKGROUND

It is generally accepted that John the apostle is the writer of the Book of Revelation. His style of writing is different than that used in the Gospel of John or the three Epistles of John. However, the difference in style is attributed to the fact that in Revelation, John recorded what he saw, and therefore less of his own style and personality is reflected in the writing. John literally functions as a scribe recording the future as it unfolds before him. He writes what he sees and hears.

Revelation was written around A.D. 95-96 during the rule of the Roman emperor Domitian. Domitian demanded Caesar worship. People had to call him God or die. Because of Domitian's hatred of Christians, they had to make a life or death choice, Christ or Caesar. Revelation became a hope and encouragement to Christians in times of tremendous persecution that evil would not prevail in the end. It is estimated that under Domitian's rule, 40,000 Christians were put to death for their faith.

Revelation comes from the Greek word "apokalupsis," which means to "unveil," "reveal," or "uncover" implying "to lift as a curtain." Revelation is an unveiling of facts and truths hidden in the mind of God that would not be known unless revealed by the Holy Spirit. Revelation is the book of unveilings of the world's future. It is a look at history beforehand, an actual record of the final phases of world history. The message is not mysterious, hidden, or confusing but illuminating and revealing. Revelation is an unveiling of Jesus Christ as King of kings and Lord of lords coming to rescue His people, judge the wicked, put an end to Satan and sin, and establish His everlasting kingdom on earth as initially intended by God.

The Bible would be incomplete without the Book of Revelation. Revelation completes God's plan and purpose for man. The Bible begins with God creating all things, including heaven and earth, and ends with God reigning over all of creation. The Bible begins human history in the Garden of Eden and ends human history in the eternal city of God. Revelation provides answers to questions about the Church, sin, curse, Satan, Israel, heaven, earth, hell, man, Jew, angels, eternity, etc.

Revelation is also a book of numbers. For example, seven is the number of perfection and completeness, and there are seven churches, seven spirits, seven stars, seven lampstands, seven seals, seven trumpets, seven bowls, seven horns, seven angels, seven thunders, seven heads, seven crowns, seven mountains, seven plagues, seven kings, seven new things, and so on.

In Revelation, God demonstrates His eternal, creative, and almighty nature and attributes of majesty, omnipotence, wisdom, omniscience, love, holiness, faithfulness, truth, righteousness, and judgment. He is referred to or called the First and the Last, Beginning and the End, Alpha and Omega, Word of God, Lamb, Lion of the tribe of Judah, Root of David, Amen, Faithful and True Witness, Beginning of the creation of God, and Lord God Almighty.

Revelation 1:3 declares a blessing for the reader and hearer of the prophecy and for those who keep the things written in Revelation. Therefore, expect and believe that you will receive a blessing while reading and studying this book on end-time prophecy and the Book of Revelation.

As further encouragement in your study, these additional scriptures of importance are provided:

2 Timothy 2:15 – *"Be diligent to present yourself approved to God, a worker who does not need to be ashamed, rightly dividing the word of truth."*

Acts 17:11 – *"These were more fair-minded than those in Thessalonica, in that they received the word with all readiness, and searched the Scriptures daily to find out whether these things were so."*

Ephesians 1:17-19 – *"...that the God of our Lord Jesus Christ, the Father of glory, may give to you the spirit of wisdom and revelation in the knowledge of Him, the eyes of your understanding being enlightened; that you may know what is the hope of His calling, what are the riches of the glory of His inheritance in the saints, and what is the exceeding greatness of His power toward us who believe, according to the working of His mighty power..."*

 OVERVIEW

GOD'S PROPHETIC TIME CHART

Daniel 9:24-27 The Prophetic Time Chart

Daniel is told by the angel Gabriel that "seventy weeks of years" or 490 years are determined regarding Israel and the holy city Jerusalem to make an end of sins, finish the transgression, make reconciliation for inequity, bring in everlasting righteousness, seal up the vision and prophecy, and anoint the Most Holy. From this prophecy, Daniel could have assumed that the Messiah's earthly kingdom (Millennium) would be established in 490 years. The "seventy weeks" literally mean "seventy segments of seven," and when multiplied and equated to years, equal 490 years. The 490-year period is divided into three parts starting with a decree to Israel to rebuild Jerusalem and the wall. The prevailing position among scholars is that the fourth decree by Artaxerxes of Persia to Nehemiah in 445 B.C., to restore and rebuild Jerusalem, started this 490-year prophetic clock. Seven weeks of years or forty-nine years later, the rebuilding of Jerusalem was completed.

Following the first period of 49 years, was a period of 62 weeks of years or 434 years to Christ's entering Jerusalem as her Messiah and His subsequent crucifixion. At this point, Jewish time stopped. In A.D. 70, the Roman General Titus destroyed the temple and the city of Jerusalem, and the Jews were dispersed throughout the world. After Pentecost, the Church Age began and has continued for almost 2000 years. Daniel did not prophetically see the Church Age. The six events pertaining to Israel, as stipulated in verse 24, are yet to occur. One segment of seven (or one week of years, or seven years) remain of the original 490 years decreed to Daniel. This remaining seven-year period is called the seventieth week of Daniel or the Tribulation Period. The prophetic stage was set in 1948, when Israel was re-gathered as a nation; and in 1967, when she regained possession of Jerusalem. The Church will be raptured (pre-Tribulation viewpoint) and God will again deal with Israel to fulfill the prophecies of verse 24.

The Prince (Antichrist) who is to come will make a covenant of peace with Israel for this seven-year period (Tribulation), but in the middle of the seven years, he will break the covenant, enter the temple and proclaim himself to be God. At this point, he will cause a tremendous persecution to come upon Israel in his attempt to destroy the nation and prevent the Second Coming of Christ and the Millennium.

Revelation 1

The apostle John is exiled to the island of Patmos and experiences visions of the end times. He is commanded to write what he sees. Chapter 1 centers on a vision of the glorified Christ. In verse 19, John is commanded to write the "things which he has seen" (vision of Christ), "the things which are" (letters to the seven churches in Asia Minor), and "the things which shall be after these things" (after the Church Age). Verse 19, therefore, becomes the natural outline for the Book of Revelation. The things that John saw are in chapter 1, "the things which are" in chapters 2 and 3, and "the things which shall take place after this" are chapters 4 through 22.

Revelation 2-3

These chapters identify letters addressed to seven literal churches in Asia Minor, but the messages can be applied to the spiritual condition of the Church at any point in the Church

Age, especially now. There are several spiritual conditions identified. Ephesus is the church that is caught up in works and has
lost its primary focus, Christ. Smyrna represents the persecuted
church that is faithful even to death. Pergamos and Thyatira represent the compromising church. Unfaithful believers in these
churches will commit spiritual adultery by following after false
teachers, e.g., Jezebel, false doctrine, complacency, and works
based on the wrong motives. Sardis represents the spiritually
dead church. People in this church may look like Christians and
appear alive; but, in fact, are spiritually dead. Many from this
church will be deceived and take the mark of the Beast. They are
the tares among the wheat. Philadelphia represents the faithful
church. The letter to this church has several admonitions but no
warnings or rebukes. The Philadelphia type church will escape the
wrath of God to come on the world in the Tribulation Period.
Laodicea is the lukewarm or complacent church. Laodiceans were
so wealthy they didn't need anyone, Rome or God. Jesus has little
tolerance for them, saying that He would spit them out of His
mouth.

Revelation 4-5

In chapter 4, God the Father is worshiped by all of heaven as
Creator; and in chapter 5, God the Son is worshiped as Redeemer.
Chapter 4 is a heavenly scene with God on the throne, surrounded by 24 elders on thrones, and four living creatures similar to
cherubim and seraphim. Chapter 5 identifies the scroll with
seven seals that no one can open but Christ Himself as the "Lion
from the tribe of Judah." This scroll appears to be the title deed
to the earth and sets forth the seal and trumpet judgments that
are to occur during the seven year Tribulation. Some believe the
scroll may only set forth the seven trumpet judgments, because
the first four seal judgments are the wrath of the Antichrist
backed by Satan. However, as it is a large scroll written on both
sides, it logically records both seal and trumpet judgments, for
the four horsemen of the seal judgments are summoned by the

living creatures. The little book of chapter 10 is open, unsealed, and apparently smaller than the seven-sealed scroll. Therefore, it sets forth the last seven bowl judgments. The remainder of the chapter shows all beings in both heaven and earth worshipping and praising God.

Revelation 6-19: The Tribulation Period

Revelation 6

This chapter describes the first six seal judgments that positionally begin or occur in the first half of the seventieth week of Daniel. Seal judgments one through four are represented as riders on horses called forth or summoned by the living creatures. These judgments depict conditions on the earth: the Antichrist and false messiahs, war, famine, pestilence, and death. The fifth seal judgment identifies believers killed for their testimony. They are seen as souls under the altar who will receive their glorified bodies at the end of the seventieth week prior to the Millennium. Many more believers will be killed in the same manner.

The sixth seal judgment begins the wrath of God. Many commentators claim all the seal judgments are the wrath of God, which doesn't appear logical, for God would be destroying his own people in seal judgment five. The first four seal judgments are the wrath of the Antichrist in his rise to power. With the sixth seal judgment, the great day of God's wrath begins. Commentators differ as to the beginning and end of the day of the Lord. Many have the "day" beginning with either the Rapture or the onset of the Tribulation and continuing through the Millennium. Including the Millennium, which is a time of blessing, as part of the day of the Lord does not fit multiple scriptures that repeatedly describe the day of the Lord as a time of judgment. Clearly in 2 Thessalonians 2:3-4, the day of the Lord will not come until the Rapture has occurred (before the Tribulation begins) and the Antichrist is revealed at mid-Tribulation. The day of the Lord is preceded in scripture by cosmic disturbances of great magnitude as seen in the sixth seal judgment. In this study, the day of the Lord is defined to be the 3 1/2-year period of time called the Great Tribulation, but it is acknowledged that the day of the Lord could strictly be applied as the literal 24-hour solar day of Christ's Second Coming. Both positions are supportable with day of the Lord scriptures.

Revelation 7

This is a parenthetical passage interjected into the main order of events to provide supplemental information necessary for a full understanding of the text. Two distinct bodies of believers are identified. The 144,000 are Jews, 12,000 from each of the 12 tribes of Israel. They are sealed by God for protection and witness for God through the execution of the trumpet judgments. After the trumpet judgments and before the bowl judgments, the 144,000 are pictured in chapter 14 as being in heaven on Mt. Zion. Since there is no indication that they physically die, they must be raptured, but separately from the "Rapture" that occurs before the Tribulation begins. The minority opinion, but the one held in this text, is that the 144,000 are raptured as the male child of Revelation 12 after the trumpet judgments. The question then becomes, when do the trumpet judgments occur? Do they occur in the first half of the seventieth week of Daniel or the second half? During the first half, Israel lives under the protection of the Antichrist. Therefore, the sealing of the 144,000 by God for protection is not as critical until the Antichrist breaks his covenant with Israel. Because the Antichrist doesn't proclaim himself to be God and begin his persecution of Israel until the middle of the Tribulation, the trumpet judgments fit better in the second half of the period. Hence, the rapture of the 144,000 occurs after the trumpet judgments in the second half of the Tribulation.

While some scholars see the woman as either the 144,000 Jews or the Church, the majority identify the woman as Israel. Because the woman and the male child are both Jewish, the 144,000 can be included as part of the woman. The woman, except for a remnant, will flee from the land of Israel into the wilderness to hide from the Antichrist during the second half of the Tribulation. However, there is no indication that the 144,000 go into hiding. In fact, if the 144,000 are witnesses for God, then they will be evangelizing, which is the probable situation, because the great multitude is saved largely as a result of their evangelistic efforts. Hence, the 144,000 are better represented as the male child than the woman.

The great multitude is the second group of believers identified in this chapter representing all nations, tribes, peoples, and tongues. They are referenced as "coming out" of the Great Tribulation, which is the second half of the seventieth week. This group is not the Church, because the Church was raptured before the Tribulation began. An elder asks who they are and where they have come from. They are in heaven because they died for their faith and for not taking the mark of the Beast or the number of his name. Following their death in the Great Tribulation, they are pictured in heaven with the martyred souls "under the altar" from Revelation 6. Both the great multitude and the martyrs receive their glorified bodies at the First Resurrection according to Revelation 20:4-5. However, the martyrs are beheaded for witnessing for Christ while the great multitude is beheaded for not taking the mark of the Beast. The great multitude is not identified as a group witnessing to others, but as the group that is witnessed to by others, i.e., the 144,000 Jews, martyrs, two witnesses, and angels.

Revelation 8

Chapter 8 describes the seventh seal judgment, and the first four trumpet judgments. The seventh seal judgment introduces the trumpet judgments, and in fact, the trumpet judgments come out of the seventh seal judgment. These four trumpet judgments affect the physical universe: trees, green grass, sea life, ships, rivers, springs of water, sun, moon, and stars. These judgments are partial in scope, affecting one-third of the designated areas.

Agricultural food products, sea life and food products from the sea, and fresh water are impacted by these judgments. The earth is dark two-thirds of each 24-hour cycle. Because of the destruction of trees, grass, green plants, the earth's atmospheric and oxygen cycles are damaged. The effect of these four trumpet judgments upsets the meteorological, hydrological, and biological systems of the planet.

Revelation 9

This chapter discusses the fifth and sixth trumpet judgments that affect God's moral creation, man. The fifth trumpet judgment is called the first woe. In this judgment, a star falls to earth from heaven with the key to the bottomless pit, which he uses to open the pit, releasing the demon locusts that have the power of scorpions to torment mankind for five months. The "star" is an angel of God. It is not a fallen angel, because a fallen angel would not be given a key to the bottomless pit (hell). God is in control and would not entrust the key to hell to a fallen angel who could release other captive beings. These locusts are not natural because they have a king, called Abaddon (Hebrew) or Apollyon (Greek), and natural locusts do not have a ruler. Secondly, a command is given to the locusts not to harm the grass, any tree, any green thing, or anyone with the protective seal of God on his/her forehead. Insect locusts would not respond to any command and by nature, would attack vegetation (grass, trees, or any green thing). The locusts only torment and do not have the power to kill. However, their sting is so painful that men will seek death, but will not be able to die.

The sixth trumpet judgment or second woe is the release of the four angels who have been bound at the great river Euphrates awaiting this fixed point in historical time, referred to as the hour, day, month, and year. An additional interpretation is that these angels will operate on the earth for thirteen months and twenty-five hours. It is obvious that these angels were prepared for this time and that their release is in the perfect timing of God. Therefore, both interpretations are applicable. Some Bible scholars believe that the four bound angels are the four satanic princes who ruled over the kingdoms of Babylon, Persia, Greece, and Rome as they oppressed Israel during the times of the Gentiles. A 200 million horsemen army follows these bound angels with the power to kill one-third of mankind with fire, smoke and brimstone, which are elements of hell. By their description, they are not natural horsemen, but demon horsemen and not natural horses, but demon animals. The elements used to kill mankind are elements of hell. Therefore, the horsemen can only be a demon army. It would appear from the context that those killed will be unbelievers, just as unbelievers were the ones tormented by the demon locusts under the fifth trumpet judgment. Unbelievers who are not killed, do not repent of their demon worship, murders, sorceries, sexual immoralities (including drugs), and thefts.

Revelation 10

This chapter divides the discussion of the judgments between the sixth and seventh trumpet to provide additional information. A mighty angel descends from heaven with a little open book in his hand. Although very majestic, this angel is not the Lord Jesus Christ. Christ is not called an angel in the Biblical text outside of being called the angel of the Lord in the Old Testament. This angel swears by someone greater than himself, i.e., the Lord Jesus Christ, eternal God and Creator of Heaven and earth. He proclaims that there should no longer be a delay in the completion of God's plan. The angel refers to the seventh trumpet angel who is about to sound and release the seven bowl judgments.

The exact contents of the little book are not specifically revealed but implied. The book is open because judgments have already been executed, and the little book describes the last seven judgments to be poured out on mankind. The book being open also demonstrates that the revelation is not to be hidden but to be shared. Because this event occurs at the sounding of the seventh trumpet in the midst of divine judgments, it is a logical conclusion that the contents and message of the little book are about further judgments to complete God's plan. Eating the book means that the message of salvation and the completion of the mystery of God is sweet as honey, but the description of the judgments to come is bitter to the stomach.

Revelation 11

Chapters 11-14 are parenthetical, occurring primarily from mid-Tribulation through the second half of Daniel's seventieth week. The first two verses of chapter 11 reveal that the temple is trodden down by the Gentiles for 42 months or the second half of the Tribulation. This occurs as the Antichrist breaks his covenant with Israel and attempts to annihilate the Jewish race. Next is the unveiling of the two witnesses for God who minister during the second half of the seventieth week, referred to as 1260 days. They have power as prophets of God to perform miracles, such as stopping the rain, turning water to blood, and striking the earth with plagues. Although the identities of the witnesses are not revealed and could be anyone, these prophets are most likely Enoch and Elijah. A majority of commentators agree to Elijah as one prophet, but fewer believe Enoch will be the second witness (rather than Moses). Enoch and Elijah have not tasted death and have not received their immortal glorified bodies, a fundamental requirement for their end-time ministry, because they are to be killed by the beast out of the bottomless pit at the conclusion of the Tribulation. The beast out of the bottomless pit is the satanic prince that empowers and controls the Antichrist. Some commentators believe this fallen angel could be the Prince of Greece, Prince of Babylon, or Prince of Assyria, each of whom was the satanic force behind a world empire that persecuted Israel during the times of the Gentiles. The Antichrist arises from the Old Grecian Empire territory as the "little horn" described in Daniel 8. At the end of the 1260 days, this satanic prince, through the agency of the Antichrist, kills the two witnesses, whose bodies then lie in the streets for three and one half days before being raised up by God.

The seventh angel announces that Christ is taking ownership of the kingdoms of the world. Heaven is opened, and the temple and ark are visible from earth. Thunderings, noises, lightning, earthquake, and great hail are manifestations of divine activity, signaling further judgment.

Revelation 12

A variety of events occur in this chapter. The woman is Israel. The great red Dragon with seven heads and ten horns is Satan. Heads and horns refer to kingdoms and kings. There are seven kingdoms that persecute Israel during the times of the Gentiles. Ten horns represent ten kings of the seventh kingdom. The heads are crowned, because Satan has had and will have control over each of those seven kingdoms. A majority of writers identify the male child as Christ, because the Bible states that He will rule the nations with a rod of iron. The male child is caught up to God, which these scholars designate as the ascension. However, the term "caught up" is a better description of the Rapture event than the ascension. Therefore, there is stronger merit for the position that the male child represents the 144,000 Jews sealed by God as described in chapter 7. A war in heaven (second heaven) is described during which Michael and his angels cast out the deceiver, Satan, and his angels. The Devil is now confined to the earth. The Devil's wrath is great as he persecutes the saints and the woman. The woman flees from the Dragon to the wilderness where she is nourished for a-times, and times, and half a time (42 months). The Dragon becomes enraged because he can't destroy the woman. Satan makes war with the woman's offspring, the remnant who remain in Jerusalem and keep the testimony of Jesus.

Revelation 13, Ezekiel 38-39, and Daniel 11

The Beast out of the sea with seven heads and ten horns is symbolic of the Antichrist. The horns are crowned, indicating that the

Antichrist has authority over the ten kings of the seventh empire. The Beast coming out of the sea portrays the Antichrist emerging from humanity. The seventh empire has the characteristics of previous empires symbolized by the lion (Babylon), bear (Medo-Persia), and leopard (Greece). Satan gives the Antichrist authority, power, and a throne. One of the heads is mortally wounded, but the deadly wound is healed, which could mean that one of the kingdoms that was defeated and destroyed in history will again be in power. Specifically, the Reconstituted Roman Empire will encompass the territories of the old Roman and Grecian Empires. Many commentators believe the Antichrist is mortally wounded and is resurrected supernaturally. Verses 12 and 14 seem to support a counterfeit resurrection. Satan does not have the power to truly resurrect anyone. During this time, the False Prophet performs signs and miracles and a counterfeit of the resurrection would deceive many people into following the Antichrist. Both applications will probably exist: the rise of a previous kingdom, and the counterfeit resurrection of the Antichrist. The Beast (Antichrist) is a very powerful political and military leader who has authority or rulership for 42 months. He speaks blasphemies against God and makes war and overcomes the saints (great multitude). Although the influence of the Antichrist is worldwide, the primary area of focus is the Middle East, Northern Africa, Europe, and Asia. Worship of the Antichrist will be worldwide.

The Antichrist makes a seven-year peace covenant with Israel that he will break at the three and one half year mark. During the first three and one half years of the seventieth week of Daniel, ten kings are in control of the Reconstituted Roman Empire territory. Just prior to the Antichrist's proclaiming himself to be God in the middle of the seventieth week, Gog, the chief prince from three powerful nations in the far north, Rosh (Russia), Meshech (Turkey), and Tubal (Turkey), along with the predominately Muslim nations of Magog (Islamic Russian territories), Persia (Iran), Ethiopia (possibly Sudan and Somalia), Libya

(Algeria, and possibly Tunisia, and Morocco), Gomer (Turkey), and Togarmah (Armenia and eastern Turkey) attack Israel. Gog is not the Antichrist, and this battle is not the battle of Armageddon. Israel is said to be dwelling safely in her land of unwalled villages at the time of this attack, which would precede the middle of the Tribulation, whereas Armageddon will be fought at the end of the seventieth week at the Second Coming of Christ. The armies of Gog will be destroyed by God Himself on the mountains of Israel to show His power, authority, and protection for Israel. At this time, God will again turn His face toward Israel, and they will be His people, and He will be their God. It will take seven months to bury the dead, and Israel will use their weapons for fuel for seven years (Ezekiel 38-39). With the threat of the armies of Gog removed, the Antichrist is able to defeat three nations from the Reconstituted Roman Empire territory, and the remaining seven will give him their power. This event will occur around the middle of the Tribulation.

Daniel describes another battle in which the King of the North (Syria or a coalition of Middle East nations including Syria) and the King of the South (Egypt or a coalition of North African nations including Egypt) attack the Antichrist in Israel and are soundly defeated by him. This battle is different from the battle described in Ezekiel 38-39 and different from the battle of Armageddon. Many scholars see this engagement preceding the battle of Armageddon. However, Daniel 11:40-45 causes that positional fit to be forced. A better and more logical scenario is to place this encounter before the battle identified in Ezekiel 38-39 that occurs prior to the middle of the seventieth week of Daniel. This encounter would then occur late in the second quarter of the Tribulation. The important point to note is that the battles of Ezekiel 38-39 and Daniel 11 may involve coalitions from areas north and south of Israel and are back-to-back military campaigns. (For more extensive discussion refer to Prophetic Keys: Daniel Military Campaign and Magog Military Campaign.)

Another Beast, called the False Prophet, exercises the power of the first Beast (Antichrist), performs great signs and miracles, causes worship of the Antichrist, and gives breath to the image of the Beast so that the image speaks. The False Prophet causes everyone to take the mark of the Beast or the number of his name. Failure to take the mark results in death. Some commentators believe that the "image" of the Beast actually refers to "images." People throughout the world will have images of the Beast in their homes. The False Prophet causes the images to speak through the operation of demons. If a person does not worship the image, the demons will know and will be instrumental in bringing about the non-worshipper's death.

Revelation 14

The 144,000 Jews are seen on the heavenly Mt. Zion in the presence of the Lamb. There exists controversy as to whether this passage is experienced in heaven or on the earth. Verse 5 says that the 144,000 are without fault before the throne. Therefore, the scene must be in heaven. Three angelic pronouncements are made. The first angel proclaims the Gospel to the whole earth, warning everyone to fear God for the hour of His judgments has come, referring to the last seven plagues. The second angel proclaims the fall of the city of Babylon that will occur at the end of the seventieth week. The third angel declares that anyone who takes the mark of the Beast or worships the Beast or his image will be eternally doomed to Hell.

The remaining verses, 14-20, describe the battle of Armageddon as the great wine press of the wrath of God and that a lake of blood will flow to the horses' bridles for 180 miles. This is figurative because an actual lake of blood would be unlikely. Millions will die in this battle and blood will be everywhere.

Revelation 15

Chapter 15 is a heavenly scene showing seven angels preparing to pour out seven bowls full of the final wrath of God. Standing on the sea of glass or floor of the throne room, are those who have victory over the Beast, over his image, over his number, and over his mark, singing the song of Moses. The song of Moses is most likely a song of triumph and resurrection. These believers are the great multitude of Revelation 7, also referred to as the overcomers of Revelation 12:11. This scene occurs near the end of the Tribulation Period.

Revelation 16

This chapter describes the seven bowl judgments that are introduced by the seventh trumpet judgment. Most commentators depict the bowl judgments as occurring throughout the last half of the seventieth week of Daniel or toward the very end of the period. However, commentators have not provided reasonable explanations for what events occur during the 30 days following the conclusion of the Great Tribulation, and why this 30-day period is specifically designated in Daniel 12. An interesting and non-traditional possibility for consideration is that the bowl judgments occur during this 30-day period referred to in Daniel 12. From Revelation 11, the two witnesses are said to minister for 1260 days or the last half of the seventieth week, and then they are killed. Their bodies lie in the street for three and one half days. At the end of the three and one half days, they are resurrected and received into heaven. Under a strict timeline application, their death and subsequent resurrection would then occur within the 30-day period following the 42-month Tribulation. If the blowing of the seventh trumpet judgment and release of the seven bowl judgments are included in this 30-day period following the last 42 months of the seventieth week of Daniel, this incongruity is satisfied. Matthew 24:29-30 further supports this contention by specifying that "immediately after the Tribulation of those days" (Great Tribulation), cataclysmic events occur to the solar system followed by the return of Christ. Therefore, cataclysmic activity and the Coming of the Lord follow the 42 months of the Great Tribulation. On the other hand, the duration of rule for the Antichrist is 42, not 43 months, and Tribulation related events use the 42-month designation. The preferred position of this study is that the bowl judgments are delivered in the 30-day period following the 42 months of the Great Tribulation. It is noted that not all questions are answered under either option. However, the significant point is that the bowl judgments occur in a time span of approximately 30-days at the end of the Tribulation, whether 42 or 43 months from the Abomination of Desolation.

The bowl judgments are called the wrath of God. These judgments are worldwide, but their greatest impact will be felt in the Beast's Empire (eighth). The trumpet judgments were partial in their destruction, while the bowl judgments are total. Malignant sores come upon those who worship the Beast, probably from the ink, chemicals, or computer chips used in the mark of the Beast. Sea and fresh waters are tainted. The sun scorches men with intense heat, and they blaspheme God. The effect is, therefore, on the unbeliever. The very throne of the Beast is effected by the fifth bowl judgment when his kingdom becomes full of darkness and people gnaw their tongues in pain. There is intense heat, darkness, and no water to drink. The great river Euphrates dries up, and demon spirits go forth from the Dragon, Beast, and the False Prophet to bring the kings of the world to battle God Almighty at Armageddon. The seventh judgment concludes the wrath of God with noises, thunderings, lightnings, and a mighty and great earthquake that divides Jerusalem into three parts, destroys Babylon, and the cities of the nations. Every island and mountain is destroyed and hailstones, weighing over 100 pounds, fall on men who continue to blaspheme God.

Revelation 17

Chapter 17 steps backward in time to look at the false religious system predominant in the first half of the Tribulation Period that controls the seventh empire comprised of the ten kingdoms.

This religious system is described as a Harlot or woman sitting on a scarlet colored beast that has committed spiritual fornication with the kings and peoples of the earth. This woman is called Mystery Babylon, the Mother of Harlots and of the Abominations of the Earth. She is the amalgamation and manifestation of all the false religions that have deceived mankind since Nimrod and his wife, Semiramis. This religious system has political clout and influence over the ten kings and is responsible for the martyrdom of many saints in the first half of the Tribulation. The ten kings hate this religious system and are happy to destroy her. After destruction of the religious system, the kings extend their allegiance to the Antichrist. The Antichrist is eager to rid himself of the Harlot, because he does not want any competition; he desires all the worship. The heads and horns are not crowned on this Beast, because it is not a kingdom or empire itself but operates within the kingdoms (woman rides the Beast). In scripture, the "Beast" is three things: a supernatural prince out of the abyss, the Antichrist, and the eighth kingdom. The Beast that John sees existed in the past as a satanic angel with demonic rulership over a country, most likely as the Prince of Greece ruling over the Grecian Empire, but possibly as the Prince of Babylon or Prince of Assyria. This satanic prince is currently locked in the abyss for release in the Tribulation. The seven heads of the Beast are also called seven mountains. From scripture, mountains refer to kingdoms, so the seven heads are seven kingdoms. Each kingdom has had or will have a king. Five kingdoms have fallen: Assyria, Egypt, Babylon, Medo-Persia, and Greece. The present kingdom, Rome, was the dominant empire in John's day, and the kingdom to come will be a reconstitution of the Roman Empire that will continue for a short time, i.e., the first half of the Tribulation. The Beast Empire, then, is the eighth kingdom, or a kingdom that had existed in the past as one of the initial five kingdoms, such as the re-formation of the Grecian Empire that will co-exist within the Reconstituted Roman Empire territory. The ten horns are ten kings that give their authority and power to the Beast for the second half of the seventieth week. The woman is also the great city Babylon, which is the center of the false religious system.

Revelation 18

This chapter is devoted to a discussion of Babylon, the city that is a habitation for demons, sorcery, and foul spirits. The city will be very rich and will commit spiritual fornication with the merchants of the earth. God commands His people to come out of her, because He will judge the city and destroy her by fire and make her desolate in one hour. The kings of the earth, merchants, and sea traders lament over her destruction, because she has made them wealthy. The city is destroyed to the point that her ruins will never be found. The prophecies concerning Babylon in the Old Testament have not been completely fulfilled, which is why Babylon must be rebuilt. Many commentators believe Babylon is actually Rome because of the scriptural references to seven hills, and Rome geographically sits on seven hills. If God was referring to "Rome," He would have said "Rome." He said "Babylon," and prophecies concerning the total destruction of Babylon have not been fulfilled. Therefore, this section must refer to a literal rebuilding of the ancient city of Babylon. The destruction of Babylon occurs under the seventh bowl judgment.

Revelation 19

Chapter 19 opens with praise in heaven followed by the marriage ceremony of the Lamb. The marriage supper of the Lamb occurs on earth after the Tribulation. The rest of the chapter describes the Second Coming of Christ and the battle of Armageddon. The heavens open up, and Christ appears on a white horse with the armies of heaven following Him. The armies or host of heaven always refer to angels, so Christ returns with His angels (2 Thessalonians 1:7). Additionally, the New Testament Church Age saints raptured before the Tribulation Period will accompany Christ and the angelic host as part of Christ's army riding on white horses and attired in white robes (Jude 14, 1 Thessalonians 3:13). Old Testament saints, the 144,000 Jewish witnesses, the two witnesses, and Tribulation saints, including the great multitude and the martyrs under the altar as identified at the fifth seal judgment, are not part of this army, because they have yet to receive their resurrected, immortal, glorified bodies. Christ does all the fighting. The Antichrist and his armies are destroyed by the brightness of Christ's Coming and by the sharp sword out of His mouth, which is the Word of God. Armageddon is referred to as the supper of the great God. The Antichrist and the False Prophet are thrown alive into the lake of fire as its first inhabitants.

Revelation 20

An angel, probably Michael, descends from heaven with the key to the bottomless pit and binds Satan in chains for 1000 years. It is assumed that demons and fallen angels are also bound with him for the 1000 years. The First Resurrection is completed when the Old Testament saints, 144,000 Jewish witnesses, two witnesses, and Tribulation saints (martyrs and great multitude) receive their resurrection bodies before the Millennium begins. At the end of this 1000-year millennial period, Satan is released for a season to again deceive the nations. The followers that join him are in number as the sands of the seashore. Satan will empower another "Gog" or leader of peoples from the land of Magog (Russia). Satan leads this army to Jerusalem in a final attack against God, but there is no battle. God destroys this army with fire and casts the Devil into the lake of fire. All unbelievers go before God's White Throne where the books are opened. No one will have an excuse. The unbelievers of all time, fallen angels, and demons are all judged and thrown into the lake of fire. Death and Hades, which some scholars believe are fallen angels, are cast into the lake of fire. The second death and resurrection are completed. Their torment in the lake of fire will be day and night forever and ever.

Revelation 21

John describes a new heaven and new earth. The great oceans and seas no longer exist. The holy city, New Jerusalem, descends from heaven prepared as a bride for the saints. The city is on a great high mountain or is literally a great mountain in structure. The city is constructed of precious gems and transparent gold. The streets are made of gold like transparent glass. The New Jerusalem is 1500 miles in length, width, and height, with walls on four sides, and three gates per side, each a giant pearl. The city has no need for the sun or the moon, because the glory of God illuminates the city. God and the Lamb are the temple, and the redeemed saints live in the very presence of God. Natural people living on the earth who endure the Tribulation, live through the Millennium, and do not follow Satan in his final revolt will live on the earth forever. They will be able to visit the city.

Revelation 22

The river of living water proceeds from the throne of God and flows through the city. On each side of the river is the tree of life with twelve kinds of fruit for the healing of the nations. There shall no longer be a curse. God is the light and temple of the city. Jesus proclaims a blessing for anyone who keeps the words of this prophecy and says that He is coming quickly. He tells John that no one should add or subtract from the words of the prophecy, and the prophecy should not be sealed up. Jesus is the Alpha and the Omega, and His command is to "come."

PART ONE

A VERSE-BY-VERSE GUIDE TO THE BOOK OF REVELATION

CHAPTER ONE

THE ALPHA AND OMEGA

Revelation 1:1-The Revelation of Jesus Christ, which God gave him to show His servants things which must shortly take place. And He sent and signified it by His angel to His servant John,

The Book of Revelation is a revelation of Jesus Christ, by Jesus Christ (Revelation 22:16), and about Jesus Christ. The message is from God, to Jesus, to His angel, to John, to the seven churches, and to general readers. God has provided this revelation to show the things or future events that must shortly come to pass. These events will climax the age. The term "must" means that these events will occur in the divine fulfillment of God's plan. History has a purpose and is not haphazard. "Shortly" indicates that when the time comes, the events will occur without delay. The definition of "signified" is to make a clear record of. The message is not to be hidden but to be revealed. The angel reveals the events in vision form to John (Revelation 22:6), who is commanded to write what he sees (Revelation 1:11).

Revelation 1:2-who bore witness to the word of God, and to the testimony of Jesus Christ, and to all things that he saw.

John is testifying that this record of future history was given to him by divine inspiration of the Holy Spirit who bears witness to the Word of God. John recorded events exactly as he saw them. This record is John's eyewitness account. To the reader, these events are prophecy, but to John they are history being recorded in advance. The "testimony of Jesus Christ" refers to the many statements made by Christ Himself to John in the Book of Revelation.

Revelation 1:3-Blessed is he who reads and those who hear the words of this prophecy, and keep those which are written in it; for the time is near.

Revelation is a prophetic book of divine origin. A blessing is bestowed upon the reader, hearers, and those who are obedient to the things written, presupposing that they all understand what is written. For the greatest understanding to occur, one must interpret the events literally wherever possible. The "reader" is in the singular tense and means reading aloud. The "hearers" are in the plural tense, which implies that the Book is being read in churches and in meeting places. If it was important for saints to read, hear, and obey Revelation in John's day, how much more important is it now when the events are much closer to being fulfilled?

Revelation 1:4- John, to the seven churches which are in Asia: Grace to you and peace from Him who is and who was and who is to come, and from the seven Spirits who are before His throne,

The Revelation message is addressed to seven literal churches in Asia Minor. "Seven" signifies completeness, totality, and perfection. John in writing to these churches was in fact writing to the whole Church. "Grace" and "peace" were the methods of greeting to the Greeks and Hebrews respectively. John affirms the eternal, infinite, and immutable attributes of God. The "seven spirits" before the throne refer to the Holy Spirit, signifying His completeness, fullness, and perfection. Seven Spirits may also refer to the manifestations and/or personality of the Holy Spirit. The seven spirits that make up the personality of the Holy Spirit are listed in Isaiah 11:2 as the spirit of the Lord, spirit of might, spirit of wisdom, spirit of counsel, spirit of understanding, spirit of knowledge, and spirit of the fear of the Lord.

Revelation 1:5-and from Jesus Christ, the faithful witness, the firstborn from the dead, and the ruler over the kings of the earth. To Him who loved us and washed us from our sins in His own blood,

Two members of the triune Godhead were mentioned in verse four. In verse five, discussion centers on the second person of the trinity, Jesus Christ, depicting His First and Second Comings.   During His First Coming, Jesus was called the Faithful Witness, because He walked on earth as a prophet, revealed God to man, did everything the Father told Him to do, said everything the Father told Him to say, and was faithful unto death.   By being the first born from the dead, Christ defeated death and broke its power through His resurrection. He was the first man to be raised up and given an immortal glorified body. At His Second Coming, Jesus will establish His rulership over the kings of the earth continuing into and throughout the Millennium during which He will rule with a rod of iron as King of kings and Lord of lords. When saints are washed in His blood, they are accepting His substitutionary sacrifice and receiving His payment of the debt for man's sins. His blood didn't just cover the sins of mankind but totally remitted them. Because of His sacrificial work, every person can become the righteousness of God in Christ Jesus.

Revelation 1:6-and has made us kings and priests to His God and Father, to be glory and dominion forever and ever, Amen.

Jesus' sacrifice provided for the re-creation or rebirth of man and completely paid man's debt. As a result, believers are called kings and priests, or literally a kingdom of priests, to minister to the Lord forever. The role of believers in this dispensation as a kingdom of priests is to intercede for others. "Glory and dominion forever" are expressions of praise.

Revelation 1:7-Behold, He is coming with clouds, and every eye will see Him, and they also who pierced Him. And all the tribes of the earth will mourn because of Him. Even so, Amen.

At the ascension, Jesus left in the clouds, and He will return in the same manner. This verse references His Second Coming during which every person will see Him, and the Jews who had Him crucified will see Him as their Messiah (Zechariah 12:10). At His Second Coming, the world will be standing in darkness so dense that men will be gnawing their tongues. The light from the sun, moon, and stars will have been diminished substantially. Out of this darkness as lightning flashes from the east to the west, Christ returns, and literally every eye will see Him. People will view Him with amazement, wonder, and horror, because the time of final judgment will have arrived.

Revelation 1:8-"I am the Alpha and the Omega, the Beginning and the End, says the Lord who is and who was and who is to come the Almighty."

In this verse, Jesus calls Himself the "Alpha and the Omega," the "Beginning and the End," who is, was, and is to come, the "Almighty." This attribute of omnipotence, the "Almighty," is ascribed to God the Father in Revelation 4:8. In Revelation 1:11, 17, and several verses in chapter 22, Jesus adds the descriptor "First and the Last." By these references to His eternal nature, Jesus is claiming equality with God the Father. The eternal nature of the Father is seen in verse four "Him who is and who was and who is to come," as well as in Isaiah 41:4; 44:6; and 48:12, where He is called the "First and the Last." The eternal nature of Christ is seen in Revelation 1:8, 11, 17, 2:8, and 22:13, where He is referred to as the "First and the Last." Therefore, both the Father and the Son are called the "First and the Last," clearly establishing the deity of Christ. In Revelation 21:6, God is called the "Beginning and the End" and the "Alpha and the Omega," while in Revelation 22:13, the same titles are ascribed to Jesus, further supporting the deity of Christ.

Revelation 1:9-I, John both your brother and companion in tribulation, and in the kingdom and patience of Jesus Christ, was on the island that is called Patmos for the word of God and the testimony of Jesus Christ.

John reminds the readers that he has shared in tribulation and persecution, specifically from the Romans for the crime of sharing the testimony of Jesus and the Word of God. John acknowledges that, in Christ's kingdom, saints are to be patient or to "occupy" until Jesus comes. The isle of Patmos was a desolate six by ten mile rocky volcanic island off the western coast of Asia Minor, approximately 30 miles from Ephesus, where criminals and political prisoners were imprisoned. According to tradition, John was dunked in boiling oil with no harmful effect, similar to the three companions of Daniel, who were thrown into the fiery furnace. Since the Romans could not successfully execute John, they exiled him to Patmos because of his testimony for Jesus and the Word of God. At Patmos, John was positioned exactly where God wanted him in order to be given this end-time prophecy.

Revelation 1:10-I was in the Spirit in the Lord's Day and I heard behind me a loud voice, as of a trumpet,

John is "in the spirit," which means he is having a vision or is in a trance. The Lord's Day is Sunday or the first day of the week. Jesus rose on Sunday and Pentecost began on a Sunday. This day is not to be confused with the day of the Lord that spans a lengthy period of time during the Tribulation and is identified with the judgments of God. A loud voice, "as of a trumpet," is the voice of Christ. In many biblical instances, an important message has been preceded by a trumpet blast.

Revelation 1:11-saying, "I am the Alpha and the Omega, the First and the Last, and, What you see, write in a book and send it to the seven churches which are in Asia: to Ephesus, to Smyrna, to Pergamos, to Thyatira, to Sardis, to Philadelphia, and to Laodicea."

Jesus calls Himself the "Alpha and the Omega" and the "First and the Last," denoting His eternal nature. He commands John to record what he sees in a book or scroll, which is Revelation, and to send it to the seven churches in Asia Minor. Each church is identified by name; and geographically, they were positioned in circular relationship to one another. John functions as a scribe, writing only what he saw or heard.

Revelation 1:12-Then I turned to see the voice that spoke with me. And having turned I saw seven golden lampstands,

John turns to see who is speaking with him and sees seven golden lampstands that, according to verse 20, represent the seven churches. Lampstands are light holders. Christ is the originator of the light, and the churches are reflectors or conveyors of the light of the Gospel to the world.

Revelation 1:13-and in the midst of the seven lampstands One like the Son of Man, clothed with a garment down to the feet and girded about the chest with a golden band.

Jesus is seen in the midst of the churches. He is the Head of the Church and has control over the Church. John sees a vision of the glorified Christ. Jesus' clothing distinguishes Him as a king or priest. In His earthly ministry, Christ, as the Son of Man, walked in the office of a prophet. Currently in Heaven, Christ, as the Son of Man, is in His high priestly or intercessory role. At His Second Coming and into the Millennium, Christ, as the Son of Man, will be King of kings.

Revelation 1:14-His head and His hair were white like wool, as white as snow, and His eyes like a flame of fire;

The description of Christ's head and hair as "white like wool" and "white as snow" is identical to the description of the Father as found in Daniel 7:9, denoting wisdom and His everlasting and eternal nature. "His eyes like flame of fire" shows omniscience, and as He judges, nothing can be hidden from Him.

Revelation 1:15-His feet were like fine brass, as if refined in a furnace, and His voice as the sound of many waters;

"His feet like fine brass" signify judgment of the ungodly. He will also judge the godly at the Judgment or "Bema" seat of Christ. "His voice as the sound of many waters" is descriptive of the voice of God as found in Ezekiel 43:2.

Revelation 1:16-He had in His right hand seven stars, out of His mouth went a sharp two-edged sword, and His countenance was like the sun shining in its strength.

"Seven stars" are in His right hand, which according to verse 20 represent the angels of the seven churches through whom this message is sent. The "two-edged sword" is a reference to the Word of God (Hebrews 4:12). The spoken Word of God is an offensive weapon to be used against the enemies of God. In Revelation 19:13, 15, Jesus defeats the armies of Antichrist with the sword out of His mouth, the Word of God. In the day-of-judgment, Satan, the Antichrist, and the False Prophet will have no defense against God's Word. Jesus' countenance, like the sun, is the manifestation of His glory as was seen on the Mount of Transfiguration in Matthew 17:2.

Revelation 1:17-And when I saw Him, I fell at His feet as dead. But He laid His right hand on me, saying to me, "Do no be afraid; I am the First and the Last."

When John sees Christ, he falls down under the power of God. John walked with Jesus in His earth ministry and saw Christ after His resurrection, but now John sees Jesus in His glorified form, which he only glimpsed on the Mount of Transfiguration. Christ comforts John, telling him not to be afraid. Jesus again refers to Himself as the "First and the Last," which denotes His eternal nature and that nothing preceded Him nor will anything or anyone continue after Him.

Revelation 1:18-"I am He who lives, and was dead, and behold, I am alive forevermore. Amen. And I have the keys

to Hades and of Death."

Jesus refers to His resurrection and His victory over death. Jesus is alive forever. He has the keys to Death and Hades, which acknowledge His authority over Death and Hell. Jesus went to Hell, paid the price for mankind, and then stripped Satan of his authority over Death and Hell.

Revelation 1:19-"Write the things which you have seen, and the things which are, and the things which will take place after this."

This is the outline verse to the Book of Revelation. John is again commanded to write. First, he is to write the "things he has seen," which is the vision of the glorified Christ. Second, he is to write the "things which are," which pertain to the letters to the seven churches in chapters 2 and 3. Lastly, he is to write the "things which will take place" after the Church Age, which is captured in chapters 4-22.

Revelation 1:20-"The mystery of the seven stars which you saw in My right hand, and the seven golden lampstands: The seven stars are the seven angels of the seven churches, and the seven lampstands which you saw are the seven churches."

A mystery in the Bible is something that man cannot figure out unless God reveals it to him. The stars and lampstands are symbols used earlier in this chapter that are now defined, so the reader and hearers will understand the message. The "seven stars" represent the angels of the seven churches, and the "seven lampstands" represent the seven churches.

CHAPTER TWO

MESSAGES TO THE CHURCH

(Refer to Prophetic Keys: Letters to the Churches and Comparative Overview of Churches of Revelation 2-3)

Ephesus

Ephesus was a great seaport and the largest city in Asia Minor with a population over 250,000. Ephesus was considered the commercial market center of Asia. Geographically, Ephesus was on the shore of the Aegean Sea about 50 miles from Smyrna, half-way between Rome and Jerusalem, and was the geographic center of the Roman Empire. The name "Ephesus" means desirable. Paul started the Ephesian church, which according to history was very mature and successful and grew to over 10,000 members. Paul wrote his letters to the Corinthian church while in residence at Ephesus. John spent the latter part of his life at Ephesus. Ephesus was a bed for every false religion, cult, and superstition. Magical arts and cult prostitution dominated the city. The temple of Diana (Artemis), considered one of the seven wonders of the ancient world, stood at Ephesus. Artemis was a multi-breasted figure and the goddess of fertility who was worshiped for sexual potency. The statue of Artemis stood 60 feet high and her temple measured 425 feet by 225 feet by 60 feet.

Revelation 2:1-3-"To the angel of the church of Ephesus write, These things says He who holds the seven stars in His right hand, who walks in the midst of the seven golden lampstands: I know your works, your labor, your patience, and that you cannot bear those who are evil. And you have tested those who say they are apostles and are not, and have found them liars;

and you have persevered and have patience, and have labored for My name's sake and have not been weary."

Jesus is seen as the One who is among the churches and the One who controls the churches. He gives ten points of commendation that include knowing their works, labor, patience, perseverance, and their non-tolerance for evil. Therefore, Ephesus is doctrinally sound, consistent under pressure, diligent to the Word, and untiring. Their works have to be based on faith, because they are commended for them.

Revelation 2:4-"Nevertheless I have this against you, that you have left your first love."

Ephesus appears to be a strong and very mature church spiritually. However, Jesus lists one point of condemnation against them; they have left their first love. They have become too caught up and involved in all their good works. They have taken their eyes off Jesus and are neglecting their personal relationship with Him. He no longer was the center of their lives. They are no longer dependent or reliant upon Him or motivated by His love. They are beginning to backslide.

Revelation 2:5-"Remember therefore from where you have fallen; repent and do the first works, or else I will come to you quickly and remove your lampstand from its place -- unless you repent."

The Ephesians are commanded to repent and be restored by returning to their former position in Christ in doing good works with the right focus or motive and with a hunger for Christ. If they do not repent, then Jesus will remove their lampstand. They will cease to be a living organism, becoming only an organization or an assembly, but no longer a lampstand or light-bearer. Because Ephesus no longer exists as a major city, it appears that they did not heed this warning of repenting and returning to their first love.

Revelation 2:6-"But this you have, that you hate the deeds of the Nicolaitans, which I also hate."

The church at Ephesus hated the deeds of the Nicolaitans as did Christ. Christ doesn't hate the people, only their deeds. The Nicolaitans were followers of a heretic named Nicholas. They taught and practiced immoral and impure doctrines separating the physical and spiritual natures of man, thus giving them license to sin, e.g., community of wives, adultery, and fornication were not considered sinful. They established an ecclesiastical, holy order or spiritual hierarchy that placed some followers closer to God than others. As a result, people were required to bring all issues of life to others in the cult who were at a higher level. Therefore, those who were higher in the order ran the lives of the people lower in the order.

Revelation 2:7-"He who has an ear let him hear what the Spirit says to the churches. To him who overcomes I will give to eat from the tree of life, which is in the midst of Paradise of God."

The overcomer is promised heaven and eternal life by eating of the tree of life in the midst of the paradise of God. In this case, they will be overcoming the works and deeds of the flesh. As an overcomer, a person would not only be a partaker of Christ's eternal nature in heaven but would be a partaker of His nature on earth with all the rights, privileges, and authority of a child of the King.

Smyrna

Smyrna means "myrrh" or bitter and is a symbol for suffering. Smyrna was a trade city with numerous guilds, a faithful ally of Rome, and a city of Caesar worship. As a great port city, it was located about 50 miles from Ephesus on the Aegean coast. During the reign of Tiberius, an earthquake devastated the city, but it survived and was rebuilt. Smyrna was wealthy and prosperous with the "street of gold" that extended from the temple of Zeus, chief of the gods, to the temple of Cybele, the goddess of nature. Today, Smyrna is a thriving port called Ismir. Polycarp, a convert of John, was the famous pastor of Smyrna who refused to say that Caesar was lord. In A.D. 155, Polycarp was placed into the arena and given the choice of cursing the name of Christ and making sacrifice to Caesar or being put to death. Polycarp replied, "86 years I have served Him, and He has done me no wrong. How can I blaspheme my King who saved me?" Polycarp was burned at the stake, but the flames did not harm him, so he was executed with a spear, and his blood put out the fire.

Revelation 2:8-"And to the angel of the church in Smyrna write, These things says the First and the Last, who was dead, and came to life."

The letter is addressed to the angel or messenger of the church of Smyrna. Jesus referred to Himself as the First and the Last, who was dead and came to life, reflecting His eternal nature and power over death.

Revelation 2:9-11-"I know your works, tribulation, and poverty (but you are rich); and I know the blasphemy of those who say they are Jews and are not, but are a synagogue of Satan. Do not fear and of those things which you are about to suffer. Indeed, the devil is about to throw some of you into prison, that you may be tested and you will have tribulation ten days. Be faithful until death, and I will give you the crown of life. He who has an ear, let him hear what the Spirit says to the churches. He who overcomes shall not be hurt by the second death."

Jesus says He knew their works, tribulation, and poverty. Smyrna Christians were under constant and tremendous persecution from the Roman government for their stand for Christ and opposition to Caesar worship. Jesus recognizes that Satan is behind the persecution. Those persecuting the Smyrna church said they were Jews but were not. In the same manner today, believers are persecuted by those who claim to be Christians and are not. Jesus tells the Smyrna church not to fear and to be "faithful unto death," which connects with why He referred to Himself as being alive after death. Tribulation in this passage does not refer to the Tribulation Period, but to the pressure, persecution, and affliction imposed upon them by those opposed to Christ. A crown of life is a martyr's crown that is promised to the overcomer who cannot be harmed by the second death or separation for eternity from God. Overcomers will be a part of the First Resurrection. Smyrna Christians were not called to repent, because their stand for Christ under intense persecution demonstrated their faith, as will the Tribulation saints demonstrate their faith through martyrdom. They say they are poor, but Jesus says they are rich, meaning they are rich in spiritual or eternal matters. They are rich in God, and their spiritual riches are far more important than material wealth.

Pergamos

Pergamos was the church infiltrated. Even though Ephesus had left their first love, and Smyrna was suffering from Roman persecution, they had both maintained sound doctrine. Pergamos, however, was a different story. This church allowed the evil doctrines of Balaamism and Nicolaitanism to gain a foothold. The doctrine of Balaamism involved spiritual idolatry and fornication, while the doctrine of Nicolaitanism involved a spiritual hierarchy. Politics and religion were heavily intertwined in Pergamos, causing temptation for Christians to compromise their beliefs for political gain.

Pergamos was located inland, about 50 miles north of Smyrna. The city was known for its great library of over 200,000 parchment scrolls. The word "parchment" is derived from Pergamum. The library was given to Cleopatra by Antony. Cleopatra had the library relocated to Alexandria, Egypt.

Pergamos was an important religious center of an imperial

cult or Caesar worship, and it had three notable temples in the city, dedicated to Zeus, Dionysos, and Athena. The altar of Zeus stood 40' high and was one of the seven wonders of the ancient world. It is supposed to still exist somewhere in West Germany. Pergamos became the headquarters for cult worshippers, and in verse 13, is referred to as Satan's seat. The altar of Zeus was even throne like in appearance. Pergamos was also known as a medical center where the god of medicine, Aesculapius, was worshiped, commonly under the sign of the coiled snake on a pole. The word for scalpel originated from this deity. Various medical practices were combined for healing, such as snake handling, dream interpretation, religious meditation, and medical arts. In addition to the imperial cult, there were many other heathen cults and cult worshippers, including temple prostitutes. The Pastor of Pergamos was Antipas, who according to tradition, was put to death by being enclosed in a burning brazen bull.

Revelation 2:12-"And to the angel of the church in Pergamos write, These things says He who has the sharp two-edged sword."

The letter is addressed to the angel or messenger of the church of Pergamos, and Christ identifies Himself as having a sharp two-edged sword. The "sharp two-edged sword" is the Word of God, which is God's counter to the false doctrines of Balaamism and Nicolaitanism.

Revelation 2:13-"I know your works, and where you dwell, where Satan's throne is. And you hold fast to My name, and did not deny My faith even in the days in which Antipas was My faithful martyr, who was killed among you, where Satan dwells."

Pergamos is commended for three actions: works, holding fast to Jesus' name, and not denying His faith. Jesus informs them that He knows where they live and where Satan's seat is located, acknowledging His understanding of the difficulty with which they must contend. Jesus calls Antipas His faithful martyr and commends their faith even to martyrdom.

Revelation 2:14-15-"But I have a few things against you, because you have there those who hold the doctrine of Balaam, who taught Balak to put a stumbling block before the children of Israel, to eat things sacrificed to idols, and to commit sexual immorality. Thus you also have those who hold the doctrine of the Nicolaitans, which I hate."

Ephesus would not have anything to do with false doctrines or its followers, but the people of Pergamos have allowed both into their midst. By entertaining or allowing these false doctrines, deception entered, causing believers to stumble in their walk and fellowship with Christ. Some of the cultic practices included preaching for money, prophesying for money, inter-marriage of Christians and pagans, eating meat or food sacrificed to idols, and committing sexual immoralities. The doctrine of the Nicolaitans was covered in the discussion on Ephesus. The doctrine of Balaam refers to Balaam as a prophet of God who misused his office and anointing for personal gain. This deception would have application to all believers who misuse the giftings, talents, and abilities they receive from God for their own purposes, rather than God's.

Revelation 2:16-17-"Repent or else I will come to you quickly and will fight against them with the sword of My mouth. He who has an ear, let him hear what the Spirit says to the churches. To him who overcomes I will give some of the hidden manna to eat. And I will give him a white stone, and on the stone a new name written which no one knows except him who receives it."

Pergamos is told to repent. If not, Jesus will fight against them with the Word of God. The Word will be the judge of their actions. The overcomer will have new manna to eat, i. e., spiritual food to replace the false doctrine. Hidden manna refers to a

word or "rhema" received from the Holy Spirit, which is the wisdom of God. The white stone symbolizes victory, which comes
from standing on and applying the Word of God. In the court
system, jury members voted or determined their verdict with a
stone, white for not guilty and black for guilty. The overcomer
receives a new name that no one knows except the receiver. This
"new name" is selected by God Himself, apparently to be used in
private communications between God and the believer.

Thyatira

Thyatira was known as the adulterous church. It was situated
about 40 miles southeast of Pergamos. Although Thyatira was
the smallest and least important of the seven cities, it was
famous for its commerce and is believed to have had more trade
guilds than any other city in Asia. There were guilds for wool
workers, linen workers, makers of outer garments, dyers, leather
workers, tanners, potters, bakers, slave dealers, and bronze-
smiths. The trade guilds were religiously based with each one
dedicated to a particular deity. Powerful women, who lived luxuriously in the city, controlled most guilds. In order to work or
operate a business in the city, guild membership was required.
However, membership meant pressure and compromise for
Christians, because they had to attend the lavish parties and eat
meat and food sacrificed to idols. Thyatira was a rich and busy
commercial city involved in the manufacture of woolen goods.
Lydia, the seller of purple mentioned in the Book of Acts, was
from Thyatira.

**Revelation 2:18-"And to the angel of the church in Thyatira
write, These things says the Son of God, who has eyes like a
flame of fire, and His feet like fine brass."**

The letter is addressed to the angel or messenger of the church of
Thyatira. Christ identifies Himself as the Son of God with eyes
a flame of fire and feet as fine brass, which are descriptive terms
of judgment. Thyatira Christians had allowed a false prophetess

and teacher into their midst and false teachings and teachers are judged by the Living Word of God.

Revelation 2:19-"I know your works, love, service, faith, and your patience; and as for your works, the last are more than the first."

Thyatira is commended for six things: works, love, service, faith, patience, and increased works or growth. Ephesus lacked love but did not tolerate evil. Thyatira exercises love but permits evil, entrusting an important teaching and leadership role to an evil prophetess.

Revelation 2:20-21-"Nevertheless I have a few things against you, because you allow that woman Jezebel, who calls herself a prophetess, to teach and beguile My servants to commit sexual immorality and to eat things sacrificed to idols. And I gave her time to repent of her sexual immorality, and she did not repent."

Jesus has four things against Thyatira: permitting Jezebel to teach, permitting Jezebel to seduce Christians to commit fornication, permitting Jezebel to seduce Christians to eat food sacrificed to idols, and tolerating Jezebel in spite of her non-repentance. Jezebel was not only immoral, but also defiant because she refused to repent. This woman is like the Jezebel in the Old Testament, who through a political marriage with Ahab, King of Israel, compromised God's kingdom with the world's kingdom. Jezebel caused Israel to worship Baal and practice paganism. The Jezebel of Thyatira is identified as a prophetess who is causing Thyatira Christians to mix idolatry and sexual immorality with Christianity, which is again compromising Christianity with the world system. The Jezebel cult, according to scholars, was deeply involved in spiritual fornication, spiritual harlotry, heathen worship, and her teachings allowed followers to participate in her pagan ceremonies, because these followers were so far advanced spiritually, that anything done in their bodies would not impact their spirits. The church is being deceived and seduced by false religious spirits. Giving her time to repent showed how long-suffering God is in providing even the most ungodly with an opportunity for repentance.

Revelation 2:22-24-"Indeed I will cast her into a sickbed, and those who commit adultery with her into great tribulation, unless they repent of their deeds. And I will kill her children with death. And all the churches shall know that I am He who searches the minds and hearts. And I will give to each one of you according to your works. But to you I say, and to the rest in Thyatira, as many as do not have this doctrine, and who have not known the depths of Satan, as they call them, I will put on you no other burden."

Judgment of the followers of this cult is an application of the law of sowing and reaping as Jesus said He would give to each one according to his/her works. Continuing to adhere to Jezebel's teachings is spiritual adultery that will cause her followers to enter into great tribulation and become sick and die. These scriptures will literally be fulfilled as the many followers of Antichrist and the False Prophet are killed during the Great Tribulation through a variety of judgments for their continual refusal to repent. Jezebel's children being killed with death refers to the ultimate doom of her converts to her paganistic teachings. The Jezebel teaching is the very depth of Satan, and a very serious sin as judged by Christ.

Revelation 2:25-29-"But hold fast what you have till I come. And he who overcomes, and keeps My works until the end, to him I will give power over the nations - He shale rule them with a rod of iron; As the potter's vessels shall be broken to pieces - as I also have received from My Father; and I will give him the morning star. He who has an ear, let him hear what the Spirit says to the churches."

The believer is told to do three things: hold fast until Christ returns, overcome, and keep His works until the end. The over-comer is to hold fast to the Word of God and keep separated from the world system and seducing spirits. In so doing, the overcomer is promised positional power and authority over the nations, ruling with a rod of iron, the morning star, which is the presence of Christ, and crushing all the resistance of the nations or victory with Christ over the evil forces of the world.

CHAPTER THREE

HEAR WHAT THE SPIRIT SAYS

(Refer to Prophetic Keys: Letters to the Churches and Comparative Overview of Churches of Revelation 2-3)

Sardis

Sardis represents the church of dead orthodoxy. She was an active, wealthy, commercial city positioned about 33 miles from Thyatira. At one time, the famous King Midas, known for his golden touch and treasures, ruled Sardis. Sardis originally stood on a hill and was almost impregnable by enemy forces. However, Cyrus of Persia defeated Sardis because of her complacency and slackness. Cyrus surrounded the city for 14 days but couldn't conquer it. A Sardinian soldier dropped his helmet over the wall and crawled down a fault in the rocks to retrieve it. The army of Cyrus crawled up the same fault and took the city at night. In A.D. 17 an earthquake destroyed the city of Sardis, but she was rebuilt by the Roman emperor Tiberius. Today only ruins remain. Cybele was the chief goddess of the city, and wealth and immorality were her reputation.

Revelation 3:1-"And to the angel of the church in Sardis write, Things says He who has the seven Spirits of God and the seven stars; I how your works, that you have a name that you are alive, but you are dead."

Jesus identifies Himself as having the "seven Spirits of God" referring to the Holy Spirit and the manifestations of the Holy

Spirit. His holding the seven stars acknowledges His authority over the churches. Sardis had a name for being alive, but Jesus says she is dead. A spiritually dead church can only be reborn by the work of the Spirit of God, which is how Christ describes Himself. From an external observation, the church was considered spiritual or had a form of godliness but without any spiritual power. What would cause a church to have a form of godliness or appear spiritual and alive but in fact be dead? The answer is "religious tradition." Jesus battled religious tradition during His earth ministry. He called the religious leaders hypocrites, which is what religious tradition causes people to be when they hold doctrines of men as doctrines of God. Jesus said in Mark 7 that the Word of God could be invalidated or become ineffectual because of man's traditions.

Revelation 3:2-3-"Be watchful, and strengthen the things which remain, that are ready to die, for I have not found your works to be perfect before God. Remember therefore how you have received and heard; hold fast and repent. Therefore if you will not watch, I will come upon you as a thief, and you will not know what hour I will come upon you."

Jesus says their works are not perfect before God. The church is not meeting the needs of the people. No one is being saved, healed, delivered, ministered to, prayed with, etc. He tells them to be watchful and to strengthen the things that remain. In other words, Sardisians are instructed to build on what little they have that was spiritually correct, before it to dies. Jesus further commands them to remember what they have seen and heard, to hold fast, and repent. If they are not watchful, He will come upon them as a thief, implying they will not be ready for His return.

Revelation 3:4-"You have a few names even in Sardis who have not defiled their garments; and they shall walk with Me in white, for they are worthy."

Even in spiritually dead Sardis, Jesus has a few followers that are worthy and righteous, that is, haven't defiled their white garments. "White" symbolically represents righteousness.

Revelation 3:5-6-"He who overcomes shall be clothed in white garments, and I will not blot out his name from the Book of Life; but I will confess his name before My Father and before His angels. He who has an ear, let him hear what the Spirit says to the churches."

Overcomers from this church are clothed in white, implying they are saved and righteous before God, will not have their names blotted out of the Book of Life, and will have their names confessed by Jesus before the Father and His angels. Expositors generally agree that everyone has their names entered into the Book of Life when they are born. If they accept Christ as Savior and Lord during their lifetime, their names will not be blotted out of the Book, but in fact, will also be entered into the Lamb's Book of Life (Revelation 13:8). If a person dies and has not accepted Christ, his/her name is blotted out of the Book of Life and of course will never be entered into the Lamb's Book of Life. During the Great Tribulation, followers of the Antichrist who take the mark of the Beast or the number of his name will have their names deleted from the Book of Life (Revelation 17:8) before they die. Once a person accepts the mark of the Beast, there is no salvation for him/her. It is interesting to note that Jesus is the One who blots names out of the Book of Life, and for those who have accepted Him as Savior, He is the One who confesses their names before the Father God.

Philadelphia

Philadelphia was the city of brotherly love or the church of the open door. It was located about 30 miles southeast of Sardis and was situated on a hill 800 feet high. Philadelphia was the youngest of the seven churches and was called the gateway to the east because of its strategic location tangent to the Roman Road, between the

Aegean and Mediterranean Seas and upper plateaus of Asia Minor. Philadelphia was described as a city full of earthquakes because after every large earthquake, the city would experience tremors for years. An earthquake destroyed Philadelphia in A.D. 17, but the city was rebuilt by the Emperor Tiberius. Philadelphia was the center of a great grape vineyard and prospered in the wine business. It was the center for the worship of Dionysos (Bacchus), the god of wine, in addition to having temples dedicated to many other gods. Philadelphia was also known for its hot springs and as a trade center for the distribution of wool.

Revelation 3:7-"And to the angel of the church in Philadelphia write, These things says He who is holy, He who is true, He who has the key of David, He who opens and no one shuts, and shuts and no one opens."

Jesus calls Himself "holy and true," the One with the key of David, and He who opens a door that no one can shut and closes a door that no one can open. The divine sovereignty of Christ is represented in the phrases "He who opens and no one shuts, and shuts and no one opens." Jesus is the standard of all holiness and truth. The key of David signifies His millennial reign on David's throne. He is a descendent of David and has the legal right to rule from Jerusalem. Jesus is the One who creates opportunities for believers, and as they operate according to His will, these opportunities and blessings cannot be stopped. Commentators have also identified the "open doors" as outreaches and evangelistic opportunities to the lost.

Revelation 3:8-9-"I know your works. See, I have set before you an open door, and no one can shut it; for you have little strength, have kept my word and have not denied My name. Indeed I will make those of the synagogue Satan, who say they are Jews and are not, but lie –indeed I will make them come and worship before you feet, and to know that I have loved you."

Jesus commends them for their works, for keeping God's Word, for not denying His Name, and for having little strength, which resulted in reliance on Him.   Keeping His Word means the Philadelphians are diligently doing or acting on His Word and that the Word of God is a way of life for them. Again, He tells them that He has set before them an open door that no one can shut. An open door refers to opportunities that become available both in the spiritual and natural realms as believers act on the Word and follow the leading of the Lord. The Holy Spirit will guide, lead, direct, and order the steps of those who are consistent, diligent, and obedient to the Word of God. Followers of Satan are in the city and many claim to be Jews but are not. They can't get a foothold in this church.

Revelation 3:10-"Because you have kept My command to persevere, I also will keep you from the hour of trial which shall come upon the whole world, to test those who dwell on the earth."

This is a key scripture, especially to those who believe in the pre-Tribulation Rapture of the Church. This church of believers, that keep the commands of Jesus and persevere, will be kept from the hour of trial or temptation that is to come upon the whole world. This verse is a promise of deliverance to the believing Church that is to be raptured before the judgments from God are poured out upon the world. Many Greek scholars argue over the correct meaning of this verse according to the original language. Some say that the Church will be protected by God *within* the sphere of persecution but will experience or will be on earth for part or all of the Tribulation. Although the Greek can be applied as these scholars describe, that is not the most accurate usage according to other scholars. The majority application is that the believing Church will be removed or kept from the hour of trial by being raptured before the Tribulation commences, and therefore, will not be on earth during the Tribulation Period when God judges sin and an ungodly world. The latter position is the one adopted in this study.

Revelation 3:11-"Behold, I come quickly! Hold fast what you have, that no one may take your crown."

Jesus tells these church believers to hold fast to what they have, that is, the Word of God, works, patience, and the name of Jesus. Jesus says He is coming quickly, meaning that when all the events begin to unfold in the end times, His Second Coming will occur within a short time period, and His appearance will be as a thief in the night to those who are not watchful and prepared.

Revelation 3:12-13-"He who overcomes, I will make him a pillar in the temple of my God and he shall go out no more. And I will write on him the name of my God, the New Jerusalem, which comes down out of heaven from My God. And I will write him My new name. He who has an ear, let him hear what the Spirit says to the churches."

Overcomers are pillars in the temple of God and remain in the temple continually. Jesus will write on the overcomers the name of God, the name of the New Jerusalem that will descend from heaven, and Jesus' new name. These names show ownership and possession.

Laodicea

Laodicea was the neutral or lukewarm church that operated on a humanistic philosophy based on the will of the people. Laodicea was a very wealthy banking and manufacturing commercial center located 45 miles southeast of Philadelphia and 40 miles east of Ephesus. The wealth of the city was generated from the manufacture of clothing from black wool, banking and finance, and a medical school known for its eye ointment, Cerryrium. Laodiceans were so wealthy that they felt they did not need Caesar or God. The church was successful, rich, prosperous, but spiritually deficient. Today, the ruins of Laodicea cannot be found. The city was named after Laodice, wife of Antiochus II, the Greek King of Syria. In A.D. 61, Laodicea was destroyed by an earthquake but rebuilt itself without the aid of Rome or the Emperor Nero.

Revelation 3:14-"And to the angel of the church of the Laodiceans write, 'These things says the Amen, the Faithful and True Witness, the Beginning of the creation of God."

As with the other letters, this one is also addressed to the angel or messenger of the church. Jesus describes Himself as the "Amen," "Beginning of the creation of God," and the "Faithful and True Witness." This city in need of no one, not even Rome, was very wealthy and caught up into themselves. Laodicea was the very pinnacle of humanistic evolution. Jesus counters their evolutionary philosophies by informing them that He was present in the beginning before creation, He is the Creator of all things, and He is the Omega, the Amen. He is the eternal, everlasting God, the Alpha and Omega, and His Word is Faithful and True.

Revelation 3:15-16-"I know your works, that you are neither hot nor cold. I could wish you were cold or hot. So then, because you are lukewarm, and neither cold nor hot, I will spew you out of My mouth."

This church obviously did some works, but Christ is not impressed and counts their works for nothing, neither hot nor cold. Not only does Laodicea not receive one commendation, but also she receives the severest criticism of all the churches. He denounces this church for her pride, dependence on material wealth, lack of concern, neutrality or indifference toward God, and says He would rather have them cold toward God than spiritually indifferent and compromising. Lukewarmness is not to be tolerated in the Church of God.

Revelation 3:17-"Because you say, I am rich, have become wealthy, and have need of nothing – and do not know that you are wretched, miserable, poor, blind, and naked."

The Laodiceans profess they are rich and in need of nothing, but

Christ says they are poor, blind, wretched, naked and miserable. Their "need for nothing" is the root of their problem. If they don't need anything, then they can never trust in or become dependent upon Christ. Laodicea speaks materially, but Jesus replies spiritually. The church is materially rich from the manufacturers of clothing, but Christ says they were naked. They are materially rich from banking, but Christ says they are poor. They are materially rich from their medical center and production of an eye ointment, but Christ says they are blind. They say they have need of nothing, implying that they are happy and content in their manner of life. Christ evaluates them as wretched and miserable.

Revelation 3:18-"I counsel you to buy from Me gold refined in the fire, that you may be rich; and white garments, that you may be clothed, that the shame of your nakedness may not be revealed; and anoint your eyes with eye salve, that you may see."

Christ informs them that He is their only answer. He counsels them to buy gold from Him, which meant that He is their true wealth. His righteousness or white garments are contrasted against their self-righteous works represented by the manufacture of black wool. He uses their production of eye salve to counsel them to anoint their own eyes so that they might see and be enlightened to the truth. In their current condition, they cannot see their own spiritual needs.

Revelation 3:19-20-"As many as I love, I rebuke and chasten. Therefore be zealous and repent. Behold, I stand at the door and knock. If anyone hears my voice and opens the door, I will come in to him and dine with him and he with Me."

Jesus says that He chastises those He loves. Laodicea is full of carnal compromising Christians, but Christ loves them and desires them to repent or turn from their ways and become spiritually right with Him. In fact, He wants them to be zealous and intensely devoted to Him. He says He is standing at the door knocking. They have to open the door to Him. Jesus will never force or impose Himself or His will upon a person. The Laodiceans or any Christians in similar circumstances must want to change, and if so, Christ will respond by dining with them. He is waiting for the invitation for personal fellowship.

Revelation 3:21-22-"To him who overcomes I will grant to sit with Me on My throne, as I also overcame and sat down with My Father on His throne. He who has an ear, let him hear what the Spirit says to the churches."

The overcomer will sit with Christ on His throne. In other words, the overcomer will have daily fellowship with Christ and will rule and reign with Him forever. By accepting Christ's substitutionary sacrifice, the worldly compromising Christian can move from a position of being "spewed out" of Jesus' mouth to ruling over the nations with Him from His throne. Repentance opens the door to victory.

CHAPTER FOUR

THE CHURCH IN HEAVEN

(Refer to Prophetic Key: Rapture)

Revelation 4:1-After these things I looked, and behold, a door standing open in heaven. And the first voice which I heard was like a trumpet speaking to me saying, "Come up here, and I will show you things which must take place after this."

"After these things" refers to the events of chapters 2 and 3 that discuss the Church Age. Therefore, "after these things" is after the Church Age, which to pre-Tribulationists is after the Rapture of the Church. According to Revelation 1:19, "after these things" will form the third and final division of the Book of Revelation. Many pre-Tribulationists believe the command to John to "come up here" foreshadows the Rapture of the Church. John sees a door open into the third heaven, signifying that John's revelations will include heaven itself. The voice speaking to John is assumed to be Christ, because in Revelation 1:10, Christ's voice is said to sound like a trumpet. Jesus is planning to show John events that will take place after the Church Age. The word "must" means that God is control, and these events will occur according to His divine plan.

Revelation 4:2-Immediately I was in the Spirit; and behold, a throne set in heaven, and One sat on the throne.

John is immediately in the spirit realm and sees God sitting on His

69

throne. The throne is a fixed or central point in this chapter with everything else in positional relationship to it. The throne symbolizes the authority, power, and majesty of God the Father.

Revelation 4:3-And He who sat there was like jasper and a sardius stone in appearance; and there was a rainbow around the throne, in appearance like an emerald.

In John's vision God is like jasper and the sardius stone in appearance. The jasper stone is a translucent crystal stone, diamond-like with a purplish hue. The color purple signifies royalty and sovereignty. The sardius stone is a transparent, blood red stone. Red signifies sacrifice and judgment. These are the first and last of the twelve precious stones set in the high priest's breastplate. Jesus is the high priest of believers and is referred to in Revelation as the "First and the Last." The emerald green rainbow around the throne represents God's mercy even in time of judgment. The circle represents eternity, and the color green stands for God's eternal nature. This description is a reminder of God's covenants and mercy in the midst of tribulation because at the White Throne judgment, the rainbow will be absent. These descriptive colors reflect the radiance and brilliance of God's Shekinah glory. Scriptures state that God is light (1 John 1:5), and He dwells in light that no man can approach (1 Timothy 6:16).

Revelation 4:4-Around the throne were twenty-four elders sitting, clothed in white robes; and they had crowns of gold on their heads.

Twenty-four literal thrones with elders sitting on them encircle God's throne. There are three major positions regarding the identity of the elders: 1) the elders represent angelic beings, 2) the elders represent the total body of believers, both Old Testament and New Testament saints, or 3) the elders represent the Church or New Testament saints only.

Position 1 - Angels

The elders are not angels, because the term "elder" is never used to describe an angel. Additionally, according to Revelation 5:11 and 7:11, the 24 elders are listed separately from both the four living creatures and angels, and are therefore, a group of beings distinct from angels. Furthermore, angels are never described as wearing crowns or sitting on thrones. Those are promises reserved for man.

Position 2 – Old Testament and New Testament Saints

An elder is a position of rank and responsibility. In the New Testament, elders are overseers and spiritual leaders in the Church. In the Old Testament, elders were the heads or leaders of families and tribes. 1 Chronicles 24 states that the priesthood was divided into 24 orders, and the elders or heads of these 24 orders represented the entire Levitical priesthood. In 1 Peter 2:5 and 2:9, believers are referred to as a holy and royal priesthood. Some scholars support the view that the 24 elders must therefore represent the entire body of believers from both Old and New Testament times with the number 24 standing for the 12 tribes from the Old Testament and 12 apostles from the New Testament. While this view has greater merit than position 1, position 3 presents the preferred interpretation.

Position 3 – The Church or New Testament Saints

Revelation 1:6 calls those believers whose sins have been washed in the blood of Christ, kings and priests or a kingdom of priests. In the letters to the seven churches (or Church) in Revelation 2 and 3, "overcomers:"
- are clothed in white
- rule with Christ
- sit down with Christ on His throne
- are pillars in the temple
- are given the crown of life

The elders fit into this class of overcomers, because they:
- are clothed in white robes, indicating their righteousness before God

- wear victors crowns received for rewards following the judgment seat of Christ
- worship God because they have been redeemed
- are a kingdom of priests
- will reign with Christ

These statements about overcomers only apply to Church Age believers. Therefore, the elders can only represent the New Testament Church. Furthermore, at the Rapture, only New Testament saints are included. The spirits and souls of Old Testament believers now in heaven will not be included in the Rapture. They will be judged for rewards and receive their immortal glorified bodies along with the Tribulation saints after the end of the Tribulation Period, thereby finalizing the First Resurrection according to Revelation 20:4.

Additionally, in Revelation 7:11-14 an elder identifies to John a group of saints that are clothed in white robes, washed in the blood of the Lamb, and who serve God day and night before the throne. These believers are Tribulation saints who are born again after the Rapture of the Church but will not minister unto God until the Millennium. By the context of these passages, the Tribulation saints are not represented by the elders who are already in heaven prior to the Tribulation saints arrival.

In Revelation 1, Jesus is seen walking among the candlesticks or in the midst of the churches or Church. In Revelation 5:6, Jesus as the Lamb is in the midst of the elders or representatives of the Church. Therefore, in summary, the elders are representative of the resurrected Church, a kingdom of priests, a chosen generation, a royal priesthood, and a holy nation who proclaim the praises of God, as seen in 1Peter 5-10, Revelation 2-3, 4:4, 8-11, 5:6, 5:8-14, 7:11-14, and 11:16-18.

Revelation 4:5-and from the throne proceeded lightnings, thunderings, and voices. And there were seven lamps of fire burning before the throne, which are the seven Spirits of God.

Thunderings, lightnings, and voices from the throne are evidence of the manifestations of the glory of God as a prelude to judgment. The seven spirits of God represent the seven manifestations of the Holy Spirit. The Holy Spirit is before the throne. His ministry in connection with the Church is completed at the Rapture of the Church. However, the Holy Spirit is omnipresent on the earth, and His role or work in the salvation of man does not change. In the Old Testament, the Holy Spirit operated through prophets, priests, and kings. During the Church Age, the Holy Spirit works through individual members of the body of Christ. In the Tribulation, the Holy Spirit will move primarily through the 144,000 Jewish witnesses, martyred saints, and the two prophets of Revelation 11.

Revelation 4:6-Before the throne there was a sea of glass, like crystal. And in the midst of the throne, and around the throne, were four living creatures full of eyes in front and in back.

The sea of glass, like crystal, before the throne is the floor of the throne room. In Revelation 15:2, overcomers are seen standing on the sea of glass. Everything in heaven is described in crystalline terms showing purity and holiness. Symbolizing the throne room floor as a sea depicts its vastness.

In the midst and around the throne are four living creatures. These living creatures are high-ranking angelic beings that dwell in the presence of God. They are similar to seraphim, described in Isaiah 6:1-8, who are above the throne, have six wings, and are continually praising God, saying "Holy, Holy, Holy." They are similar to the cherubim of Ezekiel 1:4-28, 10:8-22 who are beneath the throne, have four wings, four faces each, and are full of eyes, denoting spiritual insight, perception, and knowledge.

Some commentators see the living creatures as guardians of the throne and that nothing can get past them without being seen, although these commentators never identify from what or whom the cherubim are guarding or protecting the throne. Many

Bible expositors teach that the living creatures are cherubim. However, they appear to be an order of angel similar to seraphim and cherubim but distinct. They have six wings and continually praise God like the seraphim but are full of eyes like the cherubim. The description of their faces is different in that each living creature has a unique face, whereas each cherubim has four faces. The living creatures are listed as totaling four in number, but the Bible doesn't number the seraphim or cherubim.

Revelation 4:7-The first living creature was like a lion, the second living creature like a calf, and the third living creature had a face like a man, and the fourth living creature was like a flying eagle.

The four living creatures are described as a lion, calf (or young ox in some translations), man, and flying eagle. Several theories regarding the meaning of the different faces for each living creature are summarized as follows:

Living Creatures	Portrait of Christ in the Gospels	Attributes of Christ in Divine Government	Nature-Number 4 for Creation or World	Tabernacle Camping Order
1st living creature like a lion	Matthew King-Lion of Judah	Majesty-Power Authority	Wild Animals	East
2nd living creature-like a calf	Mark Suffering Servant	Strength	Domestic Animals	West
3rd living creature like a man	Luke Son of Man	Intelligence Moral Choice	Highest of Animal Creation	South
4th living creature like an eagle	John Divine-Son of God	Swiftness-Wisdom	Birds	North

Revelation 4:8-And the four living creatures, each having six wings, were full of eyes around and within. And they do not rest day or night, saying: "Holy, holy, holy, Lord God Almighty, Who was and is and is to come!"

The living creatures, each with six wings, are full of eyes around and within, and praise God day and night for His eternal and omnipotent nature. The repetition of "holy" in sets of three is thought to acknowledge in worship the triune Godhead, God the Father, God the Son, and God the Holy Spirit.

Revelation 4:9-11-Whenever the living creatures give glory and honor and thanks to Him who sits on the throne, who lives forever and ever, the twenty-four elders fall down before Him who sits on the throne and worship Him who lives forever and ever, and cast their crowns before the throne, saying: "You are worthy, O Lord, To receive glory and honor and power; For you created all things, And by Your will they exist and were created."

God is continually worshiped in heaven. The elders cast their victors' crowns before the throne, because in the presence of God crowns or any other possession or symbol of recognition mean nothing. The living creatures and the 24 elders, representing all of creation, worship God as the eternal Creator. In this hymn of praise, they ascribe glory, honor, and power to Him for He is worthy to receive it.

 CHAPTER FIVE

THE SEVEN SEALED SCROLL

Revelation 4 is a vision of God as Creator. Revelation 5 is a vision of God as Redeemer.

Revelation 5:1-And I saw in the right hand of Him who sat on the throne a scroll written inside and on the back, sealed with seven seals.

God the Father is seated on the throne with a scroll in His hand. Up until the second century, sheets of papyrus used in a scroll were made from strips of bulrush laid horizontally, then overlaid vertically, pressed together with Nile water, glued and beaten with a mallet, smoothed with a stone, and finally joined together horizontally. Wooden rollers were attached at each end. The scroll was unrolled with the right hand and rolled with the left. Normally a scroll was written on only one side. As an example, the Book of Revelation in scroll format would be about 15' long. In Roman times, the seal was generally made of wax and imprinted, and only an authorized person could break the seal. Once the scroll was opened, it couldn't be resealed with the same seal.

Scroll Represents Judgments

Seven signifies completeness or fullness. This scroll is a record of God's judgments in the end times. The seven seals correspond to the seven seal judgments. The scroll is written on both sides showing the fullness of God's judgments, the seal judgments on one side and the seven trumpet judgments on the other. The little, open book of chapter 10 presents the completion of God's judgments, the bowl judgments, as an extension to the seven-sealed scroll.

Scroll Represents the Title Deed to the Earth

Many commentators see the scroll as the title deed to the earth. Satan managed to usurp Adam's authority over the earth, but Jesus stripped Satan of this authority and returned it to man (Matthew 28:18-19). Jesus through His substitutionary sacrifice and the shedding of His blood purchased and redeemed the earth from Satan. The price for man's redemption has been paid in full. Satan no longer has legal authority over mankind. His only authority is exercised by deception over those who will allow it, such as unbelievers or believers who don't know their rights and privileges as children of God. With the opening of the scroll, Christ claims and subsequently takes possession of the earth by judging all sin, rebellion, and the unrighteous. The only person who can claim and possess the earth is the one who purchased it. In this sense, the scroll is a type of title deed to the earth. As long as the scroll is sealed, Satan has some time left to control the earth and deceive mankind. Satan as the god of this world has a time lease on the planet but has no legal right to possess the earth. The earth belongs to God and the time lease is running out for Satan. Following the Rapture of the Church, the Antichrist will enter into a seven-year covenant with Israel. The Tribulation Period will begin with the opening of the seven-sealed scroll. Christ will literally take possession of the earth at His Second Coming after the battle of Armageddon. Christ will then set up a theocratic government and rule the earth from Jerusalem throughout the Millennium.

Revelation 5:2-Then I saw a strong angel proclaiming with a loud voice, "Who is worthy to open the scroll and loose its seals?"

The strong angel asks who is worthy or deserving to open the scroll. One translation of this verse says, "who claims the right to open the book?"

Revelation 5:3-4-And no one in heaven or on earth or under the earth was able to open the scroll, or to look at it. So I wept much, because no one was found to be worthy to open and read the scroll, or to look at it.

No one man is able to open the scroll, because man has had nothing to do with the redemption of mankind, and therefore, does not have a legal right to open the scroll. "Man," as the understood subject of this verse, further demonstrates that the contents of the scroll are related to man and the earth. John is saddened because if no one is found worthy to open the scroll, then the earth will remain under the control of Satan.

Revelation 5:5-But one of the elders said to me, "Do not weep. Behold, the Lion of the tribe of Judah, the Root of David, has prevailed to open the scroll and loose its seven seals."

John is comforted by one of the elders, who reveals that there is hope because the "Lion of the tribe of Judah," the "Root of David," has prevailed to open the scroll and loose its seven seals. Jesus is the Lion of the tribe of Judah, having descended from the line of Judah. The "lion" was the symbol for the messianic tribe of Israel. This is His title when exhibiting power and authority, and when He returns at the Second Advent, He will return as the Lion from Judah or King of kings. The Root of David shows Christ's right, as the Messiah, to sit on David's throne. Jesus is descended from the line of David and has the legal claim in fulfillment of prophecy to rule the earth in the Millennium from the throne of David. The word "prevailed" means conquered, overcame, or achieved the victory. At Calvary, Jesus won the victory for mankind over death, hell, and the grave.

Revelation 5:6-And I looked, and behold, in the midst of the

throne and of the four living creatures, and in the midst of the elders, stood a Lamb as though it had been slain, having seven horns and seven eyes, which are the seven Spirits of God sent out into all the earth.

John in his vision sees Christ standing in the midst of the throne, living creatures, and elders as a Lamb that had been slain, i. e., the marks of the crucifixion remain visible on His body. Since Jesus came as the Lamb at His First Advent to redeem mankind, this picture of Christ points to and acknowledges His sacrificial and atoning work. Horns represent power. The "seven horns" are symbolic of complete and total power as King of kings over the world's nations, as well as expressing His divine attribute of omnipotence. The "seven eyes" symbolize that He is all knowing and all seeing, thereby expressing His divine attribute of omniscience. The seven horns and seven eyes are also identified with the seven Spirits of God demonstrating the work and presence of the Holy Spirit in heaven and on earth.

Revelation 5:7-8-Then He came and took the scroll out of the right hand of Him who sat on the throne. Now when He had taken the scroll, the four living creatures and the twenty-four elders fell down before the Lamb, each having a harp, and golden bowls full of incense, which are the prayers of the saints.

Jesus takes the scroll from the Father. Only the Father God can give the scroll, and only God the Son can receive the scroll. Immediately, the four living creatures and the elders fall down in worship. To the Jew, the harp is an instrument of praise as recorded in the Old Testament. The prayers in the golden bowls are probably those of Saints for the Second Coming of Christ and His judgment of sin.

Revelation 5:9-10-And they sang a new song, saying: "You are worthy to take the scroll, And to open its seals; For you were slain, And have redeemed us to God by Your blood Out of

every tribe and tongue and people and nation, And have made us kings and priests to our God; And we shall reign on the earth."

A new song is sung. Revelation is a book of "new things." There are new names, new songs, new heaven, new earth, new Jerusalem, as well as in Revelation 21:5 Jesus says He makes all things new. The "new" is not newness in point of time but newness in quality, form, or character that has not previously existed. The Lamb's saving work creates the situation for a new song that lauds the substitutionary sacrifice of Christ and His purchase of mankind's redemption. As a result, the saints become kings and priests, or according to some translations of the Bible, a kingdom of priests. The approach to God is open. The saints do not need the priesthood, because they are the priesthood serving God day and night (Revelation 8:15). The saints will also rule and reign with Christ (Revelation 20:4). In Revelation 4:11, the words of praise "You are worthy" are ascribed to God the Father as Creator. Identically, Christ as the Lamb, the Redeemer, is praised for His worthiness, thereby, acknowledging His deity and co-equality with the Father.

Revelation 5:11-Then I looked, and I heard the voice of many angels around the throne, the living creatures, and the elders; and the number of them was ten thousand times ten thousand, and thousands of thousands,

John sees and hears a countless number of angels around the throne in addition to the elders and the four living creatures. This number is quantified to be a hundred million plus millions.

Revelation 5:12-saying with a loud voice: "Worthy is the Lamb who was slain To receive power and riches and wisdom, And strength and honor and glory and blessing!"

This is an angelic proclamation of Christ's worthiness to receive power, riches, wisdom, strength, honor, glory, and blessing. This proclamation is a seven-fold anthem of praise, acknowledging Christ's attributes of majesty.

Revelation 5:13-14-And every creature which is in heaven and on earth and under the earth and such are in the sea, and all that are in them, I heard saying: Blessing and honor and glory and power Be to Him who sits on the throne, And to the Lamb, forever and ever! Then the four living creatures said, "Amen!" And the twenty-four elders fell down and worshiped Him who lives forever and ever.

John hears universal worship to the Father and the Son by all of creation in heaven, earth, sea, and under the earth. The implication is that even the animal kingdom praises God. The four living creature say "amen" and the elders fall down in worship of the eternal God. Through these songs of praise and worship, the deity of Christ is emphasized in a manner equal to the Father.

THE SEALS OPENED

(Refer to Prophetic Keys: Antichrist, Tribulation Period Events and Conditions on Earth During the Tribulation, Tribulation Judgments, and Matthew 24)

Introduction

Chapter six begins discussion of the seventieth week of Daniel, commonly called the Tribulation. The Antichrist makes a covenant with Israel for seven years that allows her to live in peace. However, the peace is short lived because at the mid-point of this period, the Antichrist breaks the covenant with Israel and proclaims himself to be God. During the first three and one half years, the religious system or "Mystery Babylon" (Revelation 17) strongly influences the ten kings and kingdoms of the Reconstituted Roman Empire and persecutes Israel and the saints of God. During the last half of the Tribulation, called the Great Tribulation, persecution of Israel and the saints is by Antichrist himself as he is empowered by Satan and controlled by the beast out of the abyss. Antichrist becomes obsessed with the destruction of Israel.

Revelation 6:1-Now I saw when the Lamb opened one of the seals; and I heard one of the four living creatures saying with a voice like thunder, "Come and see."

Christ, as the Lamb of God, has taken the book or scroll out of the hand of the Father who sits on the throne (Revelation 5:1, 5,

7). Christ breaks the seals one at a time. There are seven seals and seven seal judgments. As each seal is broken, the contents are revealed. John both sees and hears all the events that are occurring. Again, it is acknowledged that John is providing an eyewitness account of events of the end of the age. One of the four living creatures speaks with a voice like thunder, signifying impending judgment. The phrase "come and see" is literally "come" or "proceed," which is a calling forth of the horsemen to action. "Come" or "proceed" is not addressed to John.

Revelation 6:2-And I looked, and behold, a white horse. And he who sat on it had a bow; and a crown was given to him, and he went out conquering and to conquer.

John looks and beholds the contents of the scroll in vision form. The rider on the white horse is not Christ, because Christ is opening the seals. Christ will come to earth on a white horse at the end of the 70th week of Daniel as shown in Revelation 19. This rider is the Antichrist, who enters history as a conqueror going forth to conquer, demonstrating plan and purpose. The Antichrist conquers and wages war throughout the Tribulation. His head is crowned, signifying rulership, and he has a bow, but no arrows, signifying that he conquers not only by military might but also by deception. Satan gives him power or empowers him. The Greek word for "crown" denotes a victor's crown, and the color "white" denotes victory. The Antichrist is a false Christ, imitator of Christ, or substitute Christ who is referred to as the "little horn" in Daniel 7-8. He rises to power out of the ten kingdoms of the Reconstituted Roman Empire. At this time, not only will the Antichrist appear on the scene, but also scores of false messiahs, as stated in Matthew 24:5 "For many will come in my Name, saying I am the Christ, and will deceive many." Also Matthew 24:24 states, "many false christs and false prophets will arise..." Some commentators have theorized that the white horse rider is Gog, the military leader described in Ezekiel 38-39. However, Gog doesn't operate by deception, as does the

Antichrist, but by military might. Gog is on the geopolitical scene for only a short time, as God destroys him on the mountains of Israel. The Antichrist is not destroyed until the battle of Armageddon at the end of the age.

Revelation 6:3-When he opened the second seal, I heard the second living creature saying, "Come and see."

The second rider is summoned by a second living creature in the same manner that the first rider was summoned by the first living creature.

Revelation 6:4-And another horse, fiery red, went out. And it was granted to the one who sat on it to take peace from the earth, and that people should kill one another; and there was given to him a great sword.

The fiery red horse represents war, which is the natural result of the Antichrist as a conqueror going forth conquering. The result of the war or wars is that peace is removed from the earth, and people "kill" (in the Greek it is literally "slaughter" or "butcher") one another. "Taking peace from the earth" indicates the world will be engulfed in wars of extreme magnitude throughout the Tribulation. The "sword" is symbolic of war, bloodshed, and conflict. Insightful commentary on this time period indicates that there will be not only wars, but also racial strife, labor strikes and unrest, civil wars within nations, individual feuds, murders, rampant organized crime, and in general, a state of anarchy. Matthew 24:7 states "Nation will rise against nation and kingdom against kingdom..." Mark 13:12 refers to family members betraying one another to the point of death.

Revelation 6:5-When He opened the third seal, I heard the third living creature say, "Come and see," And I looked, and behold, a black horse, and he who sat on it had a pair of scales in his hand.

The third rider is summoned onto the scene of history by the third living creature. The black horse is symbolic of famine, which naturally follows conquest and war, the first two seal judgments. A pair of scales or balances shows scarcity of food and the severity of the famine. In the Old Testament scales refer to bread eaten by weight. The economic results of the famine are severe.

Revelation 6:6-And I heard a voice in the midst of the four living creatures saying, "A quart of wheat for a denarius, and three quarts of barley for a denarius; and do not harm the oil and the wine."

The voice in the midst of the four living creatures probably belongs to either God the Father or God the Son. A "denarius" or penny was a day's wages and could purchase a quart of wheat or three quarts of barley. Basically, all of a person's money must go for food with nothing left for rent or other required expenses. Oil and wine are products for the rich and are not to be harmed. Hence, the necessities of life for the poor are in short supply, but luxuries for the rich are in abundance. Oil could also refer to petroleum, and wine could include all intoxicating beverages, which again are "wants" of the rich. Scarcity of food will even be more extreme for Christians, because they will not be able to buy or sell during the second half of the Tribulation without the mark of the Beast, which they will not receive.

Revelation 6:7-When He opened the fourth seal, I heard the voice of the fourth living creature saying, "Come and see."

The fourth living creature calls forth the fourth rider.

Revelation 6:8-And I looked, and behold, a pale horse. And the name of him who sat on it was Death, and Hades followed with him. And power was given to them over a fourth of the earth, to kill with sword, with hunger, with death, and by the beasts of the earth.

The pale horse is actually chlorine or yellow-green in color. The rider is Death, and Hades follows after Death, but it is not stated whether or not on a horse. One interpretation is that people on the earth at this time will have to choose death, as they stand for Christ, or to follow the Antichrist and end up in hell. However, the more viable interpretation is that death visits only the ungodly, because Hades follows Death, and Hades is the abode for the unrighteous. Because the apparent onset of this event is not long after the Rapture, not many people have been saved. Hence, most of the world is unrighteous. Death of the ungodly continues throughout the Tribulation Period. Power is given to Death and Hades over one-fourth of the earth, which refers to mankind. Power implies death, because the discussion is focused on death and the methods of death. This power is of course from Satan. Death and Hades could also refer to fallen, satanic angels who rule over the nether regions. After the White Throne judgment, Death and Hades will be cast into the lake of fire, which is the eternal place of incarceration for created, spiritual beings, including the unrighteous, fallen angels, and demons.

"To kill with the sword" refers to the wars of the second seal; to kill with hunger is the famine of the third seal; and death is the result from the fourth seal judgment. Beasts of the earth can refer to a number of things, such as wild animals, poisonous snakes, or rats (remember the black plague), or ungodly, powerful, political and military dictators who are many times called "beasts." Scholars have pointed to the AIDS virus and/or other super viruses as the agents for fulfillment of this prophecy. In the year 2000 the population was approximately six billion. If, as an estimate, one billion are "born again" Christians who are raptured, then five billion unbelievers will remain on the earth. Therefore, fulfillment of this judgment could see the death of at least 1.25 billion people.

Revelation 6:9- When He opened the fifth seal, I saw under the altar the souls of those who had been slain for the word

of God and for the testimony which they held.

Souls under the altar show persons in heaven, but not with resurrected bodies. Therefore, they are saved after the Rapture of the Church. These souls are slain or martyred for the Word of God and their testimony for Christ against false religious systems, i. e., religious persecution from the Harlot religious system dominating the first half of the Tribulation and persecution from the Antichrist in the second half of the Tribulation. Many are beheaded for their stand for Christ as stated in Revelation 20:4 indicating the price for following Christ will be one's life. The Church will have been raptured and the protecting and preserving ministry of the Holy Spirit through the Church will have concluded. At this point on the prophetic timetable, it is the martyrs from the first half of the Tribulation who are seen as souls under the altar. However, they are representative of all witnesses for Christ who are martyred throughout the Tribulation Period. Other Tribulation saints, including the great multitude of Revelation 7:9, will join them in heaven. Most Tribulation saints are martyred.

Revelation 6:10-And they cried with a loud voice, saying, "How long, O Lord, holy and true, until You judge and avenge our blood on those who dwell on the earth?"

The martyrs are not crying for revenge but for justice. They are calling on the Lord as judge, not as the loving Savior. Throughout the Book of Revelation, Christ's judgments are declared to be righteous and true.

Revelation 6:11-And a white robe was given to each of them; and it was said to them that they should rest a little while longer, until both the number of their fellow servants and their brethren, who would be killed as they were, was completed.

"White robes" imply righteousness and justification. God gives the martyrs the white robes signifying that justification only comes from God. The victory is from God. The martyrs are told to rest for a while or stop crying-out, because more of their brethren will be killed in the same manner as they were killed. All the martyrs throughout the Tribulation Period will all be resurrected together as part of the First Resurrection.

Revelation 6:12-I looked when He opened the sixth seal, and behold, there was a great earthquake; and the sun became black as sackcloth of hair and the moon became like blood.

The first five seals were the result of the rise of the Antichrist. Now Christ opens the sixth seal. The sixth seal begins the wrath of God. First there is a great earthquake. This is the first of several earthquakes (Revelation 8:5; 11:13; 11:19; and 16:18; Zechariah 14:4-8) during the Tribulation week. The sun is darkened (Revelation 8:12; 9:2; 16:10; Matthew 24:29; and Joel 2:31) and the moon becomes as blood. As the sun becomes dark, the moon is correspondingly affected here (sixth seal judgment), at the fourth trumpet judgment, and at the end of the Tribulation. The magnitude of these Tribulation earthquakes will be so severe that it is believed they will be felt worldwide, because a system of faults and fractures covers the planet. This earthquake is considered "great," which should place it at least 7.0 or higher on the Richter scale. These great earthquakes will probably generate volcanic eruptions and activation of previously dormant volcanoes, plus movement of the tectonic plates.

Revelation 6:13-And the stars of heaven fell to the earth, as a fig tree drops its late figs when it is shaken by a mighty wind.

Stars, falling to the earth as figs falling from a tree, refer to meteors or asteroids impacting the earth. The mighty wind again depicts the shaking of heaven and earth. Stars are mentioned three times corresponding to the effects of the moon. Twice the stars are said to fall, here at the sixth seal judgment and at the end of the Tribulation (Matthew 24:29-31). Meteors or asteroids impacting the earth will cause catastrophic damage and destruction to the

planet, affecting all global systems, such as economic, trans-
portation, energy, healthcare, political, military, emergency serv-
ices, food and crops, communications, etc.

**Revelation 6:14-Then the sky receded as a scroll when it is
rolled up, and every mountain and island was moved out of
place.**

The sky receding and the mountains and islands moving depict
cataclysmic changes to the physical earth. Some scholars believe
the planetary devastation described above is the result of nuclear
war. Although nuclear war could produce such devastation, the
argument that these cosmic and planetary disturbances are the
wrath of God is superior. Meteors or asteroids pelting the earth,
along with a great earthquake, volcanic activity, and movement
of the tectonic plates, could produce such a shaking of planet
earth that people will believe the sky is literally being rolled up.

**Revelation 6:15-And kings of the earth, the great men, the
rich men, the commanders, the mighty men, every slave and
every free man, hid themselves in the caves and in the rocks
of the mountains,**

Seven classes of mankind are listed representing all of human
society. They know that these physical disturbances are the
wrath of God, even though they are unsaved, which weakens the
nuclear war theory. Their sinful states and fear cause them to
hide themselves in the caves as Adam and Eve hid after they
sinned against God.

**Revelation 6:16-and said to the mountains and rocks, "Fall
on us and hide us from the face of Him who sits on the
throne and from the wrath of the Lamb!"**

The unsaved are so afraid that they cry out for the mountains
and rocks to fall on them and to hide them. Judgment has come
and there is no place to hide. No repentance is mentioned. It is

interesting that the unrighteous ask to be hidden from the face of Him who sits on the throne. How did they know? Were there visions into heaven?

Revelation 6:17-"For the great day of His wrath has come, and who is able to stand?"

The great day of God's wrath begins here. This is the onset of the day of the Lord. Some commentators initiate the day of the Lord before the seventieth week of Daniel or immediately after the translation of the Church. They state that the phrase "has come" can mean a present as well as a backward application. These scholars would then include the first five seal judgments as part of the day of the Lord.

Since the day of the Lord is prophesied in several places in the Old Testament, it is not included as part of the "mystery." The "mystery" is revelation for the Church, as given by God to the New Testament writers that was previously unknown to the Old Testament prophets. For example, the Church Age and Rapture of the Church are include in the "mystery." The dispensation of the Church Age concludes with the Rapture of the Church. Because the day of the Lord is not part of the "mystery," the day of the Lord must then follow after the Rapture of the Church. Whether the first five seal judgments are included in the day of the Lord is questionable. Since cosmic disturbances are prophesied to occur at the commencement of the day of the Lord, the logical placement for the day of the Lord and the beginning of the wrath of God is at the sixth seal judgment.

The appointment for the Christian is the Rapture, while the appointment for the unrighteous is the day of the Lord.

CHAPTER SEVEN

EVANGELISM IN THE TRIBULATION

(Refer to Prophetic Key: Groups of Believers)

Revelation 7:1-After these things I saw four angels standing at the four corners of the earth, holding the four winds of the earth, that the wind should not blow on the earth, on the sea, or on any tree.

"After these things" refers to the events of the first six seal judgments. The sealing of the 144,000 Jews occurs between the sixth and seventh seal judgments. These four angels are the first four of the trumpet angels. The "four-corners" refer to the four directions of the earth, and the "winds" refer to divine judgments. The angels are restraining the divine judgments scheduled to strike the earth, sea, and trees, which are the targets of the first four trumpet judgments. Some scientific Bible commentators interpret the "winds" literally, saying angels will control the atmospheric circulation that in turn governs the winds. If there is no wind, then there won't be any rain, and a vapor canopy would develop on the earth. No other prophetic passages appear to support a vapor canopy theory at this point in the Tribulation. A vapor canopy around the earth in the new heavens and new earth after the millennial reign of Christ has merit.

Revelation 7:2-Then I saw another angel ascending from the east, having the seal of the living God. And he cried with a

loud voice to the four angels to whom it was granted to harm the earth and the sea,

Another angel appears from the east with the seal of God and instructs the four trumpet angels not to harm the earth and sea. Ascending from the east literally means coming out of the sun. The angel could be Michael, because he is the prince who stands for Israel (Daniel 10:21). The "seal of the living God" demonstrates ownership. Since the demon locusts in Revelation 9 are not allowed to harm those sealed, the "seal" must be visible both in the physical and spiritual realms. According to Revelation 14, the seal is the name of the Father, which is placed on the foreheads of the ones sealed. The seal is not for spiritual blessing, but for protection through the trumpet judgments. In Revelation 14, those sealed are seen on Mt. Zion, which is the heavenly Mt. Zion. Therefore, the 144,000 are raptured after the trumpet judgments and before the bowl judgments. During the Church Age, the Holy Spirit is the believer's seal. Later in Revelation, the Antichrist seals his followers with the "mark of the Beast" as a counterfeit.

Revelation 7:3-saying "Do not harm the earth, the sea, or the trees till we have sealed the servants of our God on their foreheads."

The ones sealed are saved because they are referred to as servants of God. The chief mission of servants of God is to communicate the Gospel of the Kingdom and Gospel of Christ. These people are saved early in the first half of the seventieth week of Daniel during the first six seal judgments and after the Rapture of the Church. The seal of God is placed on their foreheads, and until the sealing has been completed, the trumpet judgments cannot proceed.

Revelation 7:4-And I heard the number of those who were sealed. One hundred and forty-four thousand of all the tribes of the children of Israel were sealed:

The number of those sealed is 144,000, 12,000 from each of the

12 tribes of Israel. Therefore, they are Jews, representing Israel and not the Church. Although they are not said to be witnesses for God, it is certainly implied and fits the context of this chapter, i. e., the great multitude of believers who are saved during the Great Tribulation. One of the primary ways the great multitude will hear the Gospel is from these Jewish witnesses.

Revelation 7:5-8-of the tribe of Judah twelve thousand were sealed; of the tribe of Reuben twelve thousand were sealed; of the tribe of Gad twelve thousand were sealed; of the tribe of Asher twelve thousand were sealed; of the tribe of Naphtali twelve thousand were sealed; of the tribe of Manasseh twelve thousand were sealed; of the tribe of Simeon twelve thousand were sealed; of the tribe of Levi twelve thousand were sealed; of the tribe of Issachar twelve thousand were sealed; of the tribe of Zebulun twelve thousand were sealed; of the tribe of Joseph twelve thousand were sealed; of the tribe of Benjamin twelve thousand were sealed.

The 12 tribes are specifically identified. The tribe of Joseph is divided between his sons, Ephraim and Manasseh. The tribe of Levi was scattered throughout the other tribes because they were the priestly tribe. The tribes of Levi and Joseph replace the tribes of Dan and Ephraim. Therefore, Ephraim and Dan are not included in the servants of God. Ephraim led the way into civil war, which caused the tribes to divide, ten to the north and two to the south. Ephraim and Dan were the first tribes to lead Israel into idolatry. Also Dan occupied the current area encompassing Syria, which is in the region suspected to be the place of origin for the Antichrist.

Revelation 7:9-After these things I looked, and behold, a great multitude which no one could number, of all nations, tribes, peoples, and tongues, standing before the throne and before the Lamb, clothed with white robes, with palm branches in their hands,

After the sealing of the 144,000 Jews, another group is identified, called a great multitude that cannot be numbered, representing every nation, people, tribe, and tongue. This number must be vast, because the demon horsemen of Revelation 9 are numbered at 200 million. It could be concluded that the harvest of souls saved during the Tribulation would significantly exceed 200 million people. They are pictured before the throne and before the Lamb, clothed in white robes with palm leaves in their hands. White robes symbolize righteousness, and palm leaves symbolize victory and triumph. These saints are the result of the witnessing that occurs during the Tribulation by the 144,000 Jews, two witnesses (Revelation 11), martyrs, and angels. The white robes and palm leaves indicate that this group is saved, and from other passages, they are saved throughout the seven-year Tribulation. If the great multitude is raptured at the end of the Tribulation period as some postulate, then all believers would be included and there would be no saved people to enter the Millennium, except a few Jews born again at the Second Coming of Christ. However, there is no credible reference for this group being raptured. Since they are in heaven, they arrive there by being murdered for their faith by refusing to take the mark of the Beast during the Great Tribulation. Of course, some may die as a result of the judgments that hit the earth. As previously stated, the souls under the altar are martyred for their faith, evangelism, their testimony, and the Word of God. Therefore, saints represented by the martyred souls under the throne in Revelation 6:9 and the great multitude in Revelation 7:9 are martyred (beheaded) throughout the Tribulation Period. These two groups are resurrected as part of the First Resurrection stated in Revelation 20:4.

Key scripture verses are:
- Revelation 6:9-the martyrs are told to wait until their fellow servants are killed as they were
- Revelation 7:9-a great multitude from all nations of the earth

- Revelation 7:14-the great multitude comes out of the Great Tribulation
- Revelation 12:11-and they overcame him by the blood of the Lamb and the word of their testimony
- Revelation 13:7-and it was granted to him to make war with the saints and to overcome them
- Revelation 15:2-saints in heaven that are victorious over the Beast (mark, number, name)
- Revelation 20:4-martyrs killed for their testimony of Jesus, Word, and for refusal to worship the Beast

Revelation 7:10-and crying out with a loud voice, saying, "Salvation belongs to our God who sits on the throne, and to the Lamb!"

Salvation is the cry of the great multitude. Salvation is a work of God through the substitutionary sacrifice of Jesus.

Revelation 7:11-12-And all the angels stood around the throne and the elders and the four living creatures, and fell on their faces before the throne and worshiped God, saying: "Amen! Blessing and glory and wisdom, Thanksgiving and honor and power and might, Be to our God forever and ever. Amen."

Heavenly beings are pictured in concentric circles around the throne: four living creatures, then the elders, and then angels. All are on their faces in worship before God, acknowledging His attributes and qualities of blessing, glory, wisdom, thanksgiving, honor, power, and might.

Revelation 7:13-Then one of the elders answered, saying to me, "Who are these arrayed in white robes, and where did they come from?"

One of the elders asks who these people are and where they come from, indicating that the group is distinct from the Church represented by the elders. It seems that this group suddenly

appears, because the elder is surprised by their presence. Based
on the context, it could be concluded that this scene is a forward
look to the First Resurrection described in Revelation 20 when
the great multitude receive their immortal glorified bodies. The
raptured Church is present in heaven and already in glorified
form. Since the great multitude is comprised of Tribulation
saints who die in the second half of the seventieth week, they
must wait until after the Second Coming to receive their new
glorified bodies. Until that time, they are like the souls under the
altar identified in the fifth seal judgment comprised of spiritual
form and shape, but not resurrected bodies such as the one mod-
eled by Jesus after His resurrection. Additionally the fifth seal
martyrs are part of this great multitude. Arrayed in white depicts
the righteous condition of the great multitude.

**Revelation 7:14-And I said to him, "Sir, you know." So he
said to me, "These are the ones who come out of the Great
Tribulation, and washed their robes and made them white in
the blood of the Lamb."**

This scripture defines the time period pertaining to the great multitude to be the Great Tribulation or second half of the seventieth
week. Having their robes washed in the blood of the Lamb means
they have been purified and made righteous by the sacrificial work
of Christ. Based on the scriptures regarding the martyrs of
Revelation 6:9 and 20:4-5, the great multitude is killed for being
followers of Christ. Revelation 12:11 says they overcome by the
blood of the Lamb and the word of their testimony.

**Revelation 7:15-"Therefore they are before the throne of
God, and serve Him day and night in His temple. And He
who sits on the throne will dwell among them."**

The great multitude, including the martyrs of Revelation 6 and
20, have a special place of service in the temple of God, before the
throne of God where it is said that God dwells among them.
They are in the immediate, visible, Shekinah presence of God.

Many writers believe the temple in this case to be the millennial temple.

Revelation 7:16-17-"They shall neither hunger anymore nor thirst anymore; the sun shall not strike them, nor any heat; for the Lamb who is in the midst of the throne will shepherd them and lead them to living fountains of waters. And God will wipe away every tear from their eyes."

The great multitude is freed from the pain and torture of the persecutions of the Tribulation Period that they had endured. They are safe with Jesus, and He leads (shepherds) them. They don't hunger or thirst any longer. Jesus comforts them, and they are freed from the extreme heat felt during the Tribulation (Revelation 16:8).

CHAPTER EIGHT

THE TRUMPETS SOUND

(Refer to Prophetic Key: Tribulation Judgments)

Revelation 8:1-When He opened the seventh seal there was a silence in heaven for about half an hour.

The seventh seal judgment is silence in heaven for one-half hour to signify the seriousness, importance, and awesomeness of the judgments to come. The opening of the seventh seal judgment introduces the trumpet judgments.

Revelation 8:2-And I saw the seven angels who stand before God, and to them were given seven trumpets.

These angels are special angels in heaven, because they stand in the very presence of God. In the apocryphal books of Enoch and Tobit, these angels are identified as Uriel, Raphael, Raguel, Michael, Sarakiel, Gabriel, and Remiel. It is unlikely that two of the trumpet angels are the archangels Michael and Gabriel, because this activity isn't consistent with normal assignments for these archangels. These seven angels are given seven trumpets, but scripture doesn't indicate by whom. Trumpets have been a part of Jewish history as identified in the Old Testament and other Jewish works. In Israel, the trumpet was a ram's horn or "shofar" and was used to announce the beginning of festivals, assemble troops or people, or to warn of danger. The trumpet blasts by these angels are to warn of impending judgments.

Revelation 8:3-Then another angel, having a golden censer, came and stood at the altar. And he was given much incense, that he should offer it with the prayers of the saints upon the golden altar which was before the throne.

Another angel who stands in the presence of God has a golden censer to mix incense with the prayers of the saints before the golden altar. "Golden" signifies value and worth, as prayers are valuable to God. Although some commentators believe this angel to be Christ in His priestly role in heaven, he most likely is not. In Revelation 5, the elders and living creatures are seen with vials of the prayers of the saints. The only place where Christ is referred to as an angel is in the Old Testament where He is called the Angel of the Lord. These are probably prayers, yet unanswered, about the end times, Second Coming, and justice to be served on the enemies of those who have been martyred.

Revelation 8:4-And the smoke of the incense, with the prayers of the saints, ascended before God from the angel's hand.

The prayers ascend upward out of the angel's hand to God. It is assumed from the context that God hears these prayers.

Revelation 8:5-Then the angel took the censer, filled it with fire from the altar, and threw it to the earth. And there were noises, thunderings, lightnings, and an earthquake.

The response to the prayers provides additional warnings that judgment is coming, and introduces the fact that the seven trumpets are about to sound. The prayers are soon to be answered as exemplified by the mixing of the fire from the altar with the prayers. Noises, thunderings, lightnings, and an earthquake announce divine activity and God's control over nature.

Revelation 8:6-So the seven angels who had the seven trumpets prepared themselves to sound.

Trumpets in the Old Testament indicate God's intervention into history.

Revelation 8:7-The first angel sounded: And hail and fire followed, mingled with blood, and they were thrown to the earth; and a third of the trees were burned up, and all green grass was burned up.

The first four trumpet judgments affect the material earth. The first trumpet sounds as hail and fire mixed with blood are thrown to the earth resulting in the destruction of one-third of the trees and all green grass. The "one-third" signifies these judgments are partial and not total. Additionally, the "one-third" may refer to the geographical area impacted as well as the intensity of destruction. "Green grass" would also include agricultural products, such as wheat, corn, barley, etc. Hence, valuable food sources are depleted by this judgment.

Revelation 8:8-9-Then the second angel sounded: And something like a great mountain burning with fire was thrown into the sea, and a third of the sea became blood: And a third of the living creatures in the sea died, and a third of the ships were destroyed.

As the second trumpet sounds, something like a great mountain burning with fire is thrown into the sea, causing one-third of the sea to become blood, one-third of the living creatures in the sea to die, and a third of the ships to be destroyed. The "great mountain burning" refers either to a meteor (or comet or asteroid), volcanic eruption, or nuclear war. A "volcano" appears the best fit, because in a volcanic eruption, a mountain would literally be thrown or cast into the sea. If the intent of this passage was a meteor, comet, or asteroid, it would be described as falling rather than being cast. "Nuclear war" is conceivable, since the world continues to be engulfed in armed conflicts. However, this judgment is from God, and He will probably use the natural elements of the earth or cosmos, similar to His execution of the plagues in ancient Egypt. An example of the destructiveness of a volcano is Krakatua in the South Pacific that blew apart in 1883, with the sound extending for 2000 miles. Dust and debris discolored the sunsets for two years, and over one cubic mile of earth was blown into the air. This eruption will surpass anything ever experienced or conceived and could easily pollute one-third of global seas.

Scholars, however, generally favor the Mediterranean Sea as the sea referenced in this verse. Water turning to blood is similar to the first Egyptian plague. One-third of sea life dying causes the waters to become poisoned like a great red tide of dead microorganisms. Marine microorganisms constitute the lowest and most basic components of many of the world's food chains, and their destruction would potentially produce a domino effect on higher forms of life. The impact on the economy will be severe. A volcanic eruption of the magnitude described would also cause tidal waves (or tsunamis) and together with falling debris could easily destroy merchant ships in addition to many coastal regions of the world. With the revival of Babylon as a commercial trading center, many ships will be in the area and their destruction will have a significant negative effect on the world economy.

Revelation 8:10-11-Then the third angel sounded: And a great star fell from heaven, burning like a torch, and it fell on a third of the rivers and on the springs of water; and the name of the star is Wormwood; and a third of the waters became wormwood; and many men died from the water, because it was made bitter.

The third trumpet judgment is a burning meteor falling to earth from the heavens. Meteors fall, come apart, and scatter as they near the earth. However, this meteor is designated as "great," and a great or substantially large meteor could create additional catastrophes as described below in Revelation 8:12 (second paragraph). One-third of the rivers and springs of water, including wells and other subterranean sources of water, are poisoned by a "Wormwood" like substance. "Wormwood" is the name for a bitter and normally poisonous herb derived from a kind of root. The effects of this substance are drunkenness and eventual death, similar to hemlock. As a result of this judgment, drinking water will be in great demand.

Revelation 8:12-Then the fourth angel sounded; And a third of the sun was struck, a third of the moon, and a third of the stars, so that a third of them were darkened; and a third of the day did not shine, and likewise the night.

The judgment from the fourth angel is similar to the ninth Egyptian plague and the events of the crucifixion, sixth seal judgment, fifth trumpet judgment, and fifth bowl judgment. The sun, moon, and stars were set in the heavens for light. Now, a third of the sun, moon, and stars are darkened along with a third of the day that does not shine. Therefore two-thirds of the 24-hour day or 16 hours (one-third of 12 hours darkness + 12 hours of normal darkness = 16 hours of darkness) is dark rather than the current 12 hours. These are not random events of nature but controlled divine judgments on the solar system and galaxy.

Rather than having 16 hours of night, another application of this scripture is that light from the sun, moon, and stars is diminished by one-third as a result of prior judgments. The effect of a large meteor striking the earth as stated under the third trumpet judgment could easily result in tsunamis, earth-quakes, and volcanic eruptions. A large meteor impacting the earth in an ocean area could cause tsunamis that would destroy many coastal cities and depending on location, nuclear power installations resulting in meltdowns and extensive radioactive contamination. The Teutonic plates could shift resulting in worldwide earthquakes and volcanic activity including activa-tion of dormant volcanoes. Mass volcanic eruptions including the one mentioned under the second trumpet judgment would easily discolor the air and block light from the sun, moon, and stars for years. Regardless of cause, this event seemingly pro-duces greater atmospheric discoloration than that produced by the sixth seal judgment.

Revelation 8:13-And I looked, and I heard an angel flying through the midst of heaven, saying with a loud voice, "Woe, woe, woe to the inhabitants of the earth, because of the remaining blasts of the three angels who are about to sound!"

An angel is seen flying in mid-heaven proclaiming with a loud voice that all could hear saying "woe to the inhabitants of the earth because of the final three trumpet judgments that are about to sound." These three "woes" are more severe than anything mankind has faced previously. Many translations identify the angel as an "eagle" who could be one of the living creatures or a literal eagle. God has used animals to speak to men in the past, such as a donkey. However, a literal angel is the better interpretation.

CHAPTER NINE

DEMONIC ACTIVITY

**(Refer to Prophetic Keys: Tribulation Judgments,
200 Million Horsemen Army, and
Nether World Regions and Eternal Hell)**

Revelation 9:1-Then the fifth angel sounded; And I saw a star fallen from heaven to the earth. And to him was given the key to the bottomless pit.

The star falling or descending from heaven is an angel because a key was given to "him." This angel is an angel of God, because a fallen angel would not be in possession of the key to the abyss. If it was a fallen angel, he would have already released the demons bound in the pit long before it was their time to participate in the events on the earth. The abyss or bottomless pit is believed to be one of many corridors leading to hell that is in the center of the earth. This is the dwelling place or prison for Satan, fallen angels, and demons during the Millennium. The nether world compartments are:

1.   Tartarus - special prison for angels that left their first estate before the flood.

2.   Sheol-Hades - two compartments:

    a) Torments (Hell) - place of torment for the souls of unbelievers awaiting their resurrection at the Great White Throne judgment.

    b) Paradise - abode for the righteous dead until Christ conquered death, hell, and the grave. This compartment is now empty. It was also called Abraham's Bosom.

3.   Abyss or bottomless pit (referred to above). Abode for

some demons and fallen angels.

4. Lake of Fire or Gehenna - the eternal hell or final abode for the unrighteous of all time after the White Throne Judgment. Demons, fallen angels, Satan, the Antichrist, and the False Prophet will also inhabit the lake of fire for eternity.

Revelation 9:2-And he opened the bottomless pit, and smoke arose out of the pit like the smoke of a great furnace. And the sun and the air were darkened because of the smoke of the pit.

The angel opens the bottomless pit to release the inhabitants. Great masses of smoke escape to darken the sky indicating that the abyss is a place of fire and flame.

Revelation 9:3-Then out of smoke locusts came upon the earth. And to them was given power, as the scorpions of the earth have power.

Locusts emerge from the abyss. These are not ordinary locusts, but demon locusts. As will be seen, these demon locusts respond to commands unlike natural locusts. They have a king, and natural locusts do not have a king according to the Book of Proverbs. Natural locusts do not inhabit the bottomless pit and do not have the power to harm people as these locusts do. These locusts are able to recognize the mark of God on the foreheads of the 144,000 Jews, which would not be possible for natural locusts. Additionally, these locusts are not mutant locusts or men in gas masks as some commentators identify them. This event is a demonic invasion of the planet.

Revelation 9:4-They were commanded not to harm the grass of the earth, or any green thing, or any tree, but only those men who do not have the seal of God on their foreheads.

These demon locusts are commanded not to harm any green thing, such as grass and trees, which are the very items that natural locusts would devour. Additionally, they can only harm those men without the mark of God on their foreheads.

Revelation 9:5-And they were not given authority to kill them, but to torment them for five months. And their torment was like the torment of a scorpion when it strikes a man.

The demon locusts can torment men without the mark of God on their foreheads, but they are not allowed to kill anyone. The question is whether this total plague lasts five months or the torment to each individual stung is for five months, which could extend the length of the plague to ten months. The prevalent interpretation is that the plague lasts five months, and hence a person stung could be tormented for up to five months. These are spirit beings (demons) inflicting physical pain on unrepentant mankind. While the scorpion sting can set a human's nervous system on fire for several days, the tormenting sting from these demon locusts may last up to five months.

Revelation 9:6-In those days men will seek death and will not find it; they will desire to die, and death will flee from them.

As a result of the scorpion-like sting, men seek death but are unable to die. Death takes a holiday for the term of this plague. This implies that men are not even able to commit suicide, for their spirits will not leave their bodies.

Revelation 9:7-10-And the shape of the locusts was like horses prepared for battle; and on their heads were crowns of something like gold, and their faces were like the faces of men. They had hair like women's hair, and their teeth were like lions' teeth. And they had breastplates like breastplates of iron, and the sound was like the sound of chariots with many horses running into battle. They had tails like scorpions, and there were stings in their tails. And their power was to hurt men five months.

The description of the demon locusts shows a fearsome

appearance, similar to the description of locusts in Joel 2. John is not describing the appearance of natural locusts or insects, but demons. They are described as ferocious, destructive, difficult to destroy (breastplate), and existing in large numbers.

Revelation 9:11-And they had as king over them the angel of the bottomless pit, whose name in Hebrew is Abaddon, but in Greek he has the name Apollyon.

The king over the demon locusts is Abaddon, which means "destruction" in Hebrew, or Apollyon, which means "destroyer" in the Greek. This king is not Satan or the Antichrist, because they are not occupying or bound in the pit at this time.

Revelation 9:12-One woe is past. Behold, still two more woes are coming after these things.

People were warned of three woes to come in Revelation 8:13. Now one woe is completed and there are two woes left. "Woe" prophetically implies "doom."

Revelation 9:13-Then the sixth angel sounded: And I heard a voice from the four horns of the golden alter which is before God,

The second woe is the sixth trumpet judgment. The voice from the altar in heaven is God the Father or God the Son, but which one is not specified. The altar in heaven is the pattern for the earthly tabernacle.

Revelation 9:14-saying to the sixth angel who had the trumpet, "Release the four angels who are bound at the great river Euphrates."

The angels bound at the great river Euphrates are fallen angels because good angels are not bound. There is no indication as to why these four have been bound. The angels that left their first estate when they married the daughters of men in Genesis 6 are "bound in chains of darkness." Whether these four are part of that group is not known. Bible scholars have speculated that the four bound angels are the Satanic princes from Babylon, Persia, Greece, and Rome. They were the spiritual forces behind these great empires as they persecuted Israel. The Beast Empire (eighth) will be a representation of these previous empires.

The Euphrates River has held a significant place in the plan of God. It was a boundary to the Garden of Eden, boundary of Israel, boundary of Egypt, boundary of the Persian Empire, and the Tower of Babel was near the Euphrates as well as Babylon. It has been hypothesized that there are 12 vortices or openings on the earth that lead into shafts that extend into Sheol-Hades. One of these vortices is at the Euphrates River. Other vortices are over the poles, Devil's Sea, and the Bermuda Triangle.

Revelation 9:15-So the four angels, who had been prepared for the hour and day and month and year, were released to kill a third of mankind.

By reference to hour, day, month, and year, these four angels have been prepared for a fixed point in time in God's plan. While this interpretation is the preferred one, another interpretation is worthy of comment: this plague (sixth trumpet judgment) continues for 13 months and 25 hours (hour, day, month, and year). These four evil angels are released to kill one-third of mankind. At current population levels (year 2000), over 1.25 billion people could be killed under this plague. Applying the previous assumption of 5 billion unbelievers on earth after the Rapture of the Church, one-fourth or 1.25 billion are killed under the fourth seal judgment, leaving 3.75 billion inhabitants on the planet. Now another one-third of mankind or 1.25 billion people are killed under this judgment, further reducing the earth's population to 2.5 billion with the battle of Armageddon and the bowl judgments yet to come. Although this plague could be applied globally, it is more likely that the greatest impact of the plague will be on the Euphrates region, i.e., Middle East, Central Asia, and Northern Africa. Either application can be supported by this passage.

Revelation 9:16-Now the number of the army of horsemen was two hundred million, and I heard the number of them.

The army of the horsemen is 200,000,000. Each fallen angel leads an army of 50,000,000 demon horsemen to kill one-third of mankind. Several commentators see this army as Red Chinese, because the Chinese have sufficient population to field an army of this magnitude. However, these are not natural or ordinary men by description, and they just appear on the scene, indicating that they were probably bound in the same location as the fallen angels. Furthermore, the Red Chinese are not involved on the political scene at this point in the Tribulation. Activity from the kings of the East doesn't occur until the sixth bowl judgment, just prior to the Second Coming of Christ at the battle of Armageddon.

Revelation 9:17-And thus I saw the horses in the vision: those who sat on them had breastplates of fiery red, hyacinth blue, and sulfur yellow; and the heads of the horses were like the heads of lions; and out of their mouths came fire, smoke, and brimstone.

This description shows destruction and ferocity. The fire, smoke, and brimstone are elements of hell and themselves plagues. The description is not of natural horses, giving further support to a vision of a demon army.

Revelation 9:18-By these three plagues a third of mankind was killed - by the fire and the smoke and the brimstone which came out of their mouths.

One-third of mankind is killed by these three plagues: fire, smoke, and brimstone. The locusts of the fifth plague tormented, but these demons kill. Those killed are the unrepentant. The result of the fourth seal and fifth trumpet judgments is the death of one-half of mankind remaining after the Rapture or at least 2.5 billion people at current population levels.

Revelation 9:19-For their power is in their mouth and in their tails; for their tails are like serpents, having heads; and with them they do harm.

Serpent-like tails are a reference to the demonic.

Revelation 9:20-But the rest of mankind, who were not killed by these plagues, did not repent of the works of their hands, that they should not worship demons, and idols of gold. Silver, brass, stone, and wood, which can neither see no hear nor walk;

The rest of mankind, not killed by these demons, still does not repent. They witness God's judgment and omnipotence as Pharaoh did with the children of Israel, but continue in their sinful ways, worshipping demons and idols that cannot speak. In Revelation 13, it will be seen that the idols of the image of the Beast do speak.

Revelation 9:21-and they did not repent of their murders of their sorceries or their sexual immorality or their thefts.

In addition to not repenting of the worship of demons and idols, mankind does not repent of their murders, sorceries, sexual immoralities, and thefts. After seven seal judgments and six trumpet judgments, the earth stands fast in sin, and sin without apparent restraint. These moral conditions are in evidence in the world today and will continue to increase up to the time of the Antichrist and into the Tribulation Period. The moral decay is a sign of the end times. Murders are more common today, and life in many cultures is of limited value. Sorceries include the occult, astrology, witchcraft, idolatry, and drugs. Sexual immorality includes all types of sexual sins, void of any religious restraint. Complete sexual freedom and every form of perversion are the current way of life. Of course, accompanying this free life-style are all forms of sexually transmitted diseases. Theft includes all forms of lawlessness, crime, and corruption. Law and order will completely breakdown. The only authority at this time will be the Antichrist.

CHAPTER TEN

THE LITTLE OPEN BOOK

Revelation 10:1-And I saw still another mighty angel coming down from heaven, clothed with a cloud. And a rainbow was on his head, his face was like the sun, and his feet like a pillar of fire.

Between the sixth and seventh trumpet judgments, John has a vision of a mighty angel. Some writers identify this angel as Christ because of his magnitude and splendor. However, John says he saw "another" mighty angel. This is "another" angel in addition to the trumpet angels. "Another" in the Greek is another of the same kind. Angels are very active throughout the Book of Revelation. In Revelation 5, there is a strong angel, and in Revelation 18, there is an angel with great authority that illuminates the earth. These are descriptions of high-ranking angels or possibly archangels that stand in the very presence of God. "Clothed with a cloud" and a "face like the sun" indicates this angel is coming from the presence of God where he was engulfed in God's Shekinah glory. His feet as "pillars of fire" depict judgment, which is the message he is bringing. The "rainbow" always symbolizes the covenant and seems to indicate that throughout this period of judgment, God will remember His covenant, especially with Israel. An interesting note is that John seems to be positioned in this vision on earth because he sees the angel "coming down" from heaven. The angel cannot be Christ, because He will not return to earth until the Second Advent.

Revelation 10:2-And he had a little book open in his hand. And he set his right foot on the sea and his left foot on the land,

The "little open book" is not the same book or scroll displayed in Revelation 5:1. The scroll in Revelation 5:1 was sealed with seven seals, whereas this little book is open. The seven seal scroll identified judgments to come upon the earth, i.e., seal and trumpet judgments. The seventh seal opened up and contained the seven trumpet judgments. As the seven seals are opened, the entire scroll is opened. This little book contains additional information about judgments to come upon the earth, namely the seven bowl judgments that are more destructive and universal in application. The seven bowl judgments complete the wrath of God. The book is "little" because it contains seven judgments compared to 14 judgments contained in the seven-sealed scroll. By standing with one foot on the earth and one foot on the sea, the angel demonstrates universal authority over the earth, which is a prelude to Jesus taking possession of the earth.

An alternate interpretation not adopted in this study is that the seven-sealed scroll of Revelation 5 contains all God's judgments, seal, trumpet, and bowl. The little book then describes the completion of the "mystery" and/or redemptive plan of God.

Revelation 10:3-and cried with a loud voice, as when a lion roars. And when he cried out, seven thunders uttered their voices.

As with the strong angel of Revelation 5:2, this mighty angel loudly utters something unidentified, sounding like a roaring lion. A new group is mentioned but not described, called the "seven thunders." This group is most likely another class of angels.

Revelation 10:4-Now when the seven thunders uttered their voices from heaven, I was about to write; but I heard a voice from heaven saying to me, "Seal up the things which the seven thunders uttered, and do not write them."

The seven thunders utter something that is understood by John, but he is commanded, apparently by God, to seal up what they spoke and not to write down their messages. Seemingly there is more than one message, because John is commanded not to write "them" referring to the things uttered. This is the only proclamation in Revelation that is sealed up, and from the context, it must be related to judgments.

Revelation 10:5-6-And the angel whom I saw standing on the sea and on the land lifted up his hand to heaven and swore by Him who lives forever and ever, who created heaven and the things that are in it, the earth and the things that are in it, and the sea and the things that are in it, that there should be delay no longer,

The angel swears by someone greater than himself who is the Lord Jesus, the eternal Creator of heaven, earth, sea, and all things in them. He proclaims that there should be no more delay, that is, to the fulfillment of God's plan. The time for the final judgments has come.

Revelation 10:7-but in the days of the sounding of the seventh angel, when he is about to sound, the mystery of God would be finished, as He declared to His servant and prophets.

As the seventh trumpet angel sounds, introducing the seven last plagues, the "mystery" of God is finished. The mystery refers to the body of Christ that will be completed when the Jews accept Jesus as their Messiah and are born again at the Second Coming of Christ. The redemptive plan of God that has been declared throughout the Bible is finished, including God's judgment of sin on the earth. Since this event occurs at the sounding of the seventh trumpet angel in the midst of divine judgments, it is a logical conclusion that the message of the "little book" is about further judgments to complete God's plan.

Revelation 10:8-Then the voice which I heard from heaven

spoke to me again and said, "Go, take the little book which is open in the hand of the angel who stands on the sea and on the earth."

The voice from heaven again speaks to John telling him to take the open book from the angel who is standing with one foot on the earth and one foot on the sea. The book is open showing that this revelation is not hidden but is to be shared. John must take the book because revelation is received, not forced.

Revelation 10:9-10-And I went to the angel and said to him, "Give me the little book." And he said to me, "Take and eat it; and it will make your stomach bitter, but it will be as sweet as honey in your mouth." And I took the little book out of the angel's hand and ate it, and it was as sweet as honey in my mouth. But when I had eaten it, my stomach became bitter.

John asks the angel for the book. The angel instructs John to eat the book, and it will make his stomach bitter but will be sweet as honey in his mouth. Eating the book means digesting the contents as spiritual food. In the Old Testament, the prophets Ezekiel and Jeremiah experienced "eating a scroll." The "eating" is receiving the message and assimilating the revelation. The truth of the Word of God is sweet, but the message of impending judgments to fall upon mankind is bitter. In a similar application, the Gospel is sweet to those who accept the message, but bitter to those who reject it.

Revelation 10:11-And he said to me, "You must prophesy again about many peoples, nations, tongues and kings."

This message of Revelation must be given to the world, to all peoples, nations, tongues, and kings.

THE TWO WITNESSES

Revelation 11:1-2-Then I was given a reed like a measuring rod. And the angel stood saying, "Rise and measure the temple of God, the altar, and those who worship there. But leave out the court which is outside the temple, and do not measure it, for it has been given to the Gentiles. And they will tread the holy city underfoot for forty-two months."

"Measure" can mean preparation for building, restoration, or destruction. As a note, "those who worship there" refers to people, and people are not measured. Therefore, the application is not physical but spiritual. Another definition for "measure" is "evaluate." The temple is measured or evaluated and found to be in need of restoration. The Antichrist desecrates the temple in the middle of the Tribulation by proclaiming himself to be God. The Antichrist seizes the temple and his armies tread underfoot the holy city for 42 months. Forty-two months, 1260 days, and time, times and half a time, all refer to the same time period, which is the last half of the Tribulation, called the Great Tribulation. The outer court has already been given over to the Gentiles, which is why John is told not to measure it.

There is no temple in Israel at this time. The last temple, Herod's, was an expansion and remodel of the temple of Zerubbabel and was destroyed by Titus in A.D. 70. There were two temples prior to Herod's. The first temple was built by Solomon, while the second was built by Zerubbabel. The reference to

measuring the inner court could mean that only the inner sanctuary is reconstructed during the Tribulation rather than the
entire temple. Currently, the Dome of the Rock, which is a high
holy place to the Muslims, is located on the site where the Jewish
temple must be erected. Some writers conjecture that the
Antichrist's peace initiative with Israel provides for the reconstruction of the temple or inner sanctuary. The Antichrist must
be able to broker a peace accord with some desirable offering to
the Arabs, because reconstruction of a Jewish temple on the temple mount would totally infuriate the Muslims in the Middle
East. After the Tribulation temple or inner court is destroyed at
the Second Coming of Christ, a new millennial temple will be
built.

**Revelation 11:3-"And I will give power to my two witnesses,
and they will prophesy one thousand two hundred and sixty
days, clothed in sackcloth."**

According to Jewish law, two witnesses were required to validate
religious matters. These two witnesses through their prophesying validate for God the evil and depraved condition of the earth
during the Great Tribulation. God sends two witnesses or
prophets to operate on the earth during the second half of the
Tribulation. Again, 1260 days is always a reference to the second
half of the Tribulation Period. "Sackcloth" shows a message of
repentance and judgment. The two witnesses preach, prophesy,
and smite the earth with plagues in an effort to turn Israel back
to God. Because the witnesses prophesy and perform signs and
wonders, they will be two prophets, but their identity is known
only to God and will not be revealed until the Tribulation.
However, it is fun to speculate. Most expositors tend to agree that
Elijah will be one of the prophets. In Malachi 4:5-6, God says that
He will send Elijah before the great and dreadful day of the Lord.
Elijah is identified with Israel, was on the Mount of
Transfiguration with Christ, never died, and never completed his
ministry. One of the two prophets smites the earth with identical

plagues as used by Elijah in his ministry.

The choice for the second prophet is usually Moses or Enoch. Enoch is nominated because he is the other Biblical person besides Elijah who has never experienced death, having been taken by God directly into heaven. Hebrews 9:27 says it is appointed unto man once to die. Therefore, he could return and then die with Elijah at the end of the Tribulation, followed by their bodily resurrection. Enoch was a prophet of judgment to the Gentiles (Jude 14-15) and would represent God's dealing with mankind during the first 2000 years of history. Elijah would represent the next 2000 years of history and God's dealings with Israel. The Church Age follows with the Church preaching to both Jew and Gentile. The Church Age is concluded at the Rapture, followed by the Tribulation Period when God deals with both Jew and Gentile as represented by these two great prophets who return to the earth.

Moses is the other primary candidate for the second prophet. He was with Elijah on the Mount of Transfiguration, is identified with the law, and stands for Israel as Elijah stands for the prophets. The second prophet smites the earth with plagues similar to those demonstrated in the ministry of Moses. Moses will not receive his resurrected body until after the Second Coming of Christ with the other Old Testament saints at the First Resurrection. Therefore, Moses could be resurrected as Lazarus was resurrected by Jesus. However, the death of Moses is a compelling reason to discount his candidacy. Because Elijah and Enoch never died and are already in heaven in natural bodies, they are the more logical candidates to fulfill this prophecy. God has prepared and reserved them for this very time in history. For what other reason would these two prophets never see death?

Even though the majority choice among commentators for the two witnesses is Elijah and Moses, the position of this study is that Elijah and Enoch will be God's two end-time witnesses. However, it is acknowledged that the two witnesses are not identified and could be two other individuals to everyone's surprise.

Revelation 11:4-These are the two olive trees and the two lampstands standing before the God of the earth.

The reference to "two olive trees" and "two lampstands" is from Zechariah 4:11-14 and means the anointed ones. The oil from the olive tree symbolizes that these two prophets are empowered by the Holy Spirit as they speak. Their ministries demonstrated the anointing of God.

Revelation 11:5-And if anyone wants to harm them, fire proceeds from their mouth and devours their enemies. And if anyone wants to harm them, he must be killed in this manner.

Whoever tries to harm them will bring destruction on themselves. For the period of their ministry, they cannot be harmed.

Revelation 11:6-These have power to shut heaven, so that no rain falls in the days of their prophecy; and they have power over waters to turn them to blood, and to strike the earth with all plagues, as often as they desire.

The miraculous power to shut heaven and halt rainfall was performed in the ministry of Elijah. Since these two prophets can halt rainfall, turn water into blood, and strike the earth with plagues as frequently as they desire, they pose a significant threat and hindrance to the work of the Antichrist.

Revelation 11:7-Now when they finish their testimony, the beast that ascends out of the bottomless pit will make war against them, overcome them, and kill them.

The prophets are overcome by the beast out of the abyss and are killed at the end of the Tribulation when their ministry is completed. They are unable to be killed until they have fulfilled their ministry. The beast from the bottomless pit cannot be a natural man, because natural men are not in the abyss. The bottomless pit is in the spiritual realm and has been used by God as a prison house for wicked angels and demons. Therefore, this being must be an agent of Satan. He is believed by many expositors to be the Prince of Greece, the satanic authority that influenced Alexander the Great who controlled the Grecian Empire that will be revived in the end times as part of the reconstituted Roman Empire, which is the Beast or eighth empire to oppress Israel during the times of the Gentiles. It is noted that the satanic entity could be the Prince of Babylon or Prince of Assyria, because the Antichrist is called the King of Babylon and the Assyrian.

Revelation 11:8-And their dead bodies will lie in the street of the great city which spiritually is called Sodom and Egypt, where also our Lord was crucified.

The bodies of the two witnesses lie in the street of Jerusalem for three and one-half days. "Sodom" is a symbol of immorality including sexual perversions, while "Egypt" is symbolic of materialism and wickedness.

Revelation 11:9-Then those from the peoples, tribes, tongues, and nations will see their dead bodies three and a half days, and not allow their dead bodies to be put into graves.

All peoples of the world are able to view the bodies of the two witnesses lying in the street, most likely through the medium of television and satellite communications. The Antichrist doesn't allow their bodies to be buried. Because he has defeated and killed the two prophets, the world will believe that the Antichrist has greater authority and power than the witnesses with the larger deception that Satan is more powerful than God.

Revelation 11:10-And those who dwell on the earth will rejoice over them, make merry, and send gifts to one another, because these two prophets tormented those who dwell

on the earth.

The depravity of the world is demonstrated in their rejoicing over the death of the two witnesses. The plagues brought forth by these two witnesses are against the unbeliever and a torment to them. At this point, most of the world is spiritually dead.

Revelation 11:11-Now after the three and a half days the breath of life from God entered them, and they stood on their feet, and great fear fell on those who saw them.

After three and one-half days the Spirit of God raises the two witnesses back to life. Great fear or exceeding terror falls upon the people of the world, because they know this resurrection is an act of God.

Revelation 11:12-And they heard a loud voice from heaven saying to them, "Come up here." And they ascended to heaven in a cloud, and their enemies saw them.

A voice from heaven, probably God, commands the two witnesses to ascend into heaven. These are the same words spoken to John in Revelation 4:1. The two witnesses are resurrected. The Church and the 144,000 Jews were previously raptured within the last seven years. The two witnesses ascend in a cloud into heaven in the same manner that Christ rose at His ascension after His resurrection.

Revelation 11:13-In the same hour there was a great earthquake, and a tenth of the city fell. In the earthquake seven thousand men were killed, and the rest were afraid and gave glory to the God of heaven.

In the same hour as their ascension into heaven, a great earthquake occurs, a tenth of the city is destroyed, and 7000 men are killed. Many expositors equate these events with the seventh bowl judgment, but the placement of this earthquake fits better on the timeline as an event separate from and slightly preceding the seventh bowl judgment. If a very literal application of the ministry of the two witnesses is followed, as suggested by most commentators, the witnesses would minister for forty two months and be killed at the time of Armageddon and the Second Coming of Christ. The two prophets are then raised up three and one-half days later after the conclusion of these events, which does not make sense. Under the seventh bowl judgment, all cities of the nations are destroyed, and Jerusalem is divided into three parts, but at this event, a tenth of the city (Jerusalem) falls. An alternate consideration worthy of mention is that the bowl judgments occur during the 30-day period following the seven-year Tribulation. Hence, this earthquake occurs three and one-half days after the end of the forty-two months of the Great Tribulation and approximately 26 1/2 days prior to the seventh bowl judgment and the return of Christ at Armageddon. Consequently, the placement of this earthquake is at the beginning of the 30-day period identified in Daniel 12 following the 1260 days of the Great Tribulation, while Armageddon and the Second Advent are at the end of this thirty-day period. It is understood that this concept is not shared by many commentators, and although it solves some questions, others questions remain unanswered, such as the reign of the Antichrist lasting for 42 months and not 43 months.

A remnant of Israel, who are most likely the Jews in the city of Jerusalem, give glory to God. Their repentance is implied as they give glory to God. This is the only group to repent during the Tribulation.

Revelation 11:14-The second woe is past. Behold, the third woe is coming quickly.

The second woe or the sixth trumpet judgment is past, and the third woe is coming, which is the introduction of the seven bowl judgments.

Revelation 11:15-Then the seventh angel sounded: And there

were loud voices in heaven, saying, "The kingdoms of this world have become the kingdoms of our Lord and of His Christ, and He shall reign forever and ever!"

The third woe is the sounding of the seventh angel that introduces the final judgments of God. It is both a conclusion to the trumpet judgments and an introduction to the bowl judgments. This passage is a statement of the triumphs that have occurred and the final victory that is yet to occur. The first two of seven events are described in this verse. Voices in heaven loudly proclaim that God and His son, Jesus, who is the Christ, will take possession of the earth and all its kingdoms for His eternal rule. This event will come to pass very quickly, probably within thirty days under the position that the bowl judgments occur during the thirty-day period following the 1260 days or second half of the Tribulation as outlined in Daniel 12. If the bowl judgments are placed within 1260 days, these events will still occur quickly in a short span of time at the end of the period.

Revelation 11:16-18-And the twenty-four elders who sat before God on their thrones fell on their faces and worshiped God, saying: "We give You thanks, O Lord God Almighty, The One who is and was and who is to come, Because You have taken Your great power and reigned. The nations were angry, and Your wrath has come, And the time of the dead, that they should be judged, And that You should reward Your servants the prophets and the saints, And those who fear Your name, small and great, And should destroy those who destroy the earth."

At the announcement of the establishment of Christ's eternal kingdom, the 24 elders fall on their faces and worship God for His eternal and omnipotent nature and for ruling with great power. God's wrath has come, the dead will be judged, prophets and saints rewarded, and those who tried to destroy the earth will themselves be destroyed.

Revelation 11:19-Then the temple of God was opened in the heaven and the ark of His covenant was seen in His temple. And there were lightnings, noises, thunderings, an earthquake, and great hail.

God's temple in heaven is opened, and the ark of the covenant is visible. The ark in the heavenly temple is seen as a sign of God's faithfulness and grace or favor toward His people and vengeance or judgment of His enemies. Seeing the ark reminds Israel that even in the midst of God pouring out His wrath, He remembers and will honor His covenant with them. Although this ark could be the earthy ark that has been lost for centuries, it most likely is the heavenly ark after which the earthly ark was patterned. Lightnings, thunderings, noises, earthquake, and great hail are divine activity signaling that more judgments are to come. These same phenomena occur at the seventh seal judgment, seventh trumpet judgment, and seventh bowl judgment. The seventh seal judgment introduces the trumpet judgments, and the seventh trumpet judgment introduces the bowl judgments, and the seventh bowl judgment is the finalization of the wrath of God and judgment of sinful earth.

CHAPTER TWELVE

FIVE PERSONALITIES

**(Refer to Prophetic Keys: Male Child and Beasts-
Seven Heads and Ten Horns)**

Revelation 12 and 13 identify and describe seven key personalities or forces that are integral to the understanding of the events of Revelation. Five personalities are discussed in chapter 12 and two are discussed in chapter 13. Chapters 12 and 13 occur around mid-Tribulation on the prophetic timeline and are considered parenthetical or providing additional information outside the normal flow of events that is necessary to the understanding of the events. These entities operate in the natural or spiritual realms.

Revelation 12:1-Now a great sign appeared in heaven: a woman clothed with the sun, with the moon under her feet, and on her head a garland of twelve stars.

A great sign appeared or was seen in heaven, symbolizing events primarily on the earth. The sun-clothed woman is the first sign identified. The "woman" is a symbol for the Jewish nation of Israel. There are three groups of people, the Church, Israel, and Gentiles. The Church has been raptured and is in heaven, so the woman cannot be the Church. The woman does not represent Gentiles, because she is under persecution by Gentiles. Therefore, the woman must represent Israel. After Revelation 4:1, the emphasis of the Book of Revelation is Jewish with a focus on Israel. Genesis 37:9-11 describes the dream of Joseph where the woman is clothed with the sun, the moon is under her feet, and she has a crown of twelve stars, which represent Joseph's brothers who became heads of the twelve tribes of Israel, again linking the imagery to Israel. The sun, moon, and stars give off or reflect light, which is symbolic for Israel being a light bearer for God.

Revelation 12:2-Then being with child, she cried out in labor and in pain to give birth.

Pain refers to torment. The Jews are in travail (labor and pain) at this time because of the persecution they are experiencing from the ten kings or kingdoms and the whore or Mystery Babylon. Gentiles have persecuted Jews dating back to the Egyptian Empire, and the worse persecution is yet to come under the direction of the Antichrist, prior to their deliverance at the end of the Tribulation. "Being with child" means that Israel is to give birth to the male child during this period.

Revelation 12:3-And another sign appeared in heaven: behold, a great fiery red dragon having seven heads and ten horns, and seven diadems on his head.

The second sign is a "great fiery red Dragon" with "seven heads" and "ten horns." The red Dragon is Satan. He is red with the blood of martyred saints throughout the ages. This is the first reference to a seven headed, ten horned beast (Revelation 12:3, 13:1, 17:3). The seven heads stand for seven world empires that have persecuted and will persecute Israel prior to the Antichrist's rule. The first six empires were Egypt, Assyria, Babylon, Medo-Persia, Greece, and Rome. The seventh empire is the Reconstituted Roman Empire. It is a reconstitution rather than a revival of the Roman Empire, because this seventh empire is to be ruled by ten kings instead of one emperor as in ancient Rome. The heads are crowned, implying that Satan had dominated and will dominate these empires. The ten horns represent ten kings that rule in the seventh kingdom. They are not crowned because Satan gives power over these kings to the Antichrist (Revelation 13:1-3).

Revelation 12:4-His tail drew a third of the stars of heaven and threw them to the earth. And the dragon stood before the woman who was ready to give birth, to devour her Child as soon as it was born.

Although this passage is typically used to identify the number of angels that fell with Lucifer in his initial rebellion against God, the context places this event at mid-Tribulation when war breaks out in the heavenlies, and the Devil and his angels are expelled from heaven (Revelation 12:7-9). Satan's expulsion is from the second heaven. Contrary to many commentaries, Satan does not have access to the third heaven and the throne of God. Evil cannot stand in the presence of God without being consumed by the fire of His glory. The Dragon seeks to devour the woman's child as soon as he is born, i.e., delivered or brought forth.

Revelation 12:5-And she bore a male Child who was to rule all nations with a rod of iron. And her Child was caught up to God and to His throne.

The woman brings forth a "male child" who is to rule all nations with a rod of iron. The child is caught up to God and His throne. Commentators have varied interpretations on this passage of scripture. Most identify Christ as the male child and there is strong support for that interpretation. Christ was born in Israel from the tribe of Judah, and He will rule the nations with a rod of iron in the Millennium (Psalms 2:7-9). However, if Christ is the appropriate interpretation for the male child, then this is a backward look to the birth and ascension of Jesus, which doesn't flow or fit the context of chapter 12. Furthermore, there is a problem with the child being "caught up" to God and His throne, referring to the ascension of Jesus. The words "caught up" are the same words used to describe the catching away of the

Church at the Rapture. "Caught up" is a forceful and swift event or snatching away, which is not at all descriptive of the ascension of Christ (Acts 1:9-11). The less popular, but more appropriate interpretation, in this author's opinion, is that the male child represents the 144,000 Jews of Revelation 7.

Revelation 12:6-Then the woman fled into the wilderness, where she has a place prepared by God, that they should feed her there one thousand two hundred and sixty days.

Israel flees into the wilderness to a place prepared by God for 1260 days or the second half of the Tribulation. 1260 days refers to the second half of the Tribulation Period. The wilderness nations are speculated to be the land of Edom, Moab, and Ammon or the current country of Jordan. These are the only local areas to escape the control and domination of the Antichrist. Many prophecy students believe Israel will flee to the rock-fortified city of Petra. Petra lies in a large valley and is reached only through one narrow passageway, so narrow that in some places two people cannot ride abreast. The sides at the top of the canyon are so close to each other that sunlight is filtered out. The mountains that form the walls of the city on all sides are 200 to 1000 feet high. The sides of the canyon are lined with temples, houses, and tombs that have been hewn out of the rock. Jordan provides food to Israel throughout the Great Tribulation, which could secure her (Jordan) a place as a "sheep nation" during the judgment of the sheep and goat nations at the end of the age. It is noted that Petra could not totally house the nation of Israel minus a remnant, but it will be a primary place of protection for Israel. Israelites will also escape to other wilderness lands.

Revelation 12:7-And war broke out in heaven: Michael and his angels fought against the dragon; and the dragon and his angels fought,

War breaks out in heaven (second heaven) between Michael and his angels and the Dragon and his fallen angels. According to

Daniel 12:1, Michael is the chief prince that stands up for the nation of Israel. This is Satan's last attempt to overthrow God in the heavenlies. Satan's final attack against God or God's people will occur after the Millennium when Satan marshals an army from Magog and marches on Jerusalem, only to be annihilated by God.

Revelation 12:8-9-but they did not prevail, nor was a place found for them in heaven any longer. So the great dragon was cast out, that serpent of old, called the Devil and Satan, who deceives the whole world; he was cast to the earth, and his angels were cast out with him.

Satan will no longer have access to the second or stellar heavens. Many expositors state that Satan has access to the third heaven or dwelling place of God. However, Satan cannot stand in God's holy presence without literally burning up or being consumed by the glory of God, because sin cannot exist in the direct presence of a holy and righteous God. In his initial rebellion against God in the beginning (Genesis 1:2; Isaiah 12:12-14; Ezekiel 28:17), Satan, as the anointed cherub Lucifer, was cast out of the third heaven or dwelling place of God. Jesus said He saw Satan fall as lightning (Luke 10:18). After successfully deceiving Eve and Adam, who was with her, to turn over their authority to him, Satan became the prince of the power of the air in the first and second heavens. In this war, Satan and his fallen angels are cast down and confined to the earth. Satan is also referred to as the Devil, great red Dragon, or Serpent. Devil means "slanderer" or "accuser" and Satan means "adversary." Deception is identified as Satan's chief weapon.

Revelation 12:10-Then I heard a loud voice saying in heaven, "Now salvation, and strength, and the kingdom of our God, and the power of His Christ have come, for the accuser of our brethren, who accused them before our God day and night, has been cast down."

A loud heavenly voice, probably of an angel, announces the coming of God's kingdom. "Power" in this verse refers to the authority of Christ. The accuser of the brethren is cast down. Satan has accused the believer throughout the ages from the time of Adam. According to Psalm 8, Adam's dominion was over the works of God's hands, which extended into the second heaven. Some commentators have speculated that Adam's sin actually stretched into the third heaven itself. Jesus told Mary not to touch Him as He was ascending to heaven, because He had to cleanse the heavenly tabernacle. From the fall of man through Adam until Jesus led the old covenant saints into heaven, no humans occupied the third heaven with the exception of Enoch and Elijah, who both entered heaven alive. Of course, Enoch and Elijah may not have been in the third heaven, but could have been in Abraham's bosom with the rest of the Old Testament saints. Whether or not Satan somehow had access to the third heaven, excluding the throne room, during the Old Testament period based on Job 1:6-13, 2:1-6 as espoused by many commentators is speculative. However, after Christ's defeat of the Devil at the cross and His ascension into the third heaven, where He is seated at the right hand of God the Father, salvation and the kingdom of God became available to all men. Therefore, Satan's access to the third heaven to stand before God and accuse humans could not be possible or salvation has not have come to all men. Satan is evil personified, and he would literally burn up in the presence of God. The favored interpretation is that after Satan's expulsion from the third heaven, he was confined to the first and second heaven until this point at mid-Tribulation, when he is cast to the earth. Satan has always done his accusing of the brethren by influencing the brethren to accuse one another. Salvation will come to Israel and the end of the age.

Revelation 12:11-"And they overcame him by the blood of the Lamb and by the word of their testimony, and they did not love their lives to the death."

This verse references the souls under the altar of Revelation 6:9 and the great multitude of Revelation 7, who overcome the persecution of the ten kings and the harlot in the first half of the Tribulation and the Antichrist in the second half of the Tribulation. The martyred saints overcome by their testimony of Jesus and His shed blood, the same as Christians do today. These people die for their faith.

Revelation 12:12-"Therefore rejoice, O heavens, and you who dwell in them! Woe to the inhabitants of the earth and the sea! For the devil has come down to you, having great wrath, because he knows that he has a short time."

Heaven rejoices because the accuser is cast down, but woe to the inhabitants of the earth and sea, because the Devil's great wrath is manifest for he knows his time is short, referring to the last half of the Tribulation Period. Satan's time lease on the planet is running out.

Revelation 12:13-Now when the dragon saw that he had been cast to the earth, he persecuted the woman who gave birth to the male Child.

The Devil persecutes the woman who gave birth to the male child. He can't persecute the male child (or the 144,000 Jews) because of God's protection. Therefore, he vents his wrath upon the nation Israel (woman).

Revelation 12:14-But the woman was given two wings of a great eagle, that she might fly into the wilderness to her place, where she is nourished for a time and times and half a time, from the presence of the serpent.

The woman flees swiftly to Petra (and other wilderness nations) where she is nourished for a time, times, and half a time (3 1/2 years) or the second half of the Tribulation Period. Wings of an eagle describe ease and speed of flight.

Revelation 12:15-So the serpent spewed water out of his mouth like a flood after the woman, that he might cause her to be carried away by the flood

"Flood" represents armies of the Antichrist (Isaiah 59:19). The goal of these armies is to overpower and destroy the woman.

Revelation 12:16-But the earth helped the woman, and the earth opened its mouth and swallowed up the flood which the dragon had spewed out of his mouth.

Divine intervention occurs as the earth is opened into a great chasm, and these armies of the Antichrist are swallowed up in the same way as Korah of the Old Testament and his company were swallowed up (Numbers 16:29-35).

Revelation 12:17-And the dragon was enraged with the woman, and he went to make war with the rest of her off-spring, who keep the commandments of God and have the testimony of Jesus Christ.

The Dragon is unable to destroy the woman or the male child. He becomes enraged and makes war with a remnant of Israel who are believers, because they keep the commandments of God and the testimony of Jesus. This remnant resides in and around the city of Jerusalem.

CHAPTER THIRTEEN

THE TWO BEASTS

(Refer to Prophetic Keys: The Antichrist, Beasts-Seven Heads and Ten Horns, and Book of Daniel)

Revelation 13:1-Then I stood on the sand of the sea. And I saw a beast rising up out of the sea, having seven heads and ten horns, and on his horns ten crowns, and on his heads a blasphemous name.

John's position is on the earth for this part of the vision. A seven headed, ten-horned Beast rises up out of the sea. Although the "sea" typically represents people from the sea of humanity, many scholars believe the "sea" more specifically refers to the people in the Mediterranean region. This interpretation would support the prophecies of Daniel that specify the Antichrist's natural origin as coming from the Seleucid division of the old Grecian Empire. The Beast represents three things:

1) A demon prince from the abyss, possibly the Prince of Greece, who controls the Antichrist (Revelation 11:7).
2) The Antichrist or a mortal man who receives his power from the Dragon or Satan (Revelation 13:4-10, 2 Thessalonians 2:3-12).
3) The eighth and last kingdom to persecute the nation Israel during the times of the Gentiles (Revelation 17:11).

In this passage, "Beast" refers to the Antichrist and his kingdom. "Seven heads" refer to seven great empires that have or will persecute Israel during the times of the Gentiles. These seven empires are: Egypt, Assyria, Babylon, Medo-Persia, Greece, Rome, and Reconstituted Rome. The "ten horns" are the ten kingdoms and rulers of the seventh empire or the Reconstituted Roman Empire. The ten horns are crowned, symbolizing the ruling power of the individual ten kings who, in turn, give their power to the Antichrist to form the eighth or Beast Empire (Revelation 17:11). The seven heads are not crowned, because the Antichrist has not had power or control over the previous seven empires. The seven-headed, ten-horned beast of Revelation 12:3 is symbolic of Satan and is anti-God. The seven-headed, ten-horned beast of Revelation 13:1 symbolizes the Antichrist and is anti-Christ. The seven-headed, ten-horned beast of Revelation 17:3 is symbolic of the prostitute religions and is anti-Spirit. Blasphemous names are on the heads, because Satan has always blasphemed anything of God, and these empires have and will persecute Israel, God's chosen people.

Revelation 13:2-Now the beast which I saw was like a leopard, his feet were like feet of a bear, and his mouth like the mouth of a lion. And the dragon gave him his power, his throne, and great authority.

The Beast being like a bear, leopard, and lion means that the Beast empire has the characteristics of the previous empires represented by these beasts. The bear stood for Medo-Persia (Daniel 7:5), the leopard for Greece (Daniel 7:6), and the lion for Babylon (Daniel 7:4). The Antichrist receives his power, throne, and authority from the Dragon or Satan.

Revelation 13:3-I saw one of his heads as if it had been mortally wounded, and his deadly wound was healed. And all the world marveled and followed the beast.

One of the heads appears to be mortally wounded and healed. The world marvels at the healing and follows the Beast. The wounded head stands for a kingdom or empire. An interpretation is that

one of the heads, the Grecian Empire, is revived as the eighth or
Beast empire. The satanic Prince of Greece from the abyss is a
high-ranking fallen angel in Satan's kingdom who will control,
use, and empower the Antichrist to revive the former Grecian
Empire. The "mortal wound" has a second application when the
Antichrist is resurrected as a counterfeit to the resurrection of
Christ. The world marvels and follows after the Beast, because he
(Antichrist) was mortally wounded and raised up.

**Revelation 13:4-So they worshiped the dragon who gave
authority to the beast; and they worshiped the beast saying,
"Who is like the beast? Who is able to make war with him?"**

The people of the earth worship the Beast or the Antichrist and
worship Satan, who gave authority to the Beast. Worship is what
Satan has wanted since the beginning of human history. The
people of the world will believe the Antichrist to be invincible.
Worship of the Antichrist occurs in the second half of the
Tribulation. At this point the Antichrist has conquered three
nations from the seventh empire with the remaining seven
nations giving him their power. He has broken the treaty or
covenant with Israel and is waging war with her remnant. He has
witnessed the destruction of the armies under Gog on the mountains of Israel. He has destroyed the Harlot religious system that
dominated the seventh empire during the first half of the
Tribulation and has defeated the King of the North and the King
of the South.

**Revelation 13:5-And he was given a mouth speaking great
things and blasphemies, and he was given authority to
continue for forty-two months.**

The duration of the Antichrist's authority and rule is for the second half of the Tribulation Period as represented by "forty-two
months." He is a blasphemer, as is Satan. In the middle of the
Tribulation, the Antichrist breaks the covenant with Israel, enters
the temple, and desecrates it by proclaiming himself to be God.

Revelation 13:6-Then he opened his mouth in blasphemy against God, to blaspheme His name, His tabernacle, and those who dwell in heaven.

The Antichrist blasphemes God, the temple, those who dwell in heaven, and the name of God.

Revelation 13:7-And it was granted to him to make war with the saints and to overcome them. And authority was given him over every tribe, tongue, and nation.

The Antichrist and his armies wage war with the saints who are overcome, defeated, and killed. The result from this war is the great multitude of martyred saints from every nation, tongue, and tribe as described in Revelation 7.

Revelation 13:8-And all who dwell on the earth will worship him, whose names have not been written in the Book of Life of the Lamb slain from the foundation of the world.

Literally, the world will worship the Antichrist. The worshippers are unbelievers, because their names are not written in the Lamb's Book of Life. When a person accepts Jesus as Savior and Lord his/her name is entered into the Lamb's Book of Life. The Lamb slain from the foundation of the world demonstrates that the redemptive plan of God was formulated in the mind of God from the beginning of the world or the casting down of the social order under Lucifer.

Revelation 13:9-10-If anyone has an ear, let him hear. He who leads into captivity shall go into captivity; he who kills with the sword must be killed with the sword. Here is the patience and the faith of the saints.

An admonition is given to listen to what is being said. In Revelation 2-3 this admonition is repeatedly given to hear what the Spirit is saying to the churches. The absence of the word "church" is important because the Church has been raptured and is in heaven with Christ at this time. The saints are instructed to be patient, for evil will be destroyed. Evil people will reap what they have sown.

Revelation 13:11-Then I saw another beast coming up out of the earth, and he had two horns like a lamb and spoke like a dragon.

"Another Beast" means another of the same kind. The first Beast, the Antichrist, is a man, and this second Beast is also a man. His arising out of the earth is similar to the Antichrist's coming out of the sea. It symbolizes rising to prominence from among humanity. This Beast is the False Prophet or the Antichrist's religious leader. The reference to a lamb shows deception. Although he operates as a world spiritual leader, he is a beast. Also, lambs do not have horns. Horns would symbolize power and authority. The False Prophet speaks as a dragon, reflecting that he too is controlled by the Devil.

Revelation 13:12-And he exercises all the authority of the first beast in his presence, and causes the earth and those who dwell in it to worship the first Beast, whose deadly wound was healed.

The False Prophet is not a rival of the Antichrist, because he directs worship to the Antichrist from those who live on the earth. He operates in the same authority as the Antichrist. The reference to the healing of the Beast's deadly wound seems to support a deception or counterfeit of the resurrection. Satan does not have the inherent power or authority to raise anyone, but he has always counterfeited the works of God. Apparently, the world will believe the Antichrist has suffered a mortal wound that was healed. That event causes people to be deceived, believe the lie, and worship the Beast. From the context, it appears that the False Prophet develops and executes this plan. Therefore, the "deadly wound" has a two-fold application. First, it applies to the restoration of the former Grecian Empire, and secondly, to the counterfeit resurrection of the Antichrist.

Revelation 13:13-He performs great signs, so that he even makes fire come down from heaven on the earth in the sight of men.

Further deceptions by the False Prophet are identified. He performs great signs, such as causing fire to come down out of heaven, thereby counterfeiting the miracles being performed at this time by the two witnesses. Elijah in his earthly ministry called fire down out of heaven. The armies of Gog described in Ezekiel 38-39 are destroyed in the first half of the Tribulation or seventieth week of Daniel by fire and brimstone that rains on them from heaven. The False Prophet's powers of deception are significant.

Revelation 13:14-And he deceives those who dwell on the earth by those signs which he was granted to do in the sight of the beast, telling those who dwell on the earth to make an image to the beast who was wounded by the sword and lived.

Both verses 12 and 14 indicate that the False Prophet performs these miracles in the presence or in the sight of the Beast. This is an unholy trinity at work, Satan, the Antichrist, and the False Prophet, and they operate deceptively by counterfeiting miracles of God. The False Prophet directs those on earth to make an image of the Beast that was wounded and lived. Bible scholars interpret image as "images" that are distributed worldwide to followers of the Beast. People will have these images of the Beast in their homes to worship as household idols or gods.

Revelation 13:15-He was granted power to give breath to the image of the beast, that the image of the beast should both speak and cause as many as would not worship the image of the beast to be killed.

The False Prophet's granting breath to the images demonstrates the operation of demons. A demon accompanies every idol and gives voice to the idols so people are deceived into thinking the idols have life. The primary work of these demons is to watch people to see who does not worship the image of the Beast. The demons report through their satanic chain of command and believers in the Lord are put to death. The order will be to worship the image of the Beast or die. The images become a demonic surveillance ring.

Revelation 13:16-And he causes all, both small and great, rich and poor, free and slave, to receive a mark on their right hand or on their foreheads,

The False Prophet directs the application of a mark on the right hand or forehead of the followers of the Antichrist. This action counterfeits the sealing by God of the 144,000 Jews. In a three and one-half year period, it will be difficult logistically to mark every unbeliever, although technology advances may speed this process. Certainly the marking must be accomplished to followers in the more prominent parts of the Antichrist's empire, Europe, Middle East, Eurasia, and Northern Africa. The decision whether or not to take the mark is not an economic, but a spiritual decision. The Antichrist has proclaimed himself to be God. Whoever takes the mark is committing allegiance to the Antichrist and agreeing to follow and worship him as the messiah or God.

Revelation 13:17-and that no one may buy or sell except one who has the mark or the name of the beast, or the number of his name.

People need to have the mark or the number of the Antichrist's name in order to buy or sell. The mark is required to conduct any business transaction. This present generation is literally the first generation with the technological capability for this prophecy to be fulfilled. With computer technology and interconnected networks in a cash-less economy, the Antichrist will be able to control all financial transactions and literally lock people out of all financial banking systems who do not have his mark. It will be an extremely difficult, if not impossible time for Christians trying to stay alive and trying to find food for sustenance. Because of the seal and trumpet judgments, a scarcity of food will exist, even for those people with the mark.

Revelation 13:18-Here is wisdom. Let him who has understanding calculate the number of the beast, for it is the number of a man: His number is 666.

The number of the Beast is the number of a man, which is 666. The wise Christian should not only be able to read the signs of the times regarding end-time events, including revelation of the Antichrist, but also should be able to determine who the Antichrist is by an analysis of the number of his name. Scholars have pointed out that every Greek letter has a corresponding numerical value. Therefore by adding or counting the numbers, every name has a numerical value. Approximately, one in 10,000 will have the number 666. Therefore, the teachings, values, character, and actions of prominent persons on the political scene should be examined. Biblically, six is the number for man. Three sixes or 666 could also suggest the unholy trinity of the False Prophet, the Antichrist, and Satan. It is interesting to note that the number for Jesus in the Greek is 888, and every usage of His name, i.e., Lord, Christ, Christ Jesus, Jesus Christ, Jesus, Lord Jesus, Lord Christ, and Lord Jesus Christ have numerical values that are multiples of eight.

CHAPTER FOURTEEN

ANGELIC ACTIVITY

(Refer to Prophetic Key: Groups of Believers)

Revelation 14:1-Then I looked, and behold, a Lamb standing on Mount Zion, and with Him one hundred and forty-four thousand, having His Father's name written on their foreheads.

Bible scholars are divided as to whether this is the earthly Mount Zion or the heavenly Mount Zion. There are several reasons to consider this passage as referring to the heavenly Mount Zion. The Lamb refers to Christ. After His resurrection, Christ is viewed as a Lamb in heaven but not on the earth. He returns to earth as the Lion of the tribe of Judah. Therefore, He will never be seen on earth as a Lamb. In verse 3, the 144,000 Jews are singing before the throne, and in verse 5, the 144,000 Jews are said to be without guilt before the throne of God, which definitely places them in heaven. The 144,000 Jews are the same 144,000 discussed in Revelation 7. They were sealed by God to protect them through the trumpet judgments. The seal is the Name of the Father God written on their foreheads. The 144,000 Jews are in heaven but without discussion as to how they arrived there. The best explanation is that they were raptured as the male child after the conclusion of the trumpet judgments near the end of the Age.

Revelation 14:2-And I heard a voice from heaven, like the voice of many waters, and like the voice of loud thunder.

And I heard the sound of harpists playing their harps.

John hears a heavenly voice that is most likely the voice of God, and he hears harpists playing.

Revelation 14:3-And they sang as it were a new song before the throne, before the four living creatures, and the elders; and no one could learn that song except the hundred and forty-four thousand who were redeemed from the earth.

From the context, the harpists of verse two are the 144,000 Jews who also sing a new song before the throne, living creatures, and elders. This is a song that no one else could learn except the 144,000 who are redeemed from the earth. The song is of special spiritual significance to the 144,000, because they are the only ones who can sing it. The 144,000 are the first Jews saved after the Rapture of the Church.

Revelation 14:4-These are the ones who were not defiled with women, for they are virgins. These are the ones who follow the Lamb wherever He goes. These were redeemed from among men, being first fruits to God and to the Lamb.

The 144,000 Jews are called the first fruits unto God, again signifying that they are the first Jews saved after the Rapture of the Church. Not being defiled by women implies that the 144,000 are all men. The fact they are called virgins means they are unmarried. If they are to be witnesses for God in the Tribulation, then they need to be free from the ties of a family that could divert their attention from their spiritual goal in order to provide family protection. Being virgins and undefiled has a spiritual implication in demonstrating purity of character, in addition to not being polluted by spiritual fornication and the idolatrous religious system of Mystery Babylon.

Revelation 14:5-And in their mouth was found no guile, for they were without fault before the throne of God.

The 144,000 are guileless and without fault before the throne of God.

Revelation 14:6-7-Then I saw another angel flying in the midst of heaven, having the everlasting gospel to preach to those who dwell on the earth - to every nation, tribe, tongue, and people – saying with a loud voice, "Fear God and give glory to Him, for the hour of His judgment has come; and worship Him who made heaven and earth, the sea and springs of water."

An angel is seen flying in heaven with the everlasting Gospel to preach to all peoples of the earth. The Gospel message is not one of salvation and redemption, but one of fearing an omnipotent God who created all things. Up to now, only man has preached the Gospel. Man preached that judgment would be coming. The angel now proclaims, rather than preaches, that judgment has come. Since mankind has failed to respond to the Gospel of grace proclaimed by all the witnesses during the Tribulation, then maybe man will respond to the fear of judgment. The angel references God's creative power over the same parts of the earth that are the subjects of the initial trumpet judgments: earth, sea, and springs of water. God's creative abilities are proclaimed against man's evolutionary and Godless philosophies. These angels could be preaching for the entire 3 1/2 years of the Great Tribulation, but it is more probable from the placement of this scripture in the Biblical text that this incident occurs after the rapture of the male child (144,000 Jews). Therefore, the angel proclaims the Gospel throughout the duration of the bowl judgments. The 144,000 Jewish witnesses are raptured and in heaven after the trumpet judgments. The two prophets are resurrected 3 1/2 days after their 1260 days of ministry has concluded at the beginning of the bowl judgments. The greatest devastation to the planet will come as God completes His judgment of sin and unrighteous mankind by releasing the bowl judgments. Even though the 144,000 Jewish evangelists have been raptured from the planet after the trumpet judgments and the two witnesses resurrected after their 42-month ministry, God will continue to have a voice on the earth through angels who proclaim His

Gospel and issue these proclamations.

Revelation 14:8-And another angel followed, saying, "Babylon is fallen, is fallen, that great city, because she has made all nations drink of the wine of the wrath of her fornication."

Another angel announces the fall of religious and literal Babylon. The religious system fails at mid-Tribulation, when the power and authority of the seventh empire with whom the religious system is integrated is given to the Antichrist by the ten kings. The destruction of the literal city of Babylon will occur at the end of the bowl judgments at the Second Coming of Christ. This latter announcement is considered "proleptic," which means to acknowledge a future event as if it has already happened.

Revelation 14:9-11-Then a third angel followed them, saying with a loud voice, "If anyone worships the beast and his image, and receives his mark on his forehead or on his hand, he himself shall also drink of the wine of the wrath of God, which is poured out full strength into the cup of His indignation. And he shall be tormented with fire and brimstone in the presence of the holy angels and in the presence of the Lamb. And the smoke of their torment ascends forever and ever; and they have no rest day or night, who worship the beast and his image, and whoever receives the mark of his name."

The third angel gives a warning that anyone who takes the mark of the Beast or the number of his name will suffer the wrath of God and eternal damnation in a place of torments. Fire and brimstone are a reference to the lake of fire. Angels will be able to view this place of eternal torment. Receiving the mark of the Beast is signing one's eternal doom. There is no reversal once a person has taken the mark. As with the first angel in Revelation 14:6-7, this angel may provide the warning throughout the Great Tribulation, but more likely, this warning will occur during the period of the bowl judgments.

Revelation 14:12-Here is the patience of the saints; here are those who keep the commandments of God and the faith of Jesus.

Faith in God, patience, and keeping the commandments of God bring eternal rewards.

Revelation 14:13-Then I heard a voice from heaven saying to me, "Write: Blessed are the dead who die in the Lord from now on. Yes, says the Spirit, that they may rest from their labors, and their works follow them."

A voice in heaven commands John to write that those who die in the Lord are blessed. Their work is to not take the mark of the Beast even to the point of death. In heaven they will have rest. Again, this time period may refer to the Great Tribulation, but more likely to the period of the bowl judgments.

Revelation 14:14-And I looked, and behold, a white cloud, and on the cloud sat One like the Son of Man, having on His head a golden crown, and in His hand a sharp sickle.

The Son of Man is seen on a white cloud wearing a golden crown and holding a sharp sickle in His hand. This is a preview of Christ as He prepares to descend to earth to execute judgment on the unbelieving world. The golden crown is representative of His kingship. The sickle stands for judgment. The sickle in His hand demonstrates that He is ready to judge.

Revelation 14:15-16-And another angel came out of the temple, crying with a loud voice to Him who sat on the cloud, "Thrust in Your sickle and reap, for the time has come for You to reap, for the harvest of the earth is ripe." So He who sat on the cloud thrust His sickle on the earth, and the earth was reaped.

An angel, the fourth of this section, exits the temple in heaven with a message, apparently from the Father, that it is time to

reap. The delay is over, the earth is ready, and the time for judgment is here. Thrusting in the sickle represents destruction of
the Antichrist's armies at the battle of Armageddon. Christ
thrusts in the sickle and judges the earth.

**Revelation 14:17-Then another angel came out of the temple
which is in heaven, he also having a sharp sickle.**

Another angel, the fifth of the section, exits the temple with a
sharp sickle, representing angelic involvement in these final
judgments.

**Revelation 14:18-And another angel came out from the altar,
who had power over fire, and he cried with a loud cry to him
who had the sharp sickle, saying "Thrust in your sharp sickle and gather the clusters of the vine of the earth, for her
grapes are fully ripe."**

The sixth angel of this chapter comes from the altar and has
power over fire. The altar is associated with the prayers of the
saints for judgment and an end to sin. The angel with the sickle
is told to "thrust in the sickle" continuing to show angelic
involvement in the end-time judgments.

**Revelation 14:19-So the angel thrust his sickle into the earth
and gathered the vine of the earth, and threw it into the great
wine press of the wrath of God.**

The angel did as instructed. The wine press of the wrath of God
is Armageddon and the judgment of the wicked.

**Revelation 14:20-And the wine press was trampled outside
the city, and blood came out of the wine press, up to the
horses' bridles, for one thousand six hundred furlongs.**
The battle of Armageddon will be fought throughout the entire-
ty of Israel with a concentration outside Jerusalem in the valley
of Megiddo, whose dimensions are 184 miles in length by 100
miles in width. The bloodshed is extensive and the battle is

likened to a wine press that is used to crush grapes. Blood flows to the horses' bridles. Some commentators see this passage as describing an actual lake of blood. Other prophecy scholars take the passage more figuratively, because a literal lake of blood would be highly unlikely. In either case, based on millions of soldiers involved in this conflict, blood will be everywhere and on everything, including horses and bridles.

CHAPTER FIFTEEN

HEAVENLY ACTIVITY

Revelation 15:1-Then I saw another sign in heaven, great and marvelous: seven angels having the seven last plagues, for in them the wrath of God is complete.

This scene is in heaven. In chapter 12 two great signs were seen, the woman and the fiery red Dragon. This sign is not only great, but also marvelous; seven angels with the seven last plagues of the wrath of God. These seven angels are the bowl angels with the seven last judgments to be executed on the earth and the ungodly to complete God's wrath. God sent ten plagues when the children of Israel were delivered from Egyptian bondage. Those ten plagues were executed within the period of a month. Therefore, the time period for execution of the last seven plagues or bowl judgments should also be a month or less at the end of the Tribulation, culminating with the battle of Armageddon and the return of Christ.

Revelation 15:2-And I saw something like a sea of glass mingled with fire, and those who have the victory over the beast, over his image and over his mark and over the number of his name, standing on the sea of glass, having harps of God.

The sea of glass is the floor of the throne room that was not occupied in Revelation 4. The transparent glass mingled with fire reflects the glory of God throughout the throne room including the floor. The throne room is now occupied by those saints and martyrs of the great multitude of Revelation 7 who have attained victory over the Antichrist by not taking his mark, his name, the number of his name, or by not worshipping his image.

Revelation 15:3-4-And they sing the song of Moses, the servant of God, and the song of the Lamb, saying: "Great and marvelous are Your works, Lord God Almighty! Just and true are Your ways, O King of the saints! Who shall not fear You, O Lord, and glorify Your name? For You alone are holy. For all nations shall come and worship before You. For Your judgments have been manifested."

These victors or overcomers (great multitude) sing the song of Moses and the Lamb. The song of Moses is one of deliverance and victory, and the song of the Lamb is one of deliverance and victory over Satan. These songs are from psalms and show Jesus as Creator and King while declaring His attributes of holiness, justice, and truth. The reference to all nations worshipping Him points to the Millennium.

Revelation 15:5-6-After these things I looked, and behold, the temple of the tabernacle of the testimony in heaven was opened. And out of the temple came seven angels having the seven plagues, clothed in pure bright linen, and having their chests girded with golden bands.

The temple is opened in heaven, and from the temple come the seven bowl angels with the seven last plagues. These angels come from the very presence of God. They are robed in heavenly attire, bright linen and golden bands around their chests depicting their holiness, purity, and righteousness.

Revelation 15:7-Then one of the four living creatures gave to the seven angels seven golden bowls full of the wrath of God who lives forever and ever.

The living creatures that assisted Christ in calling forth the riders of the first four seal judgments now participate in execution of the bowl judgments. One of the four living creatures gives the seven angels the bowls of the wrath of God. Because the living creatures exist in the very presence of God around the throne, these judgments must then come directly from the Father God Himself.

Revelation 15:8-The temple was filled with smoke from the glory of God and from His power, and no one was able to enter the temple till the seven plagues of the seven angels were completed.

The Shekinah glory of God is manifest in the temple and no one can enter the temple until the plagues are concluded showing the awesomeness and seriousness to God of the judgments on His creation.

CHAPTER SIXTEEN

THE LAST PLAGUES

(Refer to Prophetic Key: Tribulation Judgments)

Revelation 16:1-Then I heard a loud voice from the temple saying to the seven angels, "Go and pour out the bowls of wrath of God on the earth."

The unidentified voice from the temple must be the voice of God because a command is given to the seven bowl angels to execute the wrath of God on the earth. The pouring out of the bowls implies that the judgments are sudden and occur within a short span of time at the end of the 42 months of the Great Tribulation or possibly in the thirty-day period, mentioned in Daniel 12, immediately following the end of the 1260 days. Whereas the effect of the trumpet judgments was felt in thirds, the impact of the bowl judgments is total and complete. Trumpet judgments 2-4 affected one-third of the seas, fresh waters, and light from the sun, moon, and stars. Bowl judgments 2-5 affect the remaining two-thirds sea, waters, and light from the sun not affected by the trumpet judgments. The bowl judgments are God's judgments upon men for worshipping the Beast or his image, or for taking his mark, name, or the number of his name, and for the hardness of their hearts.

Revelation 16:2-So the first went and poured out his bowl upon the earth, and a foul and loathsome sore came upon the men who had the mark of the beast and those who worshiped his image.

The first bowl judgment is delivered on the followers of the Beast who worship the Beast's image or who have taken his mark. This judgment is "foul" sores on the Antichrist's worshippers, i.e., very painful, malignant ulcers or boils. Many scholars believe the identification procedure itself causes these cancers, either from the ink, chemical used in the marking process, or from microchip implantation.

Revelation 16:3-Then the second angel poured out his bowl on the sea, and it became blood as of a dead man; and every living creature in the sea died.

The second bowl, like the second trumpet judgment, is poured out on the sea and the sea becomes as the blood of a dead man and everything in the sea dies. At a minimum, the Mediterranean Sea is tainted, if not all the seas in the Antichrist's kingdom. It is possible, if not probable, that all seas on the planet are polluted. With the death of all sea life, the stench, pestilence, and disease will be overwhelming, in addition to the absence of food products.

Revelation 16:4-Then the third angel poured out his bowl on the rivers and the springs of water, and they became blood.

Similar to the first Egyptian plague and the third trumpet judgment, rivers and springs of water become blood. Drinking water will be scarce and at a premium, because fresh water is polluted, and there has not been any rain for approximately 3 1/2 years, due to heaven being shut-up by the power of the two witnesses.

Revelation 16:5-7-And I heard the angel of the waters saying: "You are righteous, O Lord, The One who is and who was and who is to be, Because You have judged these things. For they have shed the blood of saints and prophets, And You have given them blood to drink. For it is their just due."
And I heard another from the altar saying, "Even so, Lord God Almighty, true and righteous are Your judgments."

God is praised by angels for His righteousness, eternal nature, and His judgment of those who have shed the blood of the prophets and saints. No matter what anyone thinks, God's judgments are repeatedly declared to be true and righteous.

Revelation 16:8-9-Then the fourth angel poured out his bowl on the sun, and power was given to him to scorch men with fire. And men were scorched with great heat, and they blasphemed the name of God who has power over these plagues; and they did not repent and give Him glory.

The effect of the fourth bowl judgment is on the sun as men are scorched with intense heat as fire. Again, the impact of this judgment is on unrighteous people who blaspheme God and do not repent or give Him glory. At this point, the conditions in the earth are: men scorched from the intense heat of the sun, waters polluted, and cancerous sores on the bodies of the followers of the Antichrist. The intense heat will be like having hot coals of fire on cancerous sores. Intense heat and lack of water will result in the death of multitudes. Furthermore, people exposed to the sun for an extended period may literally self-ignite. The scorching heat from the sun would cause water evaporation, resulting in extreme humidity and difficulty in breathing. Water evaporation on a large scale could alter sea levels producing coastal devastation, but the length of this judgment is probably too short to cause this degree of damage.

Revelation 16:10-11-Then the fifth angel poured out his bowl on the throne of the beast, and his kingdom became full of darkness; and they gnawed their tongues because of the pain. And they blasphemed the God of heaven because of their pain and their sores, and did not repent of their deeds.

The impact of the fifth bowl judgment is complete darkness on the throne of the Beast, Jerusalem and/or Babylon, or more extensively, the territory of the eighth or Beast Empire. This plague is similar to the darkness of the ninth Egyptian plague. It is further described in Joel 2:1-2, 10-11 as a day of darkness, gloominess, and day of clouds and thick darkness when the earth quakes, heavens rumble, sun and moon grow dark, and the stars diminish their brightness. Amos 5:18 describes this day as a day of darkness with no light. Unregenerate people will gnaw their tongues in pain from the scorching heat, malignant sores, and the fear of utter darkness. In spite of this pain, the unrighteous will continue to blaspheme God and refuse to repent of their evil deeds.

Revelation 16:12-Then the sixth angel poured out his bowl on the great river Euphrates, and its water was dried up, so that the way of the kings from the east might be prepared.

The sixth bowl judgment dries up the great river Euphrates, preparing a way for the armies from the East to move into the Holy Land. The Euphrates River is approximately 1800 miles long and forms a natural barrier between east and west. As stated previously, the Euphrates was the border of the Roman Empire, and the rebuilt city and world trade center of Babylon will sit on the Euphrates. Babylon must rely on the Euphrates for all water needs, and the drying up of the river severely impacts the life and operation of the city. Of course, the river is already polluted from the second bowl judgment. Evaporation of ice caps on nearby mountains could cause the Euphrates to dry up, but the time period for this judgment is too short. With the extensive movement of the earth from earthquakes, volcanic eruptions, and a meteor strike, the Euphrates could dry up as its waters become collected in underground caverns and fissures. However, the most probable cause is simply supernatural divine intervention. The significance of the Euphrates River, instead of other rivers, is that with the Euphrates dried-up, the pathway is open and easily accessible for the armies from the East to march into Israel for their ultimate end-time confrontation with Christ.

Revelation 16:13-16-And I saw three unclean spirits like

frogs coming out of the mouth of the dragon, out of the mouth of the beast, and out of the mouth of the false prophet. For they are spirits of demons, performing signs, which go out to the kings of the earth and the whole world, to gather them to the battle of the great day of God Almighty. "Behold, I am coming as a thief. Blessed is he who watches, and keeps his garments, lest he walk naked and they see his shame." And they gathered them together to the place called in Hebrew, Armageddon.

Three demon spirits are released by the Dragon, Beast, and the False Prophet and are sent to the kings of the earth throughout the entire world to gather armies together to wage war against God in the battle of the great day of God Almighty. The demons perform signs and operate by deception, causing kings and their armies to join the Antichrist in contention against Israel, and ultimately, against Christ for possession of the earth. The nations of the world are led to Armageddon or the valley of Megiddo. These military and world leaders probably do not know the Antichrist's true agenda and are enticed to the Armageddon site on some other grounds probably to join him in the annihilation of Israel. However, at this point mankind is so depraved that it will believe and accept any lie. Napoleon referred to Megiddo as the ideal battleground for a war involving all the armies of the world. Jesus says His Coming will be like a thief in the night and proclaims a blessing on those who are watchful, i.e., those who are ready and faithful. The fact that His Coming is likened to a thief seems to indicate that the nations and their armies are not expecting Christ to appear but are there for some other reason. The battle of Armageddon may only last for one day, because it is referred to as the "battle of the great day of God Almighty."

Revelation 16:17-Then the seventh angel poured out his bowl into the air, and a loud voice came out of the temple saying, "It is done!"

The seventh angel pours out his bowl and the voice of God in heaven from the throne proclaims that it "is done," meaning God's plan regarding the judgment of sin and unrighteous men is concluded and Christ is ready to take possession of the earth. The seventh bowl is poured into the air, which is into Satan's realm, as he is called the "prince of the power of the air."

Revelation 16:18-19-And there were noises and thunderings and lightnings; and there was a great earthquake, such a mighty and great earthquake as had not occurred since men were on the earth. Now the great city was divided into three parts, and the cities of the nations fell. And great Babylon was remembered before God, to give her the cup of wine of the fierceness of His wrath.

Noises, thunderings, and lightnings occur in addition to a great and mighty earthquake of a magnitude that has never been experienced in the history of the earth. This earthquake is described in Zechariah 14:1-5, which also tells that Jerusalem will be seized, houses rifled, women ravished, and half the city will fall into captivity. Jesus will fight against these conquering nations, the Mount of Olives will split in two as His feet touch it, and the saints will accompany Him at His Coming. Some commentators believe Revelation 11:13 also describes the events under the seventh bowl judgment. However, Revelation 11:13 states a tenth of the city is destroyed and 7000 men are killed. Furthermore, under the seventh bowl judgment, the great city is divided into three parts, the cities of the nations fall, and Babylon is judged by God. These events may all occur at the same time as the seventh bowl judgment and the Second Coming of Christ, but more likely they are separate and distinct events occurring in close proximity to one another, within a 30-day period culminating with the Second Coming.

Revelation 16:20-21-Then every island fled away, and the mountains were not found. And great hail from heaven fell

upon men, every hailstone about the weight of a talent. And men blasphemed God because of the plague of the hail, since that plague was exceedingly great.

Every island and mountain is altered, indicating that the entire landscape of the earth is reconfigured. Great hail falls from heaven weighing between 56 and 114 pounds, similar to the seventh Egyptian plague. Men continue to blaspheme God.

CHAPTER SEVENTEEN

THE HARLOT RELIGION

(Refer to Prophetic Keys: Beast-Seven Heads and Ten Horns and Religious and Literal Babylon)

Revelation 17 is a parenthetical passage that contrasts Mystery Babylon, the religious system, and the literal city of Babylon, which is fully discussed in Revelation 18. The time frame for Revelation 17 is the first half of the Tribulation culminating with the destruction of the Mother of Harlots at mid-Tribulation.

Revelation 17:1-Then one of the seven angels who had the seven bowls came and talked with me, saying to me, "Come, I will show you the judgment of the great harlot who sits on many waters."

The great Harlot refers to the religious system based on idolatry, paganism, witchcraft, occult, cults, demon worship, astrology, and every form of religious fornication. She is the embodiment of all the idolatrous religious systems and practices since Nimrod. Her sitting on many waters means that she is involved with people from all walks of life as delineated in verse 15. These are the peoples of the ten-kingdom Reconstituted Roman Empire.

Revelation 17:2-"with whom the kings of the earth committed fornication, and the inhabitants of the earth were made drunk with wine of her fornication."

Mystery Babylon is not a kingdom or political power herself, because the kings or political leaders commit fornication with her. She is a religious system with whom the kings or governments and peoples of the earth are heavily involved in her philosophies and practices. Drinking the wine of her fornication depicts involvement with her idolatrous practices, witchcraft, and demonism.

Revelation 17:3-So he carried me away in the Spirit into the wilderness. And I saw a woman sitting on a scarlet beast which was full of names of blasphemy, having seven heads and ten horns.

John is caught up in the Spirit as he is given this revelation by one of the seven bowl angels. He sees a woman sitting on a scarlet colored beast having seven heads and ten horns. The woman is the pagan religion that dominates this seventh world or Beast Empire represented by the seventh head with ten horns. She represents the religion and religious practices that have dominated all seven heads or empires. The first six of the seven heads represent the past empires of Egypt, Assyria, Babylon, Medo-Persia, Greece, and Rome, while the seventh head will be the Reconstituted Roman Empire. The ten horns are the ten kings and kingdoms that make up this seventh empire. The Beast Empire is ruled by the Antichrist after he conquers three of the ten kings and the remaining seven give him their power and authority. The "names of blasphemy" represent all the names that this false pagan religion has been called.

Revelation 17:4-The woman was arrayed in purple and scarlet, and adorned with gold and precious stones and pearls, having in her hand a golden cup full of abominations and the filthiness of her fornication.

Purple, scarlet, precious stones, pearls, and gold are examples of the wealth of this religious system. She has a golden cup containing all her spiritual abominations, which is a satanic duplication of the golden censer with the prayers of the saints described in Revelation 8:3.

Revelation 17:5-And on her forehead a name was written: MYSTERY, BABYLON THE GREAT, THE MOTHER OF HARLOTS AND OF THE ABOMINATIONS OF THE EARTH.

She is called "Mystery Babylon the Great," the "Mother of Harlots and of the Abominations of the Earth." Mystery Babylon identifies her with the religious practices of ancient Babylon. Mother of Harlots and of the Abominations of the Earth identify her with everything that is abominable to God, i.e., paganism, occult, cults, witchcraft, idolatry, spiritual fornication, etc.

Revelation 17:6-And I saw the woman, drunk with the blood of the saints and the blood of the martyrs of Jesus. And when I saw her, I marveled with great amazement.

She is drunk with the blood of the saints and martyrs, meaning that she has been responsible for the persecution and death of many of God's servants and martyrs throughout history up to mid-Tribulation.

Revelation 17:7-But the angel said to me, "Why did you marvel? I will tell you the mystery of the woman and the beast that carries her, which has the seven heads and the ten horns."

The angel explains to John the mystery of the woman and the beast. The woman and beast are separate entities; the woman represents a religious system and the beast represents a political system. The woman rides the beast, implying she has and will dominate and influence the activities of the first seven empires.

Revelation 17:8-"The beast that you saw was, and is not, and will ascend out of the bottomless pit and go to perdition.

And those who dwell on the earth will marvel, whose names are not written in the Book of Life from the foundation of the world, when they see the beast that was, and is not, and yet is.

The beast that was, is not, and yet is, who ascends out of the bottomless pit is not a person, because people are not in the abyss. The beast is a satanic prince (fallen angel) who is allowed to vacate the abyss at this time in history. The beast that "is not" means he is not associated with the Roman Empire of John's day but existed or was on the scene of history prior to Rome. The beast "that was' connects him to one or more of the five world empires before Rome: Egypt, Assyria, Babylon, Medo-Persia, or Greece. Because the Antichrist will arise from the territory of the Old Grecian Empire, one explanation for the beast from the abyss is that he is the Satanic Prince of Greece who controlled and dominated Alexander the Great as he conquered the known world of that time. The Prince of Greece would then have been bound in the bottomless pit since the fall of ancient Greece. However, it is noted that the satanic prince could be either the Prince of Babylon or the Prince of Assyria, as the Antichrist is referred to by both titles, King of Babylon and the Assyrian, and territory from both former Empires, Babylon and Assyria, fell within the boundary of the Old Grecian Empire. The phrase "yet is" means that the Beast will reappear on the scene of history to empower and control the Antichrist as he leads the eighth empire toward world domination. As has been stated previously, reference to the Beast is not only to a satanic prince, but also to the Antichrist, and the eighth kingdom ruled by the Antichrist.

Those with their names not written in the Book of Life are unbelievers who marvel at the satanically controlled Antichrist. They have rejected Christ in order to follow the Antichrist and have had their names deleted from the Book of Life.

Revelation 17:9-11-"Here is the mind which has wisdom: The seven heads are seven mountains on which the woman

sits. There are also seven kings. Five have fallen, one is, and the other has not yet come. And when he comes, he must continue a short time. And the beast that was, and is not, is himself also the eighth, and is of the seven, and is going to perdition."

The seven heads are seven mountains on which the woman sits. From this passage, many commentators believe Rome to be the seat of the Antichrist, rather than Babylon or Jerusalem. Rome is identified because it sits on seven hills. However, the context of these verses is kings and kingdoms. Also, other scriptures refer to mountains as kingdoms. Five kingdoms and their corresponding kings have fallen: Egypt, Assyria, Babylon, Medo-Persia, and Greece. The ruling government of John's day was Rome and is the kingdom that "is." The kingdom that "is to come" will be the seventh kingdom or the Reconstituted Roman Empire. When the Antichrist appears, he will be on the scene for a short time, which is 3 1/2 years or the last half of the Tribulation Period. The beast kingdom that "was" stands for one of the five fallen kingdoms identified above. The kingdom that "is not" clarifies that it is not Rome, the kingdom in John's time, but is an eighth empire. This means that ten kings rule the seventh empire independently for the first half of the seven-year Tribulation. Then the Antichrist conquers three of these ten kings (kingdoms), with the other seven giving him their power and authority, and he alone rules this new eighth empire, which is a product of the seven prior kingdoms represented by the seven heads.

Revelation 17:12-"And the ten horns which you saw are ten kings who have received no kingdom as yet, but they receive authority for one hour as kings with the beast."

This passage explains the ten kings and the seventh empire. The ten horns of the beast represent ten kings who have no kingdom in John's day but will have authority for a short time with the Beast. They exist and rule independently during the first half of the Tribulation but are led by the Antichrist during the last half of the Tribulation.

Revelation 17:13-"These are of one mind, and they will give their power and authority to the beast."

The ten kings are in agreement to give their power and authority to the Beast. This event occurs at mid-Tribulation.

Revelation 17:14-"These will make war with the Lamb, and the Lamb will overcome them, for He is Lord of lords and King of kings; and those who are with Him are called, chosen, and faithful."

The ten kings continue to exist under the rule of the Antichrist in the eighth or Beast Empire and are part of the Antichrist's armies against Christ at the battle of Armageddon. They will be defeated by Christ.

Revelation 17:15-And he said to me, "The waters which you saw, where the harlot sits, are peoples, multitudes, nations, and tongues."

This verse defines the "waters" mentioned in verse one.

Revelation 17:16-"And the ten horns which you saw on the beast, these will hate the harlot, make her desolate and naked, eat her flesh and burn her with fire."

The ten kings hate the Harlot that dominates, influences, and binds them to demonic superstitions during the first half of the Tribulation. In the middle of the Tribulation, when the Antichrist proclaims himself to be God in the holy temple in Jerusalem, the ten kings destroy the religious system called Mystery Babylon. The Antichrist tolerates the Harlot only until he has enough power to turn the worship of mankind to himself for the last half of the Tribulation. From the text, it appears that the ten kings destroy every aspect of the religious system, including all idols and religious paraphernalia, and they burn all edifices of worship. The idols are replaced with images of the Beast that speak.

Revelation 17:17-"For God has put it into their hearts to fulfill His purpose, to be of one mind, and to give their kingdom to the beast, until the words of God are fulfilled."

The ten kings give their kingdoms to the Beast, as his kingdom becomes the eighth empire. This event fulfills the divine plan of God.

Revelation 17:18-"And the woman whom you saw is that great city which reigns over the kings of the earth."

The Harlot or Mystery Babylon is the religious system that influences and dominates the Reconstituted Roman Empire under the rulership of the ten kings. The headquarters for this religious system is in the great city of Babylon.

CHAPTER EIGHTEEN

DESTRUCTION OF BABYLON

(Refer to Prophetic Key: Religious and Literal Babylon)

Revelation 17 describes the destruction of religious Babylon, while Revelation 18 describes the destruction of the literal city of Babylon. The city of Babylon is destroyed under the seventh bowl judgment at the Second Coming of Christ. Revelation 17 is parenthetical, while Revelation 18 continues the discussion of the bowl judgments.

Revelation 18:1-After these things I saw another angel coming down from heaven, having great authority, and the earth was illuminated with his glory.

"After these things" refers to after the bowl judgments. The angel described is distinct from the bowl angels and appears to be a high ranking angel coming from the presence of God, based on the descriptive terminology of "great authority" and the "earth illuminated with his glory."

Revelation 18:2-And he cried mightily with a loud voice, saying, "Babylon the great has fallen, is fallen, and has become a habitation of demons, a prison for every foul spirit, and a cage for every unclean and hated bird!"

This verse connects with Revelation 14:8 that proclaimed the fall of the great city Babylon. The proclamation is repeated for emphasis. Babylon is described as having become a habitation of demons and a prison for every foul spirit, which certainly is a primary reason for her fall. Apparently, Babylon became progressively more evil, which is not surprising, as she is the headquarters for the Antichrist and the False Prophet. The reference to "unclean and hated bird" may signify that many kinds of scavengers are present in the city to feast upon the dead flesh at the destruction of the city and/or the destruction that has been occurring throughout the area.

Revelation 18:3-"For all nations have drunk of the wine of the wrath of her fornication, the kings of the earth have committed fornication with her, and the merchants of the earth have become rich through the abundance of her luxury."

Both Mystery Babylon and literal Babylon the city have caused the kings of the nations to commit spiritual fornication. The nations identify themselves with all pagan and demonic practices of the Harlot religious system headquartered in the city during the first half of the Tribulation and the worship of the Antichrist in the second half of the Tribulation. The merchants profit greatly in their business operations in the city.

Revelation 18:4-And I heard another voice from heaven saying "Come out of her, my people, lest you share in her sins, and lest you receive of her plagues."

A voice from heaven, Christ or the Father, commands His people to get out of the city in order not to become caught up in her sins or her judgment. This warning is similar to that given to Lot and his family to leave Sodom before God destroyed it, displaying God's mercy in time of judgment.

Revelation 18:5-"For her sins have reached to heaven, and God has remembered her iniquities."

As in the time of Noah and Sodom and Gomorrah, the sins come before God. According to scholars, the term "remember" in the

Greek is remembering for judgment.

Revelation 18:6-"Render to her just as she rendered to you, and repay her double according to her works; in the cup which she has mixed, mix for her double."

Babylon's punishment is in full measure or full compensation for her sins. This is an application of the Biblical law of sowing and reaping. Babylon is to be repaid according to her deeds and sins, except the Lord's vengeance will be doubled. An additional implication could be referenced in that there are two Babylons, Mystery Babylon and the literal city of Babylon, both of which are destroyed by judgment of fire.

Revelation 18:7-"In the measure that she glorified herself and lived luxuriously, in the same measure give her torment and sorrow; for she says in her heart, I sit as a queen, and am no widow, and will not see sorrow."

Again, the same measure she glorified herself and lived in luxury is the same measure of her torment and sorrow. Babylon is personified as the queen or chief of all cities and is oblivious to her potential destruction or sorrow. She thinks this happy and opulent state will continue forever, which is typically the illusion of those in all ages who love their material riches. Babylon will be the epitome of a hedonistic, pleasure driven city.

Revelation 18:8-"Therefore her plagues will come in one day –death and mourning and famine. And she will be utterly burned with fire, for strong is the Lord God who judges her."

The judgment of Babylon is short and swift without warning or delay. The city is destroyed in one day. Verse 10 shortens the judgment to one hour. The vehicles of destruction are fire, famine, mourning, and death. Mourning, famine, and death are evident in the city as a result of the bowl judgments being executed. The great earthquake and destruction by fire occur under the seventh bowl judgment. Whereas Mystery Babylon is judged

and destroyed by the ten kings, the city of Babylon is judged and
destroyed by God Himself.

**Revelation 18:9-10-"And the kings of the earth who commit-
ted fornication and lived luxuriously with her will weep and
lament for her, when they see the smoke and burning, standing at a distance for fear of her torment, saying, Alas, alas,
that great city Babylon, that mighty city! For in one hour
your judgment has come."**

The kings rejoiced at the destruction of Mystery Babylon but
lament and weep over the destruction of this great city. They are
not weeping because they loved her but because she made them
wealthy. The kings are standing far off, so as to not be caught in
her judgment. The duration of the judgment is clarified from
one day to one hour, and the kings understand it to be judgment. Babylon's destruction must occur prior to the battle of
Armageddon, but on the same day, because the kings, merchants, and sea traders view her total annihilation.

**Revelation 18:11-14-"And the merchants of the earth will
weep and mourn over her, for no one buys their merchandise anymore: merchandise of gold and silver, precious
stones and pearls, fine linen and purple silk and scarlet,
every kind of citron wood, every kind of object of ivory,
every kind of object of most precious wood, bronze, iron,
and marble; and cinnamon and incense, fragrant oil and
frankincense, wine and oil, fine flour and wheat, cattle and
sheep, horses and chariots, and bodies and souls of men.
And the fruit that your soul longed for has gone from you,
and all the things which are rich and splendid have gone
from you, and you shall find them no more at all."**

The merchants also weep over the destruction of Babylon
because of their financial loss. Babylon is the world commercial
center and the hub of commerce. The items of merchandise and
commerce are spelled out in verses 12 and 13. Included on the

list are the bodies and souls of men, demonstrating that satanic control and possession over people are prevalent in the city. At Babylon's destruction, luxuries are no longer found in the city, having become a thing of the past.

Revelation 18:15-16-"The merchants of these things, who became rich by her, will stand at a distance for fear of her torment, weeping and wailing, and saying, Alas, alas that great city that was clothed in fine linen, purple, and scarlet, and adorned with gold and precious stones and pearls!"

As the kings stand at a distance weeping and wailing, so will the merchants who profited and were made rich by her. The kings lament over the loss of their life style, but the merchants lament over the loss of wealth.

Revelation 18:17-19-"For in one hour such great riches came to nothing. And every shipmaster, all who travel by ship, sailors, and as many as trade by the sea stood at a distance and cried out when they saw the smoke of her burning, saying, "What is like this great city? And they threw dust on their heads and cried out, weeping and wailing, and saying, Alas, alas, that great city, in which all who had ships on the sea became rich by her wealth! For in one hour she is made desolate."

Again, the one-hour period of destruction is mentioned. Now all shipmasters and sea traders stand at a distance at Babylon's judgment and weep at her destruction, for they too profited by her maritime trade. No city can compare with Babylon at this time in history. The sea traders and sea merchants weep and wail, as do the kings and merchants, at Babylon's destruction, because they too were made rich through her. All three classes of people refer to the greatness of the city. Kings stand for the governmental world, merchants for the commercial world, and sea traders for the maritime world. The sea traders acknowledge that her destruction is completed in one hour.

Revelation 18:20-"Rejoice over her, O heaven, and you holy apostles and prophets, for God has avenged you on her!"

Heaven is commanded to rejoice because justice has been executed.

Revelation 18:21-Then a mighty angel took up a stone like a great millstone and threw it into the sea, saying "Thus with violence the great city of Babylon shall be thrown down, and shall not be found anymore."

Casting of the millstone symbolizes sudden and complete destruction. Babylon is violently destroyed under the seventh bowl judgment and her ruins will never be found. This prophecy has not been fulfilled, which is another supporting reason for the rebuilding of Babylon. Because the fire from God destroys Babylon and her ruins are never to be found, it can be assumed that the heat is so intense that every element is literally disintegrated or vaporized.

Revelation 18:22-23-"The sound of harpists, musicians, flutists, and trumpeters shall not be heard in you anymore. And no craftsman of any craft shall be found in you anymore. And the sound of a millstone shall not be heard in you anymore. And the light of a lamp shall not shine in you anymore. And the voice of a bridegroom and bride shall not be heard in you anymore. For your merchants were the great men of the earth, for by your sorcery all the nations were deceived."

The sounds of the daily activities of musicians, workers, people, and craftsmen cannot be heard. Additionally, the lights of the city no longer shine. The destruction is total. All nations of the earth have been deceived by her sorceries, which in the Greek include drugs, occult, witchcraft, and astrology. Babylon is destroyed because of sorcery (v. 23); fornication (v. 3, 9); pleasures, sins, and luxuries (v. 3, 19); oppression of Israel (v. 24); martyrdom of saints (v. 24); and pride (v. 7-8).

Revelation 18:24-"And in her was found the blood of prophets and saints, and of all who were slain on earth."

Babylon is a stronghold of evil and all manner of evil is performed in the city. Many saints of God will be martyred in this great city.

CHAPTER NINETEEN

ARMAGEDDON

**(Refer to Prophetic Keys: Conditions on Earth at
Armageddon and Marriage Supper of the Lamb)**

**Revelation 19:1-After these things I heard a loud voice of a
great multitude in heaven, saying, "Alleluia! Salvation and
glory and honor and power to the Lord our God!"**

The first ten verses are parenthetical, depicting heavenly pronouncements preceding the Second Coming of Christ. "After these things" refers to events that occur after the bowl judgments and the destruction of literal Babylon as discussed in Revelation 16 and 18. John hears the voice of the great multitude praising God for His salvation, power, glory, and honor. This is the same great multitude identified in Revelation 7, made up of saints killed or martyred during the Tribulation Period.

**Revelation 19:2-3-"For true and righteous are His judgments,
because He has judged the great harlot who corrupted the
earth with her fornication; and He has avenged on her the
blood of His servants shed by her. Again they said, "Alleluia!
And her smoke rises up forever and ever!"**

God's judgments are again declared to be true and righteous. The ten kings destroy the great Harlot at mid-Tribulation while the literal city of Babylon is judged and destroyed by God at the end of the Tribulation. Both corrupt the earth with their spiritual fornication. God avenges the murder of His saints within the city. God is praised, because Babylon will never again rise from her ruins. The destruction of the city is for eternity.

Revelation 19:4-6-And the twenty-four elders and the four living creatures fell down and worshiped God who sat on the throne, saying, "Amen! Alleluia! Then a voice came from the throne saying Praise be to God, all you His servants and those who fear Him, both small and great! And I heard, as it were, the voice of a great multitude, as the sound of many waters and as the sound of mighty thunderings, saying, Alleluia! For the Lord God Omnipotent reigns!"

The 24 elders and four living creatures join with the great multitude in the worship of God. A voice from heaven, but not God, commands praise of God by all His creatures both great and small. Because the voice originated at the throne, it is probably a high-ranking angel, one of the living creatures, or an elder. In verse 10, John is commanded not to worship this being, which supports the conclusion that the voice belongs to someone other than God. This is a universal call to worship. The voice of the great multitude praises God for His omnipotence and for reigning over creation.

Revelation 19:7-10-"Let us be glad and rejoice and give Him glory, for the marriage of the Lamb has come, and His wife has made herself ready. And to her it was granted to be arrayed in fine linen, clean and bright, for the fine linen is the righteous acts of the saints. Then he said to me, Write: Blessed are those who are called to the marriage supper of the Lamb! And he said to me, These are the true sayings of God. And I fell at his feet to worship him. But he said to me, See that you do not do that! I am your fellow servant, and of your brethren who have the testimony of Jesus. Worship God! For the testimony of Jesus is the spirit of prophecy."

Most Bible commentators refer to the Church as the bride of Christ when discussing the marriage of the Lamb. Certainly, the relationship of Christ and the Church parallel a relationship of bride and groom. In Revelation 21, the New Jerusalem and her inhabitants are called the bride, the Lamb's wife. Jesus called Himself the bridegroom, and John the Baptist referred to Jesus as the bridegroom, which means newly married man. John called himself a friend of the bridegroom, which further substantiates why Old Testament saints are not members of the body of Christ. New Testament Christians are married to Christ according to the new covenant. Israel is married to God according to the old covenant but is currently separated. Israel will be restored to God in her marital relationship at the Second Coming of Christ when the prophecies of Daniel 9:24 are fulfilled. At the end of the Millennium, believers redeemed from all ages are referred to as the bride, the Lamb's wife and will dwell in the New Jerusalem throughout eternity. Natural humans on earth will be able to frequent the New Jerusalem for eternity but will not live there. They essentially live on earth but will not be considered part of the bride or the Lamb's wife.

John falls to the ground in worship of the person commanding praise to God in verse 5. Is this person an angel or redeemed saint? The message comes from the throne, so it could be delivered by one of the living creatures, by a high-ranking angel, or by one of the elders. John is told not to worship this person because he is a fellow servant of his, a brother in the Lord who has the testimony of Jesus. Most commentators identify this fellow servant to be an angel, but angels are normally not referred to as fellow servants with the testimony of Jesus. Such a description is characteristic of a reborn, redeemed saint. An elder could fit as the person making the statement. However, a similar statement in Revelation 22:8-9 identifies an angel as the one speaking. According to Revelation 1:1, God gave the Revelation to Jesus, who gave it to His angel, then to John. In Revelation 2-3, messages are sent to the angels of the seven churches. Since angel means messenger, it is noted that these angels are the pastors of the seven churches. In Revelation 5,

John is concerned about who would be qualified to open the seven-sealed scroll. An elder provides explanation to him. At this point in Revelation, the ministry of angels is in full manifestation. An elder would certainly fit the description of a fellow servant and brother, except for the usage of the word "angel" in Revelation 22:8. Regardless of who made the utterance, angel or elder, the command is to worship God.

The testimony of Jesus is the spirit of prophecy. Jesus is the provider of prophetic revelation in accordance with Revelation 1:1, and prophecy should always point to Christ with the purpose and intent to provide revelation of Christ.

Revelation 19:11-Then I saw heaven opened, and behold, a white horse. And He who sat on him was called Faithful and True, and in righteousness He judges and makes war.

This time the white horse rider is Christ Himself who returns to earth as the Lion of the Tribe of Judah. The white horse is a symbol for a conqueror and victory. He is called "Faithful" and can absolutely be trusted. His faithfulness is not dependent on man's faith. He is called "True," for He is the standard of all truth. He judges and makes war in righteousness, as there is no vindictiveness in His judgments. Christ's attribute of righteousness is offended at sin, and the sin must be judged. Anyone so judged will not have an excuse. Jesus has been long-suffering in giving as much time as possible for men to repent. During the Tribulation, He has warned mankind of the consequences of continued rebellion against God through the 144,000 Jewish witnesses, the two prophets, and even through angels. Mankind will be without an excuse.

Revelation 19:12-His eyes were like a flame of fire, and on His head were many crowns. He had a name written that no one knew except Himself.

His eyes as a "flame of fire" are symbolic for His omniscience. Nothing can be hidden from Him. On His head are many crowns, and these are royal crowns demonstrating His rulership over the kingdoms of the earth. He has various names written upon Him, but John is not told the names.

Revelation 19:13-He was clothed with a robe dipped in blood, and His name is called The Word of God.

His clothing dipped in blood could symbolize his crucifixion, and the shedding of His blood for man's sins. However, based on the location of this passage immediately preceding Armageddon, this verse more appropriately refers to the blood that will be shed at Armageddon. Jesus is called the Word of God, as He is in John 1:1.

Revelation 19:14-And the armies in heaven, clothed in fine linen, white and clean, followed Him on white horses.

Jesus' "armies in heaven" are clothed in white, clean, fine linen and also follow Christ on white horses. The armies consist of both angels and saints:

- 1 Thessalonians 3:13 *"...God and Father at the coming of our Lord Jesus Christ with all His saints."*
- 2 Thessalonians 1:7-8 *"...the Lord Jesus is revealed from heaven with His mighty angels, in flaming fire..."*
- Jude 14-15 *"...the Lord comes with ten thousands of His saints, to execute judgment on all..."*

Members of Christ's armies do not need weapons because Christ does all the fighting.

The Church Age saints in their resurrected bodies received at the Rapture of the Church return as Christ's army with the angelic host. The Old Testament saints, Tribulation saints, including the martyrs and great multitude, and the 144,000 Jewish witnesses are not a part of this army. These saints do not receive their immortal, glorified, and resurrected bodies until after the battle of Armageddon at the last stage of the First Resurrection.

One might assume that the 144,000 Jews raptured as the

male child before the bowl judgments could have received their resurrected bodies upon rapture and consequently would be included in Christ's heavenly army. However, because the 144,000 Jews are invited guests to the marriage feast and are not part of the raptured Church or Lamb's wife, they will not be included in the army returning to earth with Christ. The 144,000 Jewish witnesses do not receive their glorified bodies until the last stage of the First Resurrection.

Because the two prophets, Elijah and Enoch, are killed at the conclusion of the Great Tribulation, they also will not be included with the army of saints. They receive their immortal bodies after the battle of Armageddon, also at the last stage of the First Resurrection.

Revelation 19:15-16-Now out of His mouth goes a sharp sword, that with it He should strike the nations. And He Himself will rule them with a rod of iron. He Himself treads the wine press of the fierceness and wrath of Almighty God. And He has on His robe and on His thigh a name written: KING OF KINGS AND LORD OF LORDS.

Christ speaks a word of judgment, and it becomes a literal judgment. As He spoke the worlds into existence, He in like manner judges and destroys the nations with the words out of His mouth. In the Millennium, He will rule with a rod of iron. It will be a theocratic government where everyone conforms to God's righteous standards. The treading of the wine press is descriptive of the battle of Armageddon. Christ's destruction of the armies of the Antichrist is comparable to squashing grapes in a wine press where juice splatters everywhere. The names written on His robe and thigh are King of kings and Lord of lords, descriptive of His ownership and rulership. Jesus will rule as King and Lord over the nations in the Millennium, and the Church will rule and reign with Him.

Revelation 19:17-18-Then I saw an angel standing in the sun

and he cried with a loud voice, saying to all the birds that fly in the midst of heaven, "Come and gather together for the supper of the great God, that you may eat the flesh of kings, the flesh of captains, the flesh of mighty men, the flesh of horses and of those who sit on them, and the flesh of all people, free and slave both small and great."

Armageddon is called the supper of the great God. An angel commands the birds to gather to this supper. The birds include all scavenger types, such as hawks, eagles, vultures, falcons, etc. The birds feast on the carcasses of the Antichrist's slain armies. The unrighteous attend the supper of the great God while believers attend the wedding feast of the Lamb.

Revelation 19:19-And I saw the beast, the kings of the earth and their armies, gathered together to make war against Him who sat on the horse and against His army.

The Beast and his army and the armies of all the kings of the earth are gathered in Jerusalem to combat Christ and His armies. The battle of Armageddon probably lasts only one day and ends with the complete destruction of the Antichrist's armies.

Revelation 19:20-Then the beast was captured, and with him the false prophet who worked signs in his presence, by which he deceived those who received the mark of the beast and those who worshiped his image. These two were cast alive into the lake of fire burning with brimstone.

The Beast and the False Prophet are captured and cast alive into the lake of fire. 2 Thessalonians 2:8 states *"...the lawless one (the Antichrist)...whom the Lord will consume with the breath of His mouth and destroy with the brightness of His Coming."* Although it appears to be a contradiction, the Antichrist will be slain by Christ at His Coming, but his spirit and soul or inner man will remain alive and be cast into the lake of fire. In essence, the Antichrist is killed, resurrected, and cast into the lake of fire. The Antichrist is the first person resurrected in the Second Resurrection, and along with the False Prophet are the first inhabitants of the lake of fire.

Revelation 19:21-And the rest were killed with the sword which proceeded from the mouth of Him who sat on the horse. And all the birds were filled with their flesh

Christ destroys the armies of the Antichrist by the sword that proceeds from His mouth, which is the spoken Word of God (Revelation 19:15, 21). In addition to the spoken Word, other methods for destruction of the Antichrist's armies are:

- brightness of His Coming (2 Thessalonians 2:8)
- hailstones (Revelation 16:21)
- great earthquake (Revelation 16:18,20; Zechariah 14:1-5)
- self destruction (Zechariah 14:13)
- flesh, eyes, tongue dissolving (Zechariah 14:12)

CHAPTER TWENTY

THE MILLENNIUM AND FINAL JUDGMENT

(Refer to Prophetic Key: Millennium)

Revelation 20:1-Then I saw an angel coming down from heaven, having the key to the bottomless pit and a great chain in his hand.

In Revelation 9:1, an angel opened the bottomless pit and released the demon locusts. This angel, who may be the same as the one in Revelation 9:1, has the key to the abyss and a great chain. In 2 Peter 2:4, angels who had sinned were cast down to hell and delivered into chains of darkness. In Jude 6, God has incarcerated, held for judgment, and bound in everlasting chains under darkness angels who had not kept their proper domain. Revelation 9:13 discusses four angels bound at the great river Euphrates. It is not revealed how they are bound, only that they are. These scriptures demonstrate that fallen angels can be literally bound, and that the chains are not physical because spirit beings cannot be bound with physical chains.

Revelation 20:2-He laid hold of the dragon, that serpent of old, who is the Devil and Satan, and bound him for a thousand years.

The angel laid hold of, or became master of, subdued, or ruled over, the Devil who is further identified in this verse as Satan, the Dragon, and serpent of old. Because Satan is an angelic creation of the highest rank, it is probable that the angel who does the binding is Michael. Michael is the only angel identified by name in the Bible that has contended against Satan. Satan is bound for 1000 years, which is the period of time commonly referred to as the Millennium.

Revelation 20:3-and he cast him into the bottomless pit, and shut him up, and set a seal on him, so that he should deceive the nations no more till the thousand years were finished. But after these things he must be released for a little while.

Satan is shut up, confined, and sealed up in the bottomless pit for the duration of the Millennium. He is bound not for punishment but confinement so he will be unable to deceive the nations. Deception has been Satan's main weapon in his fight against God's people. Satan's angelic and demonic followers are also bound for the 1000 years (Isaiah 24:22-23). During His Millennial reign, Christ will rule the nations with a rod of iron without the deceptive influence of the Devil. After the 1000 years, Satan will be loosed from his confinement for a short period of time.

Revelation 20:4-And I saw thrones, and they sat on them, and judgment was committed to them. And I saw the souls of those who have been beheaded for their witness to Jesus and for the word of God, who had not worshiped the beast or his image, and had not received his mark on their fore-heads or on their hands. And they lived and reigned with Christ for a thousand years.

John sees saints sitting on literal thrones in heaven ruling with Christ, with the authority to judge having been granted to them. This verse doesn't reveal what or who the saints will be judging, only that they will. It is implied that judgment is connected with the ruling or governing of the nations with Christ. The souls referred to are the great multitude including the "souls under the altar" (Revelation 6:9). These Tribulation saints did not take the mark of the Beast, or worship the Beast or his image, which are mandates from the Antichrist during the second half of the

Tribulation Period. These souls, martyred for their witness to Jesus, are beheaded. A more literal translation of this passage is killed with an ax.

Revelation 20:5-But the rest of the dead did not live again until the thousand years were finished. This is the first resurrection.

The First Resurrection is the redemption of the body, i.e., the changing of saints' bodies to immortal, glorified forms or from mortality to immortality. The First Resurrection is completed after the binding of Satan and immediately prior to the beginning of the Millennium. The Second Resurrection occurs after the Millennium and before the White Throne judgment.

The First Resurrection occurs in stages as follows:

1. Resurrection of Christ as the first born from the dead (Revelation 1:5) or the first born among many brethren (Romans 8:29).

2. Rapture of the Church Age saints (New Testament saints that have died since Christ, and New Testament saints caught up alive to meet the Lord in the air).

3. Resurrection of the Old Testament saints, Tribulation saints (great multitude and souls under the altar), 144,000 Jewish witnesses saved during the Tribulation and raptured as the male child, and God's two witnesses or prophets raised up at the end of the Tribulation.

The wicked dead of all ages from Adam through the Millennium are confined in Sheol-Hades or Torments until after the Millennium when they are judged at the White Throne judgment and cast into the lake of fire. The Antichrist and the False Prophet are the only exceptions. They were cast into the lake of fire at the end of the Tribulation after the battle of Armageddon.

Revelation 20:6-Blessed and holy is he who has part in the first resurrection. Over such the second death has no power, but they shall be priests of God and Christ, and shall reign with Him a thousand years.

Those who are part of the First Resurrection are called blessed and holy. The Second Resurrection or second death or eternal death has no power over any saint who has a place in the First Resurrection. Again, the saints are told that they are priests of God and Christ and will reign with Him for 1000 years. John begins Revelation by referring to the millennial reign of Christ (ruling as kings and priests per Revelation 1:6) and concludes Revelation speaking of the Millennium.

Revelation 20:7-8-Now when the thousand years have expired, Satan will be released form his prison and will go out to deceive the nations which are in the four corners of the earth, Gog and Magog, to gather them together to battle, whose number is as the sand of the sea.

After the 1000-year period, Satan and his demonic legions are loosed from the abyss and immediately go to the nations throughout the earth to again deceive and tempt them into another battle to overthrow God. The term "deceive" means a deliberate misleading, to cause to wander, or go astray as it relates to doctrinal error, which Satan has always perpetrated in his perversion of Biblical truth. The amazing result is that the number of those who follow Satan will be as the "sand of the sea." These people will have experienced first hand the blessings of living in the millennial kingdom under the leadership of Christ and yet are deceived into believing that there could be improved living conditions. All men since the fall of Adam have had to choose, as an act of their will, between Satan and God. The people of the Millennium will be given the same choice. "Gog" and "Magog" stand for the hosts of evil. Gog has already died on the mountains of Israel during the Tribulation, so this isn't the same leader. However, usage of Gog and Magog seem to indicate that the rebellion forms in the territory called "Magog" or Russia/Central Asia and a natural leader arises called "Gog" who is controlled by Satan. This will be the final great attack against God.

Upon examining the book of Amos in the Septuagint, scholars linked Amos 7:1 to Revelation 20:7-8 and discovered a reference to Gog as the king of locusts. Proverbs 30:27 clearly states that locusts do not have a king. There are locusts mentioned in Revelation 9, who are not natural locusts, but demon locusts. The operation of demons is witnessed throughout the seventieth week of Daniel. This reference to Gog could then refer to a demon prince that controls a natural leader with the title Gog. The original Gog of Ezekiel 38-39 was killed on the mountains of Israel during the first half of the Tribulation. Therefore, it is this demon prince that comes on the scene after the Millennium, having been bound in the abyss with Satan for 1000 years, to lead another rebellion against God. This demon prince is likened to a previous demon prince, the prince of Greece from out of the abyss in Revelation 11 that controls and influences the Antichrist.

Revelation 20:9-They went up on the breadth of the earth and surrounded the camp of the saints and the beloved city. And fire came down from God out of heaven and devoured them.

This army of Satan surrounds Jerusalem, the beloved city, but before they can attack, they are quickly and completely destroyed by fire from God. The triumph of God is final.

Revelation 20:10-And the devil, who deceived them, was cast into the lake of fire and brimstone where the beast and the false prophet are. And they will be tormented day and night forever and ever.

The Devil becomes the third inhabitant of the lake of fire where the Antichrist and the False Prophet already exist in a state of torment day and night, forever and ever, which is the reality of eternal damnation. Satan's demons and fallen angels are cast into the lake of fire at this time, because they were already judged and condemned for their participation in the initial rebellion against God in eternity past.

Revelation 20:11-Then I saw a great white throne and Him who sat on it, from whose face the earth and heaven fled away. And there was found no place for them.

The Great White Throne is a place of judgment for the unrighteous of all time. There isn't a rainbow around the throne as was seen in Revelation 4. Lack of a rainbow signifies a time of judgment and no mercy. "White" represents the righteousness of the judgments. Some scholars use this passage to support the complete destruction of heaven and earth before creation of a new heaven and earth. However, in this context, heaven and earth fleeing away indicates that there is no place to hide. God the Father is on the throne and the time of judgment has arrived.

Revelation 20:12-And I saw the dead, small and great, standing before God, and books were opened. And another book was opened, which is the Book of Life. And the dead were judged according to their works, by the things which were written in the books.

The wicked dead are judged. The Books are opened as a testimony to His creation that His judgments are fair, true, and righteous. According to commentators the "Books" are: the Book of Law for judging those who lived under the law during the Old Testament period; the Book of Works of the Old Testament that list all of a man's works; the Book of Life where the names of every person are included at birth, but whose names can be blotted out if they are not saved by the time they die; and the Lamb's Book of Life where a person's name is entered when Christ is accepted as Savior and Lord. Everyone is judged by what is written in the Books according to their works. This judgment confirms that a person cannot be saved through works alone.

Revelation 20:13-The sea gave up the dead who were in it, and Death and Hades delivered up the dead who were in them. And they were judged, each one according to his works.

All the dead from the sea and from "Death and Hades" appear before the throne. "Death" signifies the grave and location of bodies for the Second Resurrection. "Hades" signifies the place of confinement for the souls and spirits of the unrighteous while awaiting the White Throne judgment. As stated previously, Death and Hades could refer to the angels in charge of the nether world. The "sea" includes those whose bodies have been completely lost or destroyed. It could also refer to all people lost in the Noahic flood. There is no escape from punishment regardless of the means of death.

Revelation 20:14-Then Death and Hades were cast into the lake of fire. This is the second death.

The second death is eternal separation from God in a place of everlasting torment day and night. The power over death is destroyed. This temporary hell or the angels in charge of this temporary hell are cast into the eternal hell or lake of fire, which is also called Gehenna.

Revelation 20:15-And anyone not found written in the Book of Life was cast into the lake of fire.

Anyone whose name is not found written in the Book of Life will be cast into the lake of fire. Obviously, there is not any demographic data to be able to ascertain the number of people to be judged at the White Throne judgment or how many people have ever lived on earth. Population estimates taken from internet sites project the number of people to have ever lived on earth at 105 billion. Assume at best case that 20% were believers and not subject to this judgment, then the number to be judged would be 84 billion. During the Millennium there will be virtually no death.

The population growth estimate for the Millennium is over 50 billion up to 100 billion. However, those that follow Satan in his last rebellion after the 1000 years will be in number as the sands of the seashore. Assume that number to be 5-10 billion. The result is that almost 100 billion people will be brought before the White Throne and judged. Further, suppose that it takes 5 minutes to review the books for each individual and the reviews continue nonstop for 24 hours a day, seven days a week, 52 weeks a year. The White Throne judgment would then last for close to a million years. Granted, this analysis is pure speculation. The point is that the number of persons lost is staggering, and the time to judge them from our dimension of time is staggering. God obviously will have a better system.

God already has the lake of fire prepared, initially for the Devil and his angels. Gehenna is probably a place located in the spiritual realm like Sheol-Hades, the temporary hell. In the natural realm, scientists have identified that white dwarf stars never cool off, can never burn out, and can never be quenched by any substance. White dwarf stars are in fact lakes of fire. Whether the lake of fire is located in the natural or spiritual realm, God only knows. In either case, the unrighteous of all time, as well as demons, and fallen angels will be suffering and in torment forever but will not be consumed by fire. They will be in a state of "being consumed" and burned by unquenchable fires for eternity, and will literally be dying forever.

CHAPTER TWENTY ONE

THE NEW JERUSALEM

(Refer to Prophetic Keys: Day of the Lord, Renovation of Heaven and Earth, and Postmillennial Earth or Eternity Future)

Revelation 21:1-And I saw a new heaven and a new earth, for the first heaven and first earth had passed away. Also there was no more sea.

"New" means renewed or new in freshness or character, not existence. The present heavens and earth are changed or renovated to exist in a new state. 2 Peter 3:10-13 explains that the earth's renovation is accomplished by fire where the heavens dissolve and the elements melt. Heaven and earth pass away or change from one condition to another, not cease to exist. There are actually three heavens. The first heaven is the atmospheric heaven around the earth. The second heaven is the stellar heaven or universe. The third heaven is the dwelling place of God. This passage pertains to the first and second heavens. The third heaven or residence of God would not need renovation, because the effects of the curse are not manifest there. Jesus cleansed the heavenly tabernacle when He ascended into heaven following His resurrection. "Elements melting" represent the systems of the first heavens and earth being set free, untied, and unbound from the curse, i.e., heaven and earth are loosed from the present state of bondage to the curse. This loosing is done by fervent heat with the result that the earth will be made clean and pure for man forever.

No More Sea – Position 1

To many scholars, "no more sea" means that all oceans and seas have disappeared from the earth because their necessity for mankind and earth systems has diminished, since all men on earth have glorified bodies. This last point is highly questionable. Scripture does not indicate that people who survive the Tribulation Period and live through the Millennium or are born in and live through the Millennium are to be given glorified bodies after the Millennium. Certainly, all persons who are part of the First Resurrection have received glorified bodies that will exist forever. There is, however, no indication that millennial Christians receive glorified bodies. Most likely they will enter into eternity in natural bodies not subject to death, as was the initial design for Adam's body.

No More Sea – Position 2

A more plausible interpretation for "no more sea" is that the Mediterranean Sea and great oceans cease to exist, but lakes, streams, rivers, and small seas will continue to exist. Redeemed man in his glorified form will not be affected by earth's systems and conditions. Natural man, on the other hand, will continue to live on earth after the Millennium and will be subject to earth systems, such as climate, weather, heat, food, light, water, etc. The territory presently covered by the great oceans will be needed in order to house the vast and growing population of mankind from the Millennium as a result of no death. With the removal of the curse, the perversion on the earth's climactic systems that results in storms, floods, droughts, hurricanes, tsunamis, tornados, cyclones, earthquakes, etc., will cease. The general climactic theory for weather conditions preceding the Noahic flood was a vapor canopy covering the earth, thereby producing a greenhouse effect. A mist generated by the greenhouse condition watered the earth. Without the great oceans, the climactic systems of the present earth will be significantly altered resulting in the re-formation of the vapor canopy and greenhouse effect.

Revelation 21:2-Then I, John, saw the holy city, New Jerusalem, coming down out of heaven from God, prepared as a bride adorned for her husband.

John sees the New Jerusalem descending from heaven prepared as a bride. The New Jerusalem, together with its inhabitants, is the bride of Christ. Inhabitants of the city are the saints or the redeemed of all ages including Old Testament and New Testament believers, Tribulation saints, and the 144,000 Jewish witnesses. The New Jerusalem will be the capital of God on earth in the eternal perfect state. Many scholars speculate that the New Jerusalem will actually hover over the earth as a city in space.

Revelation 21:3-And I heard a loud voice from heaven saying, "Behold, the tabernacle of God is with men, and He will dwell with them, and they will be his people, and God Himself will be with them and be their God."

Another unidentified voice, most likely angelic, proclaims that the tabernacle of God or the very presence of God is in the New Jerusalem. God the Father is among and in the midst of His people and apparently is visible to men. Redeemed man dwells in the city with God. God rules earthly man who have natural bodies, like Adam's in his pre-curse state. God never abandoned His plan for man as originally designed in the beginning. His plan was simply delayed and subsequently altered on account of the fall of man with the result that God will now have a natural man to rule over and a redeemed man to rule with Him.

Revelation 21:4-"And God will wipe away every tear from their eyes; there shall be no more death, nor sorrow nor crying; and there shall be no more pain, for the former things have passed away."

All the effects of the curse are passed away. No more sorrow, tears, crying, pain, or death. Everything that can bring sorrow to a man's life shall be removed, never to be remembered again. Death is destroyed at the end of the Millennium.

Revelation 21:5-Then He who sat on the throne said, "Behold, I make all things new. And He said to me, Write, for these words are true and faithful."

God sits on the throne and declares that He makes all things new. Again, the "new" is newness in condition not existence. Renovation or renewal of things previously cursed, such as mankind and the earth. Everything corrupted by Satan will be restored.

Revelation 21:6-7-And He said to me, "It is done! I am the Alpha and the Omega, the Beginning and the End, I will give of the fountain of the water of life freely to him who thirsts. He who overcomes shall inherit all things, and I will be his God and he shall be My son."

God refers to Himself as the "Alpha and the Omega," the "Beginning and the End." The redemptive plan of God is completed. The curse is removed. Earth is turned back to God, and God rules the universe from the New Jerusalem. Salvation is freely available to anyone who asks. The overcomer rules with God and inherits all things as sons of God.

Revelation 21:8-"But the cowardly, unbelieving, abominable, murders, sexually immoral, sorcerers, idolaters, and all liars shall have their part in the lake which burns with fire and brimstone, which is the second death."

In contrast to verses 6-7 of Revelation 21, the ungodly inherit the lake of fire, which is the second death or eternal separation from the presence of God. The lake of fire is the only place in the universe where the ungodly can be separated from God.

Revelation 21:9-11-Then one of the seven angels who had the seven bowls filled with the seven last plagues came to me and

talked with me, saying, "Come, I will show you the bride, and the Lamb's wife." And he carried me away in the Spirit to a great city, the holy Jerusalem, descending out of heaven from God, having the glory of God. And her light was like a most precious stone, like a jasper stone, clear as crystal.

One of the seven bowl judgment angels speaks with John and shows him the bride or the Lamb's wife, that is, the great city, holy New Jerusalem, descending out of heaven from God. The bride or Lamb's wife is not just the city, but the city inhabited with the redeemed saints of God, both Old and New Testament saints, Tribulation saints, and the 144,000 Jewish witnesses. John is carried in the spirit to a great and high mountain, which infers that the city sits on a mountain or is integrated with the mountain or is mountainous in shape. The glory of God is in the city and the light from the city is like precious stones and crystalline in appearance. The city literally radiates the glory of God and is designed to transmit the glory of God without limitation. The glory of God is radiated in the brilliance of light.

Revelation 21:12-14-Also she had a great high wall with twelve gates and twelve angels at the gates, and names written on them, which are the names of the twelve tribes of the children of Israel: three gates on the east, three gates on the north, three gates on the south, and three gates on the west. Now the wall of the city had twelve foundations, and on them are the names of the twelve apostles of the Lamb.

The city has a great and high wall with twelve gates, and at each gate is an angel with a name of one of the twelve tribes of Israel. Three gates exist on each side of the city, north, south, east, and west. The wall of the city has twelve foundations and on each foundation is the name of one of the twelve apostles of Jesus the Lamb. The representation of the total group of redeemed believers, both Old Testament and New Testament saints, is evident by the names of the twelve tribes on the gates and names of the twelve apostles on the foundations.

Revelation 21:15-17-And he who talked with me had a gold reed to measure the city, its gates, and its wall. And the city is laid out as a square, and its length is a great as its breadth. And he measured the city with the reed; twelve thousand furlongs. Its length, breadth, and height are equal. Then he measured its wall: one hundred and forty-four cubits, according to the measure of a man, that is of an angel.

The angel tells John to take a golden reed, normally 9 to 12 1/2 feet in length, and measure the structure. The city is laid out in a square shape at its base with the length equal to its width. The city measures 1500 miles in length, width, and height. Commentators vary as to the city's shape from a cube, to a pyramid, to a series of mountains starting with foothills inside the wall and rising to a mountain 1500 feet high upon which is located the tabernacle of God. The wall measures 225 to 300 feet. If the city is shaped like a cube, why is a wall necessary? Pyramid shapes are in many cases associated with paganism and should be ruled out. The best conclusion is that the city is shaped as a series of mountains, a fact further supported by scripture references to heaven as the mountain of His holiness, the heavenly Mount Zion, and the mount of the congregation. As a comparison, the city is half the size of the United States and as high as half the United States or nine to ten times higher than orbited satellites.

It is estimated that the number of people that have lived on the earth from Adam to the Millennium is 105 billion. If 20% are saved, then 21 billion could inhabit the city. The 20% as used in the commentary in Revelation 20:15 is only a guess derived by interpolating population statistics. The born-again Christian population in the United States slightly exceeds 40%, but is less than 10% in the rest of the world, thereby yielding at best case 20% potential inhabitants of the city. Whatever the exact number God only knows, but the dimensions of the city as described can easily accommodate 21 billion saints. People living through the Millennium on into eternity future will reside on earth outside the New Jerusalem. They will visit but not live in the New Jerusalem.

Revelation 21:18-20-And the construction of its wall was of jasper; and the city was pure gold, like clear glass. And the foundations of the wall of the city were adorned with all kinds of precious stones: the first foundation was jasper, the second sapphire, the third chalcedony, the fourth emerald, the fifth sardonyx, the sixth sardius, the seventh chrysolite, the eighth beryl, the ninth topaz, the tenth chrysoprase, the eleventh jacinth, and the twelfth amethyst.

The construction of the city is from gems and precious metals. The wall is jasper and the city is pure gold like clear glass. Each of the twelve foundations is a precious gemstone.

Revelation 21:21-22-And the twelve gates were twelve pearls: each individual gate was of one pearl. And the street of the city was pure gold, like transparent glass. But I saw no temple in it, for the Lord God Almighty and the Lamb are its temple.

Each of the twelve gates is a giant pearl probably more than a mile in diameter. The street of the city is pure, transparent gold. Most likely, these are heavenly materials unknown to man. "Street" does not mean only one street but several streets, because there are twelve gates. The entire road system of the New Jerusalem is transparent gold. According to Revelation 3:12, there is a temple in the New Jerusalem. The Father God and Christ are said to be the temple of the city and are visible to the inhabitants from any location in the city.

Revelation 21:23-And the city had no need of the sun or of the moon to shine in it, for the glory of God illuminated it, and the Lamb is its light.

The sun and moon do not shine in the city because the city is lit or illuminated by the glory of God. The sun, moon, stars, and planets still exist and are visible to the inhabitants dwelling outside the city. The light from the sun is increased seven fold in the Millennium and the light from the moon is as bright as the sun.

The sun is brighter but not hotter.

Revelation 21:24-27-And the nations of those who are saved shall walk in its light, and the kings of the earth bring their glory and honor into it. Its gates shall not be shut at all by day (there shall be no night there). And they shall bring the glory and the honor of the nations into it. But there shall by no means enter it anything that defiles, or causes an abomination or a lie, but only those who are written in the Lamb's Book of Life.

The saved nations include the sheep nations after the Tribulation. People of the nations and leaders of the nations can visit the city that is open 24 hours a day, for there is no night in the city. Nothing that is abominable or defiles can enter into the city, because persons with those natures have already been cast into the lake of fire. Only the saved whose names are written in the Lamb's Book of Life can enter into the city. The fact that there are nations and the leaders of these nations visit the New Jerusalem further suggests that natural man will continue to live on planet earth in eternity future.

CHAPTER TWENTY TWO

BEHOLD, I AM COMING QUICKLY

Revelation 22:1-And he showed me a pure river of water of life, clear as crystal, proceeding form the throne of God and of the Lamb.

The angel continues to show John scenes from heaven. He sees a "river of water of life" clear as crystal proceeding from the throne of God and the Lamb. Water is a necessity for life, and God is the source of this living water. The Old Testament prophets Zechariah and Ezekiel both experienced visions where living waters were flowing from Jerusalem and out of the temple. Jesus is on the throne with the Father God as spoken in Revelation 3:21. As the street of gold represented several streets in the city, the river of life probably represents several rivers running throughout the city. Revelation 7:17 says that the Lamb who is in the midst of the throne will lead the Tribulation saints to living fountains of water. Also, there were four rivers in Eden, providing further support for more than one river.

Revelation 22:2-In the middle of its street, and on either side of the river, was the tree of life, which bore twelve fruits, each tree yielding its fruit every month. And the leaves of the tree were for the healing of nations.

The "tree of life" is on both sides of the river bearing twelve types of fruit, apparently a different fruit for each month. The leaves of the tree are for the healing of the nations, meaning that eternal earthly man will live free from sickness and disease by eating from the tree of life for eternal health and life. Redeemed man may also eat from the tree of life according to Revelation 2:7. Therefore, man can eat and drink in eternity. Natural earthly man must eat for sustenance, while redeemed man in glorified bodily form can choose whether or not to eat and how much and how often.

Revelation 22:3-5-And there shall be no more curse, but the throne of God and of the Lamb shall be in it, and His servants shall serve Him. They shall see His face, and His name shall be on their foreheads. And there shall be no night there: They need no lamp nor light of the sun, for the Lord God gives them light. And they shall reign forever and ever.

The "curse" was initially pronounced in Genesis 3:15. Now God's plan to remove the curse is finalized, and the curse will exist no longer. Conditions on earth exist as if the curse never was. The throne of God and the Lamb are in the New Jerusalem, and the redeemed of all ages serve God. The saints are able to look upon the face of God, and His name shall be on their foreheads. In the New Jerusalem there is no night, nor is there a need for the sun or any light because the Lord God provides the light for the city. The saints are to reign with Christ forever, i.e., assisting Christ in the administration of the universe.

Revelation 22:6-Then he said to me, "These words are faithful and true." And the Lord God of the holy prophets sent His angel to show His servants the things which must shortly take place.

The angel declares that what John has seen and heard is "faithful and true" for the message is from God through His angel to show John the events of the end times. The term "shortly" is used again to signify that once the events begin to occur, they will be completed quickly.

Revelation 22:7-"Behold, I am coming quickly! Blessed is he who keeps the words of the prophecy of this book."

Jesus says He is coming quickly or in more specific terms, He is coming suddenly without any prior warning. A blessing is pronounced on anyone who keeps the words of this prophecy, which is a reiteration of the blessing pronounced in Revelation 1:3.

Revelation 22:8-9-Now I John, saw and heard these things. And when I heard and saw, I fell down to worship before the feet of the angel who showed me these things. Then he said to me "See that you do not do that. For I am your fellow servant, and of your brethren the prophets, and of those who keep the words of this book. Worship God."

John says that when he saw and heard these things he fell down to worship the angel who gave him the prophecy. The angel cautions John against worshipping him, claiming that he too is a fellow servant of God, the prophets, and those who keep the words of the prophecy. Angels are ministering spirits sent to minister to the heirs of salvation, which would include John, the prophets, and saints who keep the words of the Book of Revelation.

Revelation 22:10-And he said to me, "Do not seal the words of the prophecy of this book, for the time is at hand."

John is instructed not to seal up the words of the prophecy. The truths revealed in this Book are not to be hidden. They are to be given to those who will hear, read, and obey them.

Revelation 22:11-12-"He who is unjust, let him be unjust still; he who is filthy, let him be filthy still; he who is righteous, let him be righteous still; he who is holy, let him be holy still. And behold, I am coming quickly, and My reward is with Me, to give to every one according to his work."

A person's spiritual position for eternity will be as it was on the day the person dies. The time on earth is to determine where each person will spend eternity. There is no second chance. The Coming of Jesus is reiterated and He rewards everyone according to their works. At the judgment seat of Christ, believers receive rewards for works done while on earth. At the White Throne judgment, unbelievers will have the Books opened and are shown that their works could not and did not save them because the only work that truly counts at this time is acceptance of Christ as Savior. Unbelievers will be cast into the lake of fire.

Revelation 22:13-"I am the Alpha and the Omega, the Beginning and the End, the First and the Last."

Jesus clearly states He is God using the same terms of deity as used by the Father when He calls Himself the "Alpha and the Omega," the "Beginning and the End," and the "First and the Last." Jesus is proclaiming His equality with the Father in describing His eternal attributes.

Revelation 22:14-Blessed are those who do His commandments, that they may have the right to the tree of life, and may enter through the gates into the city.

Those who have been obedient to the commandments of God are blessed and have a right to enter the New Jerusalem and partake of eternal life from the tree of life.

Revelation 22:15-But outside are dogs and sorcerers and sexually immoral and murderers and idolaters, and whoever loves and practices a lie.

The unrighteous never enter into the New Jerusalem. They spend eternity in the lake of fire.

Revelation 22:16-"I, Jesus, have sent My angel to testify to you these things in the churches. I am the Root and the Offspring of David, the Bright and Morning Star."

Jesus says he has testified of these things through His angel to the churches. He announces His Davidic lineage and cites Revelation 2:28 when He refers to Himself as the "Bright Morning Star."

Revelation 22:17-And the Spirit and the bride say, "Come!"

And let him who hears say "Come!" And let him who thirsts come. And whoever desires, let him take the water of life freely.

This verse is a universal call to all people for salvation. The Holy Spirit and the bride or redeemed make a universal appeal for salvation. Salvation and living water are freely available to anyone who thirsts.

Revelation 22:18-19-For I testify to everyone who hears the words of the prophecy of this book; If anyone adds to these things, God will add to him the plagues that are written in this book; and if anyone takes away from the words of the book of this prophecy, God shall take away his part from the Book of Life, from the holy city, and from the things which are written in this book.

A warning is pronounced to whoever hears the words of the prophecy not to alter, add to, or take away from the prophecy. If people add to the prophecy, then the plagues contained in the prophecy will be added to them. If people take away from the prophecy, then God will remove them from the Book of Life, from the holy city, and from the blessings of the Book.

Revelation 22:20-21-He who testifies to these things says, "Surely I am coming quickly." Amen. Even so, come, Lord Jesus! The grace of our Lord Jesus Christ be with you all. Amen.

Jesus testifies to these things and reaffirms His Second Coming. Again "quickly" means suddenly, without any advance warning. The letter is closed with the normal salutation following a response to His reiteration that He is coming quickly by saying "come" Lord Jesus. The grace or favor of God is with everyone looking for the return of Christ.

PART TWO

PROPHETIC KEYS

MILLENNIUM VIEWPOINTS

There are three main views or interpretative positions pertaining to the Millennium: Premillennial, Postmillennial, and Amillennial. The view adopted will determine the interpretative approach to many passages of prophetic scripture, e.g., will there be a Rapture of the Church, literal Tribulation Period, Antichrist, battle of Armageddon, or one-thousand (1000) kingdom rule of Christ on earth?

Premillennial

The fundamental principle to follow when studying prophetic scripture is to interpret scripture literally wherever possible, and the only millennial position that adheres to this basic principle is the Premillennial view. Under this view, Christ will return to the earth at the end of the Tribulation, put down all rebellion, destroy the armies of the Antichrist, liberate Israel, and establish His physical kingdom where He will rule from Jerusalem for a literal 1000 years. During Christ's 1000 year reign, Satan will be bound in the abyss, the effects of the curse will be lifted, the covenants with Israel will be fulfilled, and peace, joy, righteousness, and justice will prevail. This is the view supported by the early Church of the first and second centuries and is the view supported by prominent prophecy scholars, such as John Walvoord, Dwight Pentecost, Tim LaHaye, Thomas Ice, Edward

Hindson, James Combs, Hal Lindsey, Chuck Missler, Mal Couch, Arnold Fruchtenbaum, Grant Jeffery, Charles Capps, Mark Hitchcock, Randall Price, and many others. Premillennialism is the most logical, consistent, clear, and defendable viewpoint as supported by Biblical exegesis of both Old and New Testament prophetic scripture and is the viewpoint followed in this text.

Postmillennial

This was the major viewpoint of the 18th and 19th centuries. Postmillennialists maintain that Christ will return to earth after the Millennium, which is the period between His First and Second Comings but not a literal 1000 years. Postmillennialists believe that the world will increasingly get better and better as the Church evangelizes and Christianizes the world. Believers will spread the Gospel throughout the world, everyone will become Christians, Christians will control the affairs of the earth, and following an ideal age under the influence of the Gospel, Christ will return to usher in eternity. As with the Amillennial view, Christ's reign is a spiritual reign, not a literal one. The idea that the world is becoming progressively better denies the reality of world conditions. As a result of the major wars of the 20th century, this viewpoint fell out of favor.

Amillennial

The letter "a" before millennial negates the word millennial rendering the meaning to be "no Millennium." The amillennialists believe there will not be a literal, future 1000-year kingdom on this earth ruled by Christ. They maintain that Christ will have a kingdom rule but not for a literal 1000 years. His kingdom will be spiritual as He rules either in the hearts of believers or in heaven over redeemed souls, depending on which facet of amillennialism is followed. The length of rule is symbolic for an undefined period of time between Christ's First and Second Advents.

Concerns with the Amillennial View

Unfortunately, this Amillennial viewpoint has widespread support among Protestant, Greek Orthodox, and Roman Catholic Church leadership. Proponents of this view deny a literal interpretation of prophetic scripture about future events, most specifically Revelation 20:1-6. They do accept a literal First Coming of Christ but deny a literal Second Coming of Christ, which results in an interpretive inconsistency. If prophecies about Christ's First Coming were literal, why wouldn't prophecies about His Second Coming be just as literal? They believe prophecies concerning Israel are applied to the Church and that Satan is bound as a result of Christ's death and resurrection. The questions to ask are: "does this present age reflect a millennial kingdom ruled by Christ?" and "do current conditions on this planet reflect a world absent Satan and his demonic legions?" I believe the answers are a resounding "no."

Furthermore, it is not necessarily surprising that this viewpoint has significant support. As the world is being prepared for the reign of the Antichrist, the strong and widespread influence of New Age and Eastern philosophies that support a "do your own thing" or "whatever makes you feel good" mentality fits perfectly with the Amillennial view. The rules to Biblical interpretation become unclear without a process or standard to follow as provided in the Premillennial view. Where is the interpretive line to determine if a passage is to be taken literally or spiritually? If scripture is left up to the individual to apply as he/she sees fit, where is scriptural accountability and responsibility? Additionally, this viewpoint is not only deceptive but also counterproductive to evangelism in that proponents do not have to concern themselves about Satan and demonic activity, the Antichrist, a coming Tribulation Period, a one-world religion or government, not to mention God's judgment of a sinful world. What is the motivation for evangelism? What is the "blessed hope" of the Church if there is no Rapture? This viewpoint is deceptive, because it promotes the idea to accept whatever comes along. Since the Devil is bound, then whatever occurs must be God's will and why fight it? When a person doesn't know God's will on a particular matter, then he/she cannot stand in faith to appropriate the answer. Faith only works where the will of God is known, and without faith it is impossible to please God (Hebrews 11:6). Finally, it is inconceivable that believers following the Amillennial viewpoint could ever walk boldly in their rights, privileges, and authority as provided by God's Word.

 PROPHETIC KEY TWO

LETTERS TO THE CHURCHES

(Refer to Revelation 2-3)

Application of the Letters:

1) Local Application-to the churches in John's day. The letters portray actual conditions that existed in seven local churches in Asia Minor.

2) Prophetical Application-to the Church throughout the dispensation of the Church Age revealing the spiritual condition in local churches.

3) Individual Application-individuals in any church in any generation may be warned and/or may profit by the failures and successes of these seven churches.

4) Historical Application-the seven churches represent seven distinct periods of Church history. Although some teachers maintain this position, it is less credible than applications 1-3.

Points of Similarity in the Letters

1) Each of the letters opens with a description of the risen Christ.

2) Each letter is addressed to the angel of the church, but the term angel can also refer to the Pastor of the church or both angel and Pastor. Hence, there is a natural and spiritual application. Angels are assigned oversight responsibilities over churches, but John is commanded to send the letters to the

churches. Directing a letter to the church would be directing the letter to a person, most likely the Pastor. Therefore, Pastors of the seven churches as the primary recipients of the letters appears to be the stronger position with a secondary consideration of angelic involvement.

3) Each letter is an appraisal of the church's spiritual standing in the opinion of Christ, the Lord, Judge, and Head of the Church.

4) Each church is commended for its works, except Laodicea.

5) Each church is rebuked or criticized, except Smyrna and Philadelphia.

6) Each church is commanded to repent, except Smyrna and Philadelphia. Thyatira has sin of which to repent but is not commanded to do so. They are apparently past redemption.

7) Warnings of judgment are given to all the churches except Smyrna and Philadelphia.

8) Each church, except Smyrna and Philadelphia, is more corrupt than its predecessor. Laodicea is the most corrupt of all, without one single virtue to commend.

9) Ten points of commendation are given to the first church, Ephesus, and ten points of criticism are given to the last church, Laodicea.

10) Each church is given promises for the overcomer.

11) Each church is admonished to hear what the Spirit has to say to the churches.

12) In each letter, John is told to write.

PROPHETIC KEY: COMPARATIVE OVERVIEW OF CHURCHES OF REVELATION 2-3

Church	Description of Christ	Commendation	Criticism	Admonition/Judgment	Promise to Overcomer
Ephesus	Holds 7 stars in right hand, walks among 7 golden lampstands	Works, labor, patience; cannot bear evil men; tested those who call themselves apostles and are not, found them to be liars; persevered; have patience; have labored for Name of Christ; have not become weary	Left their first love	Remember from where have fallen; *repent* and do first works or Jesus will remove lampstand from its place	Overcomer to eat from tree of life in the midst of the Paradise of God
Smyrna	First and Last who was dead and has come to life	Works, tribulation, and poverty (Jesus said they are rich); know blasphemy from Satan; don't fear coming suffering; cast into prison by Devil for testing; have tribulation 10 days			Overcomer shall not be hurt by the second death
Pergamos	He who has the sharp two-edged sword	Know works; where they live, where Satan's seat is; hold fast to His Name; didn't deny faith	Those who hold to doctrine of Balaam and doctrine of Nicolaitans	*Repent* or Jesus will fight with the sword of His mouth	Eat of hidden manna; given new name on white stone that no one knows except overcomer
Thyatira	Son of God, eyes like a flame of fire, feet like fine brass	Works, love, service, faith, and patience; later works more than first works	Allowed Jezebel, the prophetess, to teach and beguile servants to commit sexual immorality and eat food sacrificed to idols	Time given in order to *repent* but did not; cast into sickbed; children killed with death; gave each one according to works	Overcomer who keeps works to end will have power over nations, rule with rod of iron, receive morning star
Sardis	He who has 7 the Spirits of God and 7 stars	Works, few names that have not defiled garments; they walk with Jesus in white; haven't soiled garments	Had name that alive but Jesus said they were dead; works not found perfect before God	Be watchful and strengthen things that remain; hold fast and *repent*; if not watchful Jesus will come as a thief and no one will not know the hour	Overcomer clothed in white garments; name not blotted out of Book of Life; name confessed before Father and angels
Philadelphia	He who is holy, true, has key of David, opens and no one shuts, shuts and no one opens	Works, open door set before them that no one can shut; little strength, kept God's Word, didn't deny Name; kept command to persevere; will be kept from hour of testing			Overcomer is a pillar in the temple of God and will get to stay in temple, name of God and name of new Jerusalem written on overcomer
Laodicea	Amen, Faithful and True Witness, Beginning of creation of God		Know works; neither hot nor cold, because lukewarm. Jesus will spew them out of His mouth; said rich and in need of nothing, but Jesus said blind, wretched, miserable, and poor	Buy from Jesus gold refined in fire, white garments, eye salve to anoint eyes, be zealous and *repent*; Jesus stands at the door and knocks, who hears and opens He will come in and sup with them	Overcomer sits with Jesus on His throne as Jesus overcame and sat down with Father on His throne

SETTING THE STAGE

Scripture clearly states that no one knows the day or hour of the Lord's return, but Christians should know the season. Jesus' "coming" both at the Rapture for the saints and at His Second Advent with the saints is compared to a "thief in the night," meaning His appearances will not be expected. The world will be entirely caught off guard at the Rapture and disappearance of the Church Age saints. Similarly, as the nations are gathered at Armageddon for the destruction and annihilation of Israel, they will not be expecting the Lord to return.

Prophecy teachers sometimes take license and force fit an event after its occurrence as fulfilling a specific prophetic scripture, which can be very misleading to readers. On the other hand, many scholars caution against focusing too heavily or placing too much emphasis on current events as "signs" of the end of the age. The Rapture is a "signless" event, meaning no scripture needs to be fulfilled, and no event needs to happen before the Rapture can occur. Most signs discussed today in relation to prophecy have their actual fulfillment in the Tribulation. Pre-Tribulation signs of Tribulation events may more appropriately be referred to as "trends." Activity can be seen in this generation of many events that will finalize in the Tribulation. Therefore, examining these trends in the "macro" sense can lead Bible students to discern the "lateness of the hour" from a prophetic standpoint. As signs of Tribulation events are evidenced in this generation, then Christians know the Rapture is that much closer. In this dispensation, God does not act independently of His body, the Church, but in conjunction with the Church. He has revealed and is revealing to His Church from the pulpits across the land that the world is in its final hour, or the "last of the last days." Translating the meaning of the last of the last days into a specific time frame cannot be done, but the trends can be discerned to reveal the prophetic season. What makes this time period stand out from any other time in history is that there are multiple events with prophetic implication converging simultaneously in the world.

Listed below are indicators or trends of world situations and events that demonstrate the stage is being set for the Second Coming of Christ, and then even sooner, the Rapture of the Church. The application or significance of the event or trend is also noted.

The Septa-Millennial Theory

- God recreated the earth in six literal days and rested on the seventh.

- A day with the Lord is as 1000 years and 1000 years as a day.

- History of mankind can be divided into 1000-year segments.
  - 4000 years from Adam to Christ
  - 2000 years for the Church Age
  - 1000 years for the Millennium

- This theory was supported by the early church and is quoted frequently at this time.

Israel - The "Mega" Sign

- In 1948, Israel was recognized as a nation after having been dispersed since A.D. 70.

- In 1967, Israel came into possession of Jerusalem and the temple mount area following the six-day war.

- Daniel 9:24-27 specifically applies to the Jew and Jerusalem.

- Daniel 9:27 will have its prophetic fulfillment in the 70th week of Daniel.

- The Jews are currently preparing for the rebuilding of the

Tribulation temple or inner sanctuary.

Parable of the Fig Tree (Matthew 24:32-35, Mark 13:28-32)

- In the parable of the fig tree, the fig tree represents Israel and the trees represent the nations of the world. Jesus said when the leaves on the tree are seen, one can know that summer is near. In the same manner, when certain events occur, then Christ's appearance will be within a generation. Even though the Bible says no one knows the day or the hour of the Lord's exact return, except the Father, Christians should be able to discern the signs of the times to know the Lord's return is near, as the leaves on the fig tree revealed that summer was near.

- The Rapture is imminent, meaning that it can happen at any time, and no event needs to be fulfilled.

- All prophetic signs point to the Tribulation Period and the Second Coming of Christ.

Generation (Matthew 24:32-35, Mark 13:28-32)

- As events similar to those described in Matthew 24:5-31 and Revelation 6-20 occur, then Jesus' return (Rapture and Second Coming) is near, within one generation. In the strictest sense the generation that experiences the events of the Tribulation Period will witness the Second Coming of Christ. However, if that is the exact interpretation, as some scholars believe, then why is it necessary to speak of a generation when the time frame under discussion is only seven years? The broader application subscribed to by many Bible scholars is that the generation alive at the re-gathering of the Jews to Israel (1948) and in control of Jerusalem (1967) is the generation to experience the return of the Lord (Rapture or Second Coming).

- The Book of Revelation primarily focuses on Israel in fulfillment of Daniel's prophecy about the Jewish people and Jerusalem as stated in Daniel 9:24-27. Complete fulfillment of these passages was an impossibility until Israel was again recognized as a nation in 1948.

- The starting point is 1948, when Israel was recognized as a nation after having been scattered among the nations for almost 2000 years.

- A generation in the Bible can be 20, 40, 60, or 100 years.

- 100 or more years for a generation won't fit, as those alive when these end-time events begin to occur will not be living 100 years later.

- 20 years also doesn't fit when using a starting point of either 1948 or 1967.

- 40 or 60 years has gained popularity when defining a generation.

- 40 years for a generation has been adopted because the children of Israel roamed in the desert for 40 years following their exodus from Egypt until that unfaithful and rebellious generation died off. However, the 40 years affected people 20 years and older. The generation was actually 60 years at a minimum. Moses himself was 130 years old, Caleb 85 years old, and Joshua 110 years old at the time of their deaths.

- 40 years from 1948 is 1988, a date which has come and gone.

- 60 years from 1948 is 2008, plus or minus seven years for the Tribulation Period would equal 2001 or 2015.

- Daniel's prophecy also pertains to Jerusalem, which was not under Jewish control until 1967.

- 40 years from 1967 is 2007 and 60 years from 1967 is 2027, plus or minus seven years for the Tribulation Period would equal 2000, 2014, 2020, or 2034. Of course, the year 2000 has passed.

- A prophetic scenario comparing Israel in 1948 and 1967 to the development stages of the Jewish child would be:
  - Child born in 1948.
  - Unable to go to war until 19 years old, i.e., 1967 (6 day war for recapture of Jerusalem).
  - Life span of man is 70-80 years according to Psalm 90:10.

- Therefore, the Lord's return could be between 2018 and 2028.

- It appears from the Biblical text that a generation can best be defined as the average life span of people living during that time in history. The average life span before the Noahic flood was very long, averaging over 900 years. After the Noahic flood, the average life span continued to reduce.

  - According to scholars that have researched this subject, the average life span for the last 3000 years of history has been 70-80 years. Most of the modern developed nations of Europe and North America have average life spans of 70-80 years. The average life span in the United States today is approximately 77 years, with males slightly less and females slightly more. The average life span for people in Israel is approximately 78 years, with the average lower for males and higher for females.

  - The most reasonable conclusion is that the length of the generation referred to in Christ's Olivet discourse when he presented the parable of the fig tree is between 70-80 years based on Biblical example and Psalm 90:10.

  - If the generation referred to by Christ began with the rebirth of the nation Israel in 1948 or when Israel gained control of Jerusalem in 1967, then the generation to see the Lord's return, Rapture or Second Coming, has already been born. Under this scenario Christ could return anywhere from 2011 to 2047 ((1948 + 70 years to start of the Tribulation - 7 years for the Rapture = 2011) to (1967 + 80 years to the Rapture or Tribulation = 2047 ± 7 years depending on which event occurs at 2047)).

- All of the above "last generation" speculation serves only as an indicator that prophecy teachers and spiritual leaders see the nearness of Christ's return on the prophetic timeline, potentially anytime within the next 50 years. However, our admonition from the Lord is to "occupy until He comes," which means to always be ready for His return, even tonight or tomorrow, but live our lives as if He isn't going to return for 100 years.

Consolidation of Nations in Europe

- The world is in preparation for a power shift to the Reconstituted Roman Empire post Rapture.

- The United States will not be a major world political or military influence after the Rapture.

The Euro

- One currency now in Europe, which is preparatory for a one world economy.

- The economies of the world are linked.

- The impact on one financial market affects other global markets.

- The trend is toward cashless societies.

Globalization

- The world is becoming a smaller place.

- Global companies, global competition, and internet buying are today's norms.

- The world is in preparation for a global economy, global religion, and global government.

- A global economy will drive a global government (customs, borders, taxes, logistics).

Knowledge Will Increase (Daniel 12:4)

- Knowledge is doubling every 18 months and is projected to double every 12 months in the not too distant future.

- There is increased access to knowledge on the internet or information super highway.

- Prior generations could span hundreds of years and see little advancement, but today advancement is measured in months.

- Knowledge of prophecy and end-time events is increasing.

Technology

- An increased push for a national identification card is underway.

- The technology exists for application of the mark of the Beast (chip or tattoo).

- With computer technology and interconnected networks in a cashless society, the Antichrist could literally lock people out of financial and banking systems who do not have his mark as stated in Revelation 13. This is the first generation with such technology.

- Satellite technology is in place for the world to watch the murder of the two witnesses.

- Satellite technology will be used by the Antichrist in tracking those who do not take the mark.

- Today, there is technology sharing and linking through the internet.

- Instructions are on the internet to build and distribute atomic/nuclear bombs.

- Advances in technology have led to increased chemical and biological weapons development.

Peace and Safety

- People are afraid after the September 11, 2001 terrorist attack on America.

- People are demanding peace and the eradication of terrorism, which is preparation for the Antichrist as a world leader who can bring peace between the Jews and Arabs.

- The Antichrist will be the rider on the white horse (first seal judgment) who brokers a seven year peace covenant between Israel and the Arab world.

Coalitions of Nations

- There has been an increase in the number of coalitions, e.g., NATO, Gulf War coalition, NAFTA, European Union, United Nations, coalition against terrorism, etc.

- A key element in the war on terror is for the United States to form and maintain a coalition of supporting nations from Europe and the Middle East.

- Several Muslim nations desiring a holy war or Jihad against Christians and Jews are pushing for a coalition of Arab states, which is preparing the way for Gog from Magog.

- The King of the South and King of the North of Daniel 11 are thought to be coalitions of nations.

- Kings from the East of Revelation 16 appear to be a coalition of Asian nations that will march on Jerusalem at Armageddon.

Matthew 24:6-7 Wars and Rumors of Wars

- The rider on the red horse (second seal judgment) is war, which is the effect of a world military leader conquering nations.

- There has been an armed conflict somewhere on earth every day since WWII.

- The world is even more dangerous since the break up of the Soviet Union due to their inability to account for their inventory of nuclear devices, especially nuclear backpacks, nuke-cases, and nukepacks. It is suspected that many of these devices have fallen into the hands of terrorist organizations or terrorist supporting nations.

- The balance of power is no longer resting with the two super powers, United States and Russia.

- Approximately fifteen third world countries have nuclear capability.

- Billions of dollars are spent annually in international arms trade, while global military spending exceeds one trillion dollars annually.

- The standing armies of the world total hundreds of millions of soldiers.

- Nuclear, chemical, and biological weapons in existence today are capable of destroying the world.

- The Muslim Arab nations have weapons (nuclear, chemical, biological) capable of striking Europe.

- Over 20 Arab states surround Israel and want Israel's destruction and removal from the land of Israel. According to the Orange County Register in Southern California, the current population in these 20+ Arab states in 2002 was 280 million. By 2020, it is projected that the Arab states will have a population between 410-459 million. The pressure will continue to mount for the annihilation of Israel. The Gog / Magog war of Ezekiel 38-39 is inevitable.

- Arab military forces are greater in number than NATO forces.

- There are enough military weapons and explosive to arm every man, woman, and child on this planet.

- According to military experts, a war involving America, China, and Russia would run out of targets before running out of weapons.

- US nuclear submarines are capable of destroying military targets from submerged locations 10,000 miles away.

- Nation against nation, and kingdom against kingdom includes conflicts involving race and culture, e.g., Jews and Arabs.

- Historically, many wars have been fought over race, national origin, or religion. Muslim Jihad advocates hate both Jews and Christians. In fact, according to some Muslim teachings, if a person is not Muslim than he/she is not of God.

- During the Tribulation, war will be on-going and rampant with three major military campaigns, two in the first half of the Tribulation and one at the end of the Tribulation.

Matthew 24:7-Famine

- The rider on the black horse (third seal judgment) represents famine.

- Famine follows war as land and food sources are destroyed.

- Thousands of square miles of rain forests are being destroyed annually, ultimately leading to the devastation of planetary systems.

- Topsoil is rapidly being depleted, which harms the farming and agriculture industry.

- According to scientists, the earth cannot sustain the current population growth. Human population is trending out of control, and over population of the planet is inevitable.

- Based on global population growth estimates, it is impossible to increase food production to prevent a worldwide famine.

- Approximately one-third of mankind currently suffers from chronic hunger and malnutrition.

- In the Tribulation, food sources from land and sea, as well as fresh water, will be destroyed or polluted by the judgments.

Matthew 24:7-Pestilence-Diseases and Plagues

- Pestilence follows war and famine (Matthew 24:7).

- Twenty (20) years ago, medical science thought the end of infectious diseases was in sight. However, many new infectious diseases have emerged with no known treatment, e.g., hantavirus, ebola, lassa fever, SARS, etc..

- Other contagious diseases have re-emerged as serious threats, such as malaria, small pox, diphtheria, yellow fever, bubonic plague, anthrax, cholera (strain resistant to all known vaccines).

- A new strain of TB is claiming several million lives annually.

- Bacteria are becoming drug resistant, primarily due to misuse of antibiotics.

- There is a growing fear of a new influenza type "super bug" that would be resistant to all known antibiotics.

- Sexually transmitted diseases (STD) are on increase, largely as a result of the free life style nature of society.

- Scientists claim that there are over 50 sexually transmitted diseases.

- AIDS is at pandemic proportions and is the first politically protected disease; scientists have referred to AIDS as the biological equivalent of nuclear war.

- AIDS exists in every country and has not yet peaked.

- According to year end 2002 statistics, over 42 million people are living with HIV/AIDS.

- Mutant forms of AIDS and other viruses similar to the AIDS virus have emerged.

- Additional illnesses are developing through chemical exposure, pesticides, and toxic elements in the environment.

Matthew 24:7-Earthquakes

- Many prophecy experts indicate recorded earthquakes of magnitude 6.5+ have sharply increased over the last century. However, statistics from the USGS do not support this contention, showing major earthquake activity to be reasonably flat over this time period.

- There does appear to be a slight increase in earthquake activity greater than 6.0 over the last 20-25 years, but nothing significant enough to call a prophetic trend.

- Several million minor quakes do occur per year.

- During the Tribulation, there will be significant seismic activity as never experienced in the history of the world with earthquakes referred to as "great" and "great and mighty."

Matthew 24:24-False Christs, False Messiahs, and False Prophets

- False Christs, false prophets, and false messiahs appear on the historical scene periodically with deceptive messages. An increase in false Christs, false prophets, and false messiahs will be manifest in the Tribulation.

- The term "false Christs" is thought to also refer to false religious systems that offer a way to salvation other than through Jesus Christ.

- Today, there has been an explosion of false religious systems in our generation, such as followers of Moon, Heaven's Gate, Jim Jones, Krishna, Maharishi, L. Ron Hubbard, New Age, Eastern mysticism, the occult, etc.

- According to religious statistics, there are over one billion Catholics in the world. After the Rapture of born again believers (including born again Catholic believers), the infrastructure of the Catholic Church could be foundational to structuring the Harlot one world religion or Mystery Babylon.

- The New Age movement with its linkage to the occult, Eastern mysticism, pantheism, spiritism, reincarnation, and its "whatever makes you feel good" or "do your own thing" philosophy is preparatory for the one world religion and ultimately worship of the Antichrist.

Revelation 9:21-Murders, Sorceries, Sexual Immorality, and Theft

- The moral decay of society in evidence now will continue to grow worse in and through the Tribulation, because the "restrainer" or Church indwelt by the Holy Spirit will be removed at the Rapture.

- The city of Babylon will be a habitation for every demon and unclean spirit imaginable.

- Political leaders (kings) of the world will be totally involved in spiritual fornication, sorceries, and the occultic practices within Babylon.

- People elect candidates that support the "do your own thing" or "whatever makes you feel good" attitude so they can be free to do whatever they want under the approval of political leaders.

- Murders are common today, especially in the United States, the largest Christian country.

- The United States leads the industrialized world in murders and other violent crimes, but other nations are experiencing upward trends.

- Life in many cultures is of little value.

- Sorceries include the occult, astrology, witchcraft, idolatry, and drugs.

- Drug use has reached epidemic proportions.

- Sexual immorality includes all types of sexual sins, void of any religious restraint.

- Complete sexual freedom and every form of perversion is the basis of the "totally free" lifestyle.

- Accompanying this free life style are all forms of sexually transmitted disease.

- Theft includes all forms of lawlessness, crime, and corruption.

- Law and order will completely breakdown, and lawlessness will abound during the Tribulation.

RAPTURE

Definition

Rapture means to transport from one place to another. The word "rapture" is not specifically used in the Bible, but the event is described. In 1 Thessalonians 4:13-18 the saints are "caught up" to meet the Lord in the air, and the Greek word for caught up is "harpazo." It is the same word used when discussing how Paul was caught up to the third heaven (2 Corinthians 12:2) and when Philip was caught away after baptizing the Etheopian eunuch (Acts 9:39). Harpazo means a forceful catching away as to rescue from danger or destruction. It is a snatching away or forceful seizure. God uses a swift, resistless divine energy to move the saints through the air, which is a habitation of demons, for Satan is called the Prince of the power of the air. Harpazo has its root from the Latin word "rapturo" (or one of its derivations, such as "rapere," "rapio," or "raptus") from which the term rapture comes.

Main Rapture Viewpoints

1) Pre-Tribulation: Rapture of the Church occurs before the seventieth week of Daniel or Tribulation Period. A pre-Tribulation Rapture of the Church is the viewpoint supported in this text.

2) Mid-Tribulation: Rapture of the Church occurs in the middle of the Tribulation or 3 1/2 years into the seventieth week of Daniel.

3) Post-Tribulation: Rapture of the Church occurs at the end of

the Tribulation at the Second Coming of Christ.

4) Pre-Wrath: Rapture of the Church occurs between the sixth and seventh seal judgments midway through the second half of the seventieth week of Daniel.

5) Partial Rapture: Only the faithful, believing Christians who are waiting and watching for the Rapture will be raptured before the Tribulation begins.

Purposes for the Rapture

Christ will:

- Meet the saints in the air (1 Thessalonians 4:13-18)

- Receive the saints (New Testament believers "in Christ") to Himself (John 14:1-3)

- Take the raptured saints to heaven (John 14:1-3; 1 Thessalonians 3:13, 4:13-18)

- Settle the saints into their new dwelling places in the New Jerusalem (John 14:1-3; Hebrews 11:10,16; 12:22-23; 13:14)

- Present the saints to the Father God in heaven (1 Thessalonians 3:13)

- Make the saints whole, spirit, soul, and body (1 Thessalonians 5:23)

- Judge the saints for rewards at the judgment seat of Christ (2 Corinthians 5:10)

- Assign positions as kings and priests to rule all creation (Revelation 1:5, 2:26-27, 5:10)

- Resurrect all the saints from the New Testament Church Age (1 Thessalonians 4:13-18, Revelation 20:4-6, 1 Corinthians 15:23)

- Change the saints' bodies from mortality to immortality (1 Corinthians 15:51-56) - (glorified bodies like Christ's)

- Present the Church to Himself (Ephesians 5:27)

- Make the saints like Christ (1 John 3:2)

- Permit the coming of the man of sin (2 Thessalonians 2:7-8)

- Remove the hinderer of lawlessness from the world (2 Thessalonians 2:7-8)

- Remove the saints from the world so as not to experience the Tribulation (Revelation 3:10)

- Protect the saints from the coming wrath of God (1 Thessalonians 1:10)

- End the Church Age so God can deal exclusively with the nation of Israel (Daniel 9:24-27)

- Take the saints to heaven for the marriage of the Lamb (Revelation 19:7-10)

- Have the saints accompany Himself back to earth at (Revelation 19, Zechariah 14:1-5)

Qualifications for the Rapture

The only qualification is to be "in Christ," i.e., a born again, new creature in Christ Jesus. A person must be part of the body of Christ or the Church that came into being on the day of Pentecost. Old Testament believers are not part of the Church or body of Christ and therefore, will not be participants in the Rapture of the Church. Old Testament believers will receive their glorified bodies as part of the First Resurrection following the Tribulation and Second Coming of Christ.

Children and the Rapture

It is generally accepted that children who die before the age of accountability, normally thought to be around 10-12 years of age, when they can understand and knowingly distinguish right from wrong, go immediately to heaven to be with the Lord. The question now arises whether children under this age of account-ability will be raptured with the Church? During the time of the Noahic flood, Noah and his family were saved, while the world was destroyed. At the destruction of Sodom and Gomorrah, the angels could not destroy the cities until Lot and his family were removed. In both cases, it strongly appears that children of non-believers were destroyed. Therefore, it could be concluded that children of believers are raptured, while children of unbelieving parents enter into the Tribulation. Certainly, children in the Tribulation who die before the age of accountability will still go to be with the Lord in heaven. Whatever the case in these situations, God is faithful, compassionate, and just. True and righteous are His ways.

Time of the Rapture

Not specifically stated, but before the Tribulation and revelation of the Antichrist. According to the pre-Tribulation viewpoint, no prophecies need to be fulfilled prior to the Rapture except the shout and the sound of the trumpet of God.

Signs of the Rapture - Imminence

The Rapture is considered to be an "imminent" event, which is a theological term conveying the idea of "anytime." The imminent return of the Lord for His Church means that no special signs or events must occur before He can return. The first century Church taught that the Lord's return would be imminent, and yet He hasn't returned. Imminent doesn't mean that the Rapture will occur soon, but means that it can occur at any moment. There are no events or prophecies concerning the Rapture that must be fulfilled, but there are many prophecies about the Second Coming of Christ that are yet unfulfilled. Therefore, as Second Coming prophecies are fulfilled or trends toward fulfillment are witnessed, the Rapture is that much closer. According to the Parable of the Fig Tree, Jesus told His followers that they could discern the seasons by the leaves of the fig tree. In the same manner, the Tribulation events described in Matthew 24 will not only occur in one generation, but also the Church should be able to discern or know the season or generation that will see them fulfilled. By spiritually discerning the signs of the times, Christians should have a good idea as to the coming of the Rapture and should not be caught totally unaware.

Foreshadowing of the Rapture

Revelation 4:1 is considered by many commentators to foreshadow the Rapture of the Church. John is commanded to "come up here," meaning to enter into heaven. This verse begins the third major division of the Book of Revelation, according to Revelation 1:19 as John is shown events to occur after the Church Age. This is the most fitting place on the prophetic timeline for the Rapture to occur.

Coming of the Lord

The Rapture as well as the Second Coming of Christ are referred to as the Coming of the Lord or in the Greek, "parousia." Parousia means a bodily presence, arrival, appearance, or visit of a ruler or high official. Many commentators identify two separate and distinct Comings, one at the Rapture where Christ comes for His Church and one at the end of the Tribulation where Christ returns with His Church. The events of the two Comings are distinct from one another, but for the purposes of this study, they will be treated as one Coming that extends over a period of time at least seven years or greater. Christ's First Coming covered a period of time over thirty years from His birth through His resurrection and ascension. This Coming of the Lord or parousia has two main parts: the first, as Christ raptures His Church before the Tribulation; and the second, when Christ returns at Armageddon to destroy the Antichrist and his armies, to put an end to sin, to have Satan removed from the earth for 1000 years, and to set up His Millennial kingdom.

Fallacies Concerning the Rapture

1) *The church is to face the Antichrist and the refining fires of the Tribulation to purify, perfect, and prepare it for the Rapture.* The qualification for the Rapture is to be in Christ. Facing the

Antichrist does not place one more in Christ. God is not
going to use the Antichrist to perfect His Church. God uses
His Word to discipline, correct, and perfect (2 Timothy 3:16).
If the Church is present during the Tribulation, then the
gates of hell are prevailing against the Church, which is contrary to scriptural teaching.

2) *God takes the Church through the Tribulation and will
protect the saints from death the same as He protected Noah, Daniel,
Hebrews in the fiery furnace, and Israel from the plagues in Egypt.*
The only group promised protection during the Tribulation is
the 144,000 Jews. Saints have been killed in all ages and so it
will be in the Tribulation. Multiple passages refer to the mar-
tyring of the saints for the Word of God and their testimony
for Jesus. The Church will not be kept from testing, because
believers have been tested and persecuted in all dispensations.
Revelation 3:10 says the Philadelphia or believing Church will
be kept from the "hour of trial," which is the Tribulation.
Although this phrase can mean protection within the sphere
of conflict, the majority of Greek scholars favor the interpretation that the Church will be removed from the earth before
the Tribulation begins.

Pre-Tribulation Rapture Evidence and Scripture:

1) Dispensation-Order of Revelation-Restrainer

The Church Age is a distinct dispensation that exists between
Daniel's 69th and 70th week according to Daniel 9:24-27.
Revelation 2-3 discuss the Church. The Church is seen in heav-
en in Revelation 4-5 as symbolized by the 24 elders. The focus of
Revelation 6-19 is Israel with the Church nowhere discussed.
The Gentile persecution of Israel has nothing to do with the
Church. The Antichrist is revealed after the restrainer is
removed. The restrainer is the Church infilled by the Holy Spirit.
The Holy Spirit's ministry of infilling and empowering the
Church will be completed at the Rapture. With the restrainer

removed, the man of sin or the lawless one can be revealed according to 2 Thessalonians 2:7-8. Near the beginning of the Tribulation Period, the Antichrist is revealed at the first seal judgment as the rider on the white horse.

2) Noahic Flood

Genesis 6:7-22 discusses the flood of Noah. Righteous Noah and his family were saved before the judgment from God and destruction of the world. God protects His people before executing judgment.

3) Sodom and Gomorrah

Genesis 18-19 discusses Abraham and the destruction of Sodom and Gomorrah. God came to earth and discussed what He was about to do with His covenant partner Abraham before destroying the cities. Abraham in fact negotiated with God. God did not destroy Sodom and Gomorrah until Lot and his family had been removed, demonstrating that covenant protection was extended to Abraham's family. The righteousness of the Church in the earth today stops the wrath of God.

4) Blood Covenant

The Church is in blood covenant relationship with God and consequently God will bless and protect the Church because of the covenant.

5) Authority of the Church

The Church has authority on earth and God operates in the earth through His Church. Therefore, during this dispensation, God will not act independently of His body, and hence will not execute His wrath while the Church is present. The Church must be removed first. Then God can judge the earth.

6) Church referred to as a "Mystery"

A mystery in the Bible is something that is unknown unless

revealed by God. The following characteristics of the Church are described as a being a mystery: Jews and Gentiles are fellow-heirs and members of the body of Christ (Ephesians 3:1-12); Christ indwelling the believer (Colossians 1:24-27); and the Rapture of the Church (1 Corinthians 15:5156).

7) Israel and Hebrew Character of Revelation Chapters 6-19

God's attitude of mercy in Revelation 1-3 changes to one of judgment in chapters 6-19. The Church is mentioned 19 times in the first three chapters, but there is no mention of the Church on earth in chapters 4-21. The Church is in heaven as represented by the 24 elders in Revelation 4-5. The Church and Israel are distinct from each other with each having its own destiny. The Church is raptured before the Tribulation, whereas Israel is on earth during the Tribulation in order that Daniel 9:27 can be fulfilled. From chapter 6 forward, Israel is the subject of Revelation, and this section of Revelation is very Hebrew in character as follows:

- 285 Old Testament references in Revelation
- Lamb - connection with the sacrificial system and the Atonement
- Lion of Judah and Root of David - Jewish lineage of Christ
- 144,000 Jews
- Seal, trumpet, and bowl judgments - similar to Egyptian plagues
- Tribulation concerns Israel
- Daniel's 70th week concerns Israel
- Ministry of angels around the altar
- Altar, temple, temple worship, court, ark of the covenant, olive trees, holy city - all Jewish terms
- Woman and male child - Jewish
- Dragon with seven heads and ten horns represents nations that have persecuted Israel

- Michael the archangel stands for Israel
- Remnant is Jewish
- Babylon, Armageddon, and Millennium are connected with Israel

8) Scripture
1 Thessalonians 4:13-18

4:15-Those that are alive will not precede those who have died, indicating an order to the resurrection. The Coming of the Lord is "parousia" in the Greek, specifying the Rapture where both dead and alive saints meet the Lord in the air.

4:16-The Lord will descend from heaven at the shout of the archangel, who is Michael. The trumpet of God heralds important events. This is not one of the trumpet judgments as some mid-Tribulationists contend. The trumpet judgments are executed by angels, where as this event is signaled by God Himself. The "dead in Christ" are to be resurrected first.

4:17-The saints who are alive on the earth will be "caught up," which is the Greek word "harpazo" meaning a forceful, sudden, snatching away. The Church is transported from earth into the air in a forceful and sudden manner to meet Christ.

4:18-This message is to be a comfort to the Church, which it certainly is if the catching away occurs prior to the Tribulation. Tribulation does not comfort, but a rapture to escape the Tribulation does comfort.

1 Corinthians 15:51-57

15:51-The Rapture is described as part of the "mystery" that was unknown to the Old Testament prophets but revealed to the New Testament Church. Saints will not die but will be changed from mortality to immortality.

15:52-This transformation from mortality to immortality will occur in the twinkling of an eye, which literally is in an atomic second. Two trumpet blasts will be heard, first for those who are dead, then for those who are alive. Both the dead and those alive will meet Christ in the air where they receive their immortal, glorified bodies, never again subject to corruption by death.

John 14:1-3-Christ is preparing a place for the saints and will receive the Church to Himself. The post-Tribulation Rapture position has the Rapture and Second Coming occurring simultaneously. Therefore, this scripture negates a post-Tribulation Rapture, because Christ is going to receive the saints to Himself – **before** He returns from heaven with the saints at His Second Coming.

Revelation 3:10-The Philadelphia or believing Church will be kept from the hour of trial that is to come on the earth.

1 Thessalonians 5:9-10-God has not appointed the Church to wrath but to salvation.

1 Thessalonians 1:10-The idea in this passage is that believers are to wait (look forward to with confidence) for Jesus to deliver (or rescue) the saints from the wrath to come. The way the saints are delivered is by His rapturing the Church.

2 Thessalonians 2:1-9-The term "falling away" was actually "departure" in the earliest Bible translations. Before the day of the Lord comes, there is a departure of the Church followed by the revealing of the Antichrist or man of sin. The lawless one (the Antichrist) cannot appear on the scene of history until the restrainer, which is the Church indwelt by the Holy Spirit, is taken out of the way or removed. The removal of the restrainer opens the door for the beginning of the Tribulation. The only condition that satisfies these verses is the Rapture of the Church.

Ephesians 5:27-Jesus is going to present the Church to Himself in all her glory without spot or wrinkle. It does not appear that the Church on earth will ever be without spot or wrinkle. However, this event can occur as Christ transforms the saints in the air at the Rapture.

1 Thessalonians 3:13-This is a heavenly scene where believers are presented blameless before God the Father.

1 Thessalonians 5:23-Because of Christ's return (at His Coming), the believer's spirit, soul, and body (or the total person) will be blameless in heaven in the presence of the Lord.

1 Thessalonians 2:19-20-These scriptures reference Paul's hope and joy when believers are in the Lord's presence at His Coming.

Philippians 3:20-21-Jesus will transform the saints' natural bodies to glorious bodies. This event will occur at the Rapture of the Church.

James 5:7-9-Believers are told to wait patiently for the Lord's return as the farmer waits patiently for the rains and his crops. They can expect Christ to return for them.

Titus 2:13-Saints are to be looking for (excitedly expecting on a continual basis or joyously anticipating or continually hoping) the "blessed hope" and the glorious appearing of their God and Savior Jesus Christ. This blessed hope is the Rapture of the Church, which will occur, thus producing great joy for those who are looking for Christ's return.

Comparison of the Rapture and the Second Coming of Christ

	Rapture	Second Coming of Christ
1.	Precedes the Second Coming of the Lord by at least seven years	Occurs at least seven years after the Rapture
2.	Christ comes in the air to receive the saints, but His feet do not touch the earth. The saints are taken to heaven and presented to the Father, judged for works, and participate in the marriage of the Lamb	Christ returns from heaven with the saints. Christ stands on the Mount of Olives, which split in half
3.	Unbelievers will not see Christ	Every person will see Christ
4.	A forceful catching away of saints	Acts 1:9-11 says that Christ ascended slowly into the clouds, and He will return in the same way
5.	Occurs in the twinkling of an eye or in an atom of time	Christ's return at Armageddon will not be in a twinkling of an eye
6.	A New Testament doctrine that was part of the "mystery" and not seen by Old Testament prophets	Both a New Testament and Old Testament doctrine
7.	Believers are removed from the earth	Believers remain on the earth and enter the Millennium
8.	The saints or those "in Christ" escape the wrath of God	The unrighteous experience the wrath of God
9.	Begins the Tribulation period	Begins the 1000 year Millennium
10.	The focus is on the Church	The focus is on Israel

PROPHETIC KEY FIVE

THE UNITED STATES IN PROPHECY

As stated in the commentary for Ezekiel 38-39, scholars are in general agreement that Tarshish existed on the coastlands from Britain, southward to Spain, to the Mediterranean, or Ceylon, or the East Indies. Some students of the Bible also believe the "young lions" or "outposts of Tarshish" refer to the United States. Archaeological research has found references to Tarshish along the Mississippi River and on the west coast that would seemingly support a linkage of Tarshish to America. It is further concluded that Canada and western European nations would also be included in the outposts of Tarshish.

Even though support for the United States as an outpost of Tarshish is not universal among scholars, many do believe that the United States will diminish as a world power following the Rapture of the Church. Currently, the Church indwelt by the Holy Spirit is restraining sin and the rise of the Antichrist who is empowered by Satan. The largest concentration of Christian believers is in the United States. The current estimate by Barna Research is that 41% of Americans claim to be "born again," which projects that 78 million believers in the United States will be translated at the Rapture. These believers occupy positions in all major professions and walks of life. The Rapture will devastate the United States politically, economically, and religiously. The United States will be reduced from world power status to a position subordinate to Europe (future Reconstituted Roman

Empire).

Furthermore, the United States is the principle defender of Israel. Without support and protection from the United States, Israel would be immediately annihilated by the Middle East Muslim nations. After the Rapture, the role of protector of Israel will be assumed by the Antichrist as he brokers a seven-year peace treaty in the Middle East between Israel and her Muslim neighbors, further supporting the absence of the United States as a global power.

 PROPHETIC KEY SIX

THE ANTICHRIST

The Antichrist is a substitute Christ, false Christ, or pseudo-Christ. He represents everything Christ is not. Throughout history Satan has always had an antichrist, such as Hitler, Mussolini, Stalin, Lenin, Ghengis Khan, Mao, Roman Emperors, etc., but none have been the "Antichrist." 1 John 2:18-22 states that many antichrists have come, and the one who denies that Jesus is the Christ and denies the Father and the Son is a liar and has the spirit of antichrist. 1 John 4:3 says one who does not confess that Jesus Christ is God and has come in the flesh has the spirit of antichrist. Finally, in 2 John 7 the Antichrist is called a deceiver, and one who does not confess Jesus Christ as coming in the flesh.

Old Testament Names for the Antichrist

- The Assyrian-Isaiah 10:20-27; Isaiah 30:18-33; Isaiah 31:4-32:20; Micah 5:3-15
- The King of Babylon-Isaiah 14:4
- The Spoiler (Destroyer)-Isaiah 16:4
- The Extortioner-Isaiah 16:4
- The Nail-Isaiah 22:25
- The Little Horn-Daniel 7:8, 24; Daniel 8:9, 23
- The King of Fierce Countenance-Daniel 8:23
- The Prince That Shall Come-Daniel 9:26-27
- The Willful King-Daniel 11:36

New Testament Names for the Antichrist

- The Man of Sin-2 Thessalonians 2:3
- Lawless One-2 Thessalonians 2:8-9
- Son of Perdition-2 Thessalonians 2:3
- The Beast-Revelation 13:2
- Abomination of Desolation-Matthew 24:15, Daniel 9:27

Who is like the Beast?

- Revelation 13:2-Multitudes will make this statement.

Spiritual Origin

- The beast out of the abyss will control, influence, dominate, and demonically oppress the Antichrist (Revelation 11:7).
- The Antichrist receives his power, throne, and authority from the Dragon or Satan (Revelation 13:2).

Geographic Area

- The Antichrist will hold a position of leadership prior to the beginning of the Tribulation.
- He will rise to power as the "little horn" out of Seleucid region of the Old Grecian Empire that covered the territory of Syria, Assyria, Babylon, and eastward. This region encompasses portions of modern day Syria, Iraq, Iran, Turkey, and Lebanon.
- The people of the prince that shall come in Daniel 9:26 were the Romans, signifying that the Antichrist will come from the Reconstituted Roman Empire, but the Eastern leg.
- He is called the "Assyrian" connecting him to the Assyrian Empire that preceded the Babylonian Empire.
- He is called the "King of Babylon," connecting him to ancient Babylon and the city of Babylon will be his primary capitol. Furthermore, Micah 5:5-6 refers to the Assyrian and the land of Nimrod. Nimrod ruled from Babylon and was

the first world dictator.

- The Antichrist is, therefore, linked to both the Revived Grecian and Reconstituted Roman Empires.

- At the middle of the Tribulation, he will subdue Jerusalem and make it one of his capitol cities.

- He will have governmental influence over the nations of the world and will rule and control the territories of the Reconstituted Roman and Revived Grecian Empires.

Racial or National Origin

- Because the Antichrist does not regard the God of his fathers, he could come from Christian, Jew, or Arab lineage, since all three are monotheistic or worship one deity. However, many scholars believe that the better translation is "gods of his fathers," which means that the Antichrist could come from a family that worshiped many gods. The Antichrist himself is most likely atheistic.

- Since the Antichrist rises to power as the "little horn" out of the Seleucid division of the Old Grecian Empire, he will be strongly influenced by Muslim teachings and values, which would provide explanation for his intense hatred and subsequent persecution of Christians and Jews during the Great Tribulation. A Muslim background would be instrumental in enabling the Antichrist to broker a seven-year peace treaty with Israel that allows for the rebuilding of the temple, or more probably the inner sanctuary, on an area considered sacred to the Muslims.

- The Antichrist is a Gentile because he is called the "Assyrian" and "King of Babylon," which would negate a Jewish heritage. The Antichrist is also identified as the prince who is to come. The people of the prince who is to come were the Romans who destroyed the temple in A.D. 70. Therefore, the Antichrist is a Gentile with roots in both the Reconstituted Roman Empire and Revived Grecian Empire.

Religious Influence

- Evolutionary humanism will culminate in the worship of the Antichrist as the greatest of all men. When intellectuals decide that God does not exist, they replace him with evolution. Man becomes the pinnacle attained by evolution. Hence, a man can become God, and this man, the Antichrist, will be idolized and worshiped as God.

- The Antichrist blasphemes God (Revelation 13:5-6).

- The Antichrist speaks against God and defies God (Daniel 7:25).

- The Antichrist does as he pleases. He will be a dictator with absolute world authority. He exalts and magnifies himself above God. He honors a god of fortresses, which means power and war will be his god (Daniel 11:36-39).

- Many people worship the Beast (Revelation 13:7-8). Satan has always wanted worship.

- The False Prophet causes people to worship the Beast and/or his image (Revelation 13:12-13).

- The Antichrist sits in the temple and displays himself as God (2Thessalonians 2:4).

- The Antichrist's appearance on the scene of history is according to the working of Satan with all power, signs, and lying wonders (2 Thessalonians 2:9). With the help of Satan, the Antichrist counterfeits supernatural events.

Political Influence

- The Antichrist is an orator whose mouth utters great boasts as the mouth of a lion (Revelation 13:2).

- As the "little horn," the Antichrist has limited power and is one of many rulers (Daniel 7:8, 20).

- The Antichrist will subdue by conquest three kings of the ten-nation confederacy of the Reconstituted Roman Empire. He is a military genius. As a politician, he has a different ideology from the other kings (Daniel 7:24).

- The remaining seven of the ten kings give their power and authority to the Antichrist (Revelation 17:17).

- The Antichrist is shrewd, crafty, arrogant, and deceptive (Revelation 6:2; 13:5; Daniel 8:25).

- The Antichrist is nihilistic. He destroys laws, morals, and customs. He uses fear, terror, and death to persecute Christians and Jews (Daniel 7:25).

- The Antichrist is insolent and skilled in intrigue. He uses ambiguous speech and dark sentences, indicating his involvement with the occult (Daniel 8:23).

- The Antichrist is a covenant breaker (Daniel 9:27).

- The Antichrist has selfish ambition and no regard for anyone (Daniel 11:36-37).

- The Antichrist is lawless and operates by deception (2 Thessalonians 2:3, 8, 10, Revelation 6:2 bow and no arrows).

- The Antichrist deceives by sorcery (Revelation 18:23).

Social Influence

- The Antichrist will arise out of social chaos, because the operation of the Holy Spirit in restraining sin through the Church will have been completed at the Rapture (2 Thessalonians 2:7).

- The Antichrist has no regard or desire for women, meaning that he isn't married or as some scholars believe, he may be a homosexual (Daniel 11:37).

- The "falling away" is the Rapture of the Church that will precede the revelation of the Antichrist (2 Thessalonians 2:3).

Economic Influence

- The Antichrist will tightly control the economy. As he controls the Middle East, he controls oil and wealth. No one can buy or sell without the mark of the Beast (Revelation

13:17; Daniel 11:43).

- Babylon will be rebuilt and will be the commercial center of the world. The Antichrist will rule from Babylon predominately during the first half of the Tribulation (Revelation 18) and from both Babylon and Jerusalem during the second half of the Tribulation (Matthew 24:15).

Contemporary Scene as the Time is Nearer to the Events of the Tribulation and Revelation of the Antichrist

- Mockers in the last days will be following their own lusts.

- Pleasure in sin. The "do your own thing" or "whatever makes you feel good" attitude is a hedonistic prelude to the Antichrist. The Antichrist will come to a world prepared and waiting for him.

- Building on these "do your own thing" philosophies is the New Age movement, which is merely a repackaging of paganistic and occultic practices. The New Age movement has infiltrated all elements and branches of society. This movement strives to elevate and connect the inner self into a collective relationship or oneness with the universe. Self-realization therapy, reincarnation, channeling, yoga, visualization, imagery, pyramid power, astral projection, guided meditation, karma relationships, cosmic consciousness, astrology, psychic phenomena, abortion rights, and gay rights are but a few of the applications of New Age philosophies.

- Liberalism, intellectualism, pseudo-Christianity, and religious deception are on the rise.

- TV and movies have increased their depiction of sex, violence, looseness, terror, drugs, alternate life styles, etc.

- Alcohol and drug addiction are at epidemic proportions.

- Liberal sexual attitudes are manifest in society, including abortion, teen pregnancies, prostitution, wife swapping, adultery, promiscuity, sex magazines, sex videos, phone sex, internet sex, etc.

- Homosexuality and lesbianism are accepted as alternate lifestyles.

- Crime is out of control, especially with youth gangs. Society band-aids the problem with increased security measures rather than addressing and solving the root causes.

- The traditional family and family values have broken down.

- Music and dance especially among youth are cultic, occultic, perverted, and highly sexual.

- Cults that deny the deity of Christ are growing in their appeal, e.g., the Jehovah Witnesses and Latter Day Saints (Mormons), in addition to a host of other lesser-known cults.

- Superstition is influencing society through astrology, witchcraft, mediums, horoscopes, psychics, palm reading, spiritism, occult, etc.

- Other world religions, such as Hinduism, Islam, and Buddhism are increasing their memberships not only globally but also in the predominantly Christian United States.

- The AIDS virus is out of control with some commentators linking AIDS to the destruction of one-fourth of mankind under the fourth seal judgment.

All of the above conditions are preparing the world stage for the Antichrist (refer to Prophetic Key: Setting the Stage).

TRIBULATION PERIOD

Jacob's Trouble

Revelation 6-19 is commonly known as the Tribulation Period (or Tribulation), Jacob's trouble (Jeremiah 30:7), or the time of indignation of the Lord upon all nations (Isaiah 34:2).

Rise of the Antichrist

At the beginning of Daniel's seventieth week, Israel is under intense persecution by the ten kings of the Reconstituted Roman Empire and the corresponding religious system, the Harlot or Mystery Babylon. The Antichrist rises to power out of the ten kingdoms comprising the Reconstituted Roman Empire and forges a seven-year covenant with Israel providing her with protection. Israel will live in peace for the first 3 1/2 years. The temple is to be rebuilt during this time. It may not be the full temple, but at minimum, the inner sanctuary. Israel most likely will support the Antichrist financially in his quest to take over the ten kingdoms. At the middle of the seventieth week of Daniel, the Antichrist will break the covenant with Israel, enter the temple, and proclaim himself to be God. For the next 3 1/2 years, the Antichrist will aggressively persecute the nation of Israel and the Jewish people.

Purpose of the Tribulation

The purpose of the Tribulation is to bring Israel to repentance and complete the spiritual seed or family of Abraham (Romans

11:25-26). Israel is now temporarily blinded but will repent and be saved by the end of the Tribulation. Only one-third of Israel survives the Tribulation (Zechariah 13:8). This persecution will surpass the Jewish holocaust of World War II. Daniel 9:24 is finally fulfilled at the end of the Tribulation. The Lord Jesus judges this sin-dominated world at the judgment of nations after the Second Coming of Christ but before the Millennium.

Character of the Tribulation

The saints are severely persecuted. The wrath of God is poured out in judgment of sin, wickedness, and corruption. The ungodly defy and curse God. Thousands are saved, with most martyred for their faith (refer to the great multitude of Revelation 7).

Timing of the Tribulation

The Tribulation Period begins after the Rapture of the Church with the signing of the peace covenant, and concludes after the bowl judgments at the Second Advent of Christ. Following the Rapture of the Church the world will be in chaos, and it is during this chaotic time that the Antichrist rises to power and prominence. There probably will be some interval of time between the Rapture of the Church and onset of the Tribulation, but the interval most likely will not be long. The Antichrist must gain enough power, authority, and influence to be able to broker a covenant with Israel that provides her with seven years of peace, principally from the Muslim world. On the other hand with the United States reduced to a second rate power following the Rapture, Israel will have no protection from a Muslim jihad. Even in the midst of turmoil and confusion resulting from the disappearance of millions at the Rapture, it is inconceivable that the Middle East Arab states will delay seizing the opportunity to attack and destroy Israel. Therefore, this covenant of peace and protection must be established within a relatively short period of time following the Rapture, probably with days, weeks, or at most months, but not years, or else Israel, without protection from the United States, would be subject to annihilation by her Arab enemies.

Tribulation Worldwide?

The Tribulation will be worldwide in influence if not in actual physical territory. The major areas are the Middle East, Northern Africa, Asia Minor, and Europe, which make up the Reconstituted Roman Empire and the Antichrist's kingdom. Nations from the East and throughout the earth will be participants at Armageddon.

Judgments

Three sets of seven judgments run consecutively through this seven-year period. The seal judgments occur in the first half of the Tribulation, commencing with seal judgments one through four, known as the "four horsemen of the apocalypse." The seventh seal introduces the seven trumpet judgments in the second half of the Tribulation. The seven bowl judgments are introduced by the seventh trumpet judgment at the end of the Tribulation. The bowl judgments occur during the 42nd month of the Great Tribulation or during the next 30 days according to Daniel 12:11.

Persecution, wars, famine, and death as defined under the seal judgments actually are in evidence throughout the seventieth week of Daniel.

Prophetic Key: Events and Conditions on Earth during the Tribulation Period

War

- Armed conflicts occur throughout the Tribulation as stated in Matthew 24, "there will be wars and rumors of war." Many scholars believe several of the wars could involve nuclear, chemical, and biological exchanges.
- At approximately mid-Tribulation, the Antichrist enters the

temple in Jerusalem and declares himself to be God. He then conquers three of the ten kingdoms forming the Reconstituted Roman Empire and the remaining seven kingdoms give their power and allegiance to him.

- Two major campaigns are waged in the first half of the Tribulation:

  - First, the King of the North (Syria or coalition of nations including Syria) and the King of the South (Egypt or a coalition of nations including Egypt) attack the Antichrist but are soundly defeated by him (Daniel 11:40-45).

  - Secondly, Gog, a military leader from Magog (Russian territory-primarily the Muslim nations of Russia/Central Asia) leads an army from the North (Russian territories) and the Muslim states in the Middle East to ravage, pillage, and plunder Israel. God destroys Gog and his armies on the mountains of Israel (Ezekiel 38-39).

Famine - Food and Water Shortages

- Famines occur throughout the Tribulation.

- One-third of the agricultural products are destroyed at the first trumpet judgment.

- One-third of sea life, seafood, and ships are destroyed at the second trumpet judgment.

- All sea life is destroyed at the second bowl judgment.

- One-third of rivers and springs of water become contaminated (Wormwood), and men die at the third trumpet judgment.

- All rivers and springs become blood at the third bowl judgment.

- Food and water are scarce for everyone and especially those who refuse the mark of the Beast, Beast's name, or the number of his name.

- The average person must spend an entire day's wage just for daily food (third seal judgment).

Pestilence

- As a result of war and famine, plague and pestilence are epidemic.

- AIDS and other diseases, such as cholera, malaria, sexually transmitted diseases, TB, ecoli, ebola, super bugs, etc. are rampant, and antibiotics are ineffective against them.

Religion

- The woman on a scarlet colored beast with seven heads and ten horns stands for "Mystery Babylon the Great, the Mother of Harlots, and of the Abominations of the Earth," or the religious system that exists during the first half of the Tribulation.

- The Antichrist commits the "abomination of desolation," when at mid-Tribulation he enters the temple and proclaims himself to be God.

- The False Prophet causes the earth and those who dwell in it to worship the Beast during the second half of the Tribulation.

Cities

- When the two witnesses are killed, a tenth of Jerusalem falls.

- Babylon is destroyed in one hour at the end of the Tribulation.

- At the seventh bowl judgment, Jerusalem is divided into three parts and the cities of the nations fall.

Environmental and Cosmic Disturbances

- A great earthquake begins the wrath of God; the sun becomes black and the moon red as blood, stars of heaven fall to the earth, the sky recedes, and every mountain and island are shifted in position.

- Fire from heaven falls to earth, with noises, thunderings, lightnings, and an earthquake.

- Hail and fire mingled with blood are thrown to the earth.

- One-third of the seas become blood.

- A great mountain (volcano) burning with fire is thrown or cast into the sea.

- A great star or meteor falls from heaven burning like a torch onto the rivers and springs of water.

- One-third of the sun, moon, and stars are darkened so the light of day is diminished by one-third.

- The two witnesses turn water into blood, shut heaven from raining, smite the earth with plagues; fire proceeds from their mouths and devours their enemies.

- The seas become blood.

- The rivers and springs of water become blood.

- The sun scorches men with fire.

- The Beast's kingdom becomes totally dark, and men gnaw their tongues in pain.

- The great river Euphrates dries up to allow passage for the Kings of the East.

- At the seventh bowl judgment, noises, thunderings, lightnings, and a great earthquake occur. Mountains and islands cease to exist, and great hailstones weighing over 100 pounds fall from heaven.

Christians (including saved Jews)

- The souls of martyrs are seen under the throne.

- Saints are martyred by being beheaded with an axe.

- A great multitude that no one could number is saved during the Great Tribulation from every nation, tribe, people, and tongue.

- God's two witnesses prophesy for the last three and one-half years of the Tribulation.

- The saints in heaven participate in the marriage of the Lamb.

Jews

- The woman clothed with the sun stands for Israel.
- The woman bares a male child (144,000 Jewish witnesses).
- The 144,000 Jewish witnesses are sealed by God for protection from the Antichrist through the trumpet judgments.
- The 144,000 Jewish witnesses are raptured in the second half of the Tribulation.
- Most of Israel flees to Petra and the wilderness nations.
- A remnant of Israel remains in Jerusalem.

Unsaved

- The rider on the white horse of the first seal judgment is the Antichrist.
- The Beast that rises up out of the sea with seven heads and ten horns represents the Antichrist.
- The False Prophet is seen as another beast that comes on the earth with two horns like a lamb but speaking as a dragon.
- The False Prophet causes all the followers of the Antichrist to receive a mark on their right hand or foreheads in order to buy or sell any goods or merchandise or transact monetary business.
- People who take the mark of the Beast are eternally doomed.
- Foul and cancerous sores appear upon men who have the mark of the Beast.
- The unsaved do not repent of their murders, sorceries, sexual immoralities, or thefts.
- The unsaved hide in caves and in the rocks of the mountains and ask the mountains to fall on and hide them from the wrath of the Lamb.

Angels

- Angels continually surround the throne worshipping God.

- The living creatures summon to action the riders on the white, red, black, and pale-green horses (seal judgments 1-4).

- Four angels at the four-corners of the earth hold back the four winds (judgments) until the servants of God are sealed.

- Seven trumpet angels stand in the presence of God.

- An angel with the key to the bottomless pit opens the pit and releases the demon locusts.

- A mighty angel from heaven stands on both land and sea holding a little open book.

- Michael and his angels fight with the Devil and his angels in a heavenly war in which the Devil and his angels are cast out of heaven and confined to the earthly realm.

- Angels fly in the atmosphere, preaching the everlasting Gospel, pronouncing that Babylon has fallen, declaring that Beast worshippers and those with the mark are eternally doomed, and crying out with a loud voice that it is time for the Lord to reap the harvest of the earth.

- Angels view the torment of those who take the mark of the Beast.

- An angel proceeds from the temple with a sharp sickle.

- An angel from the altar with power over fire cries out to thrust in the sickle for the harvest.

- Seven angels in heaven have the seven last plagues completing the wrath of God.

- One of the angels with the seven last plagues shows John the judgment of the great Harlot.

- An angel with great authority shouts that Babylon has fallen.

- An angel standing in the sun calls the birds to gather together for the supper of the great God.

- The angelic host returns with Christ at His Second Coming.

- An angel descends from heaven with the key to the bottomless pit and a great chain and binds Satan and casts him into the bottomless pit for one thousand years.

Demonic Activity

- Demon locusts ascend from the abyss with the power to torment men, who have taken the mark of the Beast, with a scorpion-like sting lasting for up to five months.

- The angel of the bottomless pit, called Apollyon or Abaddon, is the king of the locust demons.

- The four angels bound at the great river Euphrates are released.

- A 200-million demon army is released with the power to kill one-third of mankind.

- The demon horsemen kill men using fire, smoke, and brimstone (elements of hell).

- The beast (satanic prince) that ascends from the bottomless pit wars against and kills the two witnesses.

- The Devil and his angels are cast to the earth (first heaven).

- Satan is seen as the great red Dragon with seven heads and ten horns.

- Babylon is a dwelling place of demons and a prison for every foul spirit.

- Three unclean spirits (spirits of demons) like frogs go out from the mouth of the Dragon, the Antichrist, and the False Prophet to entice the kings of the world to the battle of the great day of God Almighty.

- The Antichrist and the False Prophet are cast into the lake of fire.

Death

- The rider on the pale green horse (Death) with Hell following after are given power over the earth to kill one-fourth of mankind with the sword, hunger, death, and beasts of the field.

- Martyred souls under the altar are slain for the Word of God and their testimony.

- The Antichrist makes war with the saints and overcomes them.

- Demon horsemen kill one-third of mankind.

- The beast from the bottomless pit kills the two witnesses.

- The earth opens up and swallows Satan's armies pursuing Israel (woman).

- The Antichrist receives a deadly wound but is resurrected (counterfeit).

- The Beast overcomes both Jews and Saints.

- 7000 people are killed in an earthquake that occurs when the two witnesses are killed.

- The blood of those killed at Armageddon extends for 200 miles throughout a valley situated outside Jerusalem.

Prophetic Key: Tribulation Judgments
Seal Judgments

Seal	Description	Revelation
1	Rider on the white horse - conqueror out to conquer - bow with no arrows	6:1-2
2	Rider on the red horse - takes peace from the earth - people kill one another	6:3-4
3	Rider on the black horse-pair of scales in his hand - famine	6:5-6
4	Rider on the pale (green) horse - Hades follows death-power over 1/4th earth to kill with the sword, hunger, death, and beasts	6:7-8
5	Souls under the altar - those slain for the Word of God and their testimony	6:9-11
6	Wrath of God-great earthquake - sun turns black - moon turns blood red - stars of heaven fall to earth - sky recedes-mountains and islands move	6:12-17
7	Silence in heaven for ½ hour - introduction to seven trumpet angels	8:1-2

Trumpet Judgments

Trumpet	Description	Scripture
1	Hail, fire mixed with blood thrown to earth - 1/3rd trees and grass burned up	8:7
2	Great mountain burning thrown into the sea - 1/3rd sea becomes blood, 1/3rd living creatures die - 1/3rd ships destroyed	8:8-9
3	Great burning star (Wormwood) falls from heaven - 1/3rd rivers and springs of water become wormwood - many people die	8:10-11
4	1/3rd sun, moon, stars darkened - 1/3rd day doesn't shine- night increased 1/3rd	8:12
5	Star falls from heaven-has key to Abyss - demon locusts released to torment men with scorpion like sting for 5 months - men cannot die	9:1-12
6	Four angels bound at Euphrates released - lead 200 million demon army that kills 1/3rd mankind by fire, smoke, and brimstone - mankind does not repent	9:13-21
7	Seventh angel makes a proclamation - kingdoms of world have become kingdoms of our Lord and His Christ, introduces seven bowl judgments	11:15

Bowl Judgments

Bowl	Description	Scripture
1	Foul and loathsome sores come upon those with mark of the Beast	16:2
2	Sea becomes as blood - every living creature in the sea dies	16:3
3	Rivers and springs of water become blood	16:4-7
4	Heat from sun scorches men with fire - men blaspheme name of God	16:8-9
5	Throne and kingdom of the Beast in darkness - men gnaw tongues from pain - men blaspheme God	16:10-11
6	Great river Euphrates dries up - clears way for Kings from the East to gather for battle of great day of God	16:12-16
7	Noise, thunder, lightning and great earthquake - Jerusalem dived into three parts - Babylon and cities destroyed - islands and mountains removed - hail exceeding 100 lbs falls on men - men blaspheme God	16:17-21

Prophetic Key: Timeline Overview
Revelation 6-20, Daniel 11:41, and Ezekiel 38-39

Scripture	Description	1st Half	Mid Trib	2nd Half	30 Days
6:1-2	1st seal - rider on white horse - conqueror	x			
6:3-4	2nd seal - rider on the red horse - war	x			
6:5-6	3rd seal - rider on the black horse - famine	x			
6:7-8	4th seal - rider on the pale horse - death and Hades - 1/4th mankind killed	x			
6:9-11	5th seal - souls under the altar - slain for Word of God	x			
6:12-17	6th seal - cosmic disturbances - wrath of God		x		
7:1-8	Sealing of 144,000 Jews - servants of God		x		
7:9-17	Great multitude in heaven - out of the Great Tribulation			x	
8:1-2	7th seal - silence in heaven - seven trumpet angels before God			x	
8:3-5	Angel with golden censer - thunderings, earthquakes, lightnings, noises			x	
8:6-7	1st trumpet - hail, fire, blood - 1/3rd trees, all grass burned			x	
8:8-9	2nd trumpet - mountain burning - 1/3rd sea blood, 1/3rd sea life and ships destroyed			x	
8:9-11	3rd trumpet - burning star - 1/3rd rivers, springs - Wormwood			x	
8:12-13	4th trumpet - 1/3rd sun, moon, stars - 2/3rds darkness			x	
9:1-11	5th trumpet - demon locusts torment mankind for five months - 1st Woe			x	
9:12-19	6th trumpet - 4 bound angels - 200 million army - 1/3rd mankind killed – 2nd Woe			x	
9:20-21	Mankind does not repent			x	
10:1-11	Mighty angel with the little open book			x	
11:1-2	Temple to Gentiles - city trodden underfoot 42 months		x		
11:3-14	Two witnesses - 42 months - smite earth plagues – killed by beast from the abyss		x		
11:15-18	7th trumpet - kingdoms of the Lord - 3rd Woe				x
11:19	Temple of God open in heaven - thunder, lightning, hail, earthquake				x

Prophetic Key: Timeline Overview (cont.)
Revelation 6-20, Daniel 11:41, and Ezekiel 38-39

Scripture	Description	1st Half	Mid Trib	2nd Half	30 Days
12:1-2	Great sign - woman with child - travailed		x		
12:3-4	Fiery red Dragon - 7 heads, 10 horns - 1/3rd angels cast down		x		
12:5	Male child caught up to God - rule nations with rod of iron			x	
12:6	Woman flees to wilderness - 1260 days		x		
12:7-10	War in heaven - Satan cast to earth		x		
12:11-12	Saints overcome by blood of Lamb - Satan's wrath on earth		x		
12:12-17	Satan persecutes woman - woman is protected in wilderness for 42 months		x		
13:1-2	Beast from sea - 7 heads, 10 horns - Satanic authority		x		
13:3-10	Wounded head - Beast worship - 42 months - makes war and overcomes saints		x		
13:11-18	Beast from earth - causes Beast worship - image, mark, number of Beast		x		
14:1-5	Lamb and 144,000 on Mt Zion (heavenly) - before throne			x	
14:6-13	Three angelic pronouncements - judgment, Babylon, mark of the Beast				x
14:14-20	Armageddon - winepress of God's wrath				x
15:1	Seven bowl angels - in them wrath of God complete				x
15:2-4	Those with victory over the Beast - before throne				x
15:5-8	Heavenly temple open - seven bowl angels				x
16:1-2	1st bowl - malignant sores on those with mark of the Beast or worship his image				x
16:3	2nd bowl - sea becomes blood - sea life dies				x
16:4-7	3rd bowl - rivers, springs become blood - righteous judgments				x
16:8-9	4th bowl - on the sun - men are scorched with fire				x
16:10-11	5th bowl - kingdom of Beast - darkness – men gnaw tongues				x
16:12-16	6th bowl - Euphrates dries up - Kings of East - 3 demon spirits gather armies				x
16:17-21	7th bowl - Armageddon - cities fall - great earthquake, thunder, lightning				x

Prophetic Key: Timeline Overview (cont.)
Revelation 6-20, Daniel 11:41, and Ezekiel 38-39

Scripture	Description	1st Half	Mid Trib	2nd Half	30 Days
17:1-6	Scarlet beast, 7 heads, 10 horns - Mystery Babylon - saints persecuted	x			
17:7-17	Beast out of pit - heads and horns are kingdoms and kings - hate whore	x			
17:18	Woman is great city - reigns over kings	x			
18:1	Great angel - illuminates earth				x
18:2-24	Babylon fallen - one hour judgment - saints killed in Babylon				x
19:1-6	Heavenly scene - great multitude, elders, four creatures - righteous judgments				x
19:7-10	Marriage supper of the Lamb			x	
19:11-18	Armageddon - heavenly armies - Christ on white horse – war – wrath of God				x
19:19-21	Beast armies slain - Beast, False Prophet cast into lake of fire				x
20:1-3	Satan bound in pit for 1000 years				x
20:4-6	1st resurrection - heaven - souls beheaded for witness of Jesus				x
Daniel 11:41	War of the King of the North and King of the South		x		
Ezekiel 38-39	Gog leads armies from Russia and Middle East nations in attack against Israel		x		
Various	Day of the Lord		x		

Definitions:

Mid-Tribulation will contain events that occur or begin around the middle of the Tribulation period, a few months before or after the exact mid-point of the Tribulation.

30 Days refers to the last 30 days or 42nd month of the Great Tribulation or the additional 30-day period following the Great Tribulation as specified in Daniel 12:11.

GROUPS OF BELIEVERS

Martyred Souls

Revelation 6:9 – the fifth seal judgment depicts souls under the altar who are slain for the Word of God and their testimony.

Revelation 6:10 – a cry for justice; the Lord is asked how long He will refrain from judging and avenging their blood on those who dwell on the earth.

Revelation 6:11 – each person receives a white robe and is told to rest for a while longer until the number of their fellow servants and their brethren who are to be killed even as they were is complete. Although they are referred to as souls, they have spirit form, as they are given robes to wear. Their bodies are not redeemed at this point but will be redeemed as part of the First Resurrection after the Tribulation Period (Revelation 20:4).

Revelation 17: 6 – a woman, Mystery Babylon, is drunk with the blood of the saints and with the blood of the martyrs.

Revelation 20:4-5 – souls that are beheaded for the witness of Jesus, the Word of God, and for not worshipping the Beast or his image, or for not taking his mark. They live and reign with Christ for 1000 years. This is the First Resurrection. Martyrs come out of both the first and second halves of the Tribulation, as specified in Revelation 6:9 (first half) and Revelation 20:4 (second half).

144,000 Jews

Revelation 7:4 – bondservants of God who receive a seal on their foreheads from God. The number of those sealed is 144,000, 12,000 from each of the 12 tribes of Israel. The first four trumpet angels are commissioned not to harm the earth, sea, or trees until the 144,000 are sealed. This sealing process must occur after the sixth seal judgment but before the seventh. The seal is for protection through the trumpet judgments. The 144,000 appear to be in heaven before the bowl judgments as seen in Revelation 14:1-5. Although scripture doesn't say that they are evangelists, these 144,000 Jews are called "servants," and servants of God typically evangelize. Some scholars believe the 144,000 to be the "woman," since the woman is protected for 3 1/2 years (second half of the Tribulation), and the 144,000 are on Mt. Zion after the trumpet judgments (late second half of the Tribulation) but before the bowl judgments. However, the stronger and more probable position is that the 144,000 are the male child of Revelation 12.

Revelation 12:17 – the 144,000 are part of the Jewish remnant that is saved as the Antichrist wages war with remainder of the woman's offspring (remnant) who keep the commandments of God and have the testimony of Jesus.

Revelation 14:1 – the Lamb is seen standing on Mt. Zion with the 144,000 who have His name and the name of the Father on their foreheads. The 144,000 are the first Jews saved during the Tribulation and are raptured after the trumpet judgments. There is no indication that they are ever killed or martyred. This is further evidence to support the position that the 144,000 are the male child, especially since the male child is caught-up to God, which is descriptive of being raptured. When Christ is pictured as a Lamb, the scene is typically in heaven or the temple of the New Jerusalem. On earth during the Tribulation, Christ is viewed as the Lion from the tribe of Judah.

Revelation 14:3 – the 144,000 are purchased (redeemed) from the earth.

Revelation 14:4 – the 144,000 are purchased (redeemed) from among men as first fruits unto God and to the Lamb, and they follow the Lamb wherever He goes. They are celibates, not defiled by women.

Revelation 14:5 – the 144,000 are without fault before the throne of God.

Great Multitude

Revelation 7:9 – an innumerable company from every tongue, nation, people, and tribe standing before the throne and the Lamb.

Revelation 7:14 – this great multitude is a product of the Great Tribulation. The great multitude consists of saints slain by the Antichrist during the second half of the seventieth week of Daniel.

Revelation 7:15-17 – the great multitude is before the throne serving God day and night. They no longer hunger or thirst, the sun does not harm them, and God wipes away all their tears. They are freed from: hunger and thirst from the famine of the third seal judgment in the first half of the Tribulation; adverse economic conditions for refusal to take the mark of the Beast causing them to be unable to buy or sell; waters that become Wormwood and unfit to drink at the third trumpet judgment; sea and rivers becoming blood at the second and third bowl judgments; destruction of food products under the first trumpet judgment and second and third bowl judgments; and heat from the sun that scorches the skin at the fourth bowl judgment.

Revelation 12:11 – saints, including Jewish believers, overcome the Antichrist and satanic forces by the blood of the Lamb and the word of their testimony. They are willing to die for their testimony to Christ.

Revelation 12:17 – a remnant of Israel is persecuted by the Antichrist because they keep the commandments of God and have the testimony of Jesus.

Revelation 13:7 – the Beast (Antichrist) makes war with the saints and overcomes them.

Revelation 14:13 – blessed are the dead who die in the Lord from now on. This is a reference to those who die after the trumpet judgments.

Revelation 15:2 – those on the sea of glass (before the throne) represent people who are victorious over the Beast, his image, and his name. This scene occurs after the trumpet judgments and before the bowl judgments.

Revelation 18:24 – in Babylon is found the blood of prophets and saints and all those slain on the earth.

Revelation 19:1-6 – depicts a great multitude singing in heaven.

Summary

Martyred Souls under the Throne – believers killed primarily during the first half of the Tribulation but representative of believers slain throughout the seven-year Tribulation Period for the Word of God and their testimony for Jesus.

144,000 – servants of God protected after the seal judgments, through the trumpet judgments, and raptured before the bowl judgments. These 144,000 servants are the "male child."

Great Multitude – saints who are slain or martyred primarily in the second half of the Tribulation Period or Great Tribulation.

THREE MAJOR MILITARY CAMPAIGNS

(Refer to Prophetic Keys: Daniel Military Campaign, Magog Military Campaign, and Armageddon)

Three Major Military Campaigns

During the Tribulation, there will be three major campaigns fought in Israel. These three campaigns are:

1) **Daniel 11:40-47** – The King of the North and the King of the South attack and are subsequently defeated by the Antichrist in Israel.

2) **Ezekiel 38-39** – Describes the Magog invasion of Israel led by Gog in which the armies from Russia and the Muslim Russian territories combine with several Islamic nations to attack Israel and are destroyed by God on the mountains of Israel.

3) **Revelation 14:19-20; 16:12-16** – Series of battles throughout Israel during which the kings of the world, including the Kings of the East, are gathered to initially destroy Israel but then turn to fight against God Almighty. These battles include the battle of Armageddon at Mount Megiddo in the north, battle in the Valley of Jehoshaphat outside Jerusalem, and battle at Bozrah or Edom in the south.

The order and timing of these three campaigns are controversial subjects among Bible prophecy scholars. It is universally agreed that Armageddon is the final battle (war) preceding the Lord's Second Advent (Refer to Prophetic Key: Armageddon). Scholars vary as to the placement of the Magog invasion and the invasion by the Kings of the North and South (Refer to Prophetic Keys: Daniel Military Campaign and Magog Military Campaign).

Thermonuclear War or Wrath of God

These scholars believe thermonuclear exchanges will occur before or during the Tribulation, depending on placement of the Magog invasion of Israel on the prophetic timeline. They use Zechariah 14:12 as a supporting scripture: *And this shall be the plague with which the Lord will strike all the people who fought against Jerusalem: their flesh shall dissolve while they stand on their feet, their eyes shall dissolve in their sockets, and their tongues shall dissolve in their mouths.*

Since Ezekiel 39:14-15 speaks of men set apart for burying the dead from the Magog invasion, prophecy scholars further conclude that these men are set apart because of radioactive contamination resulting form a nuclear war.

The Bible speaks of wars and rumors of wars during the Tribulation where nation will rise against nation and kingdom against kingdom. Could some of these conflicts be nuclear? Quite possibly, as many third world nations currently have nuclear capability, and by the start of the Tribulation Period many additional nations should possess nuclear weapons. It isn't clear from scripture whether there will or will not be nuclear exchanges in these minor conflicts. However, the picture may be a little clearer regarding the three major military campaigns.

In the Magog campaign, God executes judgment upon Gog and his armies. In addition to a great earthquake, infighting amongst the troops, and pestilence, His divine wrath of fire, brimstone, flooding rain and great hailstones bring about Gog's destruction in the same manner as Sodom and Gomorrah were destroyed. The question of the men set apart to bury the dead is discussed in the commentary on Ezekiel 39:12-16. The dead are being buried by people of Israel before certain men are set apart for the burial process. Because it will take seven months to bury the dead, after a short period of time flesh will decompose and become contaminated with disease. For the protection of the nation, properly trained specialists should be set apart for this task. A majority of scholars place the Magog invasion before mid-Tribulation. At mid-Tribulation, the Antichrist sits on the throne in Jerusalem as a base of command and rulership with no indication of the land being plagued by radioactive fallout.

Similarly, the Daniel described war of the King of the South and King of the North against the Antichrist provides no indication of a nuclear exchange. If this war occurs before mid-Tribulation as postulated in this commentary, the Middle East area continues to be a prime focus of activity throughout the second half of the Tribulation, which would not be the case if the land was contaminated with radiation.

Some scholars place the Daniel military campaign of the Kings of the North and South with the end-time battle of Armageddon. Zechariah 14:12 certainly describes the annihilation of people who fight against Jerusalem in terms that could be characteristic of nuclear war. However, it is the contention of this commentary that Zechariah 14:12 describes the effects of the wrath of God, as the armies aligned against Christ are supernaturally destroyed at His Second Coming. The Bible also states that these armies are destroyed by the brightness of His Coming, giant hailstones, and the sharp sword out of His mouth, which is the Word of God. Revelation 14:19-20 refers to this end-time battle as the great wine press of the wrath of God and the supper of the great God.

Hence, the pouring out of God's wrath in divine judgment logically fits the destruction of the armies in these three major military campaigns better than the destructive effects caused by thermonuclear exchanges.

DANIEL MILITARY CAMPAIGN

**(Refer to Prophetic Keys:
Three Major Military Campaigns,
Magog Military Campaign, and Armageddon)**

Daniel 11 discusses the King of the South and King of the North attacking the forces of the Antichrist. Egypt has generally been considered to be the King of the South and Syria the King of the North. However, the latest prophetic research appears to favor the King of the South and King of the North as each representing a coalition of nations from their respective geographic areas, but it is noted that the term used is "King" not "Kings." The Kings (or coalitions of nations) of the South and North are soundly defeated by the Antichrist.

King of the North not the Antichrist

According to Daniel 11:40, at the time of the end, the King of the South and the King of the North shall move against the Antichrist who in turn invades their countries and overwhelmingly defeats them. Some commentators call the Antichrist the King of the North, but Daniel 11:40 clearly states that the King of the North attacks the Antichrist. Therefore, the Antichrist cannot be the King of the North and Russia is not the Northern Kingdom. The king of the North is Syria or a coalition of Middle East nations including Syria, and the King of the South is Egypt or a coalition of North African nations including Egypt.

The Antichrist arises as the eleventh horn (Daniel 7:24, 8:9) from the Seleucid portion of the Grecian Empire. The King of the North is also from this same division of the Grecian Empire. However, the Antichrist is not the King of the North. How is this issue reconciled? The Seleucid division of the Grecian Empire encompassed greater territory than Syria, including portions of Babylonia (modern day Iraq) and Assyria. The Antichrist is referred to as the King of Babylon and the Assyrian. Therefore, the Antichrist will arise in the end times as the eleventh or little horn from the Seleucid division of the Grecian Empire, probably from the region of ancient Babylon and Assyria, and will subsequently defeat the King of the North (Syria or coalition of nations from areas around Syria) and the King of the South (Egypt or a coalition of nations from northern Africa).

When Does the War Involving the King of the South and King of the North Take Place?

As with the Magog invasion, scholars are divided as to the timing of the military campaign of Daniel 11:40-44. This event occurs at the end of the age but specifically when is an interesting point for discussion:

1. At the end of the Tribulation preceding the battle of Armageddon

2. Second half of the Tribulation

3. During the first half of the Tribulation, after the Magog invasion

4. During the first half of the Tribulation, before the Magog invasion

1. At the end of the Tribulation preceding the battle of Armageddon

A traditional approach to Daniel 11:40-45 has the battle of the Antichrist against the Kings of the North and South occurring near the end of the seventieth week just before Armageddon. The

Antichrist overthrows several countries in the territory of the Reconstituted Roman Empire, including the destruction of Egypt. Verses 40-43 could fit this end-time setting. However, verse 44 is of some concern. The Antichrist is defeating countries in the Middle East when troubling news comes from the east and north, and he sets out to annihilate and destroy. However, according to the sixth bowl judgment, demon spirits go forth from Satan, the Antichrist, and the False Prophet to the kings of the world to gather them to the battle of the great day of God Almighty. The Antichrist is not attacking countries to the east and north but is enticing them to Israel. Also, there is no country of any power to the north, since the annihilation of the armies of Gog from the land of Magog. Therefore, Daniel 11:44 does not positionally fit at the time of the battle of Armageddon.

2. Second half of the Tribulation

The attack on the Antichrist from the King of the North (Syria and/or coalition of nations) and the King of the South (Egypt and/or coalition of nations) cannot fit in the second half of the Tribulation. Around mid-Tribulation the Antichrist will conquer three nations of the ten-nation confederacy of the Reconstituted Roman Empire, and the seven remaining nations will give their power to him, forming the eighth or Beast empire. For the duration of the second half of the Tribulation Period, the Antichrist will rule the Beast empire, and the King of the North and King of the South will owe allegiance to him. Therefore, the conflict presented in Daniel 11 must occur late in the first half of the seven-year Tribulation.

3. During the first half of the Tribulation after the Magog invasion

Since it is ruled out that the Daniel military campaign occurs in the second half of the Tribulation, the campaign must occur before the middle of the Tribulation and in the same general time frame of the Gog invasion of Ezekiel 38-39. The question then is whether the Daniel conflict precedes or follows the Ezekiel invasion? Neither Egypt nor Syria is mentioned as nations participating in the Gog invasion. The nations of Edom, Moab, and Ammon escape the Antichrist, and this is the area where Israel as the "woman" of Revelation 12 escapes. Libya and Ethiopia, participants of the Gog invasion, almost, but apparently do not get into this battle.

Therefore, a plausible, but not the preferred position, would be to place the Daniel military campaign around the middle of the Tribulation, during the Antichrist's rise to power following the battle of Ezekiel 38-39. The scenario would be that the army of Gog is destroyed on the mountains of Israel, which aids the Antichrist's climb to power, because at this time he does not have the military might to conquer Gog and his armies from Magog and the Muslim nations. The Kings of the North and South attack the Antichrist. He soundly defeats them, with the rest of the seventh empire kingdoms giving him their power and authority. The Antichrist breaks his covenant with Israel and becomes the Beast or eighth and last world Empire to persecute Israel during the times of the Gentiles. This scenario places the attack upon the Antichrist by the Kings of the North and South near the middle of the Tribulation – **after** the destruction of Gog's armies by God on the mountains of Israel.

However, Daniel 11:44 would not be reconciled. If Gog has already been destroyed before this conflict with the Kings of the North and South, what nation or power would be to the north that would concern the Antichrist?

4. During the first half of the Tribulation before the Magog invasion

The best and preferred position would be to place the conflict between the Antichrist and the Kings of the North and South immediately **before** the invasion of Israel by the forces of Gog. Verse 44 of Daniel 11 supports this interpretation. As the Antichrist defeats the Kings of the North and South, news to the north and east trouble him, which would be the coming invasion by Gog. The battle of the Antichrist versus the Kings of the North and South and the Gog invasion of Ezekiel 38-39 are two separate but closely related military campaigns that position the world for dictatorship under the Antichrist. Because Israel dwells safely in her homeland for 3 1/2 years or the first half of the Tribulation, these events occur within months of mid-Tribulation.

Furthermore, according to Ezekiel 38:5, Libya and Ethiopia are listed as nations aligned with Gog, but Daniel 11:43 states that the Libyans and Ethiopians follow after the Antichrist. If the Magog campaign occurs before the Daniel campaign, then Ethiopia and Libya couldn't be following the Antichrist, for they already would have been destroyed supernaturally by God on the mountains of Israel. Therefore, Daniel 11:43 and Ezekiel 38:5 clearly confirm that the Daniel military campaign must **precede** the Gog invasion.

Summary

In summary, the strongest scriptural application is to place the battles described in Daniel 11:40-44 and Ezekiel 38-39 in the same time frame with the invasion of Israel by Gog **following** the defeat of the Kings of the North and South by the Antichrist. The hypothetical scenario would be that Egypt (or coalition of North African nations including Egypt) and Syria (or coalition of Middle East nations including Syria), as the Kings of the South and North respectively, attack the Antichrist probably because of his covenant relationship with Israel. The Antichrist soundly defeats these two armies. Although the Antichrist has made the covenant to protect Israel, he doesn't have the military might to contend against Gog. The Antichrist flees as Gog moves to invade Israel. God annihilates the armies of Gog on the mountains of Israel. The Antichrist seizes the moment by conquering three nations who are part of the Reconstituted Roman Empire. Egypt and Syria may be two of the three conquered nations. The remaining seven nations making up the Reconstituted Roman and/or Grecian Empires give their power, authority, and allegiance to the Antichrist. The Antichrist enters the temple and proclaims himself to be God, breaks the covenant with Israel, and begins a persecution of Israel to the point of her annihilation during the second half of the Tribulation. Therefore, the Gog invasion would occur late in the second quarter of the Tribulation with the Antichrist defeating the three nations shortly before the middle of the seventieth week of Daniel, and then assuming full authority over the Reconstituted Roman Empire territory at the middle of the Tribulation. The Antichrist's defeat of the King of the North and King of the South under this scenario would shortly precede the Gog invasion.

PROPHETIC KEY ELEVEN

MAGOG MILITARY CAMPAIGN

**(Refer to Prophetic Keys:
Three Major Military Campaigns,
Daniel Military Campaign, and Armageddon)**

The timing of the Magog invasion is a point of controversy among Bible scholars. Historically, no battle as described in Ezekiel 38-39 has ever occurred, so the timing must be future, but scholars vary as to the placement of the Magog invasion on the prophetic timeline:

1. Preceding the Rapture of the Church
2. At the end of the Millennium
3. At the end of the Tribulation with the battle of Armageddon
4. Following the Rapture of the Church at the beginning of the Tribulation
5. Near the middle of the Tribulation

1. Preceding the Rapture of the Church

It doesn't fit scripture that the Magog invasion precedes the Rapture, because Israel's deliverance from Gog's armies is a supernatural act of God demonstrating to Israel that He is turning His face back toward them. God will only interact with Israel as a nation and the Jews as His people and turn back to them after the Church is removed at the Rapture. The Magog invasion occurs when Israel is at peace and residing safely in her land, which is not a condition pre-Rapture but happens during the first half of Daniel's seventieth week when Israel is under a covenant of protection from a world leader (the Antichrist). Additionally, this world leader, who at mid-Tribulation will be known as the Antichrist of Bible prophecy, does not emerge onto the geo-political scene and is not revealed or elevated to world leader status until after the restrainer, the Church indwelt and empowered by the Holy Spirit, is removed at the Rapture. Therefore, the Magog invasion cannot precede the Rapture.

2. At the end of the Millennium

To have the Magog invasion at the end of the Millennium doesn't fit scripture. A primary purpose for the destruction of the Magog invaders on the mountains of Israel is connected with Israel's restoration and God's demonstration that He is still the God of Israel. After the Millennium, Israel will not need to be restored, for they will have enjoyed theocratic rule under Christ for 1000 years.

3. At the end of the Tribulation with the battle of Armageddon

Many prophecy students place this war at the end of the Tribulation simultaneous with the battle of Armageddon. However, according to scripture, this battle is very different from the battle of Armageddon. At Armageddon, all the armies of the world, including the armies from the east (Middle East nations and nations of the Orient), are assembled under the leadership of the Antichrist to first destroy Israel and then to stop the return of Christ. Not all countries of the world are involved in the Magog invasion. The countries aligned with Magog are specifically designated in scripture as Islamic nations from the Middle East.

Gog, not the Antichrist, is the leader of Magog and his Islamic allies. God's influence causes Gog to invade Israel, and God Himself destroys the armies of Gog on the mountains of

Israel through supernatural means and internal strife. However, at Armageddon the zone of battle is a 200-mile stretch of land in the plains and valleys of Israel where Jesus personally destroys the armies of the Antichrist at His Second Coming.

The Magog invasion occurs when Israel is safe in her land, which must be before mid-Tribulation. After mid-Tribulation, Israel is heavily persecuted by the Antichrist, and only a remnant of the Jewish people is left in Israel with the majority having fled to Petra and wilderness nations.

Finally, the purpose of the Ezekiel campaign is to take spoil and plunder, whereas the purpose of the Armageddon campaign is to destroy the Jews and to stop Christ from setting up His millennial kingdom. Thus, the two events are separated by at least three and one-half years.

4. Following the Rapture of the Church at the beginning of the Tribulation or

5. Near the middle of the Tribulation

Gog from the land of Magog can only lead an assault on Israel during the first half of the Tribulation when Israel is covered by a peace treaty and is safely under the protection of the Antichrist. The question is when during the first half of the Tribulation does this invasion occur - at the beginning or at the end? Many prominent prophecy experts see this invasion immediately before or immediately after the commencement of the Tribulation.

However, the position of this text is to place this attack on Israel closer to mid-Tribulation. According to the Ezekiel account, God pours out His wrath destroying the armies of Gog on the mountains of Israel. At that same time, a great earthquake occurs in Israel where mountains are thrown down and walls crumble. Because such a great earthquake happens at the sixth seal judgment about mid-Tribulation and commences the wrath of God, the destruction of the armies of Gog then naturally fits simultaneously with the sixth seal judgment. Joel 2 supports this position with a discussion of the day of the Lord, and the destruction of an army by fire and flame. God shows Israel that He is still their protector, He is in their midst, and He is their God. The earth quakes, sun becomes dark, moon turns blood red, and the stars are diminished just as described under the sixth seal judgment. Hence, the Magog invasion has a better positional fit near mid-Tribulation (within seven months).

END-TIME ALIGNMENT OF NATIONS

(Refer to Prophetic Keys: Revelation 12, 13 and 17, Three Major Military Campaigns, Daniel Military Campaign, Magog Military Campaign, Daniel 7-8, 11, and Ezekiel 38-39)

Ezekiel 38:2-6—Participating Nations in the Magog Invasion

The nations listed as participating in the Gog-Magog invasion described in Ezekiel 38-39 are:

- Magog: Central Asia that would include Kazakhstan, Uzbekistan, Turkmenistan, Tajikistan, Kyrgyzstan, and possibly Afghanistan
- Rosh: Russia
- Meshech and Tubal: Turkey
- Gomer: Turkey
- Togarmah: Turkey and Armenia
- Persia: Iran
- Ethiopia (Cush): Ethiopia and possibly Sudan and/or Somalia
- Libya (Put): Libya and possibly Algeria, Tunisia, and/or Morocco

Ezekiel 38:13—Non-Participating Nations in the Magog Invasion

Nations not in the invasion but listed as commenting or

questioning the invasion:

- Sheba and Dedan: Arabian Peninsula that could include Saudi Arabia, Yemen, Oman, United Arab Emirates, Qatar, and/or Bahrain

- Tarshish: Spain or England and possibly Canada and the United States as the "young lions"

Daniel 8:8, 22—Divisions of the Grecian Empire

Upon his death, the empire of Alexander the Great was divided amongst his four generals:

- Cassander: Macedonia and Greece

- Ptolemy: Egypt and Palestine

- Seleucus: Syria and Babylonia

- Lysimachus: Thrace and Turkey

Daniel 11:40-43—King of the North and King of the South

Kings of the North and South attack the Antichrist during the first half of the Tribulation but are defeated by him:

- King of the North: Syria (could include a coalition of nations)

- King of the South: Egypt (could include a coalition of nations)

- Edom, Moab, and Ammon: Jordan—countries not conquered by the Antichrist

- Lybia and Ethiopia: Follow after the Antichrist but not brought into this battle

Revelation 12:3, 13:1, and 17:3, 9-10, Seven-Headed, Ten-Horned Beasts

The seven heads refer to the seven Gentile world empires that have and will persecute Israel during the times of the Gentiles:

- Egypt, Assyria, Babylon, Medo-Persia, Greece, Rome, and Reconstituted Rome

Daniel 2:40-42, 7:7, 20, 23-24, Revelation 17:12—Ten Toes or Ten Horns

The ten toes on the statue of Daniel 2 and the ten horns on the seven-headed, ten-horned beast of Daniel 7 stand for kings and kingdoms that will comprise the seventh empire to persecute Israel during the time of the Gentiles. The persecution by these ten kings will occur during the first half of the Tribulation. The Roman Empire or fourth empire of Daniel's visions but sixth empire to persecute Israel was divided into two branches as represented by the two legs on the statue. Scholars speculate that the countries comprising the Eastern and Western legs of the Reconstituted Roman Empire (seventh empire) could be:

- Western Leg of the Roman Empire (Five Nations): Britain, Germany, France, Spain, and Italy
- Eastern Leg of the Roman Empire (Six Nations): Egypt, Syria, Greece, Turkey, Iran, and Iraq
  (further discussion in the following sections)

Daniel 7:8, 24, 8:9, Isaiah 10:20, 14:4, Micah 5:6—the Little Horn

From the Reconstituted Roman Empire will arise another king (little horn) who is different or not one of the ten kings. The Old Grecian Empire encompassed much of the territory of the Eastern Leg of the Roman Empire. Therefore, according to Daniel 8:9 the Antichrist or the "little horn" will emerge from the territory of the Old Grecian Empire and the Eastern leg of the Roman Empire, which is the reason for assigning six nations to the Eastern leg above. More specifically, the Antichrist will come out of the Seleucid division of the Old Grecian Empire, which supports why he is also called the Assyrian and King of Babylon linking him to both these great ancient empires.

Daniel 7:8, 20, 24, Revelation 17:13—the Antichrist Subdues Three Horns

The Antichrist or 11th horn will subdue three horns or three kingdoms (nations). The remaining seven kingdoms will give their power and authority to the Antichrist and he will become the eighth or Beast Empire that will rule during the second half of the Tribulation Period or Great Tribulation.

Possible End-Time Scenario for the Alignment of Nations

No one can specifically say which nations are going to participate in the major wars during the Tribulation. Scholars are not even agreed as to the timing or placement of these wars on the prophetic timeline. However, daily knowledge is increasing and the pieces of the puzzle are coming together. The following hypothetical scenario is formulated from the scriptural passages cited above when considering the historical and future role and alignment of nations and their interaction and involvement with one another in the Tribulation:

Nations or Coalitions?

One unresolved question is "do some of the nations identified in scripture represent individual nations or coalitions?" Many consider the Kings of the North and South as representing coalitions although the term "King" is used, not "Kings." In Revelation 16, the reference for the nations from the East is the "Kings of the East." However, Daniel 11:41-42 refers to many countries that will be overthrown during this campaign.

Seven Empires

The seven empires to persecute Israel during the time of the Gentiles are: Egypt, Assyria, Babylon, Medo-Persia, Greece, Rome, and finally the Reconstituted Roman Empire that exists during the first half of the Tribulation. The Old Grecian Empire was divided into four sub-empires: Egypt, Syria, Greece, and Turkey. The territories encompassed by these Empires were greater in area than their present day boundaries. The Antichrist will ultimately emerge from one of these divisions, most likely the Seleucid division, since Antiochus, a forerunner of the Antichrist, ruled the Syrian division as the King of the North.

During Antiochus' reign, Ptolemy ruled Egypt as the King of the South. The sixth empire (fourth of the Daniel 2 statue and fourth beast in Daniel 7-8) was Rome. The two legs of the statue in Daniel 2 represented the Western and Eastern divisions of the Roman Empire. The seventh empire or the Reconstituted Roman Empire will consist of ten kings or kingdoms (nations), five from the Western leg and five from the Eastern leg. Because the Antichrist emerges from the Old Grecian Empire, he will then come from the Eastern leg of the Roman Empire. Thus, he will be connected to both the old Roman and Grecian Empires. His linkage to these empires is validated by the fact that he: is a type of Nimrod, the first world dictator from Babylon; is a type of Antiochus who ruled the Seleucid division of the Grecian Empire; and is called the Assyrian and King of Babylon. The Grecian Empire encompassed territory of the prior Persian, Babylonian, and Assyrian Empires, and the Seleucid division of the Grecian Empire also included territories that were part of these ancient empires. The Antichrist is not one of the "ten toes" or "ten horns" (kings or rulers) but is separate from them. Thus, it is the position proposed in this analysis that the Antichrist is from a nation with territorial roots to Assyria, Babylon, and the Seleucid division of the Grecian Empire.

Muslim Nations

Late in the first half of the Tribulation, the King of the North (Syria) and King of the South (Egypt) will attack the Antichrist and be defeated by him. Egypt and Syria could represent coalitions, because Daniel 11:41 states after defeating the Kings of the North and South, the Antichrist will move into Israel and many countries shall be overthrown. Daniel 11:41 indicates that Edom, Moab, and Ammon or the present day nation of Jordan will not be overrun by the Antichrist. From Daniel 11:44, the Antichrist will be troubled by news from the North and East. What could possibly bother the Antichrist from the North and East? The logical answer has to be political and military signals from Magog according to Ezekiel 38-39. A leader called Gog will amass an invasion force from Magog, which is the Russian Islamic nations (Kazakhstan, Uzbekistan, Turkmenistan, Tajikistan, Kyrgyzstan), Rosh (Russia), Meshech (Turkey), Tubal (Turkey), Gomer (Turkey), and Togarmah (Turkey and Armenia). Again ancient Turkey occupied much greater land than present day Turkey, which could include territories in the Balkens and possibly Germany. Iran (Persia), Ethiopia (ancient Cush), and Libya (ancient Put) will be aligned with Gog. Ethiopia could include the neighboring nations of Sudan and Somalia both known as terrorist nations. Libya, another known terrorist nation, could also include North African nations, such as Algeria, Tunisia, and Morocco. Ezekiel 38 continually references additional peoples joining these nations. A survey of North African nations that are predominantly Muslim includes in addition to the above: Mali, Mauritania, Niger, Chad, Eriteria, Sierra Leone, Burkina, and Western Sahara. Additional Muslim Middle East nations would include Iraq, Kuwait, Afghanistan, Lebanon, and Pakistan. Muslim nations not involved in the Gog invasion force would be those on the Arabian Peninsula (Sheba and Dedan): Saudi Arabia and possibly United Arab Emirates, Oman, Yemen, Bahrain, and Qatar. The mention of Tarshish would seem to indicate that European nations and those from North America, such as the United States and Canada will not be participants in this war, and along with Sheba and Dedan will only question the actions of Gog.

Destruction of Gog

The Muslims will seize this opportunity to join with Russia to annihilate Israel and also eliminate the Antichrist who is the emerging world leader that has brokered a covenant with Israel. The Muslim nations want to rule the world as does Russia. Gog's invasion force including allied Muslim nations as identified above will be supernaturally destroyed by God on the mountains of Israel. The destruction of Russia and her Muslim allies will eliminate them as major forces and influence in the world, thereby allowing the Antichrist to take control of the Reconstituted Roman Empire and establish the eighth or Beast Empire.

Eastern and Western Legs of the Roman Empire

The ten nations of the Reconstituted Roman Empire will not be all the nations of the empire but will be the prominent nations. There is no apparent reason at this time not to support Britain, Germany, France, Spain, and Italy as comprising the Western leg of the empire. They are the current leading western nations of the European Union, but this alignment could change in the future as history unfolds. Identification of the Eastern leg nations is more difficult, because there has been significant overlap in territories occupied by these former empires. The candidate list as previously proposed is: Egypt, Syria, Greece, Turkey, Iran, and Iraq. The Antichrist emerges from the territory now occupied by parts of Syria, Iran, Iraq, and possibly Afghanistan and Pakistan. Because the Antichrist has already defeated Egypt and Syria, those nations could be two of the three nations from the Reconstituted Roman Empire that he defeats. Who is the third nation? Turkey and Iran are annihilated in the Gog invasion, which removes them from consideration. As the Antichrist is more closely connected with Iraq than Greece, a logical candidate for the third nation to be defeated by the Antichrist is Greece. Following the defeat of the three nations, the authority and power of the remaining seven nations of the Reconstituted Roman Empire is transferred to the Antichrist.

Problems with the Eastern Leg Alignment

A significant question is raised concerning the alignment of the Eastern leg nations. It is agreed that the suggested nations of Syria, Egypt, Greece, Turkey, Iran, and Iraq are presently the more dominant nations in the region. Egypt's and Syria's defeat by the Antichrist certainly could qualify them to be two of the three conquered nations of the ten horn nations of Reconstituted Rome.

Greece could be the third nation as stated above. Having Turkey included would place the sub-kingdoms of the Old Grecian Empire as four of the five countries of the Eastern leg of the Roman Empire. The problem is that Turkey as well as Iran are destroyed in the Gog invasion. Therefore, their role as dominant Eastern leg nations doesn't appear logical, because they will have little power and authority to give to the Antichrist.

Alternate Possibilities

Another possibility would be to include one or more of the Balken states, such as Bulgaria, Romania, or Yugoslavia as Eastern leg Roman Empire nations. An alternate candidate for one of the nations could be Pakistan, because several of the great ancient empires of Assyria, Babylon, Persia, and Greece had outer boundaries that stretched into present day Pakistan. Therefore, potential alignment of the Eastern leg of the Roman Empire could include the following nations: Egypt, Syria, Greece, and two Balken states or one Balken state and Pakistan. None of these nations are among the Gog invasion force and none are involved in the Daniel 11 Antichrist versus the King of the North and King of the South battle.

Summary

In summary, the prophetic picture is reasonably clear for identification of participants in the Magog and Daniel military campaigns. However, the picture is not as clear in the alignment of nations for the Reconstituted Roman Empire. The nations speculated by some prophecy scholars to comprise the Eastern leg of the Reconstituted Roman Empire don't appear to fit when viewed in the larger panorama that includes the Gog-Magog invasion of Ezekiel 38-39 and the Antichrist's war against the Kings of the North and South as pictured in Daniel 11:40-44. As history unfolds and nations further align in the European Union, this end-time geographic picture of the alignment of nations for the Tribulation Period should come into better focus.

DAY OF THE LORD

What is the day of the Lord?

The day of the Lord is a future period or point in time when God acts in a sovereign manner in the affairs of mankind as He judges sin and unrighteousness, brings Israel to repentance, puts all rebellion under His feet, and establishes His Messianic kingdom.

Does the day of the Lord include the Rapture of the Church?

The answer is "no." According to 2 Thessalonians 2:3-4, the day of the Lord will not come until the falling away or apostasy comes first and the man of sin is revealed, the son of perdition. The apostasy or falling away is interpreted, depending on application of the Greek language, as either a back sliding of believers before the Antichrist is revealed or the departure of the Church at the Rapture. The latter position is supported by many Greek scholars (refer to *Wuest's Word Studies*) and is the primary position adopted in this writing. Therefore, the Church will be removed from the earth at the Rapture before the Tribulation begins, and the Rapture will precede and not be included in the day of the Lord.

However, it is also noted that according to Matthew 24:5, 11-12, many people will be deceived and their love will grow cold. Thus, in the first half of the Tribulation there will be a falling away from the faith or apostasy, especially upon revelation of the Antichrist for he will be perceived as the Messiah. Even though these scriptures reference a time period during the first half of the Tribulation, many scholars believe they are also representative of conditions that will exist before the Tribulation begins or preceding the Rapture. In any case, an apostasy or falling away of believers from the faith in the first half of the Tribulation period will occur, thus satisfying both interpretations of this passage from the Greek language.

The probable scenario will be that after the Rapture of the Church many people who had been ministered the Gospel of Christ and been told about biblical prophecies of the end times will realize that the disappearance of millions of people was in fact the Rapture event and turn toward the Lord. However, due to lack of grounding in the Word, no restraint of sin, persecution by the Harlot religion, and the general belief that the new emerging charismatic leader (the Antichrist) is the Messiah, they will easily be deceived and their love for the Lord and each other will grow cold. This will be the apostasy of 2 Thessalonians 2:3 and Matthew 24:11-12. By contrast, the great multitude saved primarily during the second half of the Tribulation through the ministry of the 144,000 Jewish evangelists and the two witnesses will stand for their faith even to the point of death and martyrdom.

Does the day of the Lord include the first half of the Tribulation?

The position of this text is "no." Many superb prophecy experts place the onset of the day of the Lord at the beginning of the Tribulation Period (Daniel's seventieth week) after the Rapture of the Church, thereby including the events of the first half of the Tribulation as part of the day of the Lord. However, according to 2 Thessalonians 2:4, the man of sin is clearly the Antichrist who is not revealed in his true character or identity as the "Antichrist" until the middle of Daniel's seventieth week when he enters the temple and proclaims himself to be God. Therefore, the day of the Lord cannot begin until mid-Tribulation. Additionally, Malachi 4:5 says Elijah will come before the dreadful day of the Lord, and Elijah returns as one of the two witnesses at the middle of the Tribulation.

Furthermore, if the day of the Lord includes the first half of the Tribulation, and the day of the Lord is associated with the wrath of God, then the first five seal judgments would be part of the day of the Lord and the wrath of God. Seal judgments are judgments controlled by God, as the Living Creatures call them forth onto the scene of history. However, these judgments don't appear to be the wrath of God. If the first five seal judgments are the wrath of God, then God would have to be responsible for the martyrs under the altar, as well as the Antichrist being an agent of His wrath. Throughout history, God has used other peoples or nations to test and try Israel in order to bring her to repentance, but the activities of these nations were not referred to as the wrath of God. The first four seal judgments are the effect of the wrath of Satan, which is unrestrained, since the work of the Church infilled with Holy Spirit as the restrainer of sin was completed at the Rapture of the Church (2 Thessalonians 2:7). Therefore, the day of the Lord does not include the events of the first half of the Tribulation.

Will the day of the Lord include the Millennium?

The answer is "no." Many commentators who begin the day of the Lord before or at the Rapture of the Church or at the beginning of the Tribulation, and include the seven-year Tribulation Period, the battle of Armageddon, and the Second Coming of Christ, also seem to include the Millennium, which is a time of blessing, as part of the day of the Lord. Biblically, a time of blessing has followed judgment. However, the day of the Lord scriptures do not disclose or reveal a time of blessing. Additionally, the day of the Lord is said to come as a thief in the night, but there is no need or scriptural support for the Lord appearing after the Millennium as a thief in the night, especially when He has been ruling the earth for the past 1000 years.

The key verses used for including the Millennium in the day of the Lord are 2 Peter 3:4-7, 9-10, and 12, which state *"the heavens and*

earth which now exist are...reserved for fire until the day of judgment and
perdition of ungodly men...the day of the Lord will come as a thief in the
night in which the heavens will pass away...and the elements will melt with
fervent heat; both the earth and the works that are in it will be burned
up...the heavens will be dissolved being on fire, and the elements will melt
with fervent heat...look for new heavens and a new earth..." Because such
commentators place the events described in this passage after the
Millennium or 1000 years of blessing, they must include the
Millennium in the day of he Lord. However, based on an analysis
of the day of the Lord scriptures, Old Testament scriptures on
destruction by fire at the Second Coming of Christ, the seventh
bowl judgment and battle of Armageddon scriptures, all support
and are in alignment with 2 Peter 3 as stated above. Under the seventh bowl judgment, the cities of the world are destroyed, every
island disappears, mountains disappear, Jerusalem is divided into
three parts, Babylon is utterly burned by fire as judgment from
God, the Mount of Olives is split in two, those who take the mark
of the Beast are tormented with fire and brimstone, and Jesus is
revealed from heaven with His angels in flaming fire. Hence, the
events, as described in 2 Peter 3 above, occur before the
Millennium, not after. Therefore, the conclusion is that the day of
the Lord will not include the Millennium and must conclude at
the Second Coming of Christ.

Are cosmic disturbances and God's wrath connected with the day of the Lord?

The answer is "yes." Multiple Old Testament scriptures describe
the day of the Lord as a time of cosmic disturbance and a time
when God pours out His wrath in judgment on a sinful and unbelieving world. According to Revelation 6:12-17, the earth will be
subject to cosmic disturbances as never before experienced by
mankind, and these events are called the great day of His wrath.

Is the day of the Lord a time period or a single day?

This is a very interesting question with no definitive answer. If the day of the Lord is a time period as most scholars profess, then the day of the Lord would commence when God pours out His wrath at the sixth seal judgment at mid-Tribulation and conclude with the Second Coming of Christ at the battle of Armageddon. This position has been supported by the above analysis and is the one adopted in this study. However, upon close examination of the scriptures, one could also conclude that the day of the Lord is the actual day when Christ returns at His Second Coming and not a period of time. Consider how the following events can be satisfied by the day of the Lord representing one single day:

- The Church is not subject to wrath and is raptured before the day of the Lord (pre-Tribulation).

- The Church will not be in darkness because it will be raptured before the Tribulation Period begins (pre-Tribulation).

- Peace and safety will exist for Israel for 3 1/2 years because of the seven-year covenant entered into with the Antichrist (first half of the Tribulation).

- The Antichrist is revealed in his true identity as a false-Christ before the day of the Lord (mid-Tribulation).

- Elijah will return as one of the two witnesses before the day of the Lord (mid-Tribulation).

- Cataclysmic events affect the earth, such as an earthquake, sun darkened, moon as blood, sky receding, mountains and islands moving out of position before the day of the Lord (mid-Tribulation).

- People in the world expect peace and safety under the leadership of the Antichrist but sudden and unavoidable destruction comes as labor pains come to a pregnant woman before birth (second half of the Tribulation to the end of the Tribulation).

- Cataclysmic events, such as an earthquake, darkness, shifting of land areas from their position, elements melting, etc. affect the earth as the Lord comes as a thief in the night (end of the Tribulation).

- As the armies of the world are gathered with the Antichrist in the valley of Megiddo for the battle of Armageddon, the day of the Lord will come as a thief in the night and overtake those in darkness. As a note, the world will be in darkness from effects of the fifth bowl judgment and the remaining effects from the second trumpet judgment and the sixth seal judgment (end of the Tribulation).

- Jesus returns as a thief in the night (end of the Tribulation).

- Jesus returns at His Second Coming as King of kings and Lord of lords and will shake the earth at the day of the Lord (end of the Tribulation).

- The ungodly are punished at the day of the Lord (end of the Tribulation).

In summary, the day of the Lord is the wrath of God, and the wrath of God begins with the sixth seal judgment at mid-Tribulation and continues through the Great Tribulation and Second Coming of Christ. This period would be extended to include God's wrath displayed by the seventh Trumpet judgment and ensuing bowl judgments, if the position is adopted that these judgments occur during the 30-day period following the 42-month Great Tribulation as has been proposed in this study. This outpouring of God's wrath is called the great day of His wrath. Therefore, if the day of the Lord is a period of time as most Bible teachers claim, then the length of the day of the Lord will be approximately 42-43 months following the Abomination of Desolation. As demonstrated above, the day of the Lord will not include the Rapture, first half of the Tribulation, or the Millennium. However, it must noted, an equally strong and convincing argument can be made that the day of the Lord is actually a 24-hour solar day when Christ returns at His Second Coming at the end of the seven year Tribulation (or end of the 30-days following the Great Tribulation). Either position is supportable by day of the Lord scriptures as listed below.

Scriptures - day of the Lord (also Cosmic Disturbances)

2 Thessalonians 2:2-4

...day of Christ (Lord)...for that Day will not come unless the apostasy comes first, and the man of sin is revealed, the son of perdition, who opposes and exalts himself above all that is called God...so that he sits as God in the temple of God, showing himself to be God.

I Thessalonians 5:2-4

For you yourselves know perfectly that the day of the Lord comes as a thief in the night...for when they say peace and safety then sudden destruction comes upon them as labor pains....but you brethren are not in darkness so that this Day should overtake you as a thief.

2 Peter 3:7, 9-13

...the heavens and earth which now exist are...reserved for fire until the day of judgment and perdition of ungodly men...the day of the Lord will come as a thief in the night in which the heavens will pass away...and the elements will melt with fervent heat; both the earth and the works that are in it will be burned up...the heavens will be dissolved being on fire, and the elements will melt with fervent heat...look for new heavens and a new earth...

Malachi 4:5

Behold I send you Elijah the prophet before the coming of the great and dreadful day of the Lord.

Isaiah 2:12-21

For the day of the Lord of hosts...the Lord alone will be exalted in that day but the idols He shall utterly abolish. They shall go into the holes of the rocks and into the caves of the earth, from the terror of the Lord and the glory of His majesty when He arises to shake the earth mightily...

Isaiah 13:5-13

...from the end of heaven—the Lord and His weapons of indignation to

destroy the whole land. Wail, for the day of the Lord is at hand! It will come as a destruction from the Almighty...the day of the Lord comes, cruel, with both wrath and fierce anger...He will destroy its sinners...for the stars of heaven and their constellations will not give their light; the sun will be darkened in its going forth, and the moon will not cause its light to shine...I will shake the heavens, and the earth will move out of her place, in the wrath of the Lord of hosts and in the day of His fierce anger.

Isaiah 24:19-21

The earth is violently broken, the earth is split open, the earth is shaken exceedingly. The earth shall reel to and fro like a drunkard, and shall totter like a hut; ...It shall come to pass in that day that the Lord will punish on high the host of the exalted ones, and on earth the kings of the earth.

Isaiah 34:1-8

...And the mountains shall be melted with their blood. All the host of heaven shall be dissolved, and the heavens shall be rolled up like a scroll...for it is the day of the Lord's vengeance...

Joel 1:15

Alas, for the day of the Lord is at hand; it shall come as destruction from the Almighty.

Joel 2:1-2

Blow the trumpet in Zion, and sound the alarm in My holy mountain! Let all the inhabitants of the land tremble; for the day of the Lord is coming...a day of darkness and gloominess, a day of clouds and thick darkness...

Joel 2:10-11

The earth quakes before them, the heavens tremble; the sun and moon grow dark, and the stars diminish their brightness...for the day of the Lord is great and very terrible; who can endure it?

Joel 2:30-31

And I will show wonders in the heavens and in the earth; blood and fire and pillars of smoke. The sun shall be turned into darkness, and the moon into blood, before the coming of the great and terrible day of the Lord.

Joel 3:14-16

...for the day of the Lord is near in the valley of decision. The sun and moon will grow dark, and the stars will diminish their brightness...the heavens and earth will shake...

Amos 5:18-20

Woe to you who desire the day of the Lord! For what good is the day of the Lord to you? It will be darkness, and not light...is not the day of the Lord darkness, and not light? Is it not very dark, with no brightness in it?

Obadiah 15

For the day of the Lord upon all nations is near;

Zephaniah 1:7-9

...for the day of the Lord is at hand...in the day of the Lord's sacrifice, that I will punish the princes and the king's children...

Zephaniah 1:14-18

The great day of the Lord is near...that day is a day of wrath, a day of trouble and distress, a day of devastation and desolation, a day of darkness and gloominess, a day of clouds and thick darkness...I will bring distress upon men...because they have sinned against the Lord; their blood shall be poured out like dust, and their flesh like refuse...in the day of the Lord's wrath; but the whole land shall be devoured by the fire of His jealousy...

Zephaniah 2:2-3

...before the Lord's fierce anger comes upon you, before the day of the Lord's anger comes upon you...

Zechariah 14:1-9

Behold, the day of the Lord is coming...for I will gather all nations to battle *against Jerusalem; the city shall be taken, the houses rifled, and the women ravished. Half the city shall go into captivity, but the remnant of the people shall not be cut off from the city...then the Lord will go forth and fight against those nations...and in that day His feet will stand on the Mount of Olives...and the Mount of Olives shall be split in two...thus, the Lord will come, and all the saints with Him...and the Lord shall be king over all the earth...*

Acts 2:19-20

I will show wonders in heaven above and signs in the earth beneath: blood and fire and vapor of smoke. The sun shall be turned into darkness, and the moon into blood, before the coming of the great and notable day of the Lord...

Scriptures supporting the destruction of the earth by fire at the Second Coming of Christ with a subsequent renovation of the earth at the beginning of the Millennium:

Scriptures - Destruction by Fire at the Second Coming (compare with 2 Peter 3:4-7, 9-10, 12)

Isaiah 66:15-16

For behold, the Lord will come with fire and with His chariots, like a whirlwind, to render His anger with fury, and His rebuke with flames of fire. For by fire and by His sword the Lord will judge all flesh; and the slain of the Lord shall be many.

Amos 9:5

The Lord God of hosts, He who touches the earth and it melts.

Micah 1:3-4

For behold, the Lord is coming out of His place...the mountains will melt under Him, and the valleys will split like wax before the fire...

Nahum 1:5-6

The mountains quake before Him, the hills melt, and the earth heaves at

His presence...His fury is poured out like fire, and the rocks are thrown down by Him.

Psalm 46:6

The nations raged, the kingdoms were moved; He uttered His voice, the earth melted.

Psalm 97:3-5

A fire goes before Him, and burns up His enemies round about. His lightnings light the world; the earth sees and trembles. The mountains melt like wax at the presence of the Lord...

Scripture - New Heavens and New Earth (in addition to 2 Peter 3:4-7, 9-10, 12, Revelation 21:1)

Isaiah 65:17-25

For behold, I create a new heavens and a new earth; and the former shall not be remembered or come to mind...I create Jerusalem...I will rejoice in Jerusalem...no more shall and infant from there live but a few days...for the child shall die one hundred years old...the wolf and the lamb shall feed together...they shall not hurt nor destroy in all My holy mountain...(Note: refer to Prophetic Key: Renovation of Heaven and Earth for a complete discussion of the creation of the new heavens and a new earth).

200 MILLION HORSEMEN ARMY OF REVELATION 9:16

Revelation 9:14-19-Then the sixth angel sounded: And I heard a voice from the four horns of the golden altar which is before God, saying to the sixth angel who had the trumpet, "Release the four angels who are bound at the great river Euphrates." So the four angels, who had been prepared for the hour and day and month and year, were released to kill a third of mankind. Now the number of the army of horsemen was two hundred million, and I heard the number of them. And thus I saw the horses in the vision: those who sat on them had breastplates of fiery red, hyacinth blue, and sulfur yellow; and the heads of the horses were like the heads of lions; and out of their mouths came fire, smoke, and brimstone. By these three plagues a third of mankind was killed—by the fire and the smoke and the brimstone which came out of their mouths. For their power is in their mouth and in their tails; for their tails are like serpents, having heads; and with them they do harm.

Position 1-Million Chinese Army

Many great prophecy scholars believe the 200 million horsemen are an actual army of Chinese horse soldiers. They feel this army is Chinese, since China has boasted that she could field an army of 200 million and is the only country on the planet that could do so. Additionally, this scripture is connected with Revelation 16:12 that identifies, under the sixth bowl judgment, the drying up of the great river Euphrates in order to prepare the way for the Kings from the East. In summary, their position is that at the battle of Armageddon at the end of the Tribulation, an army of 200 million soldiers from Asia will march into the Holy Land to assist the Antichrist in the destruction of Israel and subsequently, to battle against Christ for possession of the world.

Position 2-200 Million Demon Army

An alternate and preferred position is that the 200 million horsemen are not actual human beings, Chinese or otherwise, but an army of demons, and that the events of Revelation 9:16 and Revelation 16:12 are two separate and distinct events. The description of the army in Revelation 9:17-19 is non-human and demonic. These demon soldiers are led by the four angels bound at the great river Euphrates. These four angels are fallen angels and have been bound in the abyss to be released at this very time in history. Each fallen angel is to lead an army of 50 million demons. If the leaders of this army are fallen angels out of the abyss, then it stands to reason that the army itself is demonic. Additionally, the plagues used to destroy one-third of mankind are elements of hell, i.e., fire, smoke, and brimstone. Furthermore, to link the 200 million army to Armageddon pulls this passage out of context, thereby, disrupting the chronological order of judgments. The 200 million demon army is loosed under the sixth trumpet judgment in the second half of the Tribulation. The Armageddon conflict occurs under the seventh bowl judgment, near the end of the 30-day period following the seven-year Tribulation. Finally, "east" in scripture doesn't refer exclusively to the Orient, but typically refers to Middle Eastern regions, east of the Euphrates. The drying up of the Euphrates allows Middle Eastern nations as well as Asian nations to enter into Israel for the final conflict of the age.

PROPHETIC KEY FIFTEEN

MALE CHILD

(Refer to Revelation 12:5)

Male Child-Jesus

The woman brings forth a "male child" who is to rule all nations with a rod of iron. Jesus is considered the male child by most commentators. The child is "caught up" to God and His throne, which is a reference to the ascension. Caught up refers to a forceful event, a snatching away as in the Rapture of the Church. At His ascension, Jesus was taken up as the apostles watched. This was not a forceful, dynamic event. If Jesus is the male child as many scholars suggest, and caught up refers to His ascension, then this backward look causes the time line to be out of sync for these are signs occurring during the Tribulation Period.

Male Child-144,000 Jewish Witnesses

The position adopted in this book is that the male child stands for the 144,000 Jewish witnesses of Revelation 7 for the following reasons:

- The woman is Jewish, and the male child is Jewish, 12,000 from each of the twelve tribes of Israel.
- The woman represents a company of people, and the male child represents a smaller company.
- The male child or 144,000 Jews is a sub-set of the woman and is birthed from the woman.
- The 144,000 Jews are on earth and sealed by God in chapter

7, and then in chapter 14, they are seen in heaven. How did they get there? The only logical answer is that they are raptured or caught up as stated in Revelation 12:5.

- The 144,000 Jews are sealed for protection through the trumpet judgments and are in heaven when the bowl judgments are poured out on the earth.

- There is no indication that any of the 144,000 Jews are killed or martyred. Again the only conclusion is that they are raptured after the trumpet judgments.

- Revelation 14:3 says that the 144,000 Jews are redeemed from the earth. Therefore, they are in heaven and no longer on the earth.

- Revelation 14:4 says the 144,000 Jews are the first fruits unto God as they are the first Jews saved after the Rapture of the Church during the first half of the Tribulation.

- The 144,000 Jews enter the prophetic picture as a group at mid-Tribulation after the sixth seal judgment.

- The Antichrist and Satan want to devour the 144,000 Jews, but they can't because the 144,000 Jews are sealed and protected by God through the trumpet judgments.

- Because the Antichrist can't harm the 144,000 Jews, Satan turns his wrath on the woman.

- According to Isaiah 66:7-8, the male child is brought forth before Israel is saved as a nation, which occurs at the Second Coming of Christ at the end of the age. The 144,000 Jews fulfill this scripture. The bringing forth of the male child occurs at mid-Tribulation, and the catching away of the male child occurs at the end of the trumpet judgments and before the battle of Armageddon and the return of Christ.

Placement of Trumpet Judgments

Several commentators who support this interpretation of the male child representing the 144,000 place the trumpet judgments

in the first half of the Tribulation, and the rapture of the
144,000 Jews at mid-Tribulation, which could fit a chapter 12
timeline.   However, emergence of the 144,000 Jews at mid-
Tribulation and their subsequent rapture after the trumpet
judgments at the end of Daniel's seventieth week is a better timeline fit. The seal judgments that occur during the first half of
the Tribulation are the beginning of sorrows according to
Matthew 24:8.   The sixth seal judgment occurs at mid-
Tribulation as the beginning of the day of the Lord. The greater
devastation to the planet is in the second half of the Tribulation
Period, referred to as the "Great Tribulation." It is therefore,
more fitting to place the trumpet judgments in the second half
of the Tribulation. However, the position of the trumpet judgments on the prophetic timeline isn't crucial to supporting the
144,000 Jews as the male child. Additionally, the male child's
"ruling with a rod of iron" can aptly apply to the 144,000 Jews in
the sense that the believer will rule and reign with Christ in the
Millennium, and therefore, will rule with a rod of iron. The
overall support for the male child as the 144,000 out weighs the
support for Christ as the male child.

PROPHETIC KEY SIXTEEN

BEASTS - SEVEN HEADS AND TEN HORNS

Three seven headed, ten horned beasts are described in the Book of Revelation:

Revelation 12:3- Great, Fiery Red Dragon

The Dragon is another name for Satan. He is shown with seven heads and ten horns and seven diadems or crowns on his heads. Heads stand for world empires and crowns represent authority. The seven heads that are crowned signify that Satan has had or will have authority over the seven kingdoms or world empires that have persecuted and will persecute Israel during the times of the Gentiles.

Revelation 13:1-Beast Out of the Sea

The Beast out of the sea represents the Antichrist who comes to power from the sea of humanity. The horns, not heads, are crowned on this Beast signifying that the Antichrist gains power and authority over the ten kings or kingdoms that constitute the seventh head or world empire. The Antichrist conquers three of the ten kings and the remaining seven give their power or authority over to him. This action occurs at the middle of the Tribulation Period.

Revelation 17:3-Woman Sitting on a Scarlet Beast

This seven headed, ten horned beast stands for the amalgamation of all pagan religions that have existed through the ages and that will dominate the ten kings during the first half of the Tribulation. Neither the heads nor horns are crowned, indicating that this religious system has no direct authority over any of the world empires or kings of the seventh empire. A false satanically inspired religious system has influenced and dominated the first six empires and will strongly influence and dominate the seventh empire during the first half of the Tribulation. This religious system is hated by the ten kings and will be destroyed by them. The kings give their power to the Antichrist who is called the "Beast" and his Beast kingdom will be the eighth and last Gentile kingdom to persecute Israel.

Seven Heads or Kingdoms / Empires

1. Egypt
2. Assyria
3. Babylon
4. Medo-Persia
5. Greece
6. Rome
7. Reconstituted Rome (ten horns)-this kingdom occupies the territories of the old Roman Empire but is considered reconstituted, because there will be ten kings instead of one ruler or Caesar.

Eighth Empire

This empire will be ruled by the Antichrist, and according to the Book of Daniel, will actually be a revival of the Old Grecian Empire within the Reconstituted Roman Empire. The satanic prince that empowered and controlled Alexander the Great is considered by many expositors to be the beast out of the abyss of Revelation 11:7 that will control, empower, and possess, or oppress the Antichrist. Other possible identities for this satanic prince are the Prince of Babylon or Prince of Assyria, for the Antichrist will have a connection to all three prior kingdoms.

RELIGIOUS AND LITERAL BABYLON

(Refer to Revelation 17-18)

Similarities between religious and literal Babylon:

1) They both commit fornication with the kings.

2) They both shed the blood of the saints.

3) They both are made desolate.

4) They both are clothed in scarlet, purple, and precious stones.

Differences between religious and literal Babylon:

1) Revelation 18:1 states "after these things," referring to the events of chapter 18 that occur after the fulfillment of the bowl judgments of Revelation 16. Discussion of Mystery Babylon (Revelation 17) is parenthetical, inserted after the seventh bowl judgment (Revelation 16) but describing conditions existing during the first half of the Tribulation period, prior to both the trumpet and bowl judgments.

2) John is shown the destruction of Mystery Babylon by a bowl angel. "Another" or different bowl angel shows the destruction of literal Babylon.

3) Their names are different. One is Mystery Babylon the Great, Mother of Harlots and of the Abominations of the Earth while the other is merely Babylon the Great. One is a

mystery to John and the other is not. Mystery Babylon is explained to John in chapter 17, but John did not require explanation of literal Babylon.

4) The ten kings (Revelation 17:16) destroy Mystery Babylon while God destroys the literal city of Babylon (Revelation 18:19). One is destroyed by man and the other by God.

5) The ten kings rejoice over the destruction of Mystery Babylon but will lament over the destruction of the city of Babylon.

6) Mystery Babylon is destroyed in the middle of the Tribulation, but literal Babylon will be destroyed under the seventh bowl at the end of the Tribulation.

7) Mystery Babylon rides the beast where literal Babylon does not.

Babylon does not refer to Rome or some other existing city but will be a literal city rebuilt in the last days:

- The city of Babylon is the subject of Revelation 16:19 and Revelation 18.

- The great Harlot is called Mystery Babylon showing a connection with Babylon. "Mystery" defines the religious aspects of the literal city of Babylon.

- In the Bible, cities have not been renamed to identify other cities. If a city is mentioned, then all discussion pertains to that city, e.g., Tyre, Sidon, Jerusalem, Sodom, Gomorrah, etc. Why should it be different for Babylon? It is not.

- In scripture, literal Babylon is always associated with demonic religions, idolatry, occult, witchcraft, and paganism dating back to ancient Babylon.

- Babylon is the headquarters for every demon and unclean spirit (Revelation 18:2).

- Babylon is the only city named for making the nations drunk with the wine of her fornication (Revelation 18:3).

- Babylon is the only city mentioned in the last days to be the center for sorceries and enchantments (Revelation 18:23).

- Babylon is the object of God's wrath and plagues (Revelation 16:19; 18:4, 6).

- Babylon is the only city God commands his people to come out of in the last days (Revelation 18:4).

- Many prophecies about the destruction of Babylon remain unfulfilled.

- Isaiah 13-14 and Jeremiah 50-51 describe the destruction of the city of Babylon at the time of the day of the Lord.

- Jeremiah 51:26 says Babylon is to be desolate forever and no stone is to be used for a foundation of another city. This prophecy is unfulfilled. Six cities have used part of ancient Babylon in their building. When God destroys Babylon under the seventh bowl judgment, no part of the city will be used in the building of another city.

- Jeremiah 51:8 and Isaiah 13:19 state that Babylon is suddenly fallen and destroyed. Ancient Babylon was not destroyed in that manner, but the rebuilt city of Babylon will be destroyed in one hour and will not be found any longer, as the cities of Sodom and Gomorrah.

- Isaiah 13:20 says the ruins of Babylon are never to be inhabited and according to history that prophecy is yet unfulfilled.

 PROPHETIC KEY EIGHTEEN

CONDITIONS ON EARTH AT ARMAGEDDON

At the end of the age, the last battle for possession of planet earth is Armageddon. The Antichrist's forces from around the globe are marshaled outside Jerusalem in preparation to destroy Israel. The earth's population has been substantially reduced through seven years of devastation from war, famine, pestilence and the seal, trumpet, and bowl judgments of God. The situation and conditions on earth at Armageddon are as follows:

- An innumerable number of Christians, saved after the Rapture of the Church, has been martyred for their faith by having their heads chopped off with an axe. Also, many others have been killed by the natural and cosmic disasters unleashed on the planet through the judgments of God.

- Israel has fled to the rock-fortified city of Petra and to the wilderness nations. A remnant remains in Jerusalem. Only one-third of the nation of Israel will survive the Tribulation.

- The 144,000 Jewish witnesses were raptured as the male child after the Trumpet judgments.

- The two witnesses from God smote the earth with plagues, including prohibiting rain during their ministry and turning water into blood. Fire proceeds from their mouths killing those who attempt to harm them. They are killed by the beast out of the abyss but subsequently resurrected by God.

- Followers of the Antichrist have taken the mark of the Beast.

- Angels have been preaching the Gospel and warning the inhabitants of the earth to fear God and give Him glory for the hour of His judgment has arrived.

- The one-world harlot religion has been destroyed and replaced with worship of the Antichrist after he entered the temple and proclaimed himself to be God.

- Wars have been fought continuously throughout the Tribulation.

- The Antichrist has defeated the armies of the Kings of the North and South.

- The armies, from the Russian territories (Magog) and Middle East Muslim nations, led by Gog to plunder Israel were destroyed by God on the mountains of Israel.

- War, famine, pestilence, and disease are of epidemic and pandemic proportions, resulting in the death of one-fourth of mankind. These conditions exist throughout the Tribulation Period.

- Hail and fire mingled with blood destroyed one-third of all grass, trees, and agricultural products.

- A volcano (burning mountain) was cast into the sea turning the sea to blood and destroying one-third sea life and one-third of all ships. Later all seas became blood.

- A meteor fell to earth, contaminating a third of the rivers resulting in many deaths. Later all rivers turned to blood. The meteor impact produced earthquakes and tsunamis.

- A shortage of food products and water has existed throughout the Tribulation.

- A great earthquake struck the earth, the sun became black, the moon red as blood, stars (meteorites) fell from heaven, the sky receded, and every mountain and island were shifted in position.

- Demon locusts were released from the bottomless pit and for five months tormented men without the seal of God. Their sting was that of a scorpion and men wished to die, but could not.

- 200 million demon horsemen led by four fallen angels killed one-third of mankind, bringing earth's death toll to over 2 1/2 billion or half of earth's population (population projection for the year 2000) following the Rapture.

- Cancerous sores have erupted on those who display the mark of the Beast.

- The sun became so hot that it literally scorched men with fire.

- Absolute darkness engulfed the kingdom of the Beast, and men gnawed their tongues in pain.

- The great river Euphrates has dried up to allow passage for the Kings of the East into Israel.

- The great city Babylon has been destroyed.

- A tenth of Jerusalem has fallen under another great earthquake with seven thousand men killed.

- Noises, thunderings, lightnings are heard and a great and mighty earthquake, more destructive than any felt previously, has struck the earth.

- Jerusalem is divided into three parts and the cities of the world crumble.

- Mountains and islands are being moved or destroyed and hailstones weighing over 100 pounds are falling from heaven.

- The unrighteous refuse to repent and blaspheme God throughout the Tribulation Period.

ARMAGEDDON

**(Refer to Prophetic Keys:
Three Major Military Campaigns,
Daniel Military Campaign, and Magog Military Campaign)**

Wine press of the Wrath of God

The final battle before the establishment of the millennial kingdom ruled by Jesus Christ is called the battle of Armageddon. Actually, Armageddon refers not only to the battle to be fought but the location where the battle is fought, the mountain of Megiddo. Armageddon is a Greek word derived from the Hebrew words, "Har" meaning mountain and "Megiddo," a city in Israel.

- Revelation 14:19-20 refers to this battle as the great wine press of the wrath of God that is trampled outside the city of Jerusalem.

- Revelation 16:12-16 states the kings of the earth are lured to a place called in the Hebrew, Armageddon, for the battle of that great day of God Almighty.

- Revelation 19:15 says that Jesus treads the wine press of the fierceness and wrath of Almighty God.

This battle is likened to the squashing of grapes in a wine press where the juice from the grapes is scattered everywhere, as the blood of fallen soldiers will be scattered everywhere at Armageddon.

Geographic Locations of Military Campaigns in Israel

Geographically, the Valley of Esdraelon is a plain measuring 14 by 20 miles around Mount Megiddo in northern Israel, approximately 50 miles from Jerusalem. This valley is also known as the Valley of Jezreel or the plains of Megiddo. This valley or plain of Esdraelon will serve as the gathering region for the armies of the Antichrist. Many great battles have been fought in this area throughout history. Because this area is too small for all the military forces of the world to congregate, the armies, estimated to be at least 400 million strong, will be gathered throughout the Holy Land for a span of 200 miles north to south and 100 miles east to west. Additionally, there will be battles in the Valley of Jehoshaphat near Jerusalem, according to Joel 3:2, 9-12 and in Bozrah or Edom (Isaiah 34:5-10, Isaiah 63:1-6). The Valley of Jehoshaphat means the valley of God's judgment.

Destruction of the Armies of the Antichrist

Many scholars view Armageddon not as a single battle, but as a war or series of battles throughout the 20,000-square mile area of Israel. The nations of the world gather at Armageddon on the plains of Megiddo to initially join the Antichrist in his attempt to totally destroy Israel and eliminate her from the face of the earth. As Christ appears in the heavens, these armies turn their forces against Him in an effort to halt His Second Coming. Christ returns with His heavenly army consisting of the angelic host and raptured saints, but Christ's army has no weapons and will not fire any shots. The armies of the world will be annihilated by:

- The brightness of His Coming (2 Thessalonians 2:8)
- Plague (Zechariah 14:12)
- Panic (Zechariah 14:13)
- Sharp sword out of His mouth (Revelation 19:15)

Armageddon Campaign

Scholars are in general agreement as to the events that will take place in the Armageddon campaign and return of Christ. However, the order of events is open to conjecture. The following scenario appears to have the greatest support:

- The Antichrist's kingdom (throne of the Beast) is in utter darkness as a result of the fifth bowl judgment. The sixth bowl judgment dries up the river Euphrates, opening a way for the kings from the East to march into Israel. Christ streaks across the heavens as lightening, which is one way that "every eye will see Him." Christ appears at Bozrah and liberates the remnant. The armies of the nations gathered throughout Israel unite in an attempt to destroy Christ and His armies but are themselves destroyed. In his final attempt, the Antichrist invades Jerusalem and ravishes the city. Christ descends to the Mount of Olives, and as His feet touch down on the Mount, it cleaves in two. The armies of the Antichrist are destroyed in the Valley of Jehoshaphat outside Jerusalem.

Bozrah

The general consensus among scholars is that Jesus goes first to the ancient city of Bozrah, now known as the rock-fortified city of Petra located in Edom or present day Jordan. There are two reasons why Jesus goes to Bozrah:

1. Before Christ returns, the Jews must acknowledge their offense and seek His face, i.e., accept Jesus as Messiah and ask Him to free them. The Jews at Petra go through a period of national mourning.

   Hosea 5:15-6:2- *"I will return to My place till they acknowledge their offense. Then they will seek My face; in their affliction they will diligently seek Me. Come and let us return to the Lord; for He has torn, but He will heal us; He has stricken, but He will bind us up. After two days He will revive us; on the third day He will raise us up, that we may live in His sight."*

2. When Jesus leaves Petra, His robe has the blood of His enemies on it.

Isaiah 63:1-4- *"Who is this who comes from Edom, with dyed garments from Bozrah, this One who is glorious in His apparel, traveling in the greatness of His strength? I who speak in righteousness, mighty to save. Why is your apparel red, and Your garments like one who treads the wine press? I have trodden the wine press alone, and from the peoples no one was with Me. For I have trodden them in My anger, and trampled them in My fury; their blood is sprinkled upon My garments, and I have stained all My robes. For the day of My vengeance is in My heart, and the year of My redeemed has come..."*

Revelation 19:13- *"He was clothed with a robe dipped in blood, and His name is called The Word of God."*

Bozrah means sheepfold, and Petra with its high rock walls and narrow passageways is laid out as a giant sheepfold. Jesus liberates the Jewish remnant that has been protected by God for three and one-half years. Jordan is the only nation in the Middle East arena to escape direct control of the Antichrist.

Event Chronology at Armageddon

Scripture	Event
Rev 16:10-11	5th bowl judgment: the throne or kingdom of the Beast is in total darkness
Rev 16:12	6th Bowl Judgment: drying of the Euphrates to clear the way for the Kings from the East from Iraq to Asia (China, Japan, Korea, India, Pakistan, etc.)
Rev 16:17-21	7th Bowl Judgment: earthquake greater than any previous earthquake in the history of man; Jerusalem divided into three parts; cities of the nations crumble; islands removed; mountains leveled; and plague of hail with weights exceeding 100 pounds
Rev 18:10, 19 Is 13; Jer 50-51	Babylon, the great city, destroyed in one hour; complete and total destruction
Rev 16:16	Armies of the nations of the world gather on the plains of Megiddo or Armageddon to destroy Israel
Rev 19:11-14	Second Coming of Christ with angelic host and glorified saints
Zech 12:10, Rev 1:7, Hosea 5:15, 6:1-3	Israel repents; Israel realizes that Jesus who they crucified is the Messiah they have been waiting for
Is 34:5-10, Is 63:1-6, Micah 2:12	Christ rescues the remnant of Israel from Petra (Bozrah) in Jordan (Edom)
Rev 19:19	Armies of the Antichrist and the world make war against Christ and His armies
Zech 14:3, 12-13	Armies of nations destroyed throughout a 20,000 square mile area of Israel from Petra in the south to Mount Megiddo in the north (winepress of the wrath of God)
Zech 14:1-2	The Antichrist attacks Jerusalem; city captured; houses rifled; women ravished; half the city in captivity
Zech 13:7-9	Two-thirds of the Jews are killed
Zech 14:4	Christ stands on the Mount of Olives and the mountain divides in two
Joel 3:2, 9-17, Zech 12:1-9	Armies of the Antichrist destroyed in the Valley of Jehoshaphat outside Jerusalem
Rev 19:15, 17 Rev 14:14-20	Blood of the fallen soldiers from the battle (great winepress of the wrath of God) up to horses' bridles (literally everywhere) throughout the 184 mile stretch of land; birds feed on the flesh of these soldiers (supper of the great God)
Rev 19:20	The Antichrist and the False Prophet are cast alive into the lake of fire

MARRIAGE SUPPER OF THE LAMB

(Refer to Revelation 19:7-10)

Marriage Ceremony and Marriage Supper of the Lamb

Bible scholars differ on the interpretation of the marriage of the Lamb. Questions surround the location of the marriage ceremony and marriage supper and the various role participants. The best way to approach an analysis of this passage is to compare the marriage of the Lamb with the steps in an Eastern wedding:

- The fathers of the bride and bridegroom arrange the marriage in what is referred to as "betrothal." This step involves the selection of a wife and payment of a dowry. At this point a divorce decree is required in order for the couple to separate. This arrangement stage may last for a period of time prior to consummation of the marriage.

- The bridegroom prepares a house for his wife attached to his father's house.

- At the father's direction, the son or bridegroom brings his wife to their new house, at which time a private marriage ceremony is conducted.

- A wedding feast is held where friends are invited to honor the couple and celebrate the wedding.

The bridegroom is Jesus. The wife is the New Testament Church already married to Christ. Christ's substitutionary sacrifice and the shedding of His blood for man's sins is the dowry. Currently, the Church has been in the wedding arrangement stage for almost 2000 years, and during that time, Jesus has been preparing a place for the Church (John 14:1-3). The bridegroom in leaving his father's house, meeting his wife, and bringing her to her new home provides a perfect example of the Rapture of the Church. The Father commands His Son to go and get the Church. The Lord meets the Church in the air and then takes her to heaven for the wedding ceremony, which is a proclamation of Christ receiving the Church to Himself per Ephesians 5:27. The wife is arrayed in fine, clean, and bright linens, which represent the righteous acts of the saints. These acts, as righteous deeds done in the flesh, will be evaluated at the judgment seat of Christ, which takes place after the Church is in heaven. Following the wedding ceremony, the married couple slip away. In like manner, Christ and His wife (Church) will return to earth at the end of the Tribulation and set up a marriage feast that could last for the duration of the Millennium or 1000 years. The marriage supper or feast may be a 1000-year party or honeymoon thrown by the wealthiest person in the universe, the Father God Himself. The invited guests from the heavenly realm will be the Old Testament saints, Tribulation saints, 144,000 Jewish witnesses, and from the earthly realm, the survivors of the Tribulation Period. Some commentators include the angelic host as guests, but there is no indication that angels will be involved in an event reserved specifically for humans. To further support that the marriage feast will be on earth during the Millennium, Jesus said in Luke 22:16-18 that He would not eat or drink until the Kingdom of God is established, which is not until the Millennium.

Parable of the Marriage Feast

As in the parable of the Marriage Feast, both good and bad guests were brought in to fill the wedding hall. The guest without a wedding garment was cast from the feast and into outer darkness. Certainly the Old Testament saints, Tribulation saints, and the 144,000 Jewish witnesses along with believers who survive the seven-year Tribulation period are the good guests. The bad guests will be those who survive the Tribulation but have taken the mark of the Beast. For the Tribulation survivors, the casting out of the bad guests and inclusion of good guests could easily be lined up with the separation of the sheep (good) and the goats (bad) nations of Matthew 25.

 PROPHETIC KEY TWENTY ONE

MILLENNIUM

Purpose (Isaiah 9:6-7, Ezekiel 20:33-44)

The primary purposes of the Millennium are the restoration of Israel, restoration of righteousness on the earth, and the fulfillment of the everlasting covenants made to Abraham, Isaac, and Jacob as spelled out in Genesis 12-17, 26, and 28.

Satan, Fallen Angels, and Demons (Revelation 20:1-3)

An angel, presumably Michael, descends from heaven with the key to the bottomless pit and a great chain. Michael binds Satan and casts him in the abyss for 1000 years or the period of the Millennium. It is assumed that Satan's army of fallen angels and demons are also bound for the 1000 years.

Curse (Genesis 3:14-19, Genesis 9:1-5, Isaiah 65:21-23)

After the sin of Adam, God placed a curse on the earth, against the serpent, man, woman, and land. Following the Noahic flood, the nature of animals was changed and animals became food for man and each other. In the Millennium with Satan, fallen angels, and demons bound, the effects of the curse are temporarily lifted, but the permanent removal of the curse doesn't occur until after the Millennium.

Government (Isaiah 9:3-7)

The government of the Millennium is theocratic with Christ ruling from the throne of David in Jerusalem. Christ will rule in righteousness but with a rod of iron. Jesus possesses the legal and royal right to the throne of David according to Matthew 1 and Luke 1. Christ will be King of kings and His rule will be universal. No part of the earth will be outside His rulership.

Sub-Government (Ezekiel 37:21-25, Matthew 19:28, Luke 19:12-28)

The resurrected King David rules under Christ over the land of Israel. Many commentators believe Israel will also be head of the nations. Under David, the twelve apostles rule over the twelve tribes. Resurrected saints rule and reign with Christ in governmental administration over cities and nations of the earth.

Law and Judges (Isaiah 11:3-5, Isaiah 14:16-19, Isaiah 1:26)

With the continued existence of nations, laws must be established for the governing of society. There will be civil and ceremonial or religious laws, and Christ judges in perfect righteousness and justice. One such law is for representatives from nations to travel to Israel annually to worship the King and keep the Feast of Tabernacles. Failure to comply will result in no rain for the nation's land for one year and a plague. Additionally, judges are again raised up for administration of kingdom rule. The judges will be further down the governmental management chain, having the kings, redeemed saints, the twelve apostles, King David, and Christ in various hierarchal positions of leadership.

Geography (Revelation 21:1, Isaiah 35:1-2, 8, Ezekiel 36:8-38, Isaiah 11:16, Isaiah 35:8)

All lands are restored to beauty after the mass destruction of the judgments. The topography will be a gentle rolling terrain with no great mountains or islands. Climates will be warm with uniform temperatures and no storms. The deserts will blossom as a rose. Desolate waste places and ruined areas shall be restored. A major highway called the Highway of Holiness will exist in the

land. Rain will continue in the Millennium according to Isaiah
30:23, which leads to the conclusion that the great oceans still
exist. Because oceans take up three-fourths of the planet's surface, living space could become a challenge based on millennial
population projections. Mountain ranges reduced to rolling
hills could provide some offset before eternity future when the
great oceans cease to exist.

Jerusalem and Israel (Zechariah 2:10-12, Isaiah 25:15, Genesis 15:18-21)

Jerusalem will be the most prominent city of the Millennium. It
will be the Capitol of the world, the center of Israel, center for
divine government, and center of universal worship of King
Jesus. Israel will be enlarged from its current size to cover the
land originally granted by God, which includes territories into
Egypt, Syria, and Iraq. The land of Israel is to be re-apportioned
to the 12 tribes.

Jews, Redeemed Saints, Gentiles (Matthew 24:30-31, Luke 19:12-28, Revelation 2:26-27, Isaiah 11:12)

Natural Jewish believers who survive the Tribulation are to be
gathered into Israel from the four corners of the earth. The
Gentile nations (non-Jewish Tribulation saints) will be established
throughout the world and will live in the same manner as people
live today, i.e., working, marrying, raising families, attending
school, traveling, etc. The redeemed saints, consisting of all glorified saints of the First Resurrection, rule and reign with Christ.
Although natural nations will undoubtedly have some form of
self-rule, such as governors, mayors, kings, or presidents, it
appears the redeemed saints will assist in that rule.

Length of Life (Isaiah 65:20, Isaiah 11:4)

Death will virtually be non-existent in the millennial kingdom.
Natural people entering the Millennium live for the 1000-year

period. The earth's population will increase at a geometric rate to a population higher by billions of persons than any previous earth population. There will be no infant death, nor people dying of old age. The Bible states that a person who dies at 100 years of age will be as a child, and a sinner being 100 years old shall be accursed. It appears from this scripture that a person born into the Millennium has 100 years to make a decision for Christ. Failure to do so results in the person being accursed. People will still be born with sin natures in the millennial period, and certain acts of sin and violations of righteous law will warrant the death penalty.

Universal Knowledge of Christ (Habakkuk 2:14, Isaiah 11:9, Zechariah 8:23)

The earth will be filled with the knowledge of the Lord. The Millennium will be a time of intense teaching. People will have come from the Tribulation, where little opportunity existed to become a student of the Word. Biblical principles for righteous living that people were unable to learn after their salvation experience in the Tribulation will have to be taught to them in the Millennium. The teaching ministry may be one of the key roles of the redeemed saints and Jewish evangelists.

Worship (Isaiah 66:17-23, Zechariah 2:10-13)

The worship of God and Christ will be universal throughout the world with the Lord dwelling in the midst of His people, both Israel and the nations.

Economic Prosperity (Isaiah 65:21-23, Zechariah 8:11-12)

People will reap the reward of their labors. Industrialized society and technological advances continue. There will not be unemployment, labor strife, plant closures, illegal dealings, strikes, discrimination, etc. Under a righteous government, the need for all the labor laws and class protections will be non-existent. Every want and need shall be met. Abundance is the result of a worker's output. In John 10:10, Jesus said He came that we might have life and have it more abundantly.

Joy, Peace, Holiness, Comfort and Glory (Micah 4:3-4, Isaiah 12:1-6, Isaiah 35:2, 8-10)

The Millennial kingdom will be a holy and glorious kingdom full of comfort, joy, and peace. The glory of the Lord is manifest everywhere. People are comforted because all needs are met. There is individual peace without the temptations, tests, and trials brought on by Satan who is bound in the abyss. National peace exists, because war and oppression are disallowed in Messiah's kingdom.

Healing (Jeremiah 30:17, Isaiah 35:2-6)

Jesus is Jehovah Rapha, the Lord that heals, and He continues in this ministry. Hebrews 13:8 states *"Jesus Christ is the same yesterday, today, and forever."* His nature is to heal. At the onset of the Millennium, people will be physically restored. The blind will see, the deaf will hear, the dumb will talk, and the lame shall walk. Every disease and deformity will be healed. Sickness is oppression, bondage, and captivity, and is under the curse. Satan is the oppressor, and he will be bound. The curse will be lifted. Health and healing will be the order of the Millennium with the exception of sickness brought on as a result of an individual's overt sin.

Light (Isaiah 30:26)

The light from the moon will be as the current light from the sun. The light from the sun will be seven times brighter. It is important to note that the sun will be seven times brighter, but not seven times hotter. Light has restorative and healing powers. A question to consider is what will be the effects of life giving properties on the earth's flora and fauna with a sun seven times brighter?

Evangelism (Matthew 25:31-46, Zechariah 8:23)

A majority of scholars believe that anyone entering the Millennium after the Tribulation and Second Coming of Christ must be saved. The question is: will every Tribulation survivor be a born again believer for Christ or an unbeliever who took the mark of the Beast? Unlikely. It seems logical that there will be people on this planet who survive the Tribulation without having made a decision for Christ or having taken the mark of the Beast. Could these people enter the Millennium? According to the judgment of the sheep and goat nations, people may enter the Millennium based on favorable treatment of saints or Jews or be cast into everlasting punishment for unfavorable treatment of them. Further, what about people in very remote regions of the earth who had no direct participation in the events of the Tribulation Period? If they didn't take the mark of the Beast, then shouldn't they enter into the Millennium? Since the Jews are to be the evangelists of the Millennium, they could initially direct their evangelistic efforts to these people. The on-going need for evangelism will be compelling based on the staggering population growth.

Millennial Temple, Feasts, Sacrifices, and Priests (Ezekiel 40:1-46:24, Ezekiel 43:7, Isaiah 2:2-4)

The millennial temple to be constructed is detailed extensively by the prophet Ezekiel and is to be built on a mountain above the hills. The priesthood and animal sacrifices are to be re-instituted. The sacrificial system is initiated not as a way to salvation but as a memorial to the salvation provided by the substitutionary sacrifice of Christ. The glory of God will be manifest in the temple. Living water flows from the sanctuary south through the city of Jerusalem dividing the city in half, one half flowing toward the Mediterranean, and the other half to the Dead Sea, which will itself be restored. The feasts of Moses are also re-established and observed.

Animals (Isaiah 11:6-9, Isaiah 65:25)

The curse on the animal kingdom is relaxed, with animals returning to their pre-curse condition of existence as it was in the Garden of Eden. When God created the animal kingdom in the six days of re-creation, He said it was good, and so again the animal creation will be good. The animals became wild with killing natures following the curse. In the Millennium, animals will not become domesticated, but their natures will be changed. They will be freed from this killing nature and be returned to their natural nature, which may include their ability to communicate directly with humans. Eve was not shocked when the serpent approached and spoke with her, which seems to indicate that communication between animal species existed. The wolf and lamb will eat together, the leopard and young goat will lie down together, the lion shall eat straw like the ox, and toddlers will play with cobras and vipers.

Satan Released from the Abyss (Revelation 20:7-10)

At the end of the Millennium, Satan is released from his 1000-year confinement. Immediately, he proceeds to deceive the nations throughout the world. A natural leader, Gog from the land of Magog, which is present day Russia/Central Asia, will assemble massive armies from throughout the earth. Their number will be as the sands of the sea. Of course, Satan or one of his demon prices oppresses and controls Gog. Who are these people who will join Gog in an attack on God? In every dispensation, the faith of people has been tested and so it will be in the Millennium. Because there has been no deceiver or works of the evil one, the revolt will be the final test. Many people will have followed the rules of the kingdom outwardly, but in their hearts they will have not committed to Christ. These people will not only be deceived but also rebellious, thinking that Satan will provide a better alternative to the kingdom rule of the Messiah. As Satan's armies surround the holy city, Jerusalem, fire from God consumes them. God's judgment is final.

White Throne Judgment (Revelation 20:11-15)

After the 1000-year Millennium and the final rebellion of Satan, all the unrighteous dead from Adam through the Millennium will be resurrected in the Second Resurrection and brought before God for judgment. The books will be opened and everyone will be judged according to their works. Anyone whose name is not found in the Book of Life will be cast into the lake of fire. The judgment of God is true and righteous and no one will have a valid complaint.

RENOVATION OF HEAVEN AND EARTH

The heavens and earth are to be renovated by fire in order to ultimately loose them from the bondage of the curse as described in the commentary of Revelation 21:1. The question is: does this renovation occur after the Tribulation and before the Millennium, after the Millennium and the White Throne judgment, or both before and after the Millennium?

After the Millennium

Many commentators see the renovation of heavens and earth occurring after the Millennium and the White Throne judgment based on 2 Peter 3:10-13. Furthermore, by using 2 Peter 3:10-13 these commentators connect the renovation of the heavens and earth with the "day of the Lord," thereby extending the day of the Lord through the Millennium. However, as previously explained, day of the Lord scriptures describe judgment, not blessings as found in the Millennium. 2 Peter 3:10 indicates that the day of the Lord will come as a thief in the night, which is a reference to Christ's Second Coming. Christ will appear at Armageddon as a thief in the night, when no one is expecting Him, and all seems lost for Israel and the Jews. Hence, the day of the Lord concludes at the Second Coming of Christ, not after the Millennium.

After the Tribulation and Before the Millennium

In the Millennium, the curse is not totally removed, but the effects of the curse are neutralized with the binding of Satan. The earth's geography is severely altered as a result of the judgments executed on the earth. The earth has been scorched, mountains torn down, islands eliminated, cities destroyed, and seas and rivers polluted and turned to blood. Meteors have impacted the earth, volcanic eruptions and massive earthquakes have shaken the earth, and dramatic changes to the sun, moon, and stars have upset and altered the various systems of the earth. Furthermore, several Old Testament scriptures reveal destruction by fire at Christ's Second Coming where the mountains and hills melt. Millennial scriptures describe a new and gentle terrain without any great mountains. So, according to 2 Peter 3:10, some form of premillennial renovation occurs to restore the earth not only to an inhabitable, but also an idyllic state. Isaiah 65:17-25 describes the premillennial New Heavens and New Earth whereas Isaiah 66:22-24 describes a postmillennial New Heavens and New Earth.

Both Before and After the Millennium

2 Peter 3:12 refers to the "day of God," which is distinguished from the day of the Lord. The day of God occurs after the Millennium and White Throne judgment, and it is at this time that the heavens and earth are permanently renovated and permanently loosed from the effects and bondage of the curse. Therefore, 2 Peter 3:10-13 describes renovation of the earth by fire in two stages: stage one at the beginning of the Millennium triggered by the judgments of the Tribulation Period, and stage two at the end of the Millennium triggered by the supernatural destruction of Satan and his massive armies by fire from God (Gog and Magog, Revelation 20:8-9). In summary, the earth will not be completely destroyed and created anew at the end of the Millennium, but will be changed or altered to exist in a new state similar or identical to Edenic earth in the time of Adam before

his expulsion from the garden. An automatic cleansing of the first and second heavens, which are the habitation of principalities, powers, rulers of the darkness of this age, and spiritual hosts of wickedness in heavenly places (Ephesians 6:12), along with the prince of the power of the air (Ephesians 2:2), occurs with the binding of Satan and his demons and fallen angels in the bottomless pit at the beginning of the Millennium. After the Millennium, there will be a final cleansing of the heavens and earth as they are permanently loosed from the effects of the curse.

POSTMILLENNIUM EARTH OR ETERNITY FUTURE

(Refer to Revelation 21-22)

Satan, Demons, Fallen Angels, and the Unrighteous from All Ages

Satan, his fallen angels, and demons are cast in the lake of fire following the final rebellion against God at the end of the Millennium. The unrighteous of all ages from Adam through the Millennium are thrown into the lake of fire, following their judgment at the White Throne. Death and Hell are cast in the lake of fire after completion of the White Throne judgment.

Topography

The great oceans covering three-fourths of the earth's surface will disappear. With the oceans gone, a vapor canopy will likely form as existed in the Garden of Eden. Narrow seas, rivers, and lakes will exist in the postmillennial earth. The renovation by fire that began at the beginning of the Millennium is completed with heaven and earth cleansed and purged from the effects of sin and the curse. God says that all things are made new.

Curse

The curse temporarily lifted during the Millennium will be removed forever. There will be no more tears and no more death.

Natural Man and Redeemed Man

Human beings that live through the Millennium will continue to inhabit earth in a manner originally intended for Adam. Natural man's body will be eternal and never wear out, and he will continue to live in and populate the earth. Natural man will live on earth but will be able to go in and out of the New Jerusalem. Redeemed man will live in the New Jerusalem throughout eternity.

New Jerusalem

The New Jerusalem will be a great high mountain, 1500 miles in length, width, and height. Scholars conclude that the New Jerusalem will hover or be suspended over planet earth. The gates of the city are giant pearls, the streets that extend throughout the city are transparent gold, and a river of life proceeds from the throne. On each side of the river is the tree of life bearing a different fruit each month for the healing of the nations. The people of the nations will live in divine health by eating from the fruit of the tree of life. God administers the universe from the New Jerusalem.

Bride or Lamb's Wife

As the holy city, New Jerusalem, descends from heaven, the Bible refers to it as the bride or Lamb's wife. At the end of the Tribulation, the Church was considered the Lamb's wife. In the Old Testament, Israel was married to God, but after their rejection of the Messiah, became estranged. In the Millennium, Israel is reunited with God. Now in the postmillennial earth, the whole family of God, collectively with the New Jerusalem, is the bride or the Lamb's wife. The Lamb's wife is then comprised of the redeemed from all ages, Old Testament, New Testament, and Tribulation saints, and they dwell together in the New Jerusalem forever.

Temple

The Lord God Almighty and the Lamb are the temple. There is

no need for the sun or moon in the city, for the glory of God illuminates the city and there is never any night.

Animals in the Postmillennial Earth

Although scripture supports the existence of animals in the Millennium, many scholars believe that animals will not exist in the postmillennial renovated earth. If this is true, what happens to them? Does God destroy all animals on earth? Are the animals annihilated in the renovation? Such an act would be inconsistent with the character of God. It appears that God renovates and restores this postmillennial earth to its Edenic quality and condition, and if so, animals would be included, because they were natural inhabitants of Eden.

NATURAL AND SUPERNATURAL DISTURBANCES

Scriptures describing disturbances to the earth and planetary systems: earth, sun, moon, stars, sky, mountains, seas, and islands.

Matthew 24:7 - ...there will be famines, pestilences, and earthquakes.

Revelation 4:5 - lightnings, thunderings, voices from the throne.

Ezekiel 38:19, 20, 22 - ...in that day there shall surely be a great earthquake in the land of Israel...the mountains shall be thrown down...flooding rain, great hailstones, fire, and brimstone.

Revelation 6:12-16 - sixth seal judgment: a great earthquake, the sun turns black, the moon is blood red, stars fall from heaven, the sky recedes, and every mountain and island are reconfigured. This is the wrath of the Lamb (refer to Prophetic Key: Day of the Lord for additional scriptures).

Revelation 8:5 - after the seal judgments and before the first trumpet judgment a censer filled with fire is thrown to the earth

and there are noises, thunderings, lightnings, and an earthquake.

Revelation 8:8 - ...the second angel sounded: and something like a great mountain burning with fire was thrown into the sea.

Revelation 8:10 - ...the third angel sounded: and a great star fell from heaven, burning like a torch...

Revelation 8:12 - fourth trumpet judgment: one-third sun, moon, and stars darkened so that a third of the day does not shine. 16 hours of night.

Revelation 11:13 - end of the 42-month Great Tribulation and resurrection of the two witnesses. A great earthquake occurs; a tenth of Jerusalem is destroyed and 7000 men are killed.

Revelation 11:19 - after the seventh trumpet judgment the temple of God is opened and there are lightnings, thunderings, noises, earthquake, and great hail.

Revelation 16:8 - fourth bowl judgment: men are scorched from the sun's heat.

Revelation 16:10 - fifth bowl judgment: Beast's kingdom is in total darkness.

Revelation 16:18-21 - seventh bowl judgment: noises, thunderings, lightnings, and a mighty and great earthquake that has never before occurred. Jerusalem is divided into three parts and the cities of the nations fall. Babylon is not to be found, every island is moved, mountains are not found, and great hail falls from heaven weighing up to 100 pounds.

Matthew 24:29 - immediately after the Tribulation of those days, the sun will be darkened, and the moon will not give its light; the

stars will fall from heaven, and the power of the heavens will be shaken (fifth and seventh bowl judgments).

Zechariah 14:4-6 - ...His (Jesus) feet will stand on the Mount of Olives...and the Mount of Olives shall be split in two...there shall be no light; the lights shall diminish.

Zechariah 14:10 – All the land shall be turned into a plain...

2 Peter 3:10-12 - ...the day of the Lord will come as a thief in the night in which the heavens will pass away...and the elements will melt with fervent heat; both the earth and the works that are in it will be burned up...the heavens will be dissolved being on fire, and the elements will melt with fervent heat.

Revelation 21:1 - And I saw a new heaven and a new earth, for the first heaven and the first earth had passed away. Also there was no more sea.

Persecutions, Judgments, and Signs in Revelation 4-22

Revelation (Ch/Verse)	First Half of Tribulation Period	Revelation (Ch/Verse	Second Half of Tribulation Period
4:5	Lightnings, thunderings, voices from throne	7:2	144,000 Jews sealed by God
6:2	Conqueror revealed (Antichrist)	7:7-17	A great multitude slain during the Great Tribulation
6:3	War - peace taken from earth, people kill each other	8:1	Silence in heaven for 1/2 hour
6:5	Famine	8:5	Noises, thunderings, lightnings, earthquake
6:8	Death and Hades - power over 1/4th earth - to kill with sword, hunger, death, and beasts	8:7	Hail, fire, blood - 1/3rd trees and all grass burned
6:9	Souls under the altar having been killed for their testimony and the word of God	8:8	Great mountain burning - 1/3rd sea becomes blood, 1/3rd sea life dies, 1/3rd ships destroyed
6:11	Fellow servants of the souls under the altar to be killed in the same manner	8:10	Wormwood - 1/3rd rivers and spring waters made bitter - men die
6:12-17	Earthquake, sun, moon, stars, islands, mountains, sky affected - God's wrath	8:12	Sun, moon, stars are 1/3rd darker - 2/3rds of the solar day is dark
		9:1-11	Demon locusts - torment men for up to five months – 1st Woe
		9:13-21	200 million demon army - four bound angels - 1/3rd mankind killed with fire, smoke, and brimstone – 2nd Woe
		11:3-12	Two witnesses - minister 1260 days, power to shut heaven, no rain, turn water to blood, strike earth with plagues - beast from abyss revealed
		11:13	Great earthquake, 1/10th city falls, 7000 die
		11:15	Angelic pronouncements – 3rd Woe
		11:19	Lightnings, noises, thunderings, earthquake, great hail - divine activity, temple and ark seen in heaven
		12:1-5	Signs - woman, male child, Dragon
		12:7	Angelic war in heaven
		12:11	Saints martyred by Dragon
		12:13	Woman persecuted by Dragon
		12:17	Dragon makes war with woman's offspring
		13:1	Beast - 7 heads, 10 horns (Antichrist)
		13:7	Beast makes war with saints, overcomes them
		13:11	Another beast - False Prophet

Persecutions, Judgments, and Signs in Revelation 4-22 (cont.)

Revelation (Ch/Verse)	First Half of Tribulation Period	Revelation (Ch/Verse	Second Half of Tribulation Period
17:3	Woman on a scarlet covered beast - Harlot	13:13	False Prophet calls down fire, performs great signs
17:6	Harlot persecutes and martyrs saints	13:17	No one can buy or sell without mark of Beast
17:16	Harlot made desolate, naked, burned with fire	14:9-10	Wrath of God - eternal torment for Beast worshippers
		14:18-20	Angel with power over fire - winepress of wrath of God, blood spilled for 184 miles - preview of Armageddon
		16:2	Malignant sores on men with the mark
		16:3	All sea life dies
		16:4	Rivers and spring waters turn to blood
		16:8	Men are scorched with fire from the sun
		16:10	Darkness on Beast kingdom, men gnaw their tongues in pain
		16:12-14	Euphrates dries up, three demon spirits gather world's armies to Armageddon
		16:17-21	Noises, thunderings, lightnings, great earthquake, great hail, islands disappear, mountains crumble, cities fall, Jerusalem divided, Babylon destroyed
		18:8, 10, 17, 19, 21	Babylon is destroyed in one hour - burned with fire - death, mourning, famine - double portion
		18:24	Prophets, saints are persecuted and martyred in Babylon
		19:11-16	Second Coming - armies in heaven, war
		19:17-21	Armageddon - Jesus kills with sword out of His mouth, birds eat flesh of men - Antichrist, False Prophet cast into lake of fire
		20:2	Satan and his angels bound in the pit for 1000 years
		20:4	Martyrs that were beheaded for their witness
		Millennium and Eternal Future	
		20:9	Fire from God destroys Satan and Magog armies
		20:11	White Throne judgment
		20:14	Death and Hades cast into lake of fire, second death

PROPHETIC KEY TWENTY FIVE

NETHER WORLD REGIONS AND ETERNAL HELL

Sheol-Hades - Revelation 1:18, 20:13-14, Luke 16:19-31, and many other scriptures

- Temporary hell that is divided into two compartments
  - Paradise (Luke 16:22) - also called Abraham's Bosom; a compartment for the righteous dead from Old Testament times that is now empty. When Jesus rose from the dead He led the inhabitants of this compartment to heaven (Ephesians 4:8)
  - Torments (Luke 16:24) - a holding section or compartment for the unrighteous dead of all time, from Adam through the Millennium, while awaiting the White Throne judgment; place of torment and flame

Tartarus - 2 Peter 2:4, Jude 6
- Place of temporary confinement for a select group of fallen angels until they are sent to the lake of fire

Abyss or Bottomless Pit - Revelation 9:1-5, Revelation 20:1-3
- Shaft of corridor to hell
- Location of demon locusts

- Angel of the abyss - Abaddon or Apollyon
- Place of temporary confinement for Satan, demons, and fallen angels during the Millennium

Gehenna or Lake of Fire - Revelation 20:10, 14-15
- Eternal hell - (Revelation 14:9-12)
- Prepared for the Devil and his angels (Matthew 25:41)
- Second death - final separation from God
- Eternal place of incarceration for Satan, the Antichrist, the False Prophet, demons, fallen angels, and the unrighteous dead from Adam through the Millennium

Body, Soul, and Spirit at Death

	Old Testament Believers	New Testament Believers- Dead in Christ- Pre-Rapture	New Testament Believers- Alive at Rapture	Tribulation Saints- 144,000- 2 Witnesses- Post Rapture	Unbelievers of all time from Adam through the Millennium
Body	Ground	Ground	Caught up alive	Ground	Ground
Soul and Spirit	Paradise compartment of Sheol-Hades - in heaven following Christ's resurrection	Heaven	Caught up alive	Heaven	Torments compartment of Sheol-Hades
Glorified Body	1st Resurrection	Rapture	Rapture	1st Resurrection	Spirit and soul reunited with body at 2nd Resurrection after White Throne

BOOK OF MATTHEW

Matthew 24-25

**(Refer to Prophetic Keys: Tribulation Period and
Events and Conditions on Earth
during the Tribulation Period)**

Matthew 24

Matthew 24 is concerned with Israel, not the Church, and provides a chronology of events that occur during the seventieth week of Daniel or more commonly called the Tribulation. The disciples asked Jesus three questions, which He answered in Matthew 24 and Luke 21.

Matthew 24:1-Then Jesus went out and departed from the temple, and His disciples came to Him to show Him the buildings of the temple.

The disciples show Jesus the buildings of the temple.

Matthew 24:2-And Jesus said to them, "Do you not see all these things? Assuredly, I say to you, not one stone shall be left here upon another, that shall not be thrown down."

Jesus tells the disciples that the temple will be destroyed. The literal fulfillment occurred in A.D. 70, when the Roman General Titus destroyed the temple, literally stone by stone. The Jews were subsequently scattered throughout the earth until 1948.

Matthew 24:3-Now as He sat on the Mount of Olives, the disciples came to Him privately, saying, "Tell us, when will

these things be? And what will be the sign of Your coming, and of the end of the age?"

Privately the disciples asked when the temple would be destroyed? What would be the sign of Jesus' Coming? And what would be the sign of the end of the age? Two of these questions were also asked and discussed in Luke 21.

Matthew 24:4-And Jesus answered and said to them: "Take heed that no one deceives you."

Jesus warns the disciples against deception. The best defense against deception is the Word of God. A deep or solid commitment to God's Word will strengthen a person's protection against deception. Satan is known as the deceiver, and deception is his main weapon.

Matthew 24:5-"For many will come in My name, saying, I am the Christ, and will deceive many."

Verses 4-8 not only occur at the beginning of the Tribulation, but are also characteristic of the environment in the earth preceding the Tribulation and the Rapture of the Church. Many false Christs will come. False Christs represent false religious systems that offer a different way to salvation than through Jesus Christ. A result of the work of these false Christs or false religious systems is that many people will be deceived and turn away from the truth. This verse also coincides with the first seal judgment of Revelation 6 when the Antichrist, as the "false Christ," appears as the rider on the white horse.

Matthew 24:6-"And you will hear of wars and rumors of wars. See that you are not troubled; for all these things must come to pass, but the end is not yet."

"Wars and rumors of wars" coincide with the rider on the red horse in Revelation 6. These events are occurring in the beginning of the seventieth week of Daniel, and Jesus said that when the disciples see these things, the end is not yet at hand. Again war will be characteristic of the environment preceding the Tribulation and Rapture of the Church.

Matthew 24:7-"For nation will rise against nation, and kingdom against kingdom, and there will be famines, pestilences, and earthquakes in various places."

Nation against nation and kingdom against kingdom represent war (second seal judgment). The Greek word for nations also means races or cultures. Wars in the Middle East are all about race, including national origin and religion. Muslim Jihad is directly and violently opposed to Judaism and Christianity. Famines coincide with the third seal judgment and pestilence or death with the fourth seal judgment. Earthquakes occur throughout the seventieth week of Daniel. A cataclysmic earthquake will hit the earth as mentioned in the sixth seal judgment.

Matthew 24:8-"All these are the beginning of sorrows."

All preceding events are referred to as the "beginning of sorrows" or birth pangs, with worse judgments still to come in the Great Tribulation. These events are only the beginning. If Tribulation events, such as false religious systems, war, famine, and pestilence, among other events, are on the rise today, then the Church should be aware that the Rapture is that much closer.

Matthew 24:9-"Then they will deliver you up to tribulation, and kill you, and you will be hated by all nations for My name's sake."

Saints are hated for the name of Jesus, testimony to His name, and the Word of God and are severely persecuted to the point of death throughout the Tribulation. In the first half of the Tribulation, the Church is persecuted by the Harlot religious system and in the second half by the Antichrist.

Matthew 24:10-"And then many will be offended, will betray one another, and will hate one another."

The witness for Jesus offends many and causes division and strife among people. Family and friends will even betray one another (Mark 13:12, Luke 21:16).

Matthew 24:11-"Then many false prophets will rise up and deceive many."

False prophets abound resulting in the deception of many people. Many ungrounded saints and Jews will succumb to the deceptions. The battle lines between good and evil are clearly drawn. Fence riding will not be an option.

Matthew 24:12-"And because lawlessness will abound, the love of many will grow cold."

After the Rapture of the Church, the restrainer or the Church infilled with the Holy Spirit, will not be restraining sin any longer as is occurring in this dispensation. Therefore, lawlessness will abound, and many people will succumb to the pressure and turn from Christ. Why? Because they are not sufficiently grounded in the Word of God. Their spiritual houses are built on sand (Matthew 7:24-27), not on the solid rock of the Word.

Matthew 24:13-"But he who endures to the end shall be saved."

The one who endures or survives the Tribulation without taking the mark of the Beast will enter into the Millennium. Again, only one-third of the Jews will survive the Tribulation Period to enter the Millennium.

Matthew 24:14-"And this gospel of the kingdom will be preached in all the world as a witness to all the nations, and then the end will come."

The Gospel is being preached to all nations as no other time in history. The Gospel of the Kingdom is preached in several ways during the Tribulation. The martyrs who are beheaded for the Word of God and the testimony of Jesus, the 144,000 Jewish witnesses, the two Old Testament prophets, and for the first time an angel flying through mid-heaven will preach or proclaim the everlasting Gospel.

Matthew 24:15-"Therefore when you see the abomination of desolation, spoken of by Daniel the prophet, standing in the holy place" (who ever reads, let him understand),

Verse 15 occurs at the middle of the Tribulation. The Antichrist

is the Abomination of Desolation or the one who makes desolate. He enters the temple and proclaims himself to be God in
fulfillment of Daniel 9:27. It is at this time that the Antichrist
breaks the seven-year covenant of peace with Israel.

**Matthew 24:16-20-"then let those who are in Judea flee to the
mountains. Let him who is on the housetop not come down
to take anything out of his house. And let him who is in the
field not go back to get his clothes. But woe to those who are
pregnant and those with nursing babies in those days! And
pray that your flight may not be in winter or on the Sabbath."**

Israel is instructed to flee to the mountains when the Antichrist
proclaims himself to be God. The mountains are called Edom,
Moab, and Ammon, and are located in Jordan. It is believed by
most scholars that the rock-fortified city of Petra (Bozrah) in
Jordan (Edom) will be the primary sanctuary for Israel. The
direction to Israel is to flee in a hurry and not stop for clothes or
anything in the house. The hope is that the flight is not in winter or on the Sabbath or that a woman is not pregnant because
then escape would be more difficult. The Jew is restricted in the
distance that he can travel on the Sabbath.

**Matthew 24:21-"For then there will be great tribulation,
such as has not been since the beginning of the world until
this time, no, nor ever shall be."**

After the revelation of the Antichrist at mid-Tribulation, the
Great Tribulation begins and will be worse than any other period in history, including the great flood. The Great Tribulation
will be an intense period of divine wrath in the form of seven
trumpet and seven bowl judgments.

**Matthew 24:22-"And unless those days were shortened, no
flesh would be saved; but for the elect's sake those days will
be shortened."**

If the persecution by Satan, the Antichrist, and the False Prophet
is not cut short by the return of Christ at His Second Advent,
Israel would be totally destroyed. Jerusalem is at the point of

being completely plundered by the armies of the Antichrist according to Zechariah 14:2. Only one-third of the population of Israel will survive the Great Tribulation. The "elect" refers to the Jews saved during this period.

Matthew 24:23-26-**"Then if anyone says to you, Look, here is the Christ! or There! Do not believe it. For false christs and false prophets will arise and show great signs and wonders, so as to deceive, if possible, even the elect. See, I have told you beforehand. Therefore if they say to you Look, He is in the inner rooms! Do not believe it."**

Additional warnings are provided regarding false Christs and false prophets who perform signs and wonders that deceive the elect. Again, the importance of having a solid foundation in the Word of God is implied in order not to be taken-in by the deceptions. It will be difficult to become a student of the Word during these times and conditions on the earth.

Matthew 24:27-**"For as the lightening comes from the east and flashes to the west, so also will the coming of the Son of Man be."**

Jesus answers what it will be like when He returns. He will appear as lightning from the east to the west. Remember that the earth will have been through a number of judgments that affect the sun, moon, and stars, resulting in complete darkness over the earth. With the earth in darkness, suddenly it will be illuminated by the brightness of Christ's glory. No one will miss it. In addition to satellite technology, this is a definite way every person will see Him.

Matthew 24:28-**"For wherever the carcass is, there the eagles will be gathered together."**

"Carcasses and eagles gathering" refer to the battle of Armageddon. Many translations more correctly use vultures rather than eagles. Vultures and other scavenger birds probably including eagles, will feast on the dead carcasses of the fallen soldiers from the battle of Armageddon.

Matthew 24:29-"immediately after the Tribulation of those days the sun will be darkened, and the moon will not give its light; the stars will fall from heaven, and the powers of the heavens will be shaken."

Cosmic disturbances occur at the end of the Tribulation under the bowl judgments, especially the seventh. Several times the normal physical properties of the sun, moon, and stars are altered, in addition to a total shaking of the planet.

Matthew 24:30-"Then the sign of the Son of Man will appear in heaven, and then all the tribes of the earth will mourn, and they will see the Son of Man coming on the clouds of heaven with power and great glory."

With the brightness of His Coming as described in verse 27, every person will see Him. "Tribes of the earth" refer to all nations and especially to the twelve tribes of Israel who mourn when they realize that they crucified the true Messiah. "Coming on the clouds" refers to Christ's appearing in His Shekinah glory. When Jesus left in the clouds in Acts 1:9-11, it was stated that He would return in the same manner. He will return with great power to destroy the armies of the Antichrist and repossess the physical earth.

Matthew 24:31-"And He will send His angels with a great sound of a trumpet, and they will gather together His elect from the four winds, from one end of heaven to the other."

Christ sends out the angels to gather the elect (saved Jews) from around the earth. Only the angels are able to tell who are the true Jewish believers. This passage links with the separation of the wheat from the tares (Matthew 13:24-30). The "wheat" represents the Tribulation saints, including the Jewish elect, while the "tares" are the unsaved. The unsaved will be burned, i.e., sent to hell, then to the lake of fire after the White Throne judgment. The saved are brought into the barn, i.e., they enter into the Millennium with Christ. It is also believed that those persons who do not take the mark of the Beast but help the elect and/or Tribulation saints will be admitted into the Millennium, even though they have not made a personal commitment to Christ (Matthew 25:31-46). Additionally, there will be people on the

planet in remote areas who have had virtually no involvement in the events of the Tribulation who will enter the Millennium. The Jews will be the evangelists of the Millennium.

Matthew 24:32-"Now learn this parable from the fig tree: When its branch has already become tender and puts forth leaves, you know summer is near.

This is the parable of the fig tree. The fig tree represents Israel. When one sees the leaves upon the tree, he/she knows that summer is near.

Matthew 24:33-"So you also, when you see all these things, know that it is near, at the very doors."

In the same manner as the fig tree, when the signs of the Tribulation are seen as described in the beginning of sorrows and other events, then one should know that the Second Coming of Christ is very near. If the Tribulation and Second Coming of Christ are perceived to be near from the signs, then the Church should know that the Rapture is even nearer.

Matthew 24:34-"Assuredly, I say to you, this generation will by no means pass away till all these things are fulfilled."

Once people see the signs as discussed, they should know that one generation shall not pass until all the events are fulfilled, including the return of Jesus. A Biblical generation can be 20, 40, 60, or 100 years. The generation clock starts either at 1948 when Israel was recognized as a nation, or 1967 when Israel came into possession of Jerusalem. A 20-year generational period is too short while a 100-year generational period is too long based on the average human life span. A generational period of 40 years from 1948 didn't work, since 1988 has come and gone. 40 years from 1967 or 60 years from 1948 or 1967 could still be possible. The best definition for a generation is the average life span of humans at a specific point in history, which currently is 70-80 years. Psalm 90:10 supports this position. Therefore, 70-80 years from 1948 or 1967 puts the return of the Lord on the horizon. Of course, the above calculation is speculation, because no one but the Father Himself knows the exact date. However, the signs of

the times support that the world has become and is continuing to become increasingly prepared for the revelation of the Antichrist. Technological advances have positioned this generation like no other for the literal fulfillment of prophetic events, including the Rapture of the Church and Second Coming of Christ.

Matthew 24:35-"Heaven and earth will pass away, but My words will by no means pass away."

The words of Jesus are eternal and will never pass away. Even if heaven and earth were destroyed and passed away, the Word of God would not. However, heaven and earth will not be destroyed.

Matthew 24:36-"But of that day and hour no one knows, no not even my angels in heaven, but My Father only."

Only the Father knows the day and the hour of the Lord's return. However, from the previous verses, believers will be able to interpret the signs and know the season, potentially down to the year or even sooner, when Christ will return for His Church.

Matthew 24:37-"But as the days of Noah were, so also will the coming of the Son of Man be."

The Second Coming of Christ will occur in the same manner as judgment in the days of Noah.

Matthew 24:38-"For as in the days before the flood, they were eating and drinking, marrying and giving in marriage, until the day that Noah entered the ark."

Up until the time Noah entered the ark, the ungodly were oblivious to the seasons and what was about to occur. Noah warned them, but they did not listen.

Matthew 24:39-"and did not know until the flood came and took them all away, so also will the coming of the Son of Man be."

These verses do not refer to the Rapture, because the Rapture is

not the subject of this passage. The Second Coming of Christ is the subject. The flood came and took "them" away. The "them" are the ungodly of verse 38. The ungodly taken away means they were destroyed or sent to hell, destined to the lake of fire after the White Throne judgment. In like manner, at the Second Coming, the unbelievers will be sent to hell, the Torments compartment of Sheol-Hades, to await the White throne judgment after the Millennium. Believers will remain on earth, as did Noah, and will enter into the Millennium.

Matthew 24:40-41-"Then two men will be in the field; one will be taken and the other left. Two women will be grinding at the mill: one will be taken and the other left."

Additional examples are provided to emphasize the above point. Two people are in the field, one (the unbeliever) is taken while the believer remains. Another example is two women grinding at the mill and one is taken (unbeliever to hell) while the other is left (believer to the Millennium).

Matthew 24:42-"Watch therefore, for you do not know what hour your Lord is coming."

The admonition is to watch, i.e., to be ready for the return of the Lord. Even though the day and hour are not known, one should be able to interpret the signs of the times and always be ready for the Lord's return.

Matthew 24:43-44-"But know this, that if the master of the house had known what hour the thief would come, he would have watched and not allowed his house to be broken into. Therefore you also be ready, for the Son of Man is coming at an hour when you do not expect Him."

This is another scriptural admonition for people to be prepared, ready, and watchful for the Lord's return.

Matthew 24:45-Matthew 25:30

Additional parables are provided giving illustrations of people who do and do not enter the kingdom.

Matthew 25:31-46

When the Son of Man comes, the angelic host will come with Him. After the battle of Armageddon, Christ will gather and judge the nations, which will probably occur during the 45 day period that follows the 1290 days from the Abomination of Desolation as identified in Daniel 12.

The people from saved nations are called the "sheep nations" who are gathered at Christ's right hand. The "goat nations" or ungodly people are gathered at Christ's left hand. The sheep nations will enter into the Millennium and inherit the kingdom prepared from the foundation of time. They have the opportunity for eternal life. The goat nations are destined to hell, which was not originally prepared for man, but prepared for the Devil and his angels, and to everlasting punishment. The goat nations did not help Christ's people, and therefore, did not obey Christ's command to love God and love one's neighbor.

The prevalent view is that everyone entering the Millennium will be saved. However, the position supported in this presentation is that people who help the Jew and/or Tribulation saints during the Tribulation Period will also enter into the Millennium, even if they haven't personally accepted Christ as Savior and Lord. Jesus said that when people help the less fortunate, i.e., a person who is hungry, thirsty, in need of shelter, sick, or in prison, they do not just help these people, but they in effect perform these good works unto Christ Himself. Remember, during the Tribulation Period a tremendous persecution of Israel, who are God's chosen people, will take place. Helping the Jew and/or Tribulation saints may be the vehicle for some people to enter into the Millennium. This period of time is compared to the time of Noah, when the ungodly were destroyed in judgment. Noah and his household were saved, but only Noah was specifically identified as righteous. Jews are to be the missionaries or evangelists of the Millennium (Zechariah 8:23). If all people are saved upon entering the Millennium, there would be no one to evangelize for years, which doesn't make sense.

 PROPHETIC KEY TWENTY SEVEN

BOOK OF DANIEL

Overview of Daniel
(Refer to Prophetic Key: Comparison of Kingdoms and Beasts in Revelation and Daniel)

Chapter	Important Message
Daniel 2	Nebuchadnezzar's vision of a great metallic image – parts of the image stand for five world empires that have or will persecute Israel during the times of the Gentiles.
Daniel 7	From God's point of view these five world empires are seen as ferocious beasts – the little horn (Antichrist) is revealed – he emerges from the Reconstituted Roman Empire in the last days.
Daniel 8	The geographic location for the little horn (Antichrist) narrows to one of the four divisions of the Old Grecian kingdom that will be contained within the Reconstituted Roman Empire during the Great Tribulation.
Daniel 9:24-27	Prophecy of seventy weeks (sevens) of years or 490 years of Gentile persecution of Israel – one period of seven years of this prophecy is future and called the seventieth week of Daniel or the Tribulation Period.
Daniel 10	Identification of satanic fallen angels controlling the affairs of countries, e.g., the Prince of Greece and Prince of Persia.
Daniel 11	Historical battle of the King of the North and King of the South. End-time battle of the King of the North and King of the South against the Antichrist.
Daniel 12	Duration of the Great Tribulation and announcement of two additional time periods of 30 and 45 days following the completion of the seventieth week of Daniel.

Daniel 2:28-45

Daniel 2:28-"But there is a God in heaven who reveals secrets, and He had made known to King Nebuchadnezzar what will be in the latter days, Your dream and the visions of

your head upon your bed, were these:"

Daniel's interpretation of King Nebuchadnezzar's vision is that God has revealed to the king secrets concerning events that will occur in the latter days.

Daniel 2:29-30-"As for you, O king, thoughts came to your mind while on your bed, about what would come to pass after this; and He who reveals secrets has made known to you what will be. But as for me, this secret has not been revealed to me because I have more wisdom than anyone living, but for our sakes who make known the interpretation to the king, and that you may know the thoughts of your heart."

Daniel proclaims that God is the One who reveals secrets, and the One who has made known to the king what is to come to pass in the end times. Daniel accepts no credit for the dream or the interpretation.

Daniel 2:31-"You, O king, were watching; and behold, a great image! This great image, whose splendor was excellent, stood before you; and its form was awesome."

In his vision, the king sees a great image whose splendor is excellent and whose form is awesome. Each major section of the image represents an empire that has persecuted or will persecute Israel during the times of the Gentiles. These empires have operated under various forms of government. Babylon's rule under Nebuchadnezzar was a monarchy. The government of the Medes and Persians was ruled by a few leaders or limited monarchy. Greece's government was an aristocracy under Philip of Macedonia and his son, Alexander the Great, and Rome was an imperialistic form of government based on military rule.

Daniel 2:32-35-"This image's head was of fine gold, its chest and arms of silver, its belly and thighs of bronze. its legs of

iron, its feet partly of iron and partly of clay. You watched while a stone was cut out without hands, which struck the image on its feet of iron and clay, and broke them in pieces. Then the iron, the clay, the bronze, the silver, and the gold were crushed together, and became like chaff from the summer threshing floors; the wind carried them away so that no trace of them was found. And the great stone that struck the image became a great mountain and filled the whole earth."

The image's head is of gold, chest and arms of silver, belly and thighs of brass, legs of iron, and feet partly of iron and partly of clay. The image is broken in pieces by the stone "cut without hands," which became a "great mountain." Christ is the stone cut without hands, referring to His virgin birth, and the great mountain refers to Christ's kingdom that will encompass the entire earth. All the kingdoms except the kingdom of "feet and toes" have already fallen. The kingdom of the feet and toes is yet future. The stone striking the image on the feet depicts Christ destroying this future kingdom to be ruled by the Antichrist. That stone then becomes the great kingdom that fills the earth.

Daniel 2:36-40-"This is the dream. Now we will tell the interpretation of it before the king. You, O king, are a king of kings. For the God of heaven has given you a kingdom, power, strength, and glory; and wherever the children of men dwell, or the beasts of the field and of the birds of the heaven, He has given them into your hand, and has made you ruler over them all - you are his head of gold. But after you shall arise another kingdom inferior to yours; then another, a third kingdom of bronze, which shall rule over all the earth. And the fourth kingdom shall be as strong as iron, inasmuch as iron breaks in pieces and shatters all things; and like iron that crushes, that kingdom will break in pieces and crush all the others."

Babylon is the head of gold and the third Gentile kingdom (first of this vision) to oppress Israel. God gave Nebuchadnezzar

worldwide dominion over wherever people dwell, beasts roam, or birds fly. Although Nebuchadnezzar never conquered the whole world, he was given global dominion. The Medes and Persians represented by the arms of silver followed Babylon. Medo-Persia was inferior to Babylon as silver is inferior to gold. The two arms symbolized the two nations forming the duel kingdom. The limited monarchy of the Medes and Persians was not as effective a form government as the absolute monarchy of Babylon. The next kingdom represented by the belly and thighs of bronze was Greece that ruled the known world under Alexander the Great. His armies were dressed in bronze, with brass armament. The Grecian kingdom had greater territory than the preceding two kingdoms. The fourth kingdom identified by legs of iron was Rome, who was stronger than the first three kingdoms as iron is stronger than gold, silver, or bronze. The two legs represented the Eastern and Western divisions of the old Roman Empire. The Roman Empire conquered all the territories occupied by the previous empires. The worldwide dominion granted to Nebuchadnezzar was passed on to each of the other empires, even though none ever truly possessed total global dominion.

Daniel 2:41-43-"Whereas you saw the feet and toes, partly of potter's clay and partly of iron, the kingdom shall be divided; yet the strength of the iron shall be in it, just as you saw the iron mixed with ceramic clay. And as the toes of the feet were partly of iron and partly of clay, so the kingdom shall be partly strong and partly fragile. As you saw iron mixed with ceramic clay, they will mingle with the seed of men; but they will not adhere to one another, just as iron does not mix with clay."

The feet of part clay and iron represent a future seventh kingdom (fifth of the dream) to oppress Israel. The toes represent the reconstitution of the Roman Empire into ten kingdoms ruled by ten separate kings from ten separate capitols. This empire will be a divided kingdom, partially weak and partially

strong, symbolized by the two materials, clay and iron.
Commentators see two types of rule, clay signifying the rule of
the people and iron signifying the rule of the kings, and these
two forms of government do not mix as iron and clay do not mix.
The ten kings will rule until mid-Tribulation, when three kingdoms are subdued by the Antichrist, and the remaining seven
kings give their power to the Antichrist. The kingdom under the
Antichrist becomes the Beast Empire or the eighth empire to
oppress Israel during the times of the Gentiles. The Beast
Empire is not revealed in this vision.

**Daniel 2:44-45-"And in the days of these kings the God of
heaven will set up a kingdom which shall never be destroyed;
and the kingdom shall not be left to other people; it shall
break in pieces and consume all these kingdoms, and it shall
stand forever. Inasmuch as you saw that the stone was cut
out of the mountain without hands, and that it broke in
pieces the iron, the bronze, the clay, the silver, and the gold -
the great God has made known to the king what will come to
pass after this. The dream is certain, and its interpretation
is sure."**

When Christ returns at His Second Advent, He will set up the
ninth kingdom that will reign over the earth through the
Millennium. His kingdom will exist forever. Christ will destroy
the kingdoms of the world at the battle of Armageddon. He is
the stone, and His is the kingdom "cut without hands," implying
a sovereign act of God.

Daniel 7

In Daniel 2, Nebuchadnezzar is shown the Gentile world kingdoms from his day to the Second Coming of Christ, as viewed
from man's standpoint, i. e., a great metallic image. In Daniel 7,
God shows Daniel the same kingdoms from His viewpoint, ferocious wild beasts.

Daniel 7:1-3-In the first year of Belshazzar king of Babylon, Daniel had a dream and visions of his head while on his bed. Then he wrote down the dream, telling the main facts. Daniel spoke, saying, "I saw in my vision by night, and behold, the four winds of heaven were stirring up the Great Sea. And four great beasts came up from the sea, each different from the other."

In chapter 2, Daniel only interprets the dream of the king. Now Daniel describes his dream and visions regarding God's purpose and plan for the future, including end-time events. Four beasts come out of the sea, which in prophetic scripture means the sea of humanity. The four beasts represent four diverse world empires. These are the same empires symbolized by the great image in Daniel 2. The four winds stirred up are thought to represent demonically generated strife and war among countries from all compass directions in the region of the Mediterranean Sea.

Daniel 7:4-"The first was like a lion, and had eagle's wings. I watched till its wings were plucked off; and it was lifted from the earth and made to stand on two feet like a man, and a man's heart was given to it."

The first empire, Babylon, is the third empire to persecute Israel during the times of the Gentiles. The first two empires not covered in this vision were Egypt and Assyria. Babylon is compared to a lion with eagle's wings. The wings denote the swiftness of Nebuchadnezzar's conquests. The plucking of the wings could indicate the ending of the kingdom or the insanity of Nebuchadnezzar. The reference to the lion standing as a man means this great kingdom was human.

Daniel 7:5-"And suddenly another beast, a second, like a bear. It was raised up on one side, and had three ribs in its mouth between its teeth. And they said thus to it: Arise, devour much flesh!"

The second beast like a bear represents Medo-Persia. The beast

is raised on its side demonstrating that the Persians were greater than the Medes. The "three ribs" stand for the conquered empires of Egypt, Assyria, and Babylon.

Daniel 7:6-"After this I looked, and there was another, like a leopard, which had on its back four wings of a bird. The beast also had four heads, and a dominion was given to it."

The third beast is a leopard with four wings and four heads representing the Grecian Empire. Alexander the Great was the king of Greece, and the "wings" depict the swiftness of his campaigns and conquests. The "four heads" symbolize the four divisions of Alexander's empire after his death. His empire was divided among his four generals, Cassander, Ptolemy, Seleucus I, and Lysimachus.

Daniel 7:7-"After this I saw in the night visions, and behold, a fourth best, dreadful and terrible, exceedingly strong. It had huge iron teeth; it was devouring, breaking in pieces, and trampling the residue with its feet. It was different from all the beasts that were before it, and it had ten horns."

"After this" clearly indicates that the fourth beast appears after the preceding kingdoms and is not likened to any animal. The fourth kingdom symbolizes Rome and is described as a dreadful and terrible beast that is exceedingly strong with iron teeth. The iron teeth represent the great military might of the Roman Empire. The Roman Empire was stronger than the preceding empires and conquered all the territories of the preceding empires. Rome was different than the other empires in power, government, and territory dominated. The "ten horns" ("ten toes" of Daniel 2) symbolize the ten kingdoms of the Reconstituted Roman Empire of the last days or the seventh world empire to persecute Israel during the times of the Gentiles.

Daniel 7:8-"I was considering the horns, and there was another horn, a little one, coming up among them, before

whom three of the first horns were plucked by the roots. And there, in this horn, were eyes like the eyes of a man, and a mouth speaking pompous words."

The "little horn" appears after the ten horns or kingdoms are established. This little horn represents the Antichrist, who arises out of the territory of the ten kingdoms, and who conquers three kingdoms. The remaining seven kingdoms give their power and authority to the Antichrist. The "eyes" show that the Beast is intelligent and human. The Antichrist will speak blasphemies against God.

Daniel 7:9-10-"I watched till the thrones were put in place, and the Ancient of Days was seated; His garment was white as snow, and the hair of His head was like pure wool. His throne was a fiery flame, its wheels a burning fire; a fiery stream issued and came forth from before Him. A thousand thousands ministered to Him; ten thousand times ten thousand stood before Him. The court was seated, and the books were opened."

God the Father is described as the Ancient of Days sitting on the throne. Multitudes minister to Him and a 100 million stand before Him. "White" represents God's holiness and purity and "ancient" signifies His wisdom. This court scene is in heaven. The thrones are probably the 24 thrones upon which the elders are seated in Revelation 4:4. The court is in session and the books are open signifying judgment.

Daniel 7:11-"I watched then because of the sound of the pompous words which the horn was speaking; I watched till the beast was slain and its body destroyed and given to the burning flame."

The little horn or the Antichrist is a mortal man who is killed at the Second Coming of Christ, and his body is destroyed in flame. Although his body is destroyed, the Antichrist's spirit and soul

(inner man) will continue to exist forever, which is how he can die as well as be cast alive into the lake of fire, along with the False Prophet, as the first two inhabitants of the eternal hell or Gehenna.

Daniel 7:12-14-"As for the rest of the beasts, they had their dominion taken away, yet their lives were prolonged for a season and a time. I was watching in the night visions, and behold, One like the Son of Man, coming with the clouds of heaven! He came to the Ancient of Days, and they brought Him near before Him. Then to Him was given dominion and glory and a kingdom, that all peoples, nations, and languages should serve Him. His dominion is an everlasting dominion, which shall not pass away, and His kingdom the one which shall not be destroyed."

Each of the beasts prior to the Antichrist will reign for a time. The Son of Man appearing before the Ancient of Days in the clouds is a prelude to the Second Coming of Christ. In this verse, two members of the Godhead are represented. Christ's appearing before the Ancient of Days means that He cannot be the Ancient of Days, except in His oneness with the Father. His kingdom is comprised of natural peoples from all backgrounds and walks of life, is everlasting, and will never be destroyed. All peoples serving Him actually mean that all peoples worship Him, which is the purpose for the kingdom.

Daniel 7:15-17-"I, Daniel, was grieved in my spirit within my body, and the visions of my head troubled me. I came near to one of those who stood by, and asked him the truth of all this. So he told me and made known to me the interpretation of these things: Those great beasts, which are four, are four kings which arise out of the earth."

Daniel is concerned about the meaning of the vision. He is told that the great beasts are four kings who have earthly kingdoms.

Daniel 7:18-"But the saints of the Most High shall receive the

kingdom, and possess the kingdom forever, even forever and ever.”

The ninth and last empire will be the kingdom of God that the saints will inherit and possess forever.

Daniel 7:19-20-“Then I wished to know the truth about the fourth beast. Which was different from all the others, exceedingly dreadful, with its teeth of iron and its nails of bronze, which devoured, broke in pieces, and trampled the residue with its feet; and about the ten horns that were on its head, and about the other horn which came up, before which three fell, namely, that horn which had eyes and a mouth which spoke pompous words, whose appearance was greater than his fellows.”

Daniel wants to know the truth about the fourth beast kingdom that tramples the kingdoms and about the “other horn” that rises up and overthrows three of the ten horns (kingdoms). This other horn is the Antichrist who is greater than the other kings. The Antichrist speaks pompous words or blasphemy.

Daniel 7:21-22-“I was watching; and the same horn was making war against the saints, and prevailing against them, until the Ancient of Days came, and a judgment was made in favor of the saints of the Most High, and the time came for the saints to possess the kingdom.”

The Antichrist is prevailing in the war against the saints in the second half of the Tribulation, up to the Second Coming of Christ. The courts are open and the Ancient of Days rules in favor of the saints. Christ defeats the Antichrist and sets up His everlasting kingdom. Christ and the saints possess and rule the kingdom on earth from Jerusalem. After the Millennium, God the Father moves His residence from heaven to earth in the New Jerusalem.

Daniel 7:23-“Thus he said: ‘The fourth beast shall be a fourth kingdom on earth, which shall be different from all

other kingdoms, and shall devour the whole earth, trample it and break it into pieces."

The fourth kingdom or Roman Empire was stronger than the other nations and subsequently conquered all the territories of the known world.

Daniel 7:24-"The ten horns are ten kings who shall arise from this kingdom. And another shall rise after them; he shall be different from the first ones, and shall subdue three kings."

The ten kingdoms of the Reconstituted Roman Empire, seventh world empire to persecute Israel or fifth empire of this beast vision, arise out of the old Roman Empire territory. Another horn is the Antichrist who is different from the ten kings and rises to power after the ten kingdoms have been established. He then overthrows three of the kings.

Daniel 7:25-"He shall speak pompous words against the Most High, shall persecute the saints of the Most High, and shall intend to change times and law. Then the saints shall be given into his hand for a time and times and half a time."

The Antichrist persecutes the saints during the second half of the Tribulation, which is the time of his rule over the eighth empire. He changes laws and all dates and customs as they relate to Christ or the kingdom of God, such as changing or canceling Christmas, Easter, and other holidays, etc. The Antichrist speaks blasphemies against God.

Daniel 7:26-28-"But the court shall be seated, and they shall take away his dominion, to consume and destroy it forever. Then the kingdom and dominion, and the greatness of the kingdoms under the whole heaven, shall be given to the people, the saints if the Most High. This is the end of the account. As for me, Daniel, my thoughts greatly troubled me, and my countenance changed; but I kept the matter in

my heart."

As previously stated, the courtroom scene is in heaven. The convening of the court is near the end of the Tribulation. The Antichrist has been prevailing against the saints for 3 1/2 years. Christ appears as the Son of Man before the Ancient of Days and the court. The court renders a verdict against the Antichrist that his dominion is to be removed and given to the saints. Christ is to return to the earth, destroy the Antichrist's kingdom by force, and set up His everlasting kingdom where all people will worship Him.

Daniel 8

Daniel 8:1-3-In the third year of the reign of King Belshazzar a vision appeared to me - to me, Daniel - after the one that appeared to me the first time. I saw in the vision, and it so happened while I was looking, that I was in Shushan, the citadel, which is in the province of Elam; and I saw in the vision that I was by the River Ulai. Then I lifted my eyes and saw, and there, standing beside the river, was a ram which had two horns, and the two horns were high; but one was higher than the other, and the higher one came up last.

This vision of Daniel occurs two years after the vision discussed in chapter 7. A ram with two horns, of which one was higher than the other, stands for the Medo-Persian Empire. The "two horns" are two kings, Darius, King of Media and Cyrus, King of Persia. The higher horn represents Cyrus because the Persian kingdom under Cyrus was stronger, and Persia attained greater power than the Media rule under Darius.

Daniel 8:4-I saw the ram pushing westward, northward, and southward, so that no beast could withstand him; nor was there any that could deliver from his hand, but he did according to his will and became great.

The Medes and Persians conquered areas to the west, north, and south, and no nation could stand before them. Babylon and Egypt were among the countries conquered. The Medes and

Persians did what they wanted, and no one could stop them.

Daniel 8:5-And as I was considering, suddenly a male goat came from the west, across the surface of the whole earth, without touching the ground; and the goat had a notable horn between his eyes.

The "goat" was the symbol for Greece. The male goat came from the west and moved swiftly, as if not touching the ground. The notable horn stands for the King of Greece, Alexander the Great.

Daniel 8:6-7-Then he came to the ram that had two horns, which I had seen standing beside the river, and ran at him with furious power. And I saw him confronting the ram; he was moved with rage against him, attacked the ram, and broke his two horns. There was no power in the ram to withstand him, but he cast him down to the ground and trampled him; and there was no one that could deliver the ram from his hand.

The "male goat" crushed the ram or demolished the Medo-Persian Empire. Alexander the Great moved with swiftness and fury to conquer vast territories.

Daniel 8:8-Therefore the male goat grew very great; but when he became strong, the large horn was broken, and in place of it four notable ones came up toward the four winds of heaven.

The empire under Alexander became very great. At the apex of his power, Alexander died at age 32 or 33. The large horn was broken and replaced by four notable horns, representing Alexander's four generals, Cassander, Ptolemy, Seleucus I, and Lysimachus. Cassander took over the regions of Macedonia and Greece. Ptolemy ruled Egypt and Palestine. Seleucus I controlled the areas of Syria and Babylonia. Lysimachus occupied Thrace and Turkey. The combined territory appears to cover present-day Egypt, Turkey, Greece, Syria, Iran, Iraq, Afghanistan, Lebanon, Jordan, Israel, and Pakistan.

Daniel 8:9-14—And out of one of them came a little horn which grew exceedingly great toward the south, toward the east and toward the Glorious Land. And it grew up to the host of heaven; and it cast down some of the host and some of the stars to the ground, and trampled them. He even exalted himself as high as the Prince of the host; and by him the daily sacrifices were taken away, and the place of His sanctuary was cast down. Because of transgression, an army was given over to the horn to oppose the daily sacrifices; and he cast truth down to the ground. He did all this and prospered. Then I heard a holy one speaking; and another holy one said to that certain one who was speaking, "How long will the vision be, concerning the daily sacrifices and the transgression of desolation, the giving of both the sanctuary and the host to be trampled underfoot? And he said to me, For two thousand three hundred days; then the sanctuary shall be cleansed."

A "little horn" emerges from one of these territories and becomes great. The "little horn" refers both to Antiochus Epiphanes IV, who was a forerunner and type of the Antichrist, and the Antichrist of Revelation. Antiochus set up idols in the temple, ordered idol worship, sacrificed a pig on the altar in the Jewish temple, outlawed Jewish religious practices and the Jewish religion, and demanded to be worshipped as God. The host in this passage refers to the Jewish people and the prince of the host was the high priest. Antiochus put himself in the place of the high priest when he made a sacrifice in the temple. Antiochus stopped the daily sacrifice, as will the Antichrist in the Tribulation Period. In fulfillment of this prophecy, 2300 days elapsed before Judas Maccabees cleansed the temple. The Antichrist will be the latter day fulfillment of this prophecy when he enters the temple and proclaims himself to be God. He will cast down the sanctuary, destroy the altar, stop the sacrifices, and set up an image of himself to be worshipped. Christ will conquer the Antichrist, and the temple will be cleansed as it is rebuilt.

Daniel 8:15-19-Now it happened, when I, Daniel, had seen the vision and was seeking the meaning, that suddenly there stood before me one having the appearance of a man. And I heard a man's voice between the banks of the Ulai, who called, and said, "Gabriel, make this man understand the vision. So he came near where I stood, and when he came I was afraid and fell on my face; but he said to me, Understand, son of man, that the vision refers to the time of the end. Now, as he was speaking with me, I was in a deep sleep with my face to the ground; but he touched me, and stood me upright. And he said, "Look, I and making known to you what shall happen in the latter time of the indignation; for at the appointed time the end shall be."

The angel Gabriel, having the appearance of a man, is dispatched by God to help Daniel understand the meaning of the vision. Gabriel informs Daniel that the vision refers to the end times. The full realization of this prophecy will be at the Second Coming of Christ.

Daniel 8:20-22-"The ram which you saw, having the two horns - they are the kings of Media and Persia. And the male goat is the kingdom of Greece. The large horn that is between its eyes is the first king. As for the broken horn and the four that stood up in its place, four kingdoms shall arise out of that nation, but not with its power."

The "ram having two horns" represents the kings of Media and Persia. The "male goat" is the kingdom of Greece. The "large horn" is the first king or Alexander the Great. The great horn was broken at the death of Alexander and his kingdom divided among his four generals. None will equal his level of power or authority.

Daniel 8:23-"And in the latter time of their kingdom, when the transgressors have reached their fullness, a king shall arise, having fierce features, who understands sinister schemes."

The latter times of the kingdom refer to the time of the Antichrist when the Old Grecian Empire will be revived. The Antichrist will rule over the territory that at one time encompassed both the old Roman and Grecian Empires. Sin will abound. A king, the Antichrist, arises from the Seleucid division of the Grecian Empire. Since the early fulfillment of this prophecy was Antiochus ruler of the Seleucid territory, and the latter fulfillment is the Antichrist, it stands to reason that the Antichrist will come from this same region, which includes territory of Syria, Babylon, and Assyria. However, Daniel 9:26 indicates that the Antichrist will come from the Reconstituted Roman Empire, and to be more specific, the Antichrist will emerge from the Eastern division of the Reconstituted Roman Empire. Therefore, the Antichrist is linked to both the Revived Grecian and Reconstituted Roman Empires. He will be stern faced and a master of intrigue.

Daniel 8:24-"His power shall be mighty, but not by his own power; he shall destroy fearfully, and shall prosper and thrive; he shall destroy the mighty, and also the holy people."

The Antichrist will be powerful but not on his own. He is empowered by the ten kings, prince from the abyss, and Satan himself. He is prosperous, causes mass destruction, and attempts to destroy the Jewish nation.

Daniel 8:25-"Through his cunning he shall cause deceit to prosper under his hand; and he shall magnify himself in his heart. He shall destroy many in their prosperity. He shall even rise against the Prince of princes; but he shall be broken without human hand."

The Antichrist operates through deception and cunning. He breaks the covenant of peace that he established with Israel as he seeks to annihilate her. The Antichrist magnifies himself in his heart as Lucifer did when he exalted himself above God, and he will contend against the Prince of princes, Christ. The Antichrist

will be destroyed by Christ at the battle of Armageddon.

Daniel 8:26-27-"And the vision of the evenings and mornings which was told is true; therefore seal up the vision, for it refers to many days in the future. And I, Daniel, fainted and was sick for days; afterward I arose and went about the king's business. I was astonished by the vision, but no one understood it."

Shutting up the vision means the events of the vision will not be fulfilled for a long time. It has already been over 2500 years, yet these events will not occur until the Tribulation. Daniel was astonished at the vision, and no one could understand it, apart from his interpretation.

Daniel 9:24-27
Prophecy of the Seventy Weeks of Years

Daniel 9:24-27 is one of the most important passages of scripture in the Bible to the understanding of end-time events. This prophecy supports the divine origin of the Bible. God not only predicted Christ's Coming several hundred years before fulfillment in His virgin birth, but also has provided a precise look at history in advance and Israel's role at the end of the age. This prophecy focuses on Israel, not the Church, or Gentiles.

Daniel 9:24-"Seventy weeks are determined for your people and for your holy city, to finish the transgression, to make an end of sins, to make reconciliation for iniquity, to bring in everlasting righteousness, to seal up vision and prophecy, and to anoint the Most Holy."

"Seventy weeks" is literally seventy segments of seven or seventy multiplied by seven or 490 of something. In Hebrew, "seven" can refer to days, weeks, or years, depending on the context. In this case, the context clearly refers to years according to prominent theologians (refer to Daniel 9:2). Therefore, this prophecy identifies

a period of time of 490 years. In answer to Daniel's prayer and supplication in verses 3-20 regarding Daniel's people and the holy city, Jerusalem, the angel Gabriel told Daniel there would be 490 years of Gentile domination of Israel before the end of oppression by the Gentiles. The 490 years concern only Israel and Jerusalem. As far as Daniel was concerned, after 490 years Messiah would set up His kingdom. Daniel had no knowledge that there would be an interval within the 490 years and that the Church Age would exist between weeks 69 and 70. The Church Age is referred to as a "mystery" in the New Testament, and was not known to the writers of the Old Testament. The Old Testament writers knew about the events surrounding the Coming of Christ, but they did not realize that there would be a lengthy period of time between Messiah's birth and the setting up of His kingdom or His First and Second Advents. Hence, the mystery does not include the First and Second Advents of Christ, or the Millennium, but does include the body of Christ, the infilling of the Holy Spirit, spiritual gifts available to every believer, and teachings from the New Testament epistles. Additionally, the Rapture is a part of the mystery, for one of the basic rapture scriptures, I Corinthians 15:51, says *"behold, I show you a mystery..."*

Seventy weeks are "determined," or this time period is set aside or distinguished from all other time periods, for God to deal exclusively with Israel, the Jews, and Jerusalem. Six events are stated in verse 24 that have not been fulfilled and can only be fulfilled in the 70th week of the prophecy. Israel is in rebellion to God and has been broken off or separated from God for her unbelief. These six events are God's plan to bring the nation Israel into its promised blessings.

The six events are:

1) *To finish the transgression* - Jesus' work on the cross has provided redemption for sin, but Israel has not accepted God's redemptive plan. However, Israel will accept Christ's

redemption and will be saved at the end of the 70th week. Israel's sin of disobedience will be over or finished when she repents of her transgression and accepts Christ as Savior at His Second Coming.

2) *To make an end of sins* - The sins of Israel as individuals and as a nation will come to an end or be sealed up at Christ's Second Coming. The current punishment or separation from God will be removed, and Israel will then obey God forever.

3) *To make reconciliation (atonement) for inequity* - Atonement for sin was provided by Christ's substitutionary sacrifice for mankind, but Israel as a nation has not accepted Jesus' work of the cross. At the Second Coming of Christ, Israel will repent and accept their atonement through Christ's shed blood.

4) *To bring in everlasting righteousness* - When Israel's transgression of rejecting her Messiah is finished, the sin of Israel comes to an end or is sealed up. As Israel accepts the atoning work of Christ, everlasting righteousness is ushered in, which is a reference to the Millennial kingdom and Christ's ruling in righteousness or establishing an age of righteousness.

5) *To seal up the vision and prophecy* - These prophecies and God's eternal covenants with Israel and Jerusalem will be fulfilled in the Millennium under the rule of Messiah. When the prophecies are fulfilled they are considered "sealed." Until then, they are unsealed. "Prophecy" literally means prophet, i.e., there will no longer be a need for the prophets to direct or rebuke Israel in an attempt to lead her to God and righteousness. In the Millennium, all shall know the Lord.

6) *To anoint the most Holy* - Anointing the most Holy refers to the cleansing of the Holy of Holies from the abomination of desolation. It also could apply to the establishment and anointing of the Millennial Holy of Holies. Some scholars apply this anointing to a crowning of Christ. However, Christ is not to be crowned by man, but has already been crowned King of kings and Lord of lords by the Father God.

Daniel 9:25-"Know therefore and understand, that from the going forth of the command to restore and build Jerusalem until Messiah the Prince, there shall be seven weeks and sixty-two weeks; The streets shall be built again, and the wall, even in troublesome times"

A command or decree initiated the rebuilding of the temple, Holy City, street, and wall. Four decrees were given in history. The first command (Ezra 1:1-4, 6:1-5) was by Cyrus of Persia to rebuild the temple. The second decree (Ezra 6:6-12) by Darius I of Persia reaffirmed the first command to rebuild the temple. The third decree (Ezra 7:11-26) was from Artaxerxes to Ezra and concerned temple service. The fourth decree (Nehemiah 2:1-8), which is the popular and prevalent choice of prophetic teachers, was given by Artaxerxes Longimus in 445 B.C., granting the Jews permission to restore and rebuild Jerusalem, including its walls.

The 70 weeks of years or 490 years are divided into three sections. The first division is 7 weeks or 49 years, which is assumed to be the time period to complete the total rebuilding or restoration of the city. The second division of 62 weeks or 434 years, immediately followed the conclusion of the 49 years until Christ presented Himself to Israel as her Messiah in fulfillment of Zechariah 9:9, when He entered Jerusalem on Palm Sunday riding on a donkey. Zechariah 9:9 states *"Rejoice greatly, O daughter of Zion! shout, O daughter of Jerusalem! behold, your King is coming to you; He is just and having salvation, lowly and riding on a donkey, a colt, the foal of a donkey."* This was the only time that Christ allowed Himself to be recognized as King. Prior to this time, Christ

always refused recognition as King, stating His time had not yet come. Therefore, from the fourth decree issued by Artaxerxes until Messiah's entry into Jerusalem, 69 weeks or 483 years occurred. Scholars have calculated this time period to the very day as a period consisting of 173,880 days from March 14, 445 B.C. to April 6, A.D. 32, based on the Jewish calendar of 360 days per year. 483 years multiplied by 360 days per year equals 173,880 days. However, some scholars have corrected the date for Christ's triumphal entry into Jerusalem to March 29, A.D. 33 based on adjustments for Passover occurrences.

An alternate opinion, worthy of note, is that the correct decree initiating the rebuilding of Jerusalem is actually the one issued by Cyrus. The rationale for this position is that the fourth decree, which is the decree typically adopted by scholars, is not really a decree, but a request for permission to rebuild the wall. The second and third decrees pertain to building the temple and temple service. The first decree by Cyrus concerned both the building of the temple as previously stated and rebuilding the city as specified in Isaiah 44:28 and 45:13. Finally, the Daniel 9:25 prophecy of 69 weeks of years or 483 years doesn't reference the triumphal entry of Christ into Jerusalem but states "until Messiah the Prince," which would more appropriately signify His birth.

Daniel 9:26-"And after the sixty-two weeks Messiah shall be cut off, but not for Himself; and the people of the prince who is to come shall destroy the city and the sanctuary. The end of it shall be with a flood, and till the end of the war desolations are determined."

According to the biblical text, after 69 weeks or 483 years Messiah is "cut off," indicating the two divisions of 7 weeks and 62 weeks had been concluded, with an apparent break in the timeline after the 69th week. Christ being cut off points to His crucifixion. Cut off stands for a criminal receiving the death penalty. He was cut-off, not for Himself, but for all mankind.

Israel rejected her Messiah and participated in His crucifixion in fulfillment of this prophecy. The crucifixion and subsequent destruction of Jerusalem and the temple were events occurring after the end of this sixty-nine week prophetic period. The time interval between the 69th and 70th years has now lasted almost 2000 years. As a result of Israel's rejection of Jesus the Messiah, a spiritual blindness came over Israel, which will not be lifted until Christ returns at the end of the Tribulation.

"People of the prince who is to come" refers to the Romans who were in military command of Jerusalem. People are the subject of the sentence. The prince to come refers to the Antichrist who will arise out of the Old Grecian portion of the Reconstituted Roman Empire. In A.D. 70, the armies under the command of Titus destroyed Jerusalem and the temple and murdered over one million Jews. The Jews were subsequently scattered throughout the world without a homeland and without the holy city of Jerusalem. In describing the destruction of the temple, Christ said in Luke 19:44 that not one stone would be left upon another. A fire ravaged the inside of the temple and melted all the gold fixtures. Because there were so many fixtures and artifacts, the melted gold seeped to the foundation. The soldiers of Titus tore the temple apart stone by stone in pursuit of the gold, and literally one stone was not left standing upon another.

After 69 weeks or 483 years, Jewish time stopped temporarily, but it is not over, because the events listed in verse 24 have not yet occurred. One week of years, or one segment of seven, or seven years, remain for God to complete His dealings with the nation of Israel and fulfill the promises of verse 24. Before God could deal with Israel, they had to return to their homeland again, which occurred in 1948, when the state of Israel was recognized by the nations of the world. Furthermore, the Jews had to be in possession of the city of Jerusalem, which happened in 1967 after the six-day war. Now that these two events are history, the prophetic stage is set to complete the prophecies as spelled out in Daniel 9:24-27. The events of 1948 and 1967 do

not start the seventieth week, but set the stage for the seventieth week to begin. The final event to close out this interval or gap period, called the Church Age, between the 69th and 70th weeks is disclosed in Romans 11:25 *"...hardening in part has happened to Israel until the fullness of the Gentiles has come in."* "Fullness" is symbolically compared to the first drop, that when added to a full glass of a liquid, will cause an overflowing. God has determined a specific number of Gentiles to be saved by the end of the Church Age and when that count has been reached, the fullness will have been achieved; Israel will return to favored status with God; the Church will be raptured, and the seventieth week can commence upon the signing of the peace covenant. Fullness of the Gentiles is different than the "times of the Gentiles." Times of the Gentiles include the kingdoms or world empires that have persecuted the nation of Israel from Egypt through the Beast's (Antichrist) Empire.

"The end shall be with a flood" refers to war and the complete destruction of Jerusalem and the temple. "Till the end of the war" more appropriately means until the end there is war, i.e., Israel will face war and sufferings throughout the Tribulation Period, or until the 490 years have finished, at which time she will be able to rest in the Millennial kingdom.

Daniel 9:27-"Then he shall confirm a covenant with many for one week; But in the middle of the week He shall bring an end to sacrifice and offering. And on the wing of abominations shall be one who makes desolate, even until the consummation, which is determined, is poured out on the desolate."

As of 1948 and 1967, Israel is partially gathered together and God can deal with her as a nation again. This last week of seven years to come is referred to as the seventieth week of Daniel. From the pre-Tribulation Rapture viewpoint, the Church is to be raptured before the Tribulation begins. After the Rapture of the Church, the Antichrist will make a covenant or peace treaty with Israel for seven years, probably allowing Israel to rebuild

her temple or at least the sanctuary or Holy of Holies. In exchange, Israel will most likely help finance the Antichrist's takeover of the ten kingdoms. In the middle of this seven-year period, the Antichrist will break the peace treaty, enter the sanctuary and proclaim himself to be God, which is why he is referred to as the "abomination of desolation" or the one who makes desolate. He will totally desecrate the temple in the same manner that Antiochus Epiphanes did when he sacrificed a pig on the altar. The Antichrist will then seek to exterminate the Jews, because without the Jews, God cannot fulfill His covenants with them and usher in the Millennium.

Selected Verses from Daniel 10

Daniel 10:1-10

Daniel experiences another vision. In this vision, he sees Christ whose appearance is similar to John's vision in Revelation 1.

Daniel 10:11-13

The angel Gabriel was sent to Daniel because of Daniel's prayers for his people. Gabriel was held up for 21 days by the Prince of Persia until the archangel Michael came and helped him.

Daniel 10:10-14

Gabriel informs Daniel that the vision is of the latter days or end-times.

Daniel 10:15-19

Daniel is strengthened by the angel.

Daniel 10:20-Then he said, "Do you know why I have come to you? And now I must return to fight with the prince of Persia; and when I have gone forth, indeed the prince of Greece will come."
Gabriel returns to fight against the Prince of Persia. After the

Prince of Persia, the Prince of Greece enters the scene of history. The Prince of Greece is believed by many scholars to be the satanic force behind Alexander the Great that aided him in his conquest of the then known world within 13 years. The Prince of Greece or another satanic prince such as the Prince of Babylon or Prince of Assyria could be the beast out of the abyss referred to in Revelation 11, who will oppress and empower the Antichrist. These passages demonstrate the warfare in the heavenlies that occurs over nations.

Daniel 10:21-"But I will tell you what is noted in the Scripture of Truth. No one upholds me against these, except Michael your prince."

Michael is identified as the Chief Prince for the nation Israel.

Selected Verses from Daniel 11
(Refer to Prophetic Key: Daniel Military Campaign)

Daniel 11:1-"Also in the first year of Darius the Mede, I, even I, stood up to confirm and strengthen him."

After Gabriel helped Michael overthrow the Prince of Babylon, the Prince of Persia appeared on the stage of history.

Daniel 11:2-4-"And now I will tell you the truth: Behold, three more kings will arise in Persia and the fourth shall be far richer than them all; by his strength, through his riches, he shall stir up all against the realm of Greece. Then a mighty king shall arise, who shall rule with great dominion, and do according to his will. And when he has arisen, his kingdom shall be broken up and divided toward the four winds of heaven, but not among his posterity nor according to his dominion with which he ruled; for his kingdom shall be uprooted, even for others besides these."

Persia was the ruling empire at this time. Cyrus was the first

king and four other kings would rule after him. Three kings ruled Persia starting with Cyrus. Xerxes was the fourth king who was richer than the preceding three kings, and he used his wealth to obtain power. Alexander the Great was the mighty king who did as he willed for no one could stand against him. He conquered the Persian Empire that was richer and stronger than Greece and assumed rulership over the total kingdom. Alexander the Great died at age 32 or 33 from malaria, depression, and alcoholism. He was depressed because there were no more kingdoms to conquer. Alexander the Great was controlled and oppressed by the high-ranking, demonic Prince of Greece. It is believed that the beast out of the abyss in Revelation 11 could be this same satanic Prince of Greece or possibly the Prince of Babylon or Prince of Assyria, who will control and oppress the future the Antichrist.

Daniel 11:5-34

These passages provide a historical discussion of the King of the North and the King of the South. Egypt (or a coalition of nations including Egypt) is identified as the King of the South and Syria (or a coalition of nations including Syria) as the King of the North. These verses described events predicted in advance and validated by history.

Daniel 11:35-36-"And some of those of understanding shall fall, to refine them, purge them, and make them white, until the time of the end; because it is still for the appointed time. Then the king shall do according to his own will; he shall exalt and magnify himself above every god, shall speak blasphemies against the God of gods, and shall prosper till the wrath has been accomplished; for what has been determined shall be done."

The remainder of chapter 11 discusses events of the end times, along with further description of the Antichrist. These scriptures state that the Antichrist will do as he pleases, according to

his own will. He will exalt and magnify himself above every god and will speak blasphemy against God. He will prosper until the time for his judgment at the end of the Tribulation Period. God's plan will be done.

Daniel 11:37-"He shall regard neither the God of his fathers nor the desire of women, no regard any god; for he shall magnify himself above them all."

The Antichrist will not regard any god, nor the God of his fathers, deducing that the religious identification of his family could have been Jewish, Christian, or possibly Islam, for in each case, only one God is worshipped. It is unlikely that his religious background is Jewish or Christian because of his intense persecution of them. Since he probably rises up out of the Middle East (Seleucid territory), a strong possibility is that the religion of his ancestry is Islam. An alternate opinion held by scholars is that the "God of his fathers" should be interpreted "gods of his fathers," implying a polytheistic form of worship. In either case, the Antichrist himself is clearly an atheist. The Antichrist magnifies himself above everyone, including God. The Antichrist does not desire women, which has led many commentators to speculate that he may be homosexual.

Daniel 11:38-39-"But in their place he shall honor a god of fortresses; and a god which his fathers did not know he shall honor with gold and silver, with precious stones and pleasant things. Thus he shall act against the strongest fortresses with a foreign god, which shall acknowledge, and advance its glory; and he shall cause them to rule over many, and divide the land for gain."

The Antichrist does honor a god of fortresses or power and war. He worships war and material things. His military campaigns are very successful, and he apparently uses religion and worship of deities to bring people into believing he is God. In Revelation 13, it says that all inhabitants of the earth worship the Beast. All

religions of the world will merge into one religion centered on the worship of this world leader.

Daniel 11:40-"At the time of the end the king of the South shall attack him; and the king of the North shall come against him like a whirlwind, with chariots, horsemen, and with many ships; and he shall enter the countries, over-whelm them, and pass through."

The King of the North and the King of the South will attack the Antichrist but will be defeated by him.

Daniel 11:41-"He shall also enter the Glorious Land and many countries shall be overthrown; but these shall escape from his hand: Edom, Moab, and the prominent people of Ammon."

After the Antichrist defeats the King of the North and King of the South, he moves into Israel. This verse identifies that many countries are overthrown, which adds support to the King of the North and King of the South being coalitions. Three countries are noted as escaping his grasp, Edom, Moab, and Ammon. These three countries align with present day Jordan and will probably be the place of protection for the "woman" or Israel during the second half of the Tribulation. The woman flees to this hiding place, considered by most commentators to be Petra, at the middle of the seventieth week, which fits the scenario suggested above. Following the defeat of the King of the North and the King of the South by the Antichrist, Gog from the land of Magog with his Muslim allies will move against Israel. God will destroy Gog's armies on the mountains of Israel.

Daniel 11:42-43-"He shall stretch out his hand against the countries, and the land of Egypt shall not escape. He shall have power over the treasures of gold and silver, and over all the precious things of Egypt; also the Libyans and Ethiopians shall follow at his heels."

The Antichrist conquers Egypt. Libya and Ethiopia are Muslim

nations in Northern Africa that are allied with Gog. The Antichrist controls the wealth of these nations.

Daniel 11:44-"But news from the east and the north shall trouble him; therefore he shall go out with great furry to destroy and annihilate many."

As previously stated, news from the east and north that troubles the Antichrist is the Islamic Russian army from the north under Gog, joined by armies from the Muslim nations located north and east of Israel. Following the supernatural destruction of the armies led by Gog, three of the Reconstituted Roman Empire nations are conquered by the Antichrist. Egypt and Syria are most likely two of the three conquered nations. Then, the Antichrist moves to conquer the remaining seven who give their power to him, rather than engage in war. The Antichrist does not battle the Kings of the East at this time, because they will be enticed by him to come to Armageddon at the end of the Tribulation to battle against God.

Daniel 11:45-"And he shall plant the tents of his palace between the seas and the glorious holy mountain; yet he shall come to his end, and no one will help him."

The Antichrist will be defeated and cast into the lake of fire.

Daniel 12

Daniel 12:1-"At that time Michael shall stand up, the great prince who stands watch over the sons of your people; and there shall be a time of trouble, such as never was since there was a nation, even to that time. And at that time your people shall be delivered, every one who is found written in the book."

The archangel Michael is the great prince who stands for the children of Israel. The second half of the Tribulation will be a time of trouble for Israel such as has never been experienced in their history. The persecution will be so intense that at the end

of the age, only one-third of the nation will survive and be delivered or rescued. Israel as a nation will be saved and accept Jesus as their Messiah at the end of the seventieth week.

Daniel 12:2-3-"and many of those who sleep in the dust of the earth shall awake, some to everlasting life, some to shame and everlasting contempt. Those who are wise shall shine like the brightness of the firmament, and those who turn many to righteousness like the stars forever and ever."

This passage identifies two separate resurrections, called the First Resurrection and the Second Resurrection. The First Resurrection is resurrection to eternal life as the souls and spirits of saints receive their glorified bodies. The First Resurrection will occur in several stages as discussed in Revelation 20:5 but will be concluded before the onset of the Millennium. The Second Resurrection is a resurrection to damnation for the unrighteous of all time, from Adam through the millennial reign of Christ, and will take place after the Millennium but preceding the White Throne judgment. The two resurrections are then separated by the period of the Millennium.

Daniel 12:4-"But you, Daniel, shut up the words, and seal the book until the time if the end; many shall run to and fro, and knowledge shall increase."

Daniel is instructed to seal up the vision and the prophecy. To the Jew, this prophecy is sealed and will not be realized until after the middle of the Tribulation. At that time, knowledge will increase in that this prophecy will begin to have meaning to the Jews, for they will be ready to hear it. Knowledge of and about the Word of God is increasing daily as well as knowledge of Biblical prophecy as the end of the age nears. Furthermore, general knowledge is increasing at an astronomical rate. It is estimated that knowledge is doubling every 18 months and is projected to double every 12 months in the not too distant future.

Daniel 12:5-6-Then I, Daniel, looked; and there stood two others, one on this riverbank and the other on that riverbank. And one said to the man clothed in linen, who was above the waters of the river, "How long shall the fulfillment of these wonders be?"

These two beings, one on each bank of the river Tigris, are apparently angels. One asks a question of extreme interest to Daniel, i.e., how long until these things end? He did not ask how long until the end of time, but how long before these events are completed at the end of time?

Daniel 12:7-Then I heard the man clothed in linen who was above the waters of the river, when he held up his right hand and his left hand to heaven, and swore by Him who lives forever that it shall be for a time, times, and half a time; and when the power of the holy people has been completely shattered, all these things shall be finished.

The person clothed in linen is believed by most scholars to be the pre-incarnate Christ. This vision is a Christophany, or appearance of Jesus before His incarnation. The phrase "a man clothed in linen" links to Daniel 10:5-6, which in greater detail describes a certain man clothed in linen. The certain man clothed in fine linen of Daniel 10:5-6 pictures a divine visitation of Christ. This description of Christ in Daniel 10:5-6 is very similar to His description in Revelation 1:12-17. Christ answers the question posed by the angel that the time for fulfillment shall be times, times, and half a time, or 3 1/2 years. The 3 1/2 years equates with the Antichrist's severe persecution of Israel for the last half of the Tribulation after he has entered the temple and proclaimed himself to be God. During this last 42 months of the Tribulation, the Jews will be scattered and their power as a nation diluted. Most Israelites will seek refuge in Petra and accompanying wilderness areas.

Daniel 12:8-10-Although I heard, I did not understand.

Then I said, "My lord, what shall be the end of these things? And he said, Go your way, Daniel, for the words are closed up and sealed till the time of the end. Many shall be purified, made white, and refined, but the wicked shall do wickedly; and none of the wicked shall understand, but the wise shall understand."

Daniel doesn't understand and asks Jesus for clarification of events that will end this period of time. Jesus doesn't reveal any more details to Daniel. Daniel is told that the "words are closed up" until the time of the end. As time progresses, believers will continue to increase their knowledge of the Word, including the Book of Daniel and prophecies of the end. To the unrighteous, the prophetic word will remain a mystery.

Daniel 12:11-"And from the time that the daily sacrifice is taken away, and the abomination of desolation is set up, there shall be one thousand two hundred and ninety days."

An additional time period is revealed that is not elsewhere disclosed in the Word of God. The time from the abomination of desolation and the discontinuance of the daily sacrifice at the middle of the seventieth week until the end of the age shall be 1290 days. This time period represents an additional 30 days beyond the 42 months or 1260 days identified for the Great Tribulation. Commentators have not proposed solid reasons for this additional 30 days, other than time needed for cleansing of the temple or preparation for establishing the millennial kingdom. Both of these reasons appear weak. To set apart a specific 30-day period of time, God must have a greater purpose than that assumed by the majority of commentators.

An alternate position, proposed in this study, is that the additional 30 days is for execution of the bowl judgments on earth and that Armageddon and the Second Coming of Christ will occur at the end of this 30-day period. The ministry of the two witnesses supports this conclusion. In Revelation 11, the two witnesses are said to minister for 3 1/2 years, are killed, their

bodies lie in the street for 3 1/2 days, and then they are raised up and taken into heaven. They start their ministry before the seventh seal judgment and minister for 42 months, the time period of the Great Tribulation. If an exact application of the text is applied, then the witnesses would be lying in the street and resurrected 3 1/2 days after the battle of Armageddon has concluded. The two prophets smite the earth with plagues that complement the trumpet judgments, which are only partial in destruction. However, the bowl judgments are total in destruction, and additional plagues would not be necessary. The 144,000 Jews are protected during the period of the trumpet judgments and are raptured as the male child before the bowl judgments. The 144,000 Jews will not minister during the execution of the bowl judgments. It appears the same for the two prophets. The judgments will be so devastating that human witnesses for God will be removed. Angels will be God's means of evangelism during this time.

It is noted that no events are said to last longer than 42 months. The Antichrist's reign is said to be for 42 months. The Great Tribulation is for 42 months. However, this passage appears to extend the period for an additional month. Many commentators agree that the bowl judgments will be executed in a short span of time, probably the last month of Daniel's seventieth week. The question is whether the last month is 42 months or 43 months after the Antichrist breaks his covenant with Israel at mid-Tribulation and commits the abomination of desolation. Of course, the Antichrist could commit the abomination of desolation 30 days before the exact middle of the Tribulation. No blessing is mentioned for this extended 30-day time period but there is with the next 45-day period. Even though all questions regarding this additional 30-day period are not reconciled, the position proposed appears to provide a logical alternative to the standard interpretation of Daniel 12:11.

Daniel 12:12-"Blessed is he who waits, and comes to the one thousand three hundred and thirty-five days."

Another time period of 45 days beyond the 1290 days is identified. This period may be for the cleansing or reconstruction of the temple, preparation for the millennial kingdom, but more probably, it is the time period allotted for the judgment of nations. Again, there is limited commentary on the purpose for this additional time period. A blessing is pronounced for the person who survives this period, which supports the judgment of the sheep and goat nations position. The blessing would then be for those entering the Millennium as part of the sheep nations.

Daniel 12:13-"But you, go your way till the end; for you shall rest, and will arise to your inheritance at the end of the days."

This glorious promise to every believer that they will receive their inheritance and rule and reign with Christ for eternity.

Prophetic Key: Comparison of Kingdoms and Beasts in Revelation and Daniel

Revelation 17:10 Beast: Kings and Kingdoms	Revelation 17:8, 11 Beast: Kingdoms and Satanic Prince	Revelation 12:3; 13:1; 17:3 Beasts: Seven Heads and Ten Horns (17:9, 12)	Daniel 2 Great Statue (Kingdoms)	Daniel 7 Wild Beasts (Kingdoms)	Daniel 8 Little Horn (Antichrist)
Five fallen	Beast that was	Egypt (1st head) Assyria (2nd head) Babylon (3rd head) Medo-Persia (4th head) Greece (5th head)	Head of gold Arms/Chest of silver Belly/Thighs of brass	Lion with eagle's wings Bear with three ribs in its mouth Leopard with four wings and four heads	Ram with two horns Male Goat with notable horn, then four horns
One is	Beast that is not	Rome (6th head)	Legs of iron (Western and Eastern divisions of the Roman Empire)	Non-Descriptive	
One has not yet come		Reconstituted Rome (7th head with 10 horns)	Ten Toes of iron and clay	Ten horns	
Exist for a short time (Antichrist rules for the Great Tribulation)	Beast that yet is (former satanic prince) will be the Eighth (Beast Kingdom) of the seven (kingdoms)	Revived Greece within Reconstituted Rome(Beast or Eighth Kingdom)		Little Horn out of the Ten Kingdoms of Reconstituted Rome (Antichrist)	Little Horn out of the old Grecian region of Reconstituted Rome (Antichrist)

BOOK OF EZEKIEL

Ezekiel 38-39
(Refer to Prophetic Keys: United States in Prophecy and Magog Military Campaign)

Ezekiel 38:1-3-Now the word of the Lord came to me, saying, "Son of man, set your face against Gog, of the land of Magog, the prince of Rosh, Meshech, and Tubal, and prophesy against him, and say, Thus says the Lord God: Behold, I am against you, O Gog, the prince of Rosh, Meshech, and Tubal."

Based on archaeological data and other sources now available, Bible experts appear to be in general agreement as to the background of "Magog," an essential factor to understanding chapters 38-39 of Ezekiel. Magog was one of the sons of Japheth, who was one of the three sons of Noah. Magog is identified by scholars as the group of peoples called "Scythians," located in ancient Germanic areas including southern Russia, and therefore, are ancestors of present day Russia. The Scythians were savage nomads, who terrorized Russia several centuries before Christ. Josephus Flavius, in the first century B.C., said "...Scythians, who delight in murdering people and are little better than wild beasts..." Herodotus in the fifth century B.C., said of Scythians "no one confronting them can escape on foot, and if they wish not to be discovered it is impossible to engage with them. The reason is that they do not build towns or fortresses, but all of them are mounted archers and carry their homes with them...How can they fail to be invincible, and immune from attack?" Magog then encompasses the present day Muslim

Russian nations of Kazakhstan, Kyrgyzstan, Uzbekistan, Turkmenistan, Tajikistan, and possibly Afghanistan.

There is some confusion in the translation of "Rosh." It is sometimes used as a proper name and other times as the title "chief." Additionally, Rosh seems to come from the same root as Rus, from which Russia derived her name. Meshech was a son of Japheth and is identified with northern and eastern Turkey, extending north into Russia around present day Moscow. Tubal was a son of Japheth and is identified with parts of Turkey and West Central or Asiatic Russia, including the current city of Tobolsk.

A majority of prophetic scholars conclude that Russia will be eliminated as a major world power in the Magog campaign described in Ezekiel 38-39. However, because Magog consists of several Muslim republics of Russia, and the allies of Magog are all Islamic nations bent on the destruction of Israel, the war described in Ezekiel 38-39 represents an Islamic jihad against Israel. This war, following the war of the King of the South and King of the North against the Antichrist, as described in Daniel 11:40-45, results not only in the elimination of Russia as a world power, but also the elimination of Islamic nations as a major threat in the world.

"Gog" stands for a high or supreme ruler from the northern territory who will lead this end-time coalition of Russian and Muslim nations against Israel. Gog is referred to as a chief prince. Similar titles of rank could be Pharaoh, President, Czar, or King. Because this is a military campaign, an appropriate military title would be commander-in-chief. God says that He is against Gog, which is a statement of much import and significance as the events of these chapters unfold.

Ezekiel 38:4-6-"I will turn you around, put hooks into your jaws, and lead you out, with all your army, horses, and horsemen, all splendidly clothed, a great company with bucklers and shields, all of the handling swords. Persia, Ethiopia,

and Libya are with them, all of them with shield and helmet; Gomer and all its troops; the house of Togarmah from the far north and all its troops -many people are with you."

Gog leads a massive, impressive, and well-equipped army from the three power base nations of Rosh, Meshech, and Tubal. Scholars have analyzed the usage of the descriptive words and find that references to horses and horsemen with shields and swords could refer to a cavalry unit as in the writer's time, or to a mechanized army as in modern times. "Hooks in the jaw" seem to indicate that Russia will be drawn into this invasion by force, i.e. persuasion from the Muslim coalition who they have continually supported. It appears that both have their own agenda. The Muslim nations want to annihilate Israel, control the Middle East, and rule the world, while Russia under the leadership of Gog, also wants to control the Middle East and rule the world.

The allies of the northern nations are identified. Persia is from the line of Japheth, and is the ancient name for modern day Iran, which may also include parts of present day Iraq. Today, both Iran and Iraq are leaders in the Middle East, with strong Islamic influence. Ethiopia or ancient Cush is the region south of Egypt and may also include Sudan and Somalia. Cush is from the line of Ham as well as Put. Libya or ancient Put may encompass the territories of northern Africa west of Egypt, such as Algeria, Tunisia, and Morocco.

Gomer, of the Japhetic line, is sometimes identified with ancient Germania, extending into the Ukraine and the territories of the old Western USSR, but more likely represents present day Turkey. Togarmah was a son of Gomer and is identified as the area of Armenia and Eastern Turkey. It must be noted that all of the allies of Magog are Islamic or Muslim, with an intense hatred of Israel and the Jew. Islamic Jihad is directed against not only the Jew, but also the entire non-Muslim world. Their goal is to control the world, by force if necessary. Since they are committed to the destruction and annihilation of Israel, they will quickly unite

with Gog in their mutual war against Israel.

Ezekiel 38:7-"Prepare yourself and be ready, you and all your companies that are gathered about you; and be a guard for them."

"Guard" conveys being both provider and leader. Currently, and for some time, Russia has backed their Islamic allies with both weapons and technology.

Ezekiel 38:8-"After many days you will be visited. In the latter years you will come into the land of those brought back from the sword and gathered from many people on the mountains of Israel, which had long been desolate; they were brought out of the nations, and now all of them dwell safely."

The Jews had been dispersed from their homeland since A.D. 70 and had to be re-gathered before this invasion could occur. In 1948, Israel was recognized as a nation again. Today, they are in their land but not dwelling safely. Terrorism and Middle East unrest are the conditions of the day. However, after the peace covenant with the Antichrist in the first half of the seventieth week of Daniel, Israel will dwell safely in her land.

Ezekiel 38:9-"You will ascend, coming like a storm covering the land like a cloud, you and all your troops and many peoples with you."

These armies sneak attack unsuspecting Israel with great ferocity, because to the Muslims, this will be a holy war or Jihad.

Ezekiel 38:10-11-"Thus says the Lord God: On that day it shall come to pass that thoughts will arise in your mind, and you will make an evil plan: You will say, I will go up against a land of unwalled villages; I will go to a peaceful people, who dwells safely, all of them dwelling without walls, and having neither bars nor gates"

"No wall for protection" and "dwelling safely," according to some commentators, can mean not only physical safety, but also false confidence. Israel is not prepared to defend herself. Since this invasion occurs late in the first half of the seventieth week, Israel will believe she has nothing to fear because of her seven year treaty or covenant with the Antichrist.

Ezekiel 38:12-"to take plunder and to take booty, to stretch out your hand against the waste places that are again inhabited, and against a people gathered from the nations, who have acquired livestock and goods, who dwell in the midst of the land."

Israel, having been re-gathered as a nation, turns a desert environment or wasteland into a fruit bearing country. Many Bible students speculate that Israel has untapped natural resources that are desirable to the Islamic and northern European world.

Ezekiel 38:13-"Sheba, Dedan, the merchants of Tarshish, and all their young lions will say to you, Have you come to take plunder? Have you gathered your army to take booty, to carry away silver and gold, to take away livestock and goods, to take great plunder?"

Sheba and Dedan refer to the Arabian peninsula, and in addition to Saudi Arabia, could include the nations of Yemen, Oman, Qatar, UAE, and Bahrain. These nations are not included in the list of Muslim allies supporting Magog. It is the opinion of knowledgeable commentators that Iran is the main leader in the Middle East with the desire to control the Islamic Crescent.

Tarshish has been a source of speculation among commentators. Tarshish is associated with sea trade. Scholars surmise Tarshish existed on the coastlands from Britain, southward to Spain, to the Mediterranean, or Ceylon, or the East Indies. Some writers have further conjectured that the "young lions" or "outposts of Tarshish" refer to the United States with archaeological evidence supporting that conclusion. Canada

and Western European nations would also be included in the outposts of Tarshish.

Ezekiel 38:14-"Therefore, son of man, prophesy and say to Gog, Thus says the Lord God: "On that day when My people of Israel dwell safely will you not know it?"

God refers to Israel as His people. During the Church Age, estranged Israel is not considered by God to be His people. God is expressly in covenant relationship with His Church. Once the Church is raptured, God will again interact with Israel, and they will be His people. Therefore, based on this passage, the invasion by Gog cannot be pre-Rapture. Dwelling safely in the land occurs as God is dealing with Israel after the Church Age.

Ezekiel 38:15-"Then you will come from your place out of the far north, you and many peoples with you, all of them riding on horses, a great company and a mighty army."

The "far north" obviously refers to Russia and Magog (Muslim nations of Russia). The word "horses" means "leaper" and can refer to horses, birds, or even chariot-riders. Some scholars believe this 2500-year old language can easily describe a mechanized force. However, there are more horses in Russia than any other nation.

Ezekiel 38:16-"You will come up against My people Israel like a cloud, to cover the land. It will be in the latter days that I will bring you against My land, so that the nations may know Me, when I am hallowed in you, O Gog, before their eyes."

God refers to the land of Israel as His land, and again the people of Israel as His people. The reference to the "latter days" denotes an end-time prophecy. God's statement about "nations may know Him" denotes that Gog's army will see and witness first-hand His mighty power. The destruction of Gog's invading army is a direct act of God and not through the agency

of other nations as evidenced in the following scriptures.

Ezekiel 38:17-"Thus says the Lord God: "Are you he of whom I have spoken in former days by My servants the prophets of Israel, who prophesied for years in those days that I would bring you against them?""

God has declared His actions in advance through the prophets.

Ezekiel 38:18-"And it will come to pass at the same time, when Gog comes against the land of Israel," says the Lord God, "that My fury will show in My face."

God's fury is demonstrated when Gog comes against Israel. God has said to the nations that He will defend Israel. His word is on the line.

Ezekiel 38:19-20-"For in My jealousy and in the fire of My wrath I have spoken: Surely in that day there shall be a great earthquake in the land of Israel, so that the fish of the sea, the birds of the heavens, the beasts of the field, all creeping things that creep on the earth, and all men who are on the face of the earth shall shake at My presence. The mountains shall be thrown down, the steep places shall fall, and every wall shall fall to the ground."

God's wrath is manifest. A great earthquake rocks the land of Israel. The earthquake is massive and will be felt by all of God's creation: fish, birds, beasts, and creeping things. Mountains are thrown down as well as all walls. Everything will be shaken that can be shaken.

Ezekiel 38:21-22-"I will call for a sword against Gog throughout all My mountains," says the Lord God. Every man's sword will be against his brother. And I will bring him to judgment with pestilence and bloodshed; I will rain down on him, on his troops, and on the many peoples who are with

him, flooding rain, great hailstones, fire, and brimstone."

It appears that Gog's invasion force fights with one another in a state of confusion. Gog's armies are judged by God with pestilence and bloodshed. Flooding rain, great hailstones, fire, and brimstone will rain down upon the armies. Some expositors see this description as nuclear warfare. However, it is God Himself that administers divine judgment to the armies of Gog. No opposing armies are mentioned. Sodom and Gomorrah were destroyed by fire and brimstone and so shall this invasion force. The destruction of Gog and his allies will result in the elimination of the Muslim or Islamic presence as a major force in the world. However, not all Muslim nations will be involved in this conflict, e.g., Syria, Egypt, Jordan, Saudi Arabia, etc.

Ezekiel 38:23-"Thus I will magnify Myself and sanctify Myself, and I will be known in the eyes of many nations. Then they shall know that I am the Lord."

After the supernatural destruction of Gog and his armies, the nations shall look at what has occurred and know that He is Lord.

Ezekiel 39:1-2-"And you, son of man, prophesy against Gog, and say, Thus says the Lord God: Behold, I am against you, O Gog, the chief prince of Rosh, Meshech, and Tubal; and I will turn you around and lead you on, bringing you up from the far north, and bringing you against the mountains of Israel."

God is against Gog, the chief prince of Rosh, Meshech, and Tubal. From the context, it would appear that the description of Rosh refers to a land or area of a group of people rather than chief prince, because the term chief prince is already used in the sentence. It is by the will of God that the armies of Gog are brought to the mountains of Israel.

Ezekiel 39:3-5-"then I will knock the bow out of your left hand, and cause the arrows to fall out of your right hand. You shall fall upon the mountains of Israel, you and all your troops and the peoples who are with you; I will give you to birds of prey of every sort and to the beast of the field to be devoured. You shall fall on the open field; for I have spoken, says the Lord God."

Although bows and arrows are simple and ancient weapons of warfare, some scholars stretch the description to mechanized armament where an arrow could be a missile and a bow a missile launcher. The armies of Gog are killed in the open fields and on the mountains of Israel, where the beasts of the field and birds feast on the carcasses of fallen soldiers. The destruction of Gog's army and the weakening of the Muslim world will allow the Antichrist to overpower three nations of the Reconstituted Roman Empire. Ultimately, the seven remaining nations of the Reconstituted Roman Empire give their power and authority to the Antichrist, who will then be well on his way to ruling the world, or most of it.

Ezekiel 39:6-8-"And I shall send fire on Magog and on those who live in security in the coastlands. Then they shall know that I am the Lord. So I will make My holy name known in the midst of My people Israel, and I will not let them profane My holy name anymore. Then the nations shall know that I am the Lord, the Holy One in Israel. Surely it is coming, and it shall be done, says the Lord God. This is the day of which I have spoken."

God supernaturally destroys the armies of Gog so they can no longer profane His Holy Name. The wrath of God is also felt in the land of Magog and on the coastlands. Again, scholars are unsure as to the reference to "coastlands." Coastlands may simply refer to the Islamic nations located on the Mediterranean. Magog, the coastlands, Israel, and the nations, all know this judgment is from God. That which is prophesied shall be done.

Ezekiel 39:9-11-"Then those who dwell in the cities of Israel will go out and set on fire and burn the weapons, both the shields and bucklers, the bows and arrows, the javelins and spears; and they will make fires with them for seven years. They will not take wood from the field nor cut down any from the forests, because they will make fires with the weapons; and they will plunder those who plunder them, and pillage those who pillaged them," says the Lord God. It will come to pass in that day that I will give Gog a burial place there in Israel, the valley of those who pass by east of the sea; and it will obstruct travelers, because there they will bury Gog and all his multitude. Therefore they will call it the Valley of Hamon Gog."

Israel is able to burn the weapons from Gog's invading armies for fuel for seven years. If the weapons are primitive and made of wood, then they can be burned, so the energy needs of the nation can be met. Israel will not have to use any wood from the forests for fuel, and they will plunder the bodies of those who were set on plundering them. It seems that mechanized armament of modern technology would be more difficult to fit into this passage.

Because the weapons are burned for seven years, some scholars place the Gog/Magog war at the very beginning of the Tribulation. However, based on the chronological chain of events, that interpretation does not fit as well as placement toward mid-Tribulation. Shortly after the wars of Daniel 11:41-45 and Ezekiel 38-39, Israel will no longer be at peace but under persecution from the Antichrist. According to scripture, Israel is only at peace for the first three and one-half years of the Tribulation, until the peace covenant is broken. Fuel will still be needed in the Millennium. Although burning weapons for the last three and one-half years of the Tribulation and for the first three and one-half years of the Millennium does not pose significant prophetic difficulties, it does not appear to flow rationally. However, given the choices for the timing of this conflict, occurrence near mid-Tribulation, following the war listed in Daniel 11, is more compelling. Gog and his

armies are buried in Israel in the valley of Hamon Gog, which is east of the Dead Sea.

Ezekiel 39:12-16-"For seven months the house of Israel will be burying them, in order to cleanse the land. Indeed all the people of the land will be burying them, and they will gain renown for it on the day that I am glorified, says the Lord God. They will set apart men regularly employed, with the help of a search party, to pass through the land and bury those bodies remaining in the ground, in order to cleanse it. At the end of seven months they will make a search. The search party will pass through the land; and whenever anyone sees a man's bone, he shall set up a marker by it, till the buriers have buried it in the Valley of Hamon Gog. The name of the city will also be Hamonah. Thus they shall cleanse the land."

It takes seven months for Israel to bury the dead in order to cleanse the land. It appears that initially all the people will take part in burying the dead, but later "select" men are set apart and employed specifically for this task. Search parties go forth hunting for the dead to bury. When the search parties find a bone of a man, they are not to touch it, but place a marker by it for the special detail to bury. This will be the process used to cleanse the land. It would appear that, after a period of time, flesh and bones become contaminated, probably by disease, so that special training and handling are required in the burial process. Scholars, who see a nuclear exchange, believe the bodies will be radioactive, thus requiring the special burial techniques. However, if they were radioactive, all of Israel wouldn't participate in the initial burial process, because the bodies of the dead would have become contaminated immediately upon death. These bodies have been contaminated after a period of time due to their great number, decomposition, disease, and the time required to locate and to bury them all.

As previously stated, it is believed that the Daniel and Magog campaigns occur very near mid-Tribulation. At mid-Tribulation,

the Antichrist breaks the seven-year peace covenant and enters the temple or holy area in Israel and proclaims himself to be God. He then begins a campaign to exterminate the Jews and wipe Israel from the face of the earth. Because Israel will no longer be at peace, and the Jews escape Israel by whatever means possible, it is unlikely that the seven months required to bury the dead could go past mid-Tribulation. Therefore, the Magog and Daniel campaigns will most likely conclude seven months before mid-Tribulation, as the Antichrist prepares for his takeover of the Reconstituted Roman Empire

Ezekiel 39:17-29

All the nations see that this judgment is from God. God invites the birds and beasts of the field to feast upon the fallen, including the mighty and princes. From this day, the house of Israel will know that the Lord their God has returned amongst them. God previously hid His face from them for their unfaithfulness, and they were given into the hands of their enemies. God dealt with Israel according to their transgressions. Israel shall know that the Lord sent them into captivity and brought them out of captivity. God will not hide His face from them anymore, and He will pour out His Spirit upon them.

Current Locations of Ancient Nations Listed in Ezekiel 38-39

Although variance exists among researchers in identifying the modern nations that correspond to the historical nations identified in Ezekiel 38-39, the chart below reflects the predominant thinking:

Ancient Nation	Current Nation
Magog Land of Ancient Scythians	Islamic Nations of the former Soviet Union south of Russia in central Asia: Kazakhstan, Kyrgyzstan, Tajikistan, Turkmenistan, Uzbekistan, and possibly Afghanistan
Rosh Land of Ancient Scythians	Russia
Meshech Land of Ancient Scythians	Russia and parts of Turkey
Tubal	Russia and parts of Turkey
Persia	Iran and possibly parts of Iraq
Ethiopia (or Cush)	Ethiopia and possibly other nations in Africa south of Egypt, such as Somalia and Sudan
Libya (or Put)	Libya and possibly African nations west of Egypt, including Algeria, Tunisia, and Morocco
Gomar	Turkey and possibly parts of Germany
Togarmah	Turkey and Armenia
Sheba	Arabian Peninsula including Saudi Arabia and possibly Yemen, Oman, Qatar, UAE, and Bahrain
Dedan	Arabian Peninsula including Saudi Arabia and possibly Yemen, Oman, Qatar, UAE, and Bahrain
Tarshish Ancient Phoencia	Spain and/or Great Britain
Young Lions of Tarshish	Possibly United States, Canada, and/or western European nations

GLOSSARY

144,000 Jews: First Jews saved after the Rapture, 12,000 from each of the 12 tribes of Israel. They are sealed by God for protection through the trumpet judgments.

Abaddon: Hebrew name for the angel of the abyss who is king over the demon locusts.

Abomination of Desolation: Term describing the Antichrist's act of breaking the covenant with Israel at the middle of the Tribulation when he enters the temple and proclaims himself to be God.

Abyss: Bottomless pit; abode of the demon locusts. Place of incarceration for Satan, fallen angels, and demons for the Millennium.

Amillennial: No literal one-thousand year reign of Christ. A spiritual kingdom only where Christ's rulership is in the hearts of the believers or over the souls of the saved in heaven.

Angels: Spiritual beings created by God to do His will.

Antichrist: False Christ and world ruler during the second half of the Tribulation. He opposes everything Christ stands for.

Apollyon: Greek name for the angel of the abyss who is king over the demon locusts.

Armageddon: Greek word derived from the Hebrew words, "Har" meaning mountain and "Megiddo," a city in Israel. Stands for a place, Mount Megiddo, and the final battle(s) of the armies of the Antichrist against Christ and His heavenly armies, the angelic host, and redeemed saints.

Babylon the Great: City of ancient Babylon that is rebuilt on the Euphrates river as a world trade and commerce center in addition to being a dwelling place for demons and unclean spirits.

Beast Out of the Abyss: Satanic prince who empowers and controls the Antichrist during the second half of the Tribulation Period.

Beast Out of the Earth: The False Prophet who causes the earth to worship the Antichrist.

Beast Out of the Sea: Called the Antichrist. Seven headed, ten-horned beast whose horns are crowned.

Book of Life: Record of every person born in the earth. Person's name can be blotted out if he/she hasn't accepted Christ as Savior and Lord by time he/she dies.

Bowl Judgments: Last seven judgments from God during the last 30 days of the Tribulation, culminating in the battle of Armageddon and the Second Coming of Christ.

Bozrah: Current city of Petra in Jordan, historically Edom, considered the place of refuge for Israel during the Great Tribulation.

Bride of Christ: Holy city, the New Jerusalem, inhabited in eternity future by the believers from all ages; also referred to as the Lamb's wife.

Church: New Testament saints or believers, both dead and alive, who have accepted Christ as Savior and Lord.

Church Age: Period, referred to as a mystery, between Pentecost and the Rapture of the Church.

Daniel's Seventieth Week: Seven-year period of time, called the Tribulation, following the Rapture of the Church and ending with the Second Coming of Christ in which God brings Israel to salvation and also judges the ungodly for their sinfulness.

Day of the Lord: Future period (Great Tribulation) when God acts in a sovereign manner in the affairs of mankind as He judges sin and unrighteousness, brings Israel to repentance, puts all rebellion under His feet, and establishes His Messianic kingdom.

Demon Horsemen : 200 million army of demon horsemen led

by the four fallen angels currently bound at the great river Euphrates that kill one-third of mankind.

Demon Locusts: Demons released from the abyss with the power in their tails as scorpions to sting and hurt men for up to five months.

Elect: Jews saved during the Tribulation.

Eternal State: Period following the Millennium under the perfect rule of God.

Euphrates: River in the Middle East. The city of Babylon will be rebuilt on the Euphrates river.

Fallen Angels: One-third of the angels that followed Lucifer in his initial rebellion against God and were cast out of the third heaven.

False Prophet: Third person of the satanic trinity who performs great signs and causes those who dwell in the earth to worship the Beast during the Great Tribulation.

First Resurrection: Consists of several stages where believers' bodies are changed from mortality to immortality, including the resurrection of Christ, the Rapture of Church Age saints, rapture of the 144,000 Jewish witnesses, resurrection of the two witnesses, and the resurrection of Old Testament saints and Tribulation saints (martyrs included).

Forty-two Months: Length of the second half of the Tribulation Period referred to as the Great Tribulation. Also called one thousand two hundred and sixty days or time, times, and half a time.

Goat Nations: Unsaved and/or unworthy nations (people) who after the Tribulation and battle of Armageddon are not allowed to enter into the Millennium period.

Gog : Leader of the Russian and Muslim coalition that marches against Israel approximately seven months before the middle of the Tribulation.

Great Multitude: Innumerable number of people from every

nation, tribe, and tongue who are saved during the Great Tribulation.

Great Red Dragon: Called Satan or the Devil. Seven headed, ten-horned beast that deceives the world.

Great Tribulation: Second three and one-half years of the seven-year Tribulation Period.

Image of the Beast: Image of the Antichrist worshipped by his followers.

Judgment Seat of Christ: Called the "bema" seat of Christ where believing Christians are judged for rewards. This event occurs in heaven simultaneously with the Tribulation Period occurring on earth.

King of the North: Leader of Syria, or coalition of nations including Syria, that attacks the Antichrist shortly before mid-Tribulation and immediately preceding the Gog/Magog invasion.

King of the South: Leader of Egypt, or coalition of North African nations including Egypt, that attacks the Antichrist shortly before mid-Tribulation and immediately preceding the Gog/Magog invasion.

Kings of the East : Rulers of kingdoms east of the Euphrates river that are summoned by the satanic trinity to the final battle of Armageddon against Israel and God.

Lake of Fire: Gehenna, or the eternal hell or final abode of the unrighteous dead, demons, fallen angels, Satan, Antichrist, and the False Prophet.

Lamb's Book of Life: Record of every individual that has accepted Christ as Savior and Lord; person's name recorded at time of salvation.

Lamb's Wife: New Testament saints or the Church before the Millennium. Saints from all ages who live in the New Jerusalem after the Millennium in eternity future.

Little Open Book: Book that provides additional information

on God's final set of seven judgments during the Tribulation, i.e., the bowl judgments.

Living Creatures: Four high-ranking angelic beings around the throne of God, similar to cherubim and seraphim that praise God day and night.

Magog: Territory to the far north of Israel consisting of Russian Muslim states.

Male Child: 144,000 Jews sealed by God for protection through the trumpet judgments and caught up to heaven or raptured after the trumpet judgments.

Mark of the Beast: Mark on the forehead or right hand of the Antichrist's followers allowing them to be able to buy or sell.

Marriage Ceremony of the Lamb: Marriage of the bridegroom and His wife, the Church, that occurs in heaven while the Tribulation is occurring on earth.

Marriage Supper of the Lamb: Post-Tribulation feast on earth following the celebration of the marriage ceremony of the Lamb; attended by Old Testament and Tribulation saints, including the 144,000, as guests of the bridegroom.

Martyrs: Saints slain during the Tribulation Period for the Word of God and their testimony for Christ.

Millennium: The literal, one-thousand year kingdom rule of Christ on earth after the Tribulation Period and His Second Coming.

Mother of Harlots: Apostate religions that persecute the saints during the first half of the Tribulation.

Mount Zion: Heavenly mount on which the 144,000 Jews appear with Jesus following their rapture after the trumpet judgments.

Mount of Olives: Location where Jesus' feet touch earth at His Second Coming. The mount will split in two.

Mystery: New Testament doctrines that would not be known

unless revealed by God, including the Church, gospel, salvation in Christ, Christ in the believer, baptism with the Holy Spirit, speaking in tongues, the Rapture, etc.

New Testament Saints: Believers born again during New Testament times.

Number of Beast's Name: Number of a man, six hundred and sixty six.

Old Testament Saints: Righteous people of Old Testament times.

Olivet Discourse: The mount where Jesus was sitting as He explained to His disciples the signs of His Second Coming and the end of the age.

Premillennial: Christ's Second Coming will precede the establishment of His one-thousand year, literal and physical kingdom rule of earth from Jerusalem.

Postmillennial: A spiritual kingdom only where Christ's rule is in the hearts of believers. The world becomes progressively better through the preaching of the Gospel, ultimately resulting in the return of Christ as He ushers in eternity.

Rapture: Catching away of the Church before the Tribulation Period.

Remnant of Israel: Born again Jews alive at the Second Coming of Christ.

Satan: A fallen angel, previously called Lucifer, the anointed cherub. Satan is also called the Devil and the great red Dragon.

Scarlet Beast: Apostate religious system of the first half of the Tribulation.

Sea of Glass: Floor of the throne room.

Seal Judgments: First seven judgments of the Tribulation that begin in the first half of the period.

Second Coming of Christ: Physical return of Christ at the

battle of Armageddon to rescue Israel and judge sin and the unrighteous.

Second Resurrection: Resurrection and judgment of the unrighteous dead of all ages at the Great White Throne of God following the Millennium.

Seven Churches: Seven literal churches in Asia Minor to whom the Book of Revelation was sent.

Seven Lampstands: Symbolic for the seven churches.

Seven Sealed Book: Scroll written on the inside and back describing the seal and trumpet judgments; a title deed to the earth.

Seven Stars: Symbolic for the angels of the seven churches.

Seventy Weeks of Daniel: Daniel's prophetic vision of 490 years concerning Israel and the holy city Jerusalem.

Sheep Nations: Nations (people) judged worthy to enter into the Millennium.

Temple: Holy place of worship for the Jews.

Times of the Gentiles: Gentile persecution of national Israel by eight empires from Egypt through the Beast empire.

Three Woes: Fifth, sixth, and seventh trumpet judgments.

Tribulation Period: Last seven years preceding the Millennium during which God restores Israel to Himself and judges sin and the unrighteous of the earth.

Tribulation Saints: Believers saved during the Tribulation Period.

Trumpet Judgments: Second or middle set of seven judgments that occur during the second half of the Tribulation.

Twenty-four Elders: New Testament believers that are representative of the Church in heaven.

Two Witnesses: Special witnesses for God, most likely Enoch

and Elijah, who prophesy and strike the earth with plagues during the second half of the Tribulation.

White Throne Judgment: God's throne where the unrighteous of all ages will be judged following the Millennium.

Woman: National Israel.

Wrath of God: God's judgment and punishment of sinful mankind; begins at the sixth seal judgment.

Author's Salvation Statement

In the mid-seventies, my salvation experience came through the prophecy channel as I read *The Late Great Planet Earth* by Hal Lindsey. At that time Hal's classic book addressed questions that had been on my heart since childhood. I learned that God has a plan for His people and the future of this planet, and that plan is detailed in the Bible. The Book of Revelation opens the door to understanding future events that will culminate this age in the finalization of God's plan of redemption.

The Father is a loving God, not desiring any person to be lost, but for all to come to the knowledge of the truth and accept His plan of salvation and the atoning sacrifice of His son, Jesus Christ. However, God in creating man as a spiritual being gave him a gift not possessed by any other of His creation. This gift is "free will" or the ability and right of choice. Man is a spirit being created to operate by faith, the same as God. Man can choose to follow God or choose to reject God. God has placed such a high value on man's right of choice that He will honor either decision, one that leads to eternal fellowship with Him or the other that leads to eternal separation from Him.

We are quickly approaching the return of Christ. The stage is set. During a seven year period called the Tribulation, God will fulfill His covenants with Israel, judge the earth, sin, rebellious people, and a one world kingdom under the rulership of the Antichrist. This will be a time of destruction, devastation, persecution, famine, war, calamity, and physical catastrophe unprecedented in human history. Millions will be saved but will have to make a bold stand for Christ resulting in martyrdom. But God doesn't want His children to experience this Tribulation Period. He has a better plan. The Bible says that God will deliver His people from the wrath to come. He has not appointed His children to experience this outpouring of wrath but to obtain salvation through the Lord Jesus Christ. In His love God will remove

His Church from this planet before the Tribulation begins. This event is called the "Rapture," where the body of believers who have individually and personally accepted Jesus as Savior and Lord will be "caught up" or raptured alive to meet the Lord in the air, according to 1 Thessalonians 4:13-18.

It is my hope that this book has clearly outlined the events that will take place after the Rapture. If you have not already accepted Christ as your personal Savior, I encourage you not to wait any longer. Salvation is a free gift of God. You cannot "do anything" or be "good enough" to earn or merit salvation. God's gift of salvation is received by faith. By confessing with your mouth that Jesus is Lord and by believing in your heart that God raised Him from the dead, you shall be saved. The Bible says with the heart man believes resulting in righteousness and with the mouth confession is made unto salvation (Romans 10:9-10).

I encourage and exhort you to say the following prayer out loud and then sign and date this prayer at the bottom of the page. Your signature then forever testifies that on this date you made Jesus your Savior and Lord and entered into eternal life with God, your Father.

Father in the Name of Jesus,
The Bible says that whosoever shall call upon the Name of the Lord shall be saved. I believe that Jesus is the Son of God, and as an act of my will I make Jesus the Lord and Savior of my life. I believe in my heart and confess with my mouth that God raised Jesus from the dead. I renounce Satan and all his works. I am free from the bondage to sin. I am a new creature in Christ Jesus. I am saved. I am a born again Christian, a child of Almighty God, and I have eternal life with God. Thank you for my salvation.

_____   _____

Signature   *Date*

REFERENCES AND ADDITIONAL
STUDY MATERIALS

Benware, Paul N. *Understanding End Times Prophecy*

Beshore, F. Kenton *The Millennium, The Apocalypse, and Armageddon*

Biederwolf, William E. *The Prophecy Handbook*

Campbell, Stan and Bell Jr., James S. *Complete Idiot's Guide to the Book of Revelation*

Capps, Charles *End Time Events*

Combs, James *Rainbows From Revelation*

Couch, Mal *A Bible Handbook to Revelation*

Couch, Mal *The hope of Christ's Return*

Dake, Finis Jennings *Revelation Expounded*

Dake, Finis Jennings *The Rapture and the Second Coming of Christ*

Dake, Finis Jennings *Annotated Bible*

Dobson, Ed *The End*

Duck, Daymond, R. *Daniel God's Word for the Biblically-Inept*

Duck, Daymond, R *Prophecies of the Bible God's Word for the Biblically-Inept*

Duck, Daymond, R. *Revelation God's Word for the Biblically-Inept*

Fogle, Lerry W. *Revelation Explained*

Fruchtenbaum, Arnold *A Review of the Pre-Wrath Rapture of the Church*

Fruchtenbaum, Arnold *A Study Guide of Israel, Historical & Geographical*

Fruchtenbaum, Arnold *Messianic Christology*

Gentile, Ernest B. *The Final Triumph*

Goodman, Phillip *The Assyrian Connection*

Gregg, Steve *Revelation Four Views A Parallel Commentary*

Hagee, John *Beginning of the End*

Hagee, John *From Daniel to Doomsday*

Hall, John *Prophecy Marches On! Vol 1 and 2*

Hammond, Mac *The Last Millennium*

Hindson, Edward *Approaching Armageddon*

Hindson, Edward *Final Signs*

Hindson, Edward *Revelation, Unlocking the Future*

Hindson, Edward & Fredrickson, Lee *Future Wave*

Hitchcock, Mark *101 Answers*

Hitchcock, Mark *After the Empire*

Hitchcock, Mark *Bible Prophecy*

Hitchcock, Mark *Is America in Bible Prophecy?*

Hitchcock, Mark *Is the Antichrist Alive Today?*

Hitchcock, Mark *Seven Signs of the End Times*

Hitchcock, Mark *The Coming Islamic Invasion of Israel*

Hitchcock, Mark *The Second Coming of Babylon*

Hitchcock, Mark *What On Earth is Going On?*

Horvath, James *He's Coming Soon*

Ice, Thomas and Demy, Timothy *Prophecy Watch*

Ice, Thomas and Demy, Timothy *When the Trumpet Sounds*

James, William T. et. al. *Prophecy at Ground Zero*

Jeffery, Grant R. *Apocalypse*

Jeffery, Grant R. *Armageddon, Appointment with Destiny*

Jeffery, Grant R. *NIV Prophecy Study Bible*

Jeffrey, Grant R. *Triumphant Return*

Jeffery, Grant R *War on Terror*

Jeremiah, David *Escape the Coming Night*

Jeremiah, David *The Handwriting on the Wall*

Johnian, Mona *Life in the Millennium*

Kirban, Salem and Cohen, Gary *Revelation Visualized*

Kirban, Salem *Guide to Survival*

Kirban, Salem *The Rise of the Antichrist*

LaHaye, Tim *No Fear of the Storm*

LaHaye, Tim *Prophecy Study Bible*

LaHaye, Tim *The Merciful God of Prophecy*

LaHaye, Tim *Revelation*

LaHaye, Tim *Revelation Unveiled*

LaHaye, Tim & Ice, Thomas *Charting The End Times*

LaHaye, Tim & Ice, Thomas *The End Times Controversy*

LaHaye, Tim and Jenkins, Jerry *Are We Living in the End Times?*

Larkin, Clarence *The Book of Revelation*

Larson, Bob *Larson's New Book of Cults*

Levy, David M. *Revelation*

Lindsay, Gordan *The Prophecies of Daniel*

Lindsey, Hal *Planet Earth, 2000 A.D.*

Lindsey, Hal *Planet Earth, The Final Chapter*

Lindsey, Hal *The Everlasting Hatred The Roots of Jihad*

Lindsey, Hal *The Late Great Planet Earth*

Lindsey, Hal *The Rapture*

Lindsey, Hal *There's a New World Coming*

Missler, Chuck *The Magog Invasion*

Missler, Chuck *Update, August 2002*

Missler, Chuck *Update, November 2002*

Morris, Henry *The Revelation Record*

Newell, William R. *Revelation*

Pentecost, J. Dwight *Things to Come*

Phillips, John *Exploring Revelation: An Expository Commentary*

Phillips, John *Exploring the Future*

Price, Randall *Charting the Future*

Price, Randall *Fast Facts on the Middle East Crisis*

Price, Randall *Unholy War*

Reagan, David *Wrath and Glory*

Swihart, Stephen D. *Armageddon*

Sutton, Hilton *Revelation*

Sutton, Hilton *The Book of Revelation Revealed*

Swaggart, Jimmy *God's Plan for the Ages*

Swaggart, Jimmy *The Book of Daniel*

Swaggart, Jimmy *The Book of Revelation*

Swaggart, Jimmy *A Study in Bible Prophecy*

Van Impe, Jack *Final Mysteries Unsealed*
Van Impe, Jack *Revelation Revealed*
Walvoord, John F. *Every Prophecy of the Bible*
Walvoord, John F. *Prophecy*
Walvoord, John F. *Prophecy in the New Millennium*
Walvoord, John F. *The Prophecy Knowledge Handbook*
Walvoord, John F. *The Rapture Question*
Wilmington, H. L. *The King is Coming*
Wuest, Kenneth S. *Wuest's Word Studies Prophetic Light in the Present Darkness*

CD, Video, Cassette Tape, and Seminar Presentations

Bigalke Jr., Ron *Current PreTribulationism and Jewish Questions of the End* (article – seminar presentation)

Brindle, Wayne *Biblical Evidence for the Imminence of the Rapture* (article – seminar presentation)

Couch, Mal *Posttribulationism and 2 Thessalonians 2:1-12* (article – seminar presentation)

Dake, Finis Jennings *God's Plan for Man* (cassette series)

Fruchtenbaum, Arnold *Rabbinic Quotations of the Old Testament and How It Relates to Joel 2 and Acts 2* (article – seminar presentation)

Goodman, Phillip *7 Heads and 10 Kings* (CD)

Goodman, Phillip *7 Heads and 10 Horns* (article – seminar presentation)

Gromacki, Robert *Israel, Past, Present, and Future – Romans 9-11* (article – seminar presentation)

Hall, John *Prophecy Seminar* (cassette series)

Johnson, George *Revelation* (cassette series)

McAvoy, Steve *The Day of the Lord and Certain So-Called Precursors* (article – seminar presentation)

Missler, Chuck *Roots of War* (video)

Missler, Chuck *The Book of Revelation* (CD)

Niemela, John *Sequence in Daniel 7:1-28* (article – seminar presentation)

Stallard, Mike *An Analysis of the Use of Cosmic-Sign Passages by Proponents of the Pre-Wrath Rapture Theory* (article – seminar presentation)

Sutton, Hilton *Revelation* (cassette series)

Swaggart, Jimmy *The Book of Revelation* (cassette series)

Van Impe, Jack *Armageddon* (video)

Vlack, Michael *Variations within Supersessionism* (article – seminar presentation)

Yandian, Bob *The Rapture Question* (cassette series)

Subject Index

Abaddon, 25, 110, 262, 345, 405

Abode, 87, 107-108, 405, 408

Abomination of Desolation, 33, 248, 258, 298, 349-350, 356, 376, 380, 388-389, 405

Abraham, 107, 134, 239, 254, 325, 344

Abyss, 14, 34, 83, 107-108, 122-123, 137, 139, 168, 189, 192-193, 213, 248, 262, 305, 310, 314, 325, 329, 331, 344-345, 372, 381-382, 405-407

Adam, 78, 90, 133-134, 191-192, 198-199, 202, 221, 325, 332, 334, 336-337, 344-345, 386

Aegean Sea, 47, 49, 62

Afghanistan, 285, 290-291, 369, 393, 404

Africa, 29, 111, 143, 256, 276, 385, 394, 404

AIDS, 87, 230, 253, 258, 278

Alexander the Great, 123, 168, 286, 310, 358, 360, 363, 369, 371, 381-382

Alexandria, 51

Algeria, 30, 285, 290, 394

Almighty (God), 18, 33, 42, 74, 126, 154, 158, 161, 186, 203, 262, 272, 277, 300, 317, 337, 414

Alpha and the Omega, 18, 37, 39, 41-45, 65, 200, 208

Altar, 22, 24, 36, 52, 87-88, 96, 98, 102, 110, 119, 135, 150, 158, 190-191, 240, 261, 263, 268, 295, 304, 370, 380

America, 224, 226, 228, 245, 290

Amillennial, 213-216, 405

Ammon, 132, 278, 286, 289, 350, 384

Ancient of Days, 364-366, 368

Angel, 19, 25-28, 31, 34, 36, 39, 47, 50, 52, 54, 59, 62, 65, 71, 74, 78, 93-94, 102-108, 110, 112, 115-119, 125-126, 134, 139, 147-150, 158-162, 167-168, 173, 178, 182-184, 186-187, 189-190, 201-202, 205-208, 217, 261-262, 304-305, 311, 325, 340, 345, 349, 371, 374, 380, 387, 405, 410

Angels, 12, 18, 24-26, 28, 31, 35-36, 45-46, 61, 70-71, 81, 87, 93-94, 96-97, 101-102, 106-108, 110-112, 115-116, 123, 131-133, 147-148, 153-155, 157, 159, 165-166, 173, 183-185, 189, 194-196, 200-201, 207, 217, 236, 240-241, 261-262, 269, 296, 304-305, 315-316, 323, 325, 335-336, 344-345, 352, 354, 356-357, 387, 389, 405, 407-408, 411

Animals, 26, 87, 106, 325, 331, 338

Anointing, 53, 122, 376

Antichrist, 14-15, 20-24, 27-31, 33-34, 36, 45, 56, 61, 78, 83-85, 87-89, 94-95, 108, 110, 113-114, 119-120, 122-123, 125, 130-132, 135-144, 148, 150, 154, 158-159, 161, 166, 168-170, 174, 186-188, 190-191, 194, 213, 215, 226, 231, 236-239, 242, 245-258, 260, 262-263, 269-272, 274-280, 282-283, 286-295, 297-298, 305, 307, 309-310, 314-315, 318-320, 345, 347-352, 354, 357, 359,

361, 364-368, 370-373, 378-385, 387, 389, 393, 395-396, 400-401, 403, 405-406, 408-409, 413

Antiochus (Epiphanes), 64, 288-289, 370, 372, 380

Apocalypse, 9, 12, 256

Apollyon, 25, 110, 262, 345, 405

Arab(s), 120, 226-228, 249, 255-256, 286, 290

Arabian Peninsula, 286, 290, 396, 404

Armageddon, 14, 30-31, 33, 35-36, 78, 85, 111-112, 125, 150, 153, 161, 170, 176, 181, 183, 185-187, 191, 213, 220, 227, 237, 241, 256, 263, 272-277, 281-283, 295-298, 305, 307, 314, 317-319, 333, 351, 356, 361, 373, 385, 389, 405-408, 411

Armenia, 30, 285, 290, 394, 404

Artaxerxes, 19, 376-377

Asia, 11, 20, 29, 40, 43-44, 47, 54, 62, 111, 193, 217, 256-257, 285, 305, 331, 411

Asia Minor, 20, 40, 43-44, 47, 62, 217, 256, 411

Assyria, 27, 34, 123, 130, 138, 166, 168-169, 248, 276, 286, 288-289, 292, 310, 362-363, 372, 381-382

Assyrian, 123, 168, 248-249, 276, 287, 289

Assyrian Empire, 289

Atonement, 240, 375

Babylon, 167, 248, 276, 312-313, 405

Babylon the Great, 167, 173, 258, 311, 405

Babylonia, 276, 286, 369

Babylonian, 248, 289

Babylonian Empire, 248

Bahrain, 286, 290, 396, 404

Balaam, 11, 53

Balaamism, 51-52

Balak, 53

Balken(s), 290, 292

Bear, 10, 29, 47, 138, 362

Beast Empire, 34, 111, 138-139, 159, 166, 170, 277, 288, 291, 361, 411

Beast-Seven Heads, 165

Beasts, 12, 86-87, 137-139, 141, 143, 263, 286, 309, 357, 359-363, 365, 392, 398, 400, 403

Beginning and the End, 18, 42, 200, 208

Believers, 16, 21-24, 32, 41, 51, 53, 62-64, 70-72, 78, 93, 95-96, 136, 143, 145, 183, 187, 195, 199, 201, 207, 214, 216, 231, 234-236, 238, 242-243, 245, 268, 270-271, 293-294, 324, 327, 352, 354-355, 388, 405-407, 410-411, 414

Bema Seat, 45, 408

Blood, 27, 31, 41, 50, 70-72, 78, 80, 88-89, 97-98, 103-104, 122, 130, 134-135, 150-151, 158-159, 167, 179, 181, 185, 239, 257-259, 263, 268, 270-271, 284, 297, 300-302, 311, 314-315, 317, 319-320, 323, 334, 339, 375

Blood Covenant, 239

Book of Law, 194

Book of Life, 11, 61, 140, 168, 194-195, 204, 209, 332, 406, 408

Book of Works, 194

Bottomless Pit, 25, 27, 36, 107-108, 110, 122-123, 167-168, 189-190, 261-263, 315, 325, 335, 344, 405

Bowl Judgments, 22-23, 26, 32-33, 78, 94, 111, 116, 125-127, 147-149, 153, 155, 157, 173, 175, 181, 186, 255-256, 269-271, 298, 307, 311, 314, 341, 350, 352, 389, 406, 409

Bozrah, 272, 318-320, 350, 406

Brass, 45, 54, 113, 359-360

Bride, 10-11, 37, 178, 182-183, 199, 201, 208-209, 322, 337, 406

Bride of Christ, 11, 182, 199, 406

Bright Morning Star, 208

Britain, 245, 287, 291, 396, 404

Bronze, 176, 358-361, 366

Bulgaria, 292

Burkina, 290

Caesar, 17, 49-50, 52, 64, 310

Canada, 245, 286, 290, 396, 404

Cancerous Sores, 159, 260, 316

Cassander, 286, 363, 369

Cataclysmic Changes (Events), 11, 32, 90, 297, 348

Catholic Church, 215, 231

Central Asia, 111, 193, 257, 285, 331, 404

Chief Prince, 29, 133, 381, 393, 399

China, 228, 304

Chinese, 112, 304-305

Christ, 9, 11, 21, 40-41, 44, 144, 184, 235, 356, 414

Christian, 2, 67, 91, 144, 202, 232, 245, 249, 253, 383, 414

Christianity, 55, 348

Christians, 17, 21, 50-51, 53-55, 66-67, 86-87, 135, 144, 183, 198, 214, 220, 222, 227-228, 234, 236, 249, 251, 259, 314, 408

Church Age, 13, 19-20, 35, 46, 69, 72-73, 91, 94, 121, 185, 191, 217, 220-221, 234-235, 237-238, 374, 379, 397, 406-407

Churches, 9, 11, 18, 20-21, 39-40, 43-50, 53, 56, 59-61, 64-65, 67, 71-72, 140, 183, 208, 217-219, 411

Churches of Revelation, 47, 59, 219

Coalitions, 30, 227, 275, 288-289, 384

Coastlands, 245, 396, 400

Coming of Christ, 14, 20, 30, 35, 80, 96, 112, 117, 120-121, 125, 148, 162, 173, 181, 183, 215, 221-222, 234-237, 255, 295-298, 302, 307, 330, 333, 353-355, 361, 364-366, 371, 374-375, 389, 406, 410

Cosmic (Disturbances), 22, 90-91, 252, 258, 296, 299, 314, 352

Creator, 21, 26, 65, 75, 77, 81, 117, 154

Crime, 43, 85, 114, 232, 253

Cush, 285, 290, 394, 404

Cyrus, 59, 368, 376-377, 382

Daniel Military Campaign, 30, 272-275, 277-279, 281, 285, 317, 381

Darius, 368, 376, 381

David, 11, 18, 62, 79, 208, 240, 325-326

Day of the Lord, 15, 22-23, 43, 91, 120, 197, 242, 284, 293-302, 308, 313, 333-334, 339, 341, 406

Dead Sea, 330, 402

Death, 17, 21-22, 24-25, 27, 31-32, 36, 41, 46, 50-52, 56, 79, 85-87, 105, 107, 109, 113, 121, 124, 134, 143, 149, 158-159, 167, 175, 192, 195, 198-200, 215, 238, 242, 251, 256, 262-263, 286, 294, 315-316, 327-328, 336, 345, 348, 363, 371, 378, 402

Dedan, 286, 290, 396, 404

Demon, 25-26, 33, 94, 96, 108-110, 112, 137, 142, 161, 165, 189, 193, 232, 261-263, 277, 305, 312, 315-316, 331, 344, 405-407

Demons, 31, 35-36, 87, 107-110, 112-113, 123, 142-143, 161, 173-174, 193-194, 196, 233, 262, 305, 325, 335-336, 345, 405, 407-408

Destruction of Babylon, 35, 173, 175-177, 179, 313

Destruction of Gog, 278, 290, 397, 399-400

Devil, 28, 36, 50, 111, 131, 133-135, 141, 189-190, 193, 196, 216, 261-262, 345, 356, 408, 410

Eagle, 10, 74, 106, 135, 362

Earth, 10, 12, 14-15, 17-18, 21-22, 25-28, 31, 34-35, 37, 41-42, 45, 49, 60, 63, 73, 78-90, 93-94, 96, 102-108, 111, 113, 115-118, 120-124, 126-127, 129, 131, 133-137, 139-142, 145-147, 149-150, 153, 157, 159-163, 165-168, 171, 173-174, 176, 178-179, 181, 183-187, 192-195, 197-200, 202, 204, 206-208, 213-214, 221, 227, 229, 235, 237-243, 256, 258-263, 268-271, 284, 293, 295-303, 306-307, 311, 314-318, 323, 325-331, 333-339, 341, 346-348, 351-352, 354-355, 359, 361-362, 365-369, 384, 386, 389, 398, 403, 406-413,

Earthquakes, 62, 89, 105, 160, 198, 230-231, 315, 334, 339, 348

East Indies, 245, 396

Eastern Leg (Roman Empire), 248, 287, 289, 291-292

Eastern Turkey, 30, 393-394

Eden, 17, 111, 205, 331, 336, 338

Edom, 132, 272, 278, 286, 289, 318-320, 350, 384, 406

Egypt, 11, 30, 34, 51, 103, 111, 123, 130, 138, 166, 168-169, 223, 238, 257, 275-279, 286-289, 291-292, 310, 327, 362-363, 369, 379, 382, 385, 394, 399, 404, 408, 411

Egyptian, 104-105, 130, 153, 158-159, 163, 240

Egyptian Empire, 130

Eighth Empire, 123, 168-169, 171, 310, 361, 367

Elam, 368

Elders, 11, 14, 21, 70-72, 75, 79-82, 97, 102, 126, 146, 182-183, 238, 240, 364, 411

Elect, 232, 350-352, 407

Elijah, 11, 27, 120-122, 134, 142, 186, 294, 297, 299, 412

Empire, 27, 29-30, 33-34, 47, 83-84, 111, 123, 130, 137-139, 141, 143, 148, 159-160, 165-166, 168-171, 225, 246, 248-250, 254, 256-257, 276-280, 286-289, 291-292, 309-310, 357-358, 360-363, 366-369, 372, 378-379, 382, 385, 400, 403, 411

Empires, 29, 111, 130, 137-138, 166-168, 249, 280, 286-289, 291-292, 309-310, 357-358, 360, 362-363, 372, 379, 411

End Times, 9, 11-12, 20, 64, 77, 102, 113, 123, 206, 276, 294, 358, 371, 383

England, 286

Enoch, 27, 101, 121, 134, 186, 411

Ephesus, 21, 43, 47-49, 51, 53, 55, 64, 218

Eriteria, 290

Esdraelon, 318

Eternal, 17-18, 26, 40, 42, 44-45, 49-51, 65, 70, 74-75, 82, 87, 107-108, 117, 126, 148-149, 159, 192, 194-195, 199-200, 205-206, 208, 337, 344-345, 354, 356, 365, 375, 386, 407-408, 413-414

Eternal Hell, 107-108, 195, 344-345, 365, 408

Eternal State, 407

Eternity Future, 197, 202, 204, 327, 336, 406, 408

Ethiopia, 29, 278-279, 285-286, 290, 385, 393-394, 404

Euphrates (River), 25, 33, 110-111, 160, 189, 259, 262, 304-305, 316, 319, 405, 407-408

Eurasia, 143

Europe, 29, 143, 224-225, 227-228, 245, 256

European Union, 227, 291-292

Eve, 90, 133, 331

Evil, 17, 47-48, 51, 55, 57, 111, 120, 131, 134, 141, 160, 174, 179, 192, 331, 349, 395

Faith, 17, 24, 48, 51-53, 55, 96, 135, 140, 149, 184, 216, 255, 293-294, 314, 331, 413-414

Faithful and True Witness, 18, 65

Faithful Witness, 41

Fallen Angels, 36, 87, 107-108, 110, 112, 132-133, 189, 194, 196, 305, 316, 325, 335-336, 344-345, 357, 405, 407-408

False Christ(s), 84, 231, 247, 347, 351, 405

False Messiahs, 22, 84, 231

False Prophet, 29-31, 33, 36, 45, 56, 108, 141-144, 161, 174, 187-188, 191, 193, 250, 258, 260, 262, 277, 345, 350, 365, 406-408

False Prophets, 84, 231, 348-349, 351

Famine(s), 22, 86-87, 175, 229, 256-258, 270, 314-315, 339, 348, 413

Father, 18, 21, 41-42, 44, 56, 61, 67, 70, 75, 77, 80-83, 86, 94, 110, 134, 145, 149, 155, 174, 185, 194, 199, 203, 205, 208, 222, 234, 243, 247, 269, 322-323, 353-354, 364-366, 376, 413-414

Fiery Red Dragon, 130, 153, 309

Fig Tree, 89, 222, 224, 236, 353

Final Judgment, 42, 189, 191, 193, 195

Fire, 15, 26, 35-36, 44, 50, 54, 66, 72, 87, 102-103, 108-109, 112, 115, 122, 131, 142, 148, 150, 153, 159, 170, 175, 178, 184-185, 187-188, 191, 193-197, 200, 204, 208, 258-259, 261-262, 273, 284, 296, 299-305, 314-316, 318, 331-334, 336, 339-341, 344-345, 352, 355, 364-365, 378, 385, 398-401, 408

First and the Last, 18, 42-45, 50, 70, 208

First Resurrection, 24, 36, 51, 72, 89, 96, 98, 121, 185-186, 191-192, 198, 235, 268, 327, 386, 407

Food, 24, 53-55, 86, 90, 103-104, 118, 132, 144, 158, 198, 229, 257-258, 270, 315, 325

France, 287, 291

Future, 11, 13, 15-17, 39, 148, 197, 202, 204, 214-215, 225, 245, 281, 288, 291, 293, 327, 336, 357, 359-360, 362, 373, 382, 387, 406, 408, 413

Gabriel, 19, 101, 371, 374, 380-381

Garden of Eden, 17, 111, 331, 336

Gate, 201, 203, 231

Gehenna, 108, 195-196, 345, 365, 408

Generation, 72, 143, 217, 220, 222-224, 226, 231, 236, 353-354

Gentile, 121, 238, 249, 286, 310, 327, 357, 359, 361, 374, 411

Gentiles, 26-28, 119, 121, 123, 129-130, 137-138, 240, 278, 286-288, 309, 327, 357-358, 361-363, 373-374, 379, 411

Germania, 394

Germany, 52, 287, 290-291

Goat Nations, 132, 330, 356, 390, 407

Godhead, 41, 74, 365

Gog, 29-30, 36, 84-85, 139, 142, 192-193, 227-228, 257, 272-273, 277-283, 290-292, 315, 331, 334, 384-385, 392-395, 397-402, 407-408

Gog-Magog, 285, 292

Gold, 10-11, 37, 50, 66, 70, 109, 113, 166, 176-177, 202-203, 205, 337, 358-361, 378, 383, 385, 396

Gomer, 30, 285, 290, 394, 404

Gomorrah, 174, 235, 239, 273, 312-313, 399

Government, 50, 78, 169, 186, 215, 225, 325, 327-328, 358, 360-361, 363

Great Multitude, 24, 29, 32, 36, 88, 95-99, 135, 140, 153-154, 181-182, 185, 190-191, 255, 259, 270-271, 294, 407

Great Red Dragon, 28, 133, 262, 408, 410

Great Tribulation, 23-24, 32-33, 56, 61, 83, 95-98,

119-120, 125, 132, 147-149, 157, 186, 249, 256, 259, 270-271, 288, 298, 308, 340, 348, 350-351, 357, 388-389, 406-408

Great White Throne, 107, 194, 411

Grecian Empire(s), 27, 29, 34, 123, 137, 139, 141, 168, 248-249, 276, 280, 286-289, 292, 310, 357, 360, 363, 372, 378

Greece, 26-27, 29, 34, 111, 123, 130, 137-139, 166, 168-169, 193, 286-288, 291-292, 310, 357-358, 360, 363, 369, 371, 381-382

Hades, 36, 46, 86-87, 195

Harlot, 10, 34, 88, 135, 139, 165, 167, 169-171, 174, 181, 231, 254, 261, 294, 312, 315, 348

Harpazo, 233, 241

Heaven, 10, 14-15, 17-18, 21-26, 28, 31-32, 35-37, 44, 49, 64, 69, 71-73, 75, 79-82, 88-89, 91, 96-98, 101-102, 104, 106-107, 110, 115-118, 121-122, 124, 126-127, 129-135, 140-142, 145, 147, 149-150, 153-154, 158-159, 162-163, 173-174, 178, 181-182, 184-185, 187, 189-190, 193-194, 197, 199, 201-202, 205, 214, 231, 233-238, 240-243, 258-262, 269, 271, 296, 299-300, 302-303, 307, 315-316, 323, 325, 333, 336-337, 339-341, 344, 352, 354, 357, 359, 361-362, 364-370, 382, 387, 389, 405, 407-409, 411

Hell, 18, 25-26, 31, 46, 79, 87, 107-108, 112, 189, 195-196, 238, 262, 305, 336, 344-345, 352, 355-356, 365, 408

Highway of Holiness, 326

Holiness, 18, 62, 73, 154, 202, 326, 329, 364

Holy, 9-12, 17, 19, 37, 39-40, 49, 54, 59, 62-63, 71-75, 80, 88, 94, 119-120, 122, 133, 148, 154, 160, 170, 178, 192, 199, 201, 206-207, 209, 227, 231, 238, 240, 242, 245, 251, 282, 295, 300, 303, 305, 318, 329, 331, 337, 349, 370, 372-374, 376, 378, 380, 385, 387, 395, 400, 403, 406, 410-411

Holy City, 19, 37, 119, 199, 209, 331, 337, 373-374, 376, 378, 406, 411

Holy Land, 160, 305, 318

Holy of Holies, 376, 380

Holy One, 370, 400

Holy Spirit, 9-12, 17, 39-40, 54, 59, 63, 73, 75, 80, 88, 94, 122, 209, 231, 238, 242, 245, 251, 282, 295, 349, 374, 410

Horns, 12, 18, 28, 34, 80, 110, 129-130, 137-138, 141, 165-167, 169-170, 240, 258, 260, 262, 287, 289, 304, 309-310, 363-364, 366-369, 371, 406

Image, 31-32, 113, 142-143, 148, 153-154, 157-158, 187, 190, 250, 268, 271, 357-359, 361-362, 371, 408

Image of the Beast, 31, 113, 142-143, 408

Iran, 29, 248, 285, 287, 290-292, 369, 394, 396, 404

Iraq, 248, 276, 287, 290-291, 327, 369, 394, 404

Iron, 28, 41, 56-57, 109, 131, 176, 186, 190, 306, 308, 326, 359-361, 363, 366

Islam, 253, 383

Islamic, 29, 272, 282, 290, 385, 393-396, 399-400, 404

Israel, 10-11, 14, 18-20, 23, 26-30, 53, 55, 78-79, 83, 85, 94-95, 101, 111, 113, 115, 119-121, 123, 125, 127, 129-139, 150, 153, 160-161, 178, 183, 192-193, 201, 213, 215, 220-224, 226, 228, 235, 238, 240-241, 246, 249, 254-255, 257, 260, 263, 269, 271-274, 277-284, 286-290, 293, 295, 297, 305-307, 309-310, 314-319, 325-328, 333, 337, 339, 346, 350-353, 356-363, 367, 370, 373-376, 378-381, 384-387, 389, 393-403, 405-413

Italy, 287, 291

Jerusalem, 11-12, 16, 19-20, 28, 33, 36-37, 47, 62, 64, 78, 81, 123, 125, 133, 136, 150, 159, 162, 169-170, 183, 187, 193, 197, 199-206, 208, 213, 221-224, 227, 234, 249, 252, 257-258, 260, 263, 269, 272-274, 296, 302-303, 312, 314, 316-319, 325, 327, 330-331, 337, 340, 350, 353, 366, 374-379, 406, 408, 410-411

Jesus Christ, 9, 17-18, 26, 39-41, 43, 136, 144, 185, 209, 231, 243, 247, 317, 329, 347, 413

Jew, 18, 80, 121, 221, 249, 350, 356, 386, 394

Jewish, 19, 23, 27, 36, 73, 95, 101, 120, 129, 147, 184-186, 191, 199, 201, 222-223, 240-241, 249, 254-255, 260, 269-270, 283, 294, 306, 314, 320, 323-324, 327-328, 349, 352, 370, 372, 377-378, 383, 407

Jewish Witnesses, 36, 73, 95, 147, 184-186, 191, 199, 201, 260, 306, 314, 323-324, 349, 407

Jews, 14, 19, 23-24, 28, 31, 42, 50-51, 62-63, 93, 95-96, 108, 117, 124-125, 130, 132, 135, 143, 145-147, 185-186, 221-222, 226-228, 238, 240, 249, 251, 259-260, 263, 269, 281, 283, 306-308, 319, 327, 330, 333, 346, 349, 351-353, 356, 374, 376, 378-380, 386, 388-389, 395, 403, 405, 407, 409-411

Jezebel, 11, 21, 55-56

Jihad, 227-228, 255, 348, 393-395

Jordan, 132, 286, 289, 319-320, 350, 370, 384, 399, 406

Judah, 11, 18, 21, 79, 95, 131, 145, 184, 240, 269

Judgment, 10-11, 18, 22, 24-26, 28, 32-33, 35-36, 42, 45, 54, 56, 70, 72-73, 80, 84, 87, 89-91, 98, 101-105, 107-108, 110-113, 115, 117, 120-121, 124-125, 127, 132, 147, 149-150, 158-160, 162, 165, 173-178, 185-186, 189-191, 193-196, 201, 207-208, 215, 218, 226-227, 229, 234, 239-240, 253, 255-261, 268-270, 273-274, 277, 283-284, 295-299, 305, 307-308, 311, 313, 315, 318-319, 323, 330-334, 336, 339-340, 344, 347-348, 352, 354-356, 364, 366, 383, 386, 389-390, 398-400, 403, 408, 411-412

Judgment Seat of Christ, 72, 207, 234, 323, 408

Judgments, 14, 16, 21-27, 31-33, 43, 56, 63, 77-78, 83-84, 86, 88, 91, 93-94, 96, 101, 103, 105-107, 111-113, 115-118, 125-127, 144-145, 147-150, 153-155, 157-159, 173, 175, 181, 184, 186, 194, 229, 234, 241, 255-256, 260-261, 263, 269-271, 295, 298, 305, 307-308, 311, 314, 326, 334, 339,

341, 348, 350-352, 389, 405-406, 409-411

Kazakhstan, 285, 290, 393, 404

King, 10, 15, 17, 25, 30, 34, 41, 44, 49-50, 55, 59, 64, 79-80, 108, 110, 123, 139, 154, 168, 170, 186, 193, 227, 247-249, 257, 262, 272, 274-277, 280, 286-289, 292, 298, 301-302, 326-327, 357-359, 361-363, 368-369, 371-373, 376-377, 381-382, 384, 393, 405, 408

King of Babylon, 123, 168, 248-249, 276, 287, 289, 362

King of Greece, 363, 369

KING OF KINGS AND LORD OF LORDS, 17, 41, 186, 298, 376

King of the North, 15, 30, 139, 227, 257, 272, 274-277, 280, 286, 288-289, 292, 357, 382, 384, 393, 408

King of the South, 15, 30, 139, 227, 257, 272, 274-277, 280, 286, 289, 292, 357, 382, 384, 393, 408

Kingdom, 10, 17, 19, 28-29, 33-34, 41, 43, 55, 71-72, 81-82, 85, 94, 126, 131, 133-134, 137-139, 158-159, 166, 168-169, 171, 192, 213-215, 228, 237, 256, 259, 273, 275, 283, 293, 310, 316-317, 319, 323, 326-327, 329, 331, 340, 348-349, 355-357, 359-363, 365-368, 371-372, 374-375, 379, 382, 388, 390, 405-406, 409-410, 413

Kingdoms, 26, 28-29, 33-34, 83-84, 126, 130, 138, 166, 169, 171, 185, 254, 257, 278, 287-289, 303, 309-310, 357, 359-361, 363-367, 371, 379-380, 382, 408

Kings, 12, 17-18, 28-29, 33-35, 41, 44, 71, 73, 79-81, 83, 90, 112, 118, 130-131, 135, 138, 148, 160-161, 165-166, 169-171, 174, 176-177, 181, 186-187, 192, 204, 227, 232, 234, 250-251, 254, 259, 262, 272-279, 286-289, 292, 298, 300, 305, 309-312, 315-317, 319, 326-327, 359-361, 365-368, 371-372, 376, 381-382, 385, 408

Kuwait, 290

Kyrgyzstan, 285, 290, 393, 404

Lake of Fire, 36, 87, 108, 148, 187-188, 191, 193-196, 200, 204, 208, 262, 332, 336, 344-345, 352, 355, 365, 385, 408

Lamb, 10-12, 18, 31, 35, 37, 61, 72, 80-83, 90, 95-99, 134, 140-141, 145-146, 148, 154, 170, 181-183, 186-187, 194, 201, 203-206, 235, 240, 260, 269-270, 303, 322, 331, 337, 339, 406, 408-409

Lampstands, 12, 18, 44, 46-47, 122, 411

Laodicea, 21, 43, 64-66, 218

Lawless One, 187, 239, 242

Legs of Iron, 359-360

Leopard, 10, 29, 138, 331, 363

Libya, 29, 278-279, 285, 290, 385, 394

Lion, 10-11, 18, 21, 29, 74, 79, 116, 138, 145, 184, 240, 250, 269, 331, 362

Literal Babylon, 148, 165, 173-174, 181, 311-312

Little Horn, 27, 84, 248-250, 276, 287, 357, 364, 370

Little Open Book, 26, 77, 115-117, 261, 408

Living Creatures, 21-22, 71, 73-75, 80-84, 86, 97, 102-103, 106, 146, 154-155, 182-183, 261, 295, 409

Locusts, 25-26, 94, 108-110, 112, 189, 193, 261-262, 315, 344, 405, 407

Lord God, 18, 74, 126, 154, 158, 175, 182, 203, 206, 302, 337, 392, 395, 397-402

Lord Jesus, 18, 26, 117, 144, 185, 209, 255, 356, 413

Lucifer, 131, 133, 140, 373, 407, 410

Lybia, 286, 404

Lysimachus, 286, 363, 369

Macedonia, 286, 358, 369

Magog, 29-30, 36, 133, 192-193, 227-228, 257, 272-279, 281-285, 290, 292, 315, 317, 331, 334, 384, 392-394, 396-397, 400-404, 408-409

Magog Invasion, 272-274, 276-278, 281-285, 408

Magog Military Campaign, 30, 272-273, 275, 281, 285, 317, 392

Male Child, 15, 23-24, 28, 129-132, 135-136, 145, 147, 186, 191, 260, 269, 271, 306-308, 314, 389, 409

Male Goat, 369, 371

Mali, 290

Mankind, 25-26, 34, 41, 46, 78-81, 87, 90, 106, 109, 111-113, 118, 121, 147, 161, 170, 184, 198, 200, 221, 229, 253, 262-263, 293, 296, 304-305, 315-316, 375, 378, 406-407, 412

Man of Sin, 235, 239, 242, 293-294, 299

Mark of the Beast, 15, 21, 24, 31-33, 61, 86, 94, 96-97, 143-144, 148-149, 153-154, 157-158, 187, 190, 226, 251, 257, 260-262, 268, 270, 296, 315-316, 324, 330, 349, 352, 409

Marriage Ceremony, 35, 322, 409

Marriage Feast, 186, 323

Marriage Supper, 7, 35, 181-182, 322-323, 409

Martyrs, 24, 36, 88-89, 96, 98, 153, 167, 185, 259, 268, 295, 349, 407, 409

Mauritania, 290

Medes, 358, 360, 363, 368-369

Mediterranean (Sea), 62, 104, 137, 158, 198, 245, 330, 362, 396, 400

Medo-Persia, 29, 34, 130, 138, 166, 168-169, 286, 288, 310, 360, 362, 369

Medo-Persian Empire, 368-369

Megiddo, 11, 150, 161, 272, 298, 317-318, 405

Meshech, 29, 285, 290, 392-394, 399, 404

Messiah, 19, 42, 79, 117, 143, 293-294, 319, 329, 331, 337, 352, 374-378, 386

Meteors, 89-90, 104, 334

Michael, 28, 36, 94, 101, 132-133, 190, 241, 261, 325, 380-381, 385-386

Mid-Tribulation, 22, 27, 129, 131, 134, 148, 165, 167, 170, 181, 233, 256, 258, 274, 277, 279, 282-

284, 294, 297-298, 307-308, 350, 361, 389, 401, 403, 408

Middle East, 29-30, 111, 120, 143, 227, 246, 251, 255-257, 274-275, 277, 279, 282, 290, 315, 320, 348, 383, 394-396, 407

Millennial, 36, 62, 93, 99, 120, 190, 192, 198, 213-215, 237, 283, 317, 327-330, 334, 375-376, 379, 386, 388, 390

Millennial Temple, 99, 120, 330

200 Million (Army) 26, 96, 107, 304, 305, 316

Moab, 132, 278, 286, 289, 350, 384

Moon, 24, 37, 42, 89, 105, 129-130, 157, 160, 203, 231, 258-259, 284, 297, 300-302, 315, 329, 334, 338-340, 351-352

Morning Star, 56-57, 208

Morocco, 30, 285, 290, 394, 404

Moses, 11, 27, 32, 121, 154, 223, 330

Most High, 365-367

Most Holy, 19, 373, 376

Mother of Harlots, 34, 165, 167, 258, 311, 409

Mount Megiddo, 272, 318, 405

Mount of Olives, 162, 296, 302, 319, 341, 346, 409

Mount of Transfiguration, 45, 120-121

Mount Zion, 145, 202, 409

Mountain, 33, 37, 90, 103, 163, 201-202, 258-259, 300, 303, 315, 317, 327, 330, 337, 339-340, 359, 361, 385, 405

Mountains, 12, 18, 30, 34, 85, 90, 132, 139, 160, 162, 168-169, 192-193, 202, 257, 259-260, 272, 278-279, 282-283, 290, 296-297, 300, 302-303, 315-316, 326, 334, 339-340, 350, 384, 395, 398-400

Mt. Zion, 15, 23, 31, 94, 269

Muslim(s) , 29, 120, 227-228, 246, 249, 255, 257, 272, 278, 289-290, 315, 348, 384-385, 392-394, 396-397, 399-400, 407, 409

Muslim Jihad, 228, 255, 348

Muslim Nations, 29, 227, 246, 257, 278, 289-290, 315, 385, 393-394, 397, 399

Mystery, 27, 34, 46, 83, 91, 116-117, 130, 146, 165-167, 170-171, 174-176, 231, 239-241, 254, 258, 268, 311-312, 374, 388, 406, 409

Mystery Babylon, 34, 83, 130, 146, 165-167, 170-171, 174-176, 231, 254, 258, 268, 311-312

Name of Jesus, 64, 348, 414

NATO, 227-228

Nebuchadnezzar, 357-362

New Age, 215, 231, 252

New Earth, 37, 81, 93, 197, 296, 299, 303, 334, 341

New Heavens, 93, 296, 299, 303, 334

New Jerusalem, 11-12, 37, 64, 81, 183, 197, 199-204, 206, 208, 234, 269, 337, 366, 406, 408

New Testament Saints, 70-72, 191, 201, 406, 408, 410

Nicolaitans, 11, 49, 53

Niger, 290

Nimrod, 34, 165, 248, 289

Noah, 174, 235, 238-239, 354-356, 392

Noahic Flood, 195, 198, 224, 235, 239, 325

North African, 30, 275, 279, 290, 408

North America, 224, 290

Northern Africa, 29, 111, 143, 256, 276, 385, 394

Northern Kingdom, 275

Nuclear, 90, 103, 105, 226-228, 230, 256, 273-274, 399, 402

Oil, 43, 86, 122, 176, 251

Old Grecian Empire, 27, 137, 168, 248-249, 287-289, 292, 310, 357, 372, 378

Old Testament Saints, 14, 36, 121, 134, 183, 185, 191, 323-324, 407, 410

Olivet Discourse, 224, 410

Oman, 286, 290, 396, 404

Overcomers, 32, 51, 61, 64, 71-73, 154

Pakistan, 290-292, 370

Palestine, 286, 369

Palm Sunday, 377

Paradise, 49, 107, 344

Parousia, 237, 241

Partial Rapture, 234

Patmos, 20, 43

Pentecost, 19, 43, 213, 235, 406

Pergamos, 21, 43, 51-54

Persia, 19, 26, 29, 59, 111, 285, 290, 292, 357, 368, 371, 376, 380-382, 393-394, 404

Persian Empire, 111, 289, 368, 382

Pestilence, 22, 158, 229, 258, 273, 314-315, 348, 398-399

Petra, 132, 135, 260, 283, 314, 319-320, 350, 384, 388, 406

Pharaoh, 113, 393

Philadelphia, 21, 43, 61-62, 64, 218, 238, 242

Philip of Macedonia, 358

Phoencia, 404

Population, 47, 87, 111-113, 195-196, 198, 202, 228-229, 314, 316, 327-328, 330, 351

Post-Tribulation, 233, 242, 409

Postmillennial, 197, 213-214, 334, 336-338, 410

Postmillennial Earth, 197, 336-338

Postmillennialists, 214

Praise, 35, 41, 74-75, 80-82, 182-183, 409

Pre-Tribulation, 13, 15, 20, 63, 220, 233, 236, 238, 297, 380

Pre-Wrath Rapture, 234, 415

Premillennial, 13, 15, 213, 215, 334, 410

Premillennialism, 214

Priests, 11, 41, 71-73, 81, 192, 234, 330

Prince, 20, 27, 29, 34, 94, 123, 133, 137, 139, 162, 168, 193, 233, 247-249, 262, 310, 335, 357, 370, 372-373, 376-378, 380-382, 385-386, 392-393, 399, 406

Prince of Assyria, 27, 34, 123, 168, 310, 381-382

Prince of Babylon, 27, 34, 123, 168, 310, 381-382

Prince of Greece, 27, 34, 123, 137, 139, 168, 193, 357, 381-382

Prince of Persia, 357, 380-381

Prophecy, 13-16, 18-19, 37, 40, 43, 79, 87, 121-122, 132, 143, 151, 178, 182, 184, 206-207, 209, 213, 220, 222-224, 226, 230, 245, 272-273, 282-283, 292, 294, 304, 313, 357, 370-378, 386-387, 392, 397, 413

Ptolemy, 286, 289, 363, 369

Put, 285, 290, 394, 404

Pyramid, 202, 252

Qatar, 286, 290, 396, 404

Ram, 101, 368-369, 371

Rapture, 13-15, 22-23, 28, 63, 69, 72-73, 78, 87-88, 91, 94, 111, 113, 121, 132, 146-147, 185-186, 191, 213, 215, 220-222, 224-225, 231, 233-238, 240-243, 245-246, 251, 255, 281-283, 293-295, 298, 306-308, 314, 316, 323, 347-349, 353-354, 374, 380, 405-407, 409-410, 414

Reconstituted Roman Empire, 29-30, 34, 83-84, 123, 130, 138, 165-166, 169, 171, 225, 245, 248-250, 254, 256-257, 277, 279-280, 287-289, 291-292, 310, 357, 363, 367, 372, 378, 385, 400, 403

Redeemed, 37, 72, 78, 80, 146, 183, 198-199, 201, 206, 209, 214, 268, 270, 307, 320, 326-328, 337, 405

Redeemed Man, 198-199, 206, 337

Redeemed Saints, 37, 201, 326-328, 405

Redeemer, 21, 77, 81

Redemptive Plan, 13, 15, 17, 37, 116-117, 140, 200, 375

Remnant (of Israel), 14, 23, 28, 125, 132, 136, 139, 241, 260, 269, 271, 283, 302, 314, 319-320, 410

Renovation, 7, 197, 200, 302-303, 333-334, 336, 338

Repentance, 56, 67, 90, 120, 125, 254, 293, 295, 406

Resurrection, 24, 29, 32, 36, 41, 45-46, 51, 72, 89, 96, 98, 107, 121, 124, 139, 141-142, 145, 185-186, 188, 191-192, 195, 197-198, 215, 235, 237, 241, 268, 327, 332, 340, 386, 407, 411

Revived Grecian Empire, 249, 372

Righteous, 61, 88, 98, 107, 133, 158-159, 181-182, 186, 194, 207, 236, 239, 323, 328, 332, 344, 356, 410

Rod of Iron, 28, 41, 56-57, 131, 186, 190, 306, 308, 326

Roman Empire, 29-30, 34, 47, 83-84, 123, 130, 138, 160, 165-166, 168-169, 171, 225, 245, 248-250, 254, 256-257, 277, 279-280, 287-289, 291-292, 310, 357, 360, 363, 367, 372, 378, 385, 400, 403

Roman General Titus, 19, 346

Romania, 292

Rome, 21, 26, 34-35, 47, 49, 65, 111, 130, 138, 166, 168-169, 286, 288-289, 291, 310, 312, 358, 360, 363

Root of David, 11, 18, 79, 240

Rosh, 29, 285, 290, 392-394, 399, 404

Russia, 29, 36, 193, 227-228, 257, 272, 275, 285, 290, 331, 392-395, 397, 404

Sackcloth, 11, 89, 120

Sacrifices, 330, 370

Saints, 14, 18, 28-29, 34-37, 40-41, 43, 51, 70-73, 80-81, 83, 88, 96-98, 102, 121, 126, 130, 134-135, 140-141, 149-150, 153-154, 158-159, 162, 167, 178-179, 181-183, 185-186, 190-193, 199, 201-202, 205-207, 220, 233-235, 238, 241-243, 253, 255, 259-260, 263, 268, 270-271, 302, 311, 318, 323-324, 326-328, 330, 337, 348-349, 352, 356, 365-368, 386, 405-411

Salvation, 27, 61, 73, 97, 133-134, 147, 181, 200, 207, 209, 231, 242, 328, 330, 347, 377, 406, 408, 410, 413-414

Sardis, 21, 43, 59-61

Satan, 14-15, 17-18, 21, 28-29, 36-37, 45-46, 50, 52, 56, 62-63, 78-79, 83-84, 87, 107-108, 110, 123, 130-131, 133-135, 137-139, 141-142, 144, 154, 162, 189-194, 196, 200, 213, 215, 233, 237, 245, 247-248, 250, 262-263, 277, 295, 307, 309, 325, 329, 331-332, 334-336, 345, 347, 350, 372, 405, 408, 410, 414

Satanic, 25, 27, 34, 87, 111, 123, 139, 143, 166, 168, 177, 262, 270, 310, 357, 381-382, 406-408

Satellite, 123, 226, 351

Saudi Arabia, 286, 290, 396, 399, 404

Savior, 61, 88, 140, 194, 208, 243, 356, 375, 406, 408, 414

Scarlet Beast, 166, 309, 410

Scroll, 10, 21-22, 44, 77-81, 83-84, 90, 116, 118, 184, 300, 411

Scythians, 392, 404

Sea, 10, 24, 28-29, 32-33, 35, 47, 73, 82, 93-94, 103-104, 111, 116-118, 135, 137, 141, 147, 153, 157-159, 176-178, 192, 195, 197-198, 229, 257, 259-261, 269-271, 309, 315, 330-331, 340-341, 362, 396, 398, 401-402, 406, 410

Sea of Glass, 10, 32, 73, 153, 271, 410

Seal, 19, 21-22, 24-25, 36, 77, 84-87, 89, 91, 93-94, 98, 101, 105, 108, 111-113, 116-117, 127, 144-145, 154, 190, 207, 226-227, 229, 234, 239-240, 253, 256, 258, 260-261, 263, 268-271, 283-284, 295, 297-298, 307-308, 314, 316, 339, 347-348, 373, 375, 386, 389, 410-412

Seal Judgments, 21-22, 77, 84, 86, 91, 93-94, 113, 154, 234, 256, 261, 263, 271, 295, 308, 339, 410

Second Advent, 79, 115, 125, 220, 255, 273, 350, 361

Second Coming, 14, 20, 23, 30, 35, 41-42, 44, 64, 78, 80, 96, 98, 102, 112, 117, 120-121, 125, 148, 162, 173, 181, 183, 209, 215, 221-222, 224, 234-237, 242, 255, 261, 274, 283, 295-298, 302, 307, 318, 330, 333-334, 353-355, 361, 364-366, 371, 375, 389, 406, 409-410

Second Resurrection, 188, 191-192, 195, 332, 386, 411

Seleucid, 137, 248-249, 276, 287-289, 372, 383

Seleucus, 286, 363, 369

Semiramis, 34

Serpent, 133, 135-136, 189, 325, 331

Seven, 11-15, 18-22, 26, 28, 30-32, 34-35, 39-40, 43-47, 52, 54, 59-61, 71-73, 77, 79-81, 83-84, 90, 93, 101-102, 113, 116-117, 124-126, 129-130, 137-139, 153-155, 157, 165-169, 183, 196, 200-201, 203, 217-218, 222-223, 226, 237, 240, 251, 254-258, 260-262, 274, 277, 280, 284, 286, 288, 291, 298, 309-310, 314, 316, 329, 350, 357, 361, 364, 374, 376, 378, 380, 385, 396, 400-403, 406-411, 413

Seven Churches, 11, 18, 20, 39-40, 43-46, 61, 71, 183, 217-218, 411

Seven Empires, 138, 167, 288

Seven-Headed, Ten-Horned Beasts, 138, 286-287

Seven Heads, 15, 18, 28, 34, 130, 137-138, 166-169, 240, 258, 260, 262, 286, 309-310

Seven Lampstands, 18, 44, 46, 411

Seven Sealed Book, 411

Seven Spirits, 18, 40, 59, 72-73, 80

Seven Stars, 18, 45-47, 59-60, 411

Seventieth Week, 15, 20, 22-24, 27, 29-32, 35, 83, 91, 94, 98, 142, 193, 233-234, 254, 256, 270, 276, 280, 282, 294, 308, 346-348, 357, 379-380, 384, 386, 388-389, 395-396, 406

Seventy Weeks of Daniel, 411

Seventy Weeks of Years, 19, 357, 373

Sexual Immorality, 53, 55, 113, 231-232

Sheba, 286, 290, 396, 404

Sheep Nations, 204, 356, 390, 411

Shekinah (Glory), 70, 98, 115, 155, 352

Sheol-Hades, 107, 111, 191, 196, 344, 355

Sierra Leone, 290

Sign, 52, 113, 127, 129-130, 153, 221, 347, 352

Silver, 113, 176, 358-361, 383, 385, 396

Signs, 29, 31, 120, 142, 144, 153, 161, 187, 220, 222, 236, 250, 302, 306, 351, 353-355, 407, 410

Sin, 17-18, 49, 56, 63, 78, 80, 113, 117, 133-134, 147, 150, 162, 184, 218, 235, 237, 239, 242, 245, 251-252, 255, 293-295, 299, 325, 328-329, 336, 349, 372, 375, 406, 411, 413-414

Smyrna, 21, 43, 47, 49-51, 218

Sodom, 11, 123, 174, 235, 239, 273, 312-313, 399

Somalia, 29, 85, 290, 394, 404

Son of God, 54, 414

Son of Man, 44, 149, 351-352, 354-356, 365, 368, 371, 392, 397, 399

Son of Perdition, 293, 299

Sorceries, 26, 113, 178, 231-232, 260, 313

Souls, 22, 24, 72, 87-88, 96, 98, 107, 135, 176-177, 190-191, 195, 214, 259, 263, 268, 271, 386, 405

Soviet Union, 227, 404

Spain, 245, 286-287, 291, 396

Spirit, 9-12, 17-18, 39-41, 43, 49-50, 53-54, 56, 59-61, 63-65, 67, 69, 73, 75, 80, 88, 94, 109, 122, 124, 140, 149, 166, 173-174, 182, 184, 187, 189, 201, 208-209, 218, 231-232, 234, 238, 242-243, 245, 247, 251, 262, 268, 282, 295, 312, 349, 364-365, 374, 403, 410, 413

Spirit of God, 60, 124

Spirit Says, 49-50, 53, 56, 59, 61, 63-65, 67

Spirits, 12, 18, 33, 35, 40, 56-57, 59, 72-73, 80, 109, 160-161, 195, 207, 262, 277, 386, 405

Statue, 47, 287, 289

Sudan, 29, 285, 290, 394, 404

Supernatural Disturbances, 339

Superstition, 47, 253

Syria, 30, 64, 95, 248, 257, 275-279, 286-289, 291-292, 327, 369, 372, 382, 385, 399, 408

Tabernacle, 11, 110, 134, 140, 154, 197, 199, 202

Tajikistan, 285, 290, 393, 404

Tarshish, 245, 286, 290, 396-397, 404

Tartarus, 107, 344

Technology, 143, 226, 351, 395, 401

Temple, 11, 14, 19-20, 27-28, 37, 47, 50, 52, 64, 71, 98-99, 119-120, 127, 139-140, 149-150, 154-155, 157, 161, 170, 203, 205, 221-222, 240, 249-250, 254, 257-258, 261, 269, 280, 294, 299, 315, 330, 337, 340, 346-347, 350, 370-371, 376-380, 388, 390, 403, 405, 411

Ten Horns, 28, 34, 129-130, 137-138, 165-167, 169-170, 240, 258, 260, 262, 287, 289, 309-310, 363-364, 366-367

Ten Toes, 287, 289, 363

Ten-Horned Beast(s), 138, 286-287

Terror, 124, 227, 251-252, 299

Terrorism, 226-227, 395

Thermonuclear War, 273

Thessalonica, 18

Three Major Military Campaigns, 228, 272-275, 281, 285, 317

Three Woes, 106, 110, 411

Three, 3, 10, 21, 29, 31-33, 36-37, 40, 52, 62, 67, 69-73, 75, 77, 79-83, 87, 90-91, 95-99, 102, 107-108, 131, 134, 138, 145-146, 153, 155, 159, 162, 182-183, 191, 194-196, 200, 205-206, 208, 248, 259, 261, 270-271, 274, 306, 319, 325-326, 332-334, 336-337, 339, 344, 352, 355, 364, 386, 409-412

Thunderings, 28, 33, 72-73, 102, 127, 162, 182,

258-259, 316, 339-340

Thyatira, 21, 43, 54-56, 59, 218

Times of the Gentiles, 26-28, 123, 137-138, 278, 286, 309, 358, 361-363, 379, 357

Title Deed, 21, 78, 411

Togarmah, 30, 285, 290, 394, 404

Torments, 107, 148, 191, 344, 355

Tower of Babel, 111

Tree of Life, 3, 11, 37, 49, 205-206, 208, 337

Tribulation, 13-15, 20-24, 27, 30, 32-37, 43, 50-51, 56, 61, 63, 70, 72-73, 78, 83-89, 93, 95-99, 101, 107, 112-113, 119-122, 125-126, 130, 132, 135, 139, 142, 146-149, 153, 157, 165, 169-170, 174, 181, 184-186, 190-193, 198-199, 201, 204-205, 213, 215, 220, 222-224, 228-242, 248-249, 252, 254-260, 263, 268-274, 276-283, 286-289, 292-295, 297-298, 305-312, 314-316, 323-324, 327-328, 330, 333-334, 337, 340, 346-353, 356-357, 366-368, 370, 373, 378-380, 383-389, 401, 405-414

Tribulation Judgments, 83, 101, 107, 157, 263

Tribulation Period, 15, 20-22, 32-33, 35, 51, 63, 72, 78, 83, 87-89, 96, 99, 113, 120-121, 132, 135, 139, 169, 181, 191, 198, 213, 215, 222-223, 233, 239, 254-256, 268, 271, 273, 277, 288, 292, 294-295, 297, 306, 308-309, 311, 315-316, 323-324, 330, 334, 346, 349, 356-357, 370, 379, 383, 406-411, 413

Tribulation Saints, 36, 51, 72, 88, 98, 185, 190-191, 199, 201, 205, 323-324, 327, 337, 352, 356, 407, 409, 411

Trumpet Judgments, 21, 23-25, 33, 77, 93-94, 101, 103, 106, 112-113, 115-116, 126-127, 144-145, 147, 157, 241, 256, 260, 269, 271, 307-308, 314, 389, 405, 409, 411

Tubal, 29, 285, 290, 392-394, 399, 404

Tunisia, 30, 285, 290, 394, 404

Turkey, 29-30, 248, 285-288, 290-292, 369, 393-394, 404

Turkmenistan, 285, 290, 393, 404

Two Witnesses, 11, 14-15, 24, 27, 32, 36, 96, 119-121, 123-125, 127, 142, 147, 158, 191, 226, 258-259, 262-263, 294-295, 297, 314, 340, 389, 407, 411

Ukraine, 394

Unbelievers, 26, 36, 78, 87, 107, 111, 140, 168, 208, 355

United Arab Emirates, 286, 290, 404

United Nations, 227

United States, 16, 202, 224-225, 227, 232, 245-246, 253, 255-256, 286, 290, 392, 396, 404

Unrighteous, 78, 87, 91, 108, 147, 159-160, 162, 187, 194-196, 208, 316, 332, 336, 344-345, 386, 388, 408, 411-412

Uzbekistan, 285, 290, 393, 404

Valley of Esdraelon, 318

Valley of Hamon Gog, 401-402

Valley of Jehoshaphat, 272, 318-319

Valley of Jezreel, 318

Valleys of Megiddo, 11

West Germany, 52

Western European, 245, 397, 404

Western Leg (Roman Empire), 287, 289, 291

White Throne Judgment, 70, 87, 107-108, 191, 195-196, 208, 332-334, 336, 344, 352, 355, 386, 412

Wine, 31, 62, 86, 148, 150-151, 162, 165-166, 174, 176, 186, 274, 312, 317, 320

Wings, 73-74, 135, 362-363

Woe, 25, 106, 110, 125-126, 135, 301, 350

Woman, 10, 15, 23-24, 28, 34-35, 55, 129-132, 135-136, 153, 166-169, 171, 228, 240, 258, 260, 263, 268-269, 278, 297, 306-307, 325, 350, 384, 412

Word of God, 3, 9, 13, 18, 36, 39, 43, 45, 52-55, 57, 60, 63-64, 87-88, 96, 118, 185, 188, 190, 238, 263, 268, 271, 274, 320, 347-349, 351, 354, 387-388, 409

Wormwood, 104, 257, 270

Worship, 17, 26, 29, 31, 33-34, 49-50, 52, 55, 62, 72, 74-75, 80, 82, 97, 113, 119, 126, 139-143, 147-148, 154, 158, 165, 170-171, 174, 182-184, 190, 207, 231, 240, 249-250, 258, 315, 326-328, 365, 368, 370, 383-384, 406-407, 411

Wrath of God, 21-22, 31, 33, 89-91, 116, 127, 148, 150, 153-155, 157, 235, 239, 255, 258, 261, 273-274, 283, 295, 298, 317, 400, 412

Yemen, 286, 290, 396, 404

Yugoslavia, 292

Zion, 15, 23, 31, 94, 145, 202, 269, 300, 377, 409